T5-BYL-086

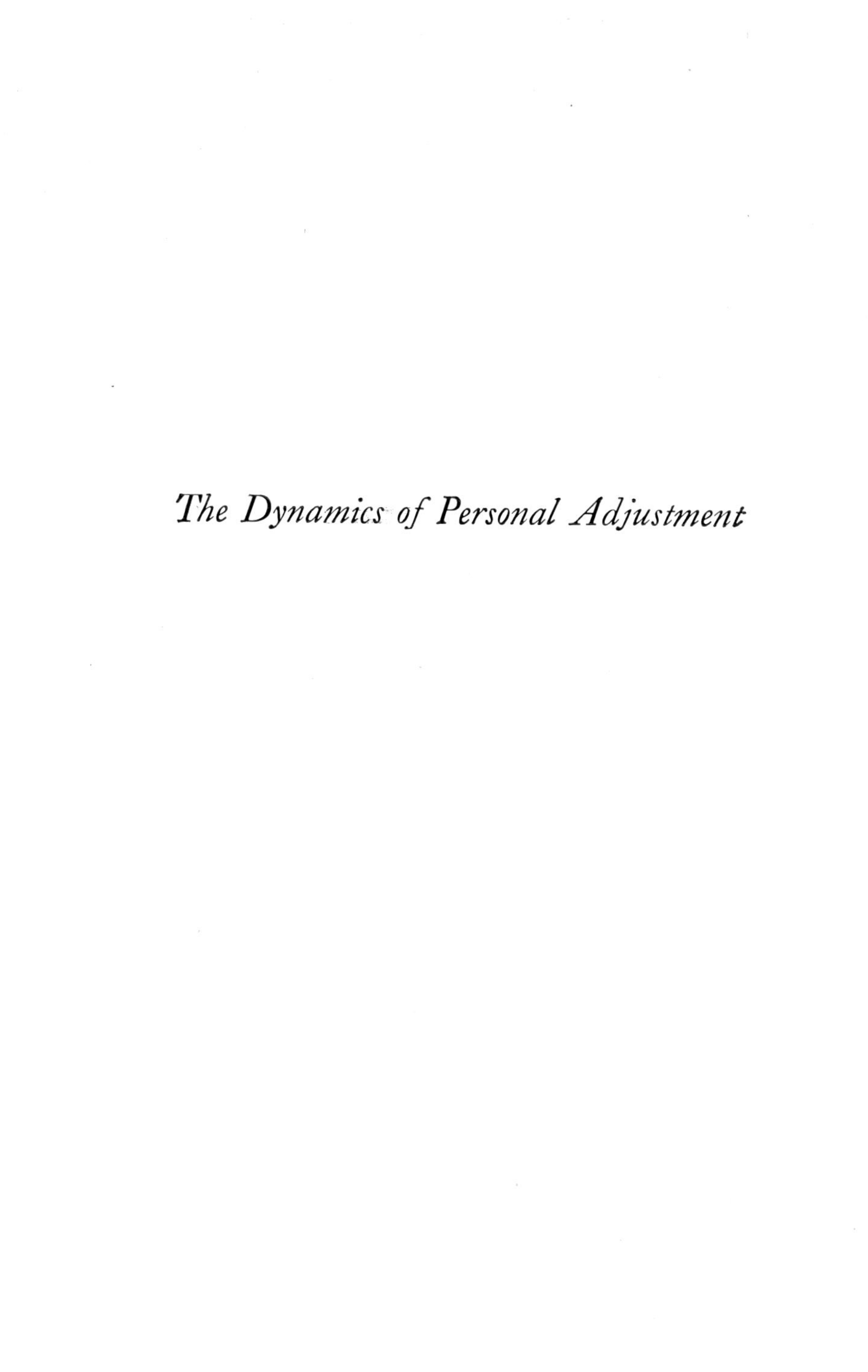

The Dynamics of Personal Adjustment

The Dynamics

SECOND EDITION

of Personal Adjustment

GEORGE F. J. LEHNER

Professor of Psychology

University of California, Los Angeles

ELLA KUBE

Social Psychologist

Occidental College

PRENTICE-HALL, INC.

Englewood Cliffs, N. J.

SECOND EDITION

The Dynamics of Personal Adjustment

LEHNER AND KUBE

Printed in the
United States of America.
Library of Congress
Catalog Card No. 64-11438.

Designed by Harry Rinehart

C-22204

PRENTICE-HALL PSYCHOLOGY SERIES

PRENTICE-HALL INTERNATIONAL, INC., *London*
PRENTICE-HALL OF AUSTRALIA, PTY. LTD., *Sydney*
PRENTICE-HALL OF CANADA, LTD., *Toronto*
PRENTICE-HALL FRANCE, S.A.R.L., *Paris*
PRENTICE-HALL OF INDIA PRIVATE LIMITED, *New Delhi*
PRENTICE-HALL OF JAPAN, INC., *Tokyo*
PRENTICE-HALL DE MEXICO, S.A., *Mexico City*

Preface to the First Edition

We would not expect to cross the desert in a boat or the ocean in an automobile, but many of us fail to realize that it is just as unrealistic to expect inadequate behavior patterns to carry us satisfactorily through the journey of life. We tend to take ourselves and our behavior for granted. We tend to coast along, blind to the potentialities we are wasting, deaf to the danger signals manifest in our personalities, dumb in our inability to release the tensions we have suppressed.

The purpose of this book is to attempt to bring into sharper focus certain factors that may facilitate or hinder the journey—to offer suggestions concerning problems that may be encountered, solutions that may be discovered, goals that may be attained, personal relationships that may be established, and pleasures and satisfactions that may be enjoyed.

Throughout the book the motivational and goal-directed aspects of behavior are stressed—i.e., that we do not merely act; we act with a purpose. An attempt is made not merely to describe behavior but to *explain* it, to reveal the inner workings, to interpret surface phenomena by exposing the deeper-lying dynamics. The expression *dynamics of adjustment* is intended to convey the multiple facets that operate to influence the relationships between needs, the blocking of these needs, the appearance, disappearance, and shifting of coping and defense mechanisms—the innumerable factors that determine the way in which each individual behaves. The expression implies learning and re-learning—especially in the area of social relations. It implies emphasis not on physiological structure but on psychological strain, not on physiological tonus but on psychological tension. Problems are viewed as a challenge to new learning. Since deviant behavior results from learning, just as does normal behavior, then re-learning may change deviant behavior into normal behavior.

What is a well-adjusted person? How can he remain well-adjusted? How can he reconcile his needs and his social relations? What do his characteristics reveal about himself? How can he handle his problems in order to achieve optimum adjustment—with or without special help? How can he best utilize his capacities and his experiences? These are some of the questions the book considers, from the viewpoint of both a clinical and a social psychologist, in an attempt to show the process of interaction between personal and social needs.

In this book we have tried to present material that we believe will be helpful to students taking courses in introductory psychology and to include, as well, certain ideas and concepts generally found only in more advanced courses and therefore lost to students who must limit the amount of time they can devote to the study of psychology. In discussing this material, we have attempted to avoid theoretical considerations and to stress, instead, the personal experiences of the student or general reader. It was our hope to eliminate technical terms without sacrificing the precision which they convey.

We want to express thanks to our respective wife and husband who have contributed to this book, not only through their general support and encouragement, but also because of their special skills—to Eleanor Lehner for her help in writing and editing, and to Kemper Nomland, Jr., for his help in the choice and preparation of the illustrative material. Our thanks also go to Wilbur Mangas of Prentice-Hall, Inc., for his valuable assistance throughout the preparation of the book.

Preface to the Second Edition

Since *The Dynamics of Personal Adjustment* first appeared in May, 1955, we have received many appreciative comments from both teachers and students. We feel that these comments obligate us not only to retain or to improve the aspects of the book that elicited them, but also to modify and develop other elements that might further enhance its value.

In its revised form the book has been divided into the following four parts: *Fundamentals of Adjustment, Misdirected Adjustment, Areas of Adjustment,* and *Achieving Adjustment.* The first part defines adjustment and discusses the fundamentals that contribute to the type of adjustment we attain. The second describes what happens when people are unable to adjust satisfactorily. The third discusses the various sets of circumstances to which all of us must learn to adjust in the course of a lifetime. The fourth focuses on attitudes and methods that can help us to adjust satisfactorily.

In preparing the material we have kept in mind that everyone, regardless of his field of specialization, can benefit from a better understanding of the factors affecting personal adjustment. Consequently, we have tried to avoid overemphasizing technical terms and to concentrate, instead, on presenting the important concepts in such a way that they will be understandable not only to psychology majors but also to those students who have had less technical training. Yet, at the same time, we have been aware that to deprive such students of the chance to become familiar with significant psychological terminology would be to do them an injustice. Thus, both the choice of material and the manner of presenting it has been influenced by our desire to help *any* student (*including* psychology majors) to understand more about the field of psychology as well as about himself as a human being. In other words, we have tried to enable the student to understand *himself* better by understanding *psychology* better.

We offer the book to the many teachers who strive with us to clarify for *all* students the research findings and conceptualizations of the fascinating field of psychology.

George F. J. Lehner
Ella Kube

THIS BOOK IS DEDICATED
TO ELEANOR B. LEHNER
WHOSE EDITORIAL SKILLS
HAVE MADE THIS A MORE
READABLE BOOK.

Contents

PART ONE

The Fundamentals of Adjustment

PART THREE

Areas of Adjustment

PART FOUR

Achieving Adjustment

P A R T   O N E

The Fundamentals of Adjustment

A. The Psychological Approach to Adjustment

HOW WE ADJUST: THE ADJUSTMENT PROCESS

A Process of Interaction

A Continuous Process

A Process of Causes and Effects

HOW WE REFLECT ADJUSTMENT: OUR BEHAVIOR

HOW WE EXPLORE ADJUSTMENT: SCIENTIFIC PROCEDURE

The Scientific Method

HOW WE IMPROVE ADJUSTMENT

Increased Self-Awareness

Increased Other-Awareness

Increased Problem-Awareness

B. Alternative Approaches to Adjustment

THEORIES AS AIDS TO SECURITY AND ADEQUACY

The Spirit Theory

Religious Theory

Astrology and Related Pseudo-Sciences

Popular Superstitions

Wishful Thinking

An Introduction to Adjustment

1

A. The Psychological Approach to Adjustment

Every organism
attempts to relate to its physical environment
in a way that will satisfy its needs.
Man, our concern in this book, must,
like the other organisms,
satisfy such *physiological* needs
as hunger, thirst, and protection from harm
by *adjusting* to his physical environment.

But man must also *adjust* to environments that are not common to all organisms. In addition to the physical, he must relate to *psychological* and *sociocultural* environments. He must, that is, satisfy such *psychological* needs as those for emotional security, acceptance, affection, self-esteem, and self-fulfillment. And he must satisfy these needs in a sociocultural setting.

How We Adjust: The Adjustment Process

With so many needs and such a complex environment, how can man achieve satisfactory adjustment? We shall need the entire book to answer this question; but, at the start, three fundamental points should be made, points that pertain to any type of adjustment. Adjustment is (1) a process of interaction; (2) a continuous—and therefore never completed—process; and (3) a process in which cause-and-effect relationships can be observed.

A Process of Interaction

Personal adjustment is a process of interaction between ourselves and our environments. In this process we can either *adapt* to the environment or *alter* it. We can, that is, modify our surroundings, either directly or indirectly, or we can modify our own behavior. Whichever we do, however, we are interacting successfully if we achieve a satisfactory relationship. Satisfactory personal adjustment depends on successful interaction.

Some people believe that to adjust means to conform. But conformity is only one kind of adjustment, one kind of interaction; and the quality of adjustment it produces depends on circumstances. In choosing a career, for example, one young man may be content to conform to his parents' wishes because these correspond to his own desires and abilities and because he has confidence in his parents' judgment. To another, who finds himself in conflict with his parents and suppressed by their authority, conformity may mean a surrender, damaging his self-esteem and leaving him in a state of doubt about himself. Still a third may lack the abilities for the career his parents want him to enter, and conformity to their wishes might mean job failure.

Interaction between ourselves and our environment is an integral part of living. At the outset our environment involves principally the members of our families. As we interact with these people we unconsciously acquire from them certain methods of adjusting, methods which we modify to suit our needs. As we grow older we interact with larger groups of people and acquire additional methods for adjusting. During this process of interaction—and often without being aware of what we are doing—we experiment with methods we have observed in others and so evolve the behavior patterns that constitute our own individual pattern of adjustment.

A Continuous Process

Adjustment is a process of *continuous* interaction. Neither the individual nor his world is static. Both are being acted on and modified continually, even though at times these modifications may be so minute that the individual's efforts to adjust to them are imperceptible. Every one of these changes, either in the individual himself or in his environment, alters his relationship to the environment. Every time we encounter another person or problem, something new is introduced into our environment that necessitates adjusting to a new set of circumstances. Even our viewpoint toward our surroundings changes. Our approach to everything that happens to us today, for example, may be influenced by feelings aroused in us by the attendant who parked our car this morning—by whether his friendliness gave us a lift or his grouchiness depressed us.

Recognition of this process of continuous interaction leads us to realize that no human adjustment is ever complete or ideal. That is why we speak of adjustment as an *attempt* to relate satisfactorily to the environment. Because of the continuous modifications in ourselves and our environments, there will always be (except perhaps for very brief periods) some disharmony between ourselves and our environment, some gap between our needs and their complete satisfaction. A *relatively* satisfying adjustment is the best we can achieve.

Since our adjustment involves a process of dealing with changes—in ourselves, in others, in our environment—it is never completed. As long as we live we shall encounter new problems demanding a continuous readiness on our part to adjust to them. We cannot avoid these problems; we can only learn to handle them as they arise.

A Process of Causes and Effects

In studying adjustment we assume that there are orderly, lawful relationships between any behavior and its antecedent conditions—between causes and effects. The effect of a cause can also be described as a response to a stimulus. Thus, Dick hits Jimmy (stimulus), and then Jimmy hits Dick (response).

But maybe Jimmy doesn't hit Dick. Maybe he runs away, or calls his mother, or sits down and cries. Maybe he even ignores Dick. He may react in a variety of ways, but whatever the reaction, the cause in this instance is apparent. We would be reasonably safe in assuming that whatever Jimmy did he did in response to Dick's having hit him.

But why did Dick hit Jimmy to begin with? Possibly there were many reasons, all of them interrelated. This is frequently the case, and for this reason it is more accurate to speak of cause*s* and effect*s* than cause and effect. Only in a few simple instances might we be able to identify a single causative factor in someone's actions. Usually there are a number of contributing causes, some of them obscure, others easily identifiable. This *multiplicity* of causes complicates the study of human behavior and personal adjustment and explains why personal adjustment problems are frequently puzzling and difficult so solve. Seemingly identical causes can have a number of different effects, while seemingly identical effects can stem from a number of different causes.

Let us look at two examples. First, three students fail the same college course. One failed because he was not interested in the subject, the second because he lacked the necessary ability, and the third because of a severe conflict between himself and his instructor. Here we see similar effects stemming from different causes. Secondly, let us consider three teen-age girl friends who live in similar homes in the same suburb. Their fathers are business associates; their mothers belong to the same civic club; and the girls attend the same school and church. When a new, attractive girl moves into the neighborhood, the first girl wants to welcome her into their group; the second girl agrees but does everything she can to make the new girl feel uncomfortable; the third girl abandons the group and attaches herself to another set of companions. Here we have different effects produced from seemingly identical background factors (causes).

Obviously these seemingly identical background factors are interrelated with other causative factors that may not be easy to discover. That other causes do exist here, however, is apparent to the experienced therapist. What they may be and how to deal with them so that they will not develop into serious adjustment problems are questions he cannot answer without an opportunity to study the individuals involved. Such a study forms the basis of psychotherapy and will be discussed in Chapter 15, but we should like here to emphasize one point. In any attempt to identify causative factors we must observe carefully and describe accurately the dynamic forces affecting the individual *at the moment of observation.* His environment, his needs and goals, and his past experiences must be studied in relation to his present situation.

Awareness of the multiplicity of causative factors that influence behavior helps us to take a tolerant, understanding attitude toward those whose behavior is not generally socially approved. For example, we have modified our attitudes toward alcoholics since we have learned that alcoholism is not caused merely by a "weak will." Similarly, we now realize that people who behave in an excessively hostile or aggressive manner are not merely being "ornery." We have learned to try to discover what makes them behave this way.

How We Reflect Adjustment: Our Behavior

If we wish to determine the quality of a person's adjustment we must observe his *behavior.* Some forms of behavior indicate satisfactory adjustment. Others may be recognized as danger signals, warning that maladjustive behavior patterns are being established. Still others indicate the presence of neuroses or psychoses. How to recognize satisfactory and unsatisfactory behavior patterns, so that we can utilize the former and avoid the latter, constitutes the principal subject matter of this book. Here, therefore, we shall just make a few introductory remarks.

For purposes of this discussion we shall define *behavior* as everything we do that is consciously or unconsciously selective—every action that is determined by conscious or unconscious choice from among various possibilities. Behavior is consciously selective when we are aware of what we are doing and why we are doing it. Behavior is unconsciously selective when we do not realize what we are doing or why —when, for example, we "feel impelled" to do things we cannot explain even to ourselves, things about which we later might say, "Now why

Our behavior reflects the quality of our adjustment. The man is dozing at a railroad siding; the boys are taking part in a city cleanup drive. Their contrasting behavior indicates the type of adjustment each has achieved. (From Monkmeyer, by Lowber Tiers, and Nancy Hays.)

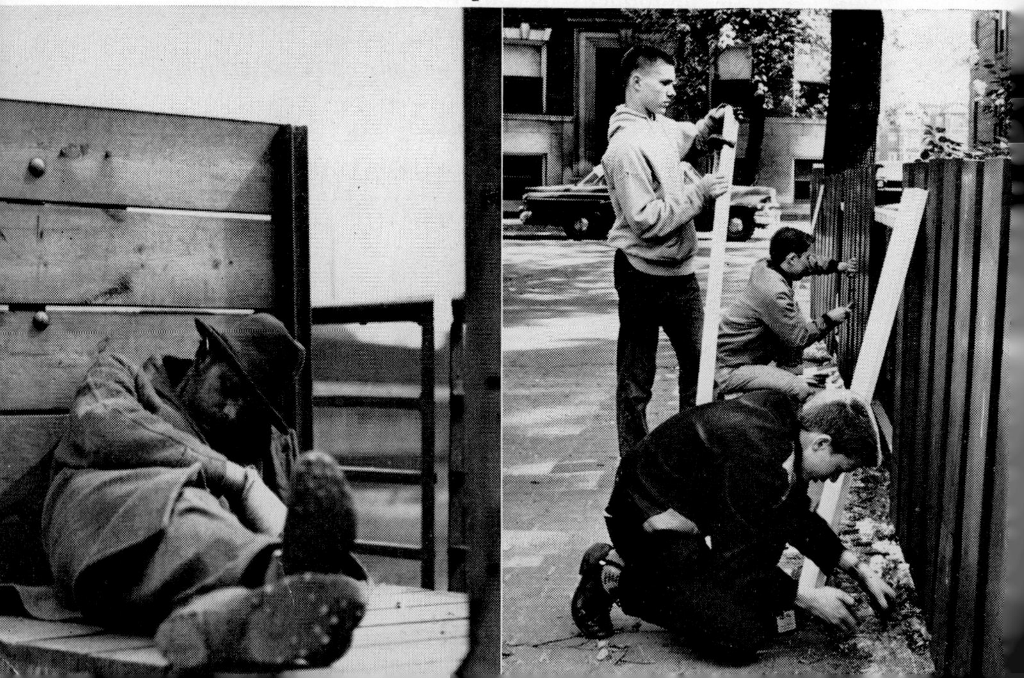

did I do that?" In psychological terminology, this behavior is motivated by our *unconscious*.

When we study the dynamics of personal adjustment we learn that we can—to a certain extent—control the responses of others by consciously controlling our own behavior. Most of us want other people to react favorably toward us. Once we find out, therefore, what kind of behavior produces either welcome or unwelcome responses, we learn how to behave in order to bring about the preferred responses. Although he may not be aware of it, this is one of the first things a growing child learns. He discovers that if he obeys his mother she will probably reward him and that if he disobeys she will probably punish him. To a certain extent, therefore, he can control his mother's behavior by behaving in a particular way himself.

All behavior is directed toward interacting with others or with our environment in ways that will satisfy our needs or solve our problems. Thus all behavior indicates *some* sort of adjustment. But we must realize that some behavior is unacceptable to those around us, even if it seems to accomplish what we ourselves desire. Such behavior may indicate maladjustment. Acceptable forms of behavior, on the other hand, usually indicate satisfactory adjustment. In studying adjustment we learn to distinguish between the two so that we can make acceptable choices.

Well-adjusted people interact with each other in a mutually satisfying manner. In other words, they control their own behavior in such a way as to please other people as well as themselves. In achieving satisfactory adjustment, therefore, we learn that by behaving a certain way we not only influence others to *behave* a certain way but also to *feel* a certain way.

Let us look at an example of how our behavior might affect another's feelings. Suppose you have a friend, Terry, who is very sensitive about the fact that he is only five feet tall. He is shy with girls and has little social life. A club to which you both belong is giving a dance, and Terry asks you to get him a date for it. You know two eligible girls. Both are pretty. Both are good company. One is five feet tall. The other is five feet eight. Which one do you invite? Probably the short one, because you know it would embarrass Terry to dance with the tall girl. The significance of this particular incident is that you were able to control your behavior in such a way as to contribute to Terry's pleasure. If you had chosen to do so, you could just as easily have controlled your behavior in such a way as to cause him discomfort.

Once we gain this concept and learn to understand the important contribution our behavior can make to the way others behave and feel, we see how far-reaching its effects can be and how very much we need to learn which way to control it. But we cannot effectively control the behavior at our end of the interaction process until we gain some insight into the factors that motivate it. These factors will be discussed in Chapter 3.

One further point. Our behavior produces certain effects, which we shall call the *consequences* of our behavior. In many instances people fail to see the cause-and-effect relationship between certain things they do and certain other things that just seem to "happen." A mother, for example, may not be aware that spanking arouses hostility in her child that may express itself in various forms later on. We frequently hear people comment—after their behavior has led to unfortunate consequences—"Oh, I never expected this to happen!" or "Why did this have to happen?" or "What did I ever do to deserve this?"

When we behave in a certain way, and then are surprised at the consequences—whether pleasant or unpleasant—we betray the fact that we were ignoring—or were unaware of—the various possible consequences such behavior could bring about. The extent to which we are aware of these possible consequences depends upon the number and degree of consequences we have consciously experienced in the past, and upon the efforts we have made to learn to *predict* consequences. A small child, having had limited experiences, is limited in his ability

Exploring personal adjustment scientifically. (Top) what the boy says and does to the models of family members and other authority figures in this miniature home setting alerts the therapist to problems that may be affecting his adjustment. The scene was photographed at the Washington University Child Guidance Clinic, St. Louis. (St. Louis Post Dispatch *from Black Star.)*

Among other methods frequently utilized to explore adjustment are laboratory experiments (left: electrodes being attached to head of subject in a dream laboratory) and public opinion polls (right). (Left: from Kleitman, 1960, reproduced with permission from Scientific American. *Right: courtesy* Facts Consolidated, *Los Angeles.)*

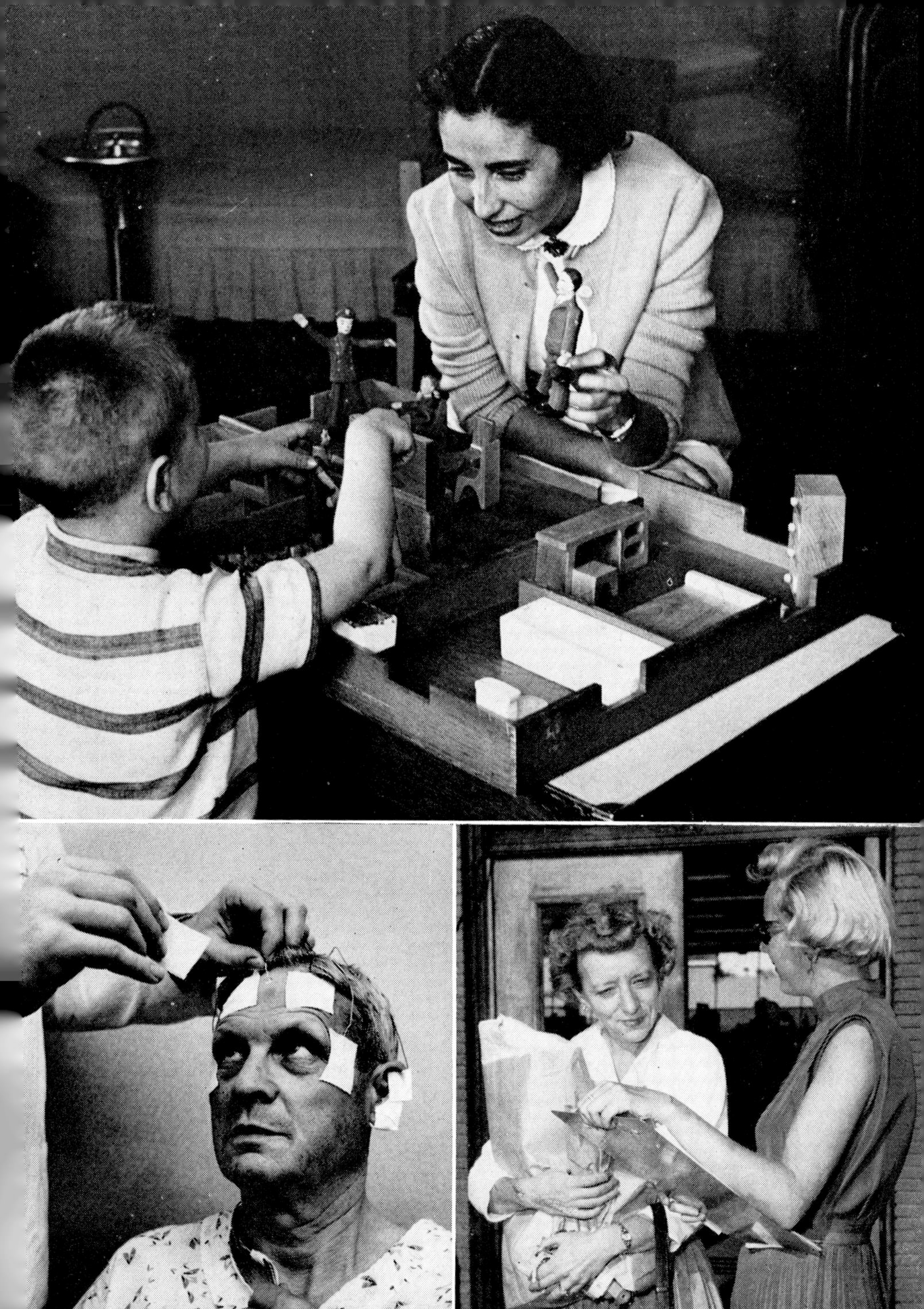

to predict or control the consequences of his behavior. By the time that he has finished school and gone to work, however, his ability to do so should have improved considerably; and the older he grows the more skillful he may become at predicting and controlling consequences.

Awareness of consequences and the ability to predict them are critical factors in personal adjustment; for unless we can foresee the direction in which our behavior will lead us, we shall find it difficult to behave effectively. Satisfactory adjustment to our environment, satisfactory adjustment to others, and satisfactory adjustment to ourselves can be achieved only as consequences of effective behavior.

How We Explore Adjustment: Scientific Procedure

In any study of behavior and adjustment, knowledge of the methods used to obtain relevant information is essential to an accurate interpretation of that information. Suppose, for example, someone tells us that morale is poor on a certain college campus or in a certain factory. How did he arrive at this conclusion? Did he rely on casual observations or did he investigate by controlled observations, that is, *scientifically*? Did he, for example, interview a *representative cross-section* of the student body or the workers (controlled observation), or did he casually talk to a few articulate gripers (and thereby obtain unreliable, unsubstantiated data)?

In psychology, as in any other field of scientific investigation, progress depends on the development and use of appropriate methods of inquiry. The development of intelligence tests, for example, meant a great step forward in our study and understanding of human intelligence. True, casual observations of others may reveal certain of their habits or attitudes and enable us sometimes to predict their behavior. We know, for example, that a certain friend will always be late for appointments, that another will never remember to return a book we have lent him. Nevertheless, such observations hardly constitute sure bases for conclusions. At best they provide us with ideas or impressions —or, if we express it in scientific terminology, with reasonable *hy-*

potheses. These hypotheses must be checked and tested before they can be accepted as valid conclusions.

The Scientific Method

What are the essentials of a scientific approach to the study of human behavior? We can distinguish five steps in scientific procedure: (1) formulating a hypothesis, (2) selecting a research design, (3) collecting data, (4) analyzing data and drawing conclusions, and (5) interpreting the conclusions in a theoretical framework.

FORMULATING A HYPOTHESIS Hypotheses may be formulated either as questions or as assertions of certain relationships. Thus we might ask: "How does age at marriage affect the rate of divorce?" Or we might state: "Having a voice in decision-making increases the productivity of workers." A good hypothesis must be amenable to investigation. The question, "How many angels can dance on the head of a pin?" does not lend itself to scientific inquiry. There can be no procedure or plan for counting angels. How relevant a hypothesis may be to our understanding of human behavior will vary greatly, depending on the experience, wisdom, and skill of the person formulating and investigating it. Sometimes knowledge is advanced because an investigator breaks out of a traditional way of looking at certain phenomena and formulates a revolutionary question or hypothesis.

SELECTING A RESEARCH DESIGN In selecting our research design, the second step, we may decide to employ a previously established method that seems appropriate for our purposes, or we may develop a new type of exploratory program. The type of design we select depends on the observations we wish to make and the data we hope to collect. For some investigations *controlled experimentation*—in which laboratory conditions are created to isolate and control variables—may be possible. Where controlled experimentation is impossible, we may get our information through clinical case studies, that is, through interviews, clinical observations, questionnaires, and tests.

COLLECTING DATA As the third step in our procedure we collect whatever data the methods employed in our research design supply us with. The data must be carefully observed and recorded, and the *validity* and *reliability* of our measurements must be verified. By reliability we mean that repeated measurements will give the same results. By validity we mean that our methods actually measure what we intend them to measure.

The conditions under which we make our measurements must also be noted. Is the subject answering a questionnaire he thinks may help him get a job, or does he think he is merely cooperating in a check on the usefulness of the questionnaire? The subject's motives will affect his attitude, and his attitude will affect his answers. Are we, for example, studying competitive behavior among children at a playground? Then we must note whether the adults in charge encourage competition or cooperation. We must also note whether the toys and games are preponderantly competitive or cooperative, as well as other elements that might influence the behavior of the children.

ANALYZING DATA AND DRAWING CONCLUSIONS Our fourth step, analyzing our findings and drawing conclusions from them, requires us to organize the data so that they contribute answers to the questions raised in the hypothesis. Sometimes these answers disprove the hypothesis; but even refutation is valuable since it eliminates that hypothesis from further consideration. Sometimes the findings may be ambiguous, indicating that a sharpening of the hypothesis or a refining of the methods may be necessary. Frequently the information obtained results in the raising of additional questions, which serve as guides for further investigations.

INTERPRETING CONCLUSIONS IN A THEORETICAL FRAMEWORK The last step, interpreting the conclusions, is closely related to the fourth. Interpretation means relating the evidence obtained to a larger body of scientific knowledge and evaluating it in a theoretical framework. We may, for example, want to compare our findings with results from related studies. Our findings may support what is already known, or they may add something new, perhaps making it necessary to modify a previous interpretation or to reformulate an established theory. In our conclusion we then make a summarizing statement of what the investigation has achieved.

Scientific procedure provides us with the best method we know for *understanding* the phenomena we study, whether we are studying the earth, as in geology, or ourselves, as in psychology. And although the attempt to understand the world and ourselves is in itself most rewarding, what we learn may also give us a basis for making *predictions.* We may be able to anticipate certain future effects as the result of certain known causative factors. Correct predictions test the validity of scientific conclusions or principles. Correct scientific explanations can help us not only to account for and understand behavior but also to predict the kind of behavior that will occur under certain conditions. The greater our knowledge, the greater is our ability to predict.

With understanding and the ability to predict may come also the desire and need to *control,* that is, to regulate and direct behavior of an organism or of some physical phenomenon. Suppose, for example, we administer an intelligence test to a 14-year-old boy. The results will enable us (1) to *understand* the level of his mental abilities, and this understanding will enable us (2) to *predict* whether he will be able to complete the requirements for a college degree. If we find, for example, that his IQ is below normal we know that he will be limited in what he is able to learn and that he would therefore encounter frustration and failure in college. By advising him of our predictions we may (3) *control* his behavior to the extent that he follows our suggestions about what activities he can most successfully pursue. Thus, through the process of understanding, predicting, and controlling we help him to avoid loss of time and feelings of failure and disappointment.

Scientific study of human behavior by investigators in the field of psychology has opened up areas of knowledge undreamed of until the closing years of the nineteenth century. These investigations have provided the information that enables us to study personal adjustment.

How We Improve Adjustment

We have seen that adjustment is a continuous process of interaction and that not all processes of interaction are satisfactory. We have seen that our behavior reflects the quality of our adjustment, and that cause-and-effect relationships determine this behavior. Finally, we have seen that scientific investigators have developed reliable methods for checking and verifying their observations about human behavior. With this information as background, we can consider what we must do to begin to improve our own personal adjustment.

When we study the dynamics of adjustment we are really trying to learn *how* we interact with others, *why* we interact as we do, and how we can *improve* our process of interaction. We are seeking, in other words, an improved method, an *appropriate* and *effective* method, to apply—consciously or unconsciously—to the solution of our problems. Everyone learns *some* method for dealing with problems, but not all methods are appropriate or effective. Suppose, for example, our problems provoke us to temper tantrums or sulkiness, to overeating or heavy drinking, to threats to run away or maybe even shoot ourselves. Such methods bring us no closer to a solution; but they disrupt our relationships with other people, who find them unacceptable no matter how justified we may feel in using them. Such methods are *maladjustive,* and if we constantly employ them we must consider ourselves *maladjusted.* To improve our adjustment and avoid maladjustment, then, we must look for the most effective, appropriate and acceptable methods of dealing with our problems. And to do this we must increase our: (1) *self-awareness;* (2) *other-awareness;* and (3) *problem-awareness.*

Increased Self-Awareness

To increase our self-awareness we must learn to see ourselves as we relate to others and to our environment. We must develop the objectivity that enables us to study ourselves critically and dispassionately, with a minimum of self-deception and camouflage.

Many of us know very little about ourselves. If we stop to think we may realize we know more about cars, clothes, or postage stamps. We may not know, for example, what motivates us, how we communicate with others, or how sensitive we are to the needs of others. We may be unaware of the conditions that affect our emotional ups and downs. We actually seem reluctant to take a close look at ourselves—almost as though we are afraid of what we might find. Yet to take that close look is the first step in forming a realistic basis for solving the problems we face in meeting our needs.

What must we learn about ourselves? To begin with, we should become increasingly aware of our strong points so that we may be able to utilize them to better advantage. Secondly, we should discover our weak points, paying particular attention to personal idiosyncrasies that may be compelling us to cling habitually to faulty, inappropriate methods of interaction, methods that are not solving our problems. Until we modify or discard such methods, we shall not feel free to experiment with new ones. Ability to recognize and apply alternative methods of dealing with problems is essential to satisfactory personal adjustment.

Thirdly, we should become more fully aware of how we affect our environment and how our environment affects us. We should realize that our social existence is one of interconnected, interdependent relationships and that in order to understand ourselves we must understand others.

Increased Other-Awareness

We cannot interact successfully if we are aware only of our own needs, desires, and ways of doing things. It is important to try to be aware of others also—to realize that they have needs and desires similar to ours and to respect their individual ways of doing things. The well-adjusted person does not try to satisfy his needs at another person's expense or to solve his problems by burdening them on someone else.

By other-awareness, then, we mean sensitivity to the needs and feelings of others. We can develop this sensitivity if we make it a point to notice how certain people behave under certain conditions. A mother's sensitivity to her child's needs, for example, helps her to know when she must be tactful and when she can be direct and explicit without upsetting him. It guides her in her choice of disciplinary procedures. A sensitive mother respects the feelings of her child.

By training ourselves to notice and to remember, we may, over a period of time, learn to anticipate how others will react. We may then try to modify our own behavior accordingly, in the interest of achieving a mutual feeling of satisfaction.

Being aware of others will help us to know when they need our support, our interest, our companionship. If we are sensitized to their reactions as well as to our own, if we are aware of their needs as well as ours, our relationships with them can be greatly enriched.

Increased Problem-Awareness

By increasing problem-awareness we mean maximizing our awareness of both the problems we must solve and the situations in which we must solve them. To do so it may help us to learn (1) to avoid oversimplification; (2) to consider the problem from several points of view; and (3) to be aware of the relationship between means and ends.

1. Each of us has some kind of an adjustment problem. We oversimplify it if we assume that it results from a single cause, and thus overlook other significant factors that need to be considered before it can be solved. If we are not interacting with other people as well as we think we should, and we would like to improve our social relationships, it is important to try to discover as many causes as we can that might be contributing to the difficulty. The fat boy who assumes that people avoid him simply because he is fat and the homely girl who blames her lack of popularity on her face are ignoring the fact that many other fat or homely people have wide circles of friends. If each of them will consider other factors, the problem may be solved. One of the ways they can do this, of course, is to increase their self-awareness.

2. If a problem has us stymied, possibly we are approaching it from only one angle. If we can discover no other possible approach on our own then it might help to consult someone else and to get his point of view. From where he stands the problem may look quite different, like a mountain that can be climbed on one side but not on the other. What we have to do is to keep going around the mountain until we find our way to the top. If we stay where we are we may never find it.

3. What we want is one thing. How to get it is another. It is not enough simply to *want* to improve our interaction with others. We must also be willing to *do something about it,* and to select means consistent with our ends.

B. Alternative Approaches to Adjustment

The psychological theories of personal adjustment presented in this book are less than one hundred years old. Before studying them in detail, therefore, it may be interesting to take a brief look at some other ideas that have guided man's efforts to adjust.

For as long as men have inhabited the earth they have been trying to adjust to their world and to each other. In their journey through history they have tried one system after another, some founded on superstition, others developed around a factual basis. But superstition or fact, all of these theory systems have evolved out of man's efforts to satisfy his needs and solve his problems—efforts directed toward achieving, as an end result, feelings of *security* and *adequacy.*

Theories as Aids to Security and Adequacy

Efforts at personal adjustment are aimed at acquiring the feelings of security and adequacy that come from *knowing how to interact with others and with the environment.* All of us know that we feel more secure in familiar surroundings than we do in unfamiliar places. We like to know our way around. It gives us a feeling of security to run across familiar sights and faces as we go about our daily chores. Occasionally we do take trips and explore unfamiliar surroundings, but we agree, almost unanimously, that "it always feels good to get home again."

Furthermore, all of us want to feel that we are capable of doing the things we want to do or are supposed to do. We want, that is, to feel adequate. If we do not feel adequate, we are likely to contrive various excuses to try to explain our deficiencies.

In needing to feel secure and adequate we are no different from any of the generations that have preceded us. The problem of knowing how to interact with others and with the environment is one that man has always faced; and, for this reason, he has sought *explanations,* has striven to erect *systems of thought* that would aid him in understanding more about himself, about other men, and about the universe. In his search for understanding man has been motivated not so much by curiosity or intellectual restlessness as by this need to feel secure and adequate. Frightened and puzzled by the unpredictability of nature, man has tried to relate the unknown to the known, an effort that has often led him to accept *imagined* systems that seemed to explain otherwise incomprehensible factors and forces.

If the imagined system was one in which he could believe implicitly, it helped him to feel secure and adequate, no matter how far-fetched it might be. An imagined system can serve the same function psychologically as a realistic one if it offers acceptable answers to our questions and if it happens to be the system that the majority of our fellows believe in too. But as man has acquired more knowledge about himself and the world, the answers provided by imagined systems have ceased to satisfy him, and he has abandoned or become impatient with systems that served satisfactorily in the past. Sometimes, however, it is very difficult for a group of people, and especially for an entire society, to replace old, inaccurate views with newer, more accurate ones. New discoveries and ideas usually have to struggle against stern resistance before they become generally accepted. New systems of thought have to demonstrate their value.

This applies to psychological theories as well. Until the late nineteenth century no one had ever heard of the ideas that now form the basis of psychological theory. And since our current theories of personal adjustment are so new historically it seems natural to ask why we need them now when we managed to survive for so long without them. The best way to answer this question would seem to be to look at some of the other systems of thought that have influenced—and still are influencing—man's behavior. We can try to determine whether they can adequately serve his needs. Then, as we learn more about the psychological approach to personal adjustment, we shall have acquired a frame of reference that will help us to evaluate the system of reasoning that supports it.

When we refer to each of these systems of thought as a *theory*, we use the word to indicate a sphere of speculative thought not necessarily founded on fact; that is to say, an intelligent or fanciful guess. In scientific terminology, on the other hand, a theory is a general principle supported by considerable data, more solidly supported than a hypothesis, less firmly established than a law, but covering a wider range than a single law.[1]

We shall examine each of these theory-systems in the light of two questions:

1. To what extent has the theory been validated scientifically? The more positive its scientific validation, the more enduring it is, the more it provides us with a reliable guide for further exploration and understanding.

2. How can it help modern man to adjust?

Theories, it should be remembered, influence behavior. They lead to action. They have consequences. If, for example, we support the theory that crime and delinquency are the result of certain innate characteristics and that the person born with them will become a criminal regardless of his rearing and other experiences, then our ultimate aim can only be to lock these criminals up for life so that they can cause no trouble. Such a theory provides no suggestion for preventing a person from becoming a criminal or for changing him if he does become one. But if we believe that criminal behavior is a result of childhood experiences and environmental forces—that the criminal, in other words, is a product of environment rather than heredity—this theory will lead to an entirely different set of actions.

Let us look now at some of the theory-systems that have influenced man's efforts to adjust.

The Spirit Theory

Ancient man developed the spirit theory to account for natural phenomena he could not understand. Based on superstition, the spirit theory ascribed human qualities, a personal life-force or spirit, to everything that seemed to be a potential source of assistance or danger. Spirits controlled clouds, pushed rocks,

[1] H. B. English and A. C. English, *A Comprehensive Dictionary of Psychological and Psychoanalytical Terms* (New York: Longmans, Green, 1958).

created rain, drove the sun across the sky, rustled the leaves on the trees. But spirits were unpredictable. No one could tell when they might appear or disappear, and to try to predict events on the basis of past performance was futile.

The spirit theory was extended to account for human behavior as well. If a person behaved in an acceptable manner—was guilty of no sins or transgressions against the tribal mores—it was a sign that he was inhabited by good spirits. But if his behavior was strange and unacceptable, this was taken as a sign that evil spirits had gained the upper hand. A person afflicted with evil spirits had to submit to being "purged" by such measures as bloodletting, whipping, dunking, or

The spirit theory of human behavior. Artistic conceptions. Left: a demon's flight from the body of a possessed woman. Right: a fit of demoniac fury with twisting of bodily members. (Courtesy, The Huntington Library, San Marino, California.)

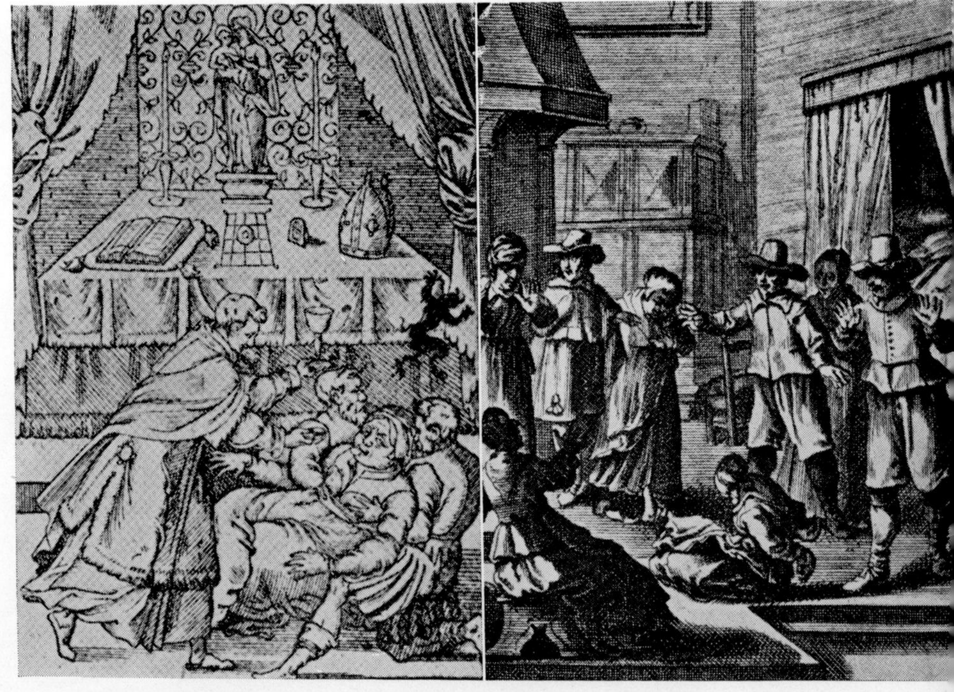

having holes bored in his skull or his body exposed to fire. It was also believed that good and bad spirits might inhabit the same body at different times or even at the same time, in which case there might occur a tremendous struggle between the good and evil spirits for control of the body they were occupying.

No cause-and-effect principle was in effect where spirits were concerned. They could do whatever they pleased, be mischievous or malicious. They could even turn men into animals. Man was helpless in their power.

Not all persons who acted strangely, however, were believed to be possessed by *evil* spirits. Healers and prophets who derived inspiration from trances, epileptic seizures, somnambulism, and other such phenomena, were very much admired and sought after. In ancient Egypt people would travel great distances to hear such people speak and make predictions about the future, passing along messages transmitted to them by the spirits. Even the Greeks sought the advice of such persons, called oracles.

Has the spirit theory been validated scientifically? Not as far as we know. It does not lend itself to scientific investigation. To our knowledge, no scientist has ever conducted an experiment that caused a spirit to materialize.

Yet for centuries the spirit theory did serve a function in primitive society (as it continues to do today in some areas). It guided man's efforts to adjust to other men and to the environment. It made the universe meaningful for him and spared him the responsibility of working out his own destiny. The spirits ruled and man's initiative succumbed to their caprice. He felt secure in the knowledge that the spirits were in control and that he was not required to make decisions on his own. He was like a child who feels secure in the knowledge that his parents will take care of him, even though he knows they may need to punish him at times for his transgressions. As for the need for adequacy, this did not trouble man as long as he felt that little was expected of him as an individual. He did not even need to be an adequate interpreter of the spirits. The magicians would do it for him.

Can the spirit theory help modern man to adjust? Modern, *informed, intelligent,* man would scoff at any suggestion that his life was masterminded by spirits. As modern beings living in a sophisticated, civilized society, we cannot ask the advice of an oracle when we have a need to satisfy or a problem to solve. Nor can we confer with the spirits. We must seek a more reasonable, realistic method for working our way out of our difficulties.

Religious Theory

Religion has been defined as "a system of attitudes, practices, rites, and beliefs by means of which individuals or a community put themselves in relation to God or to a supernatural world and often to each other, and from which the religious person derives a set of values by which to judge events in the natural world." [2]

Religions developed out of man's efforts to replace superstitions

[2] English and English, *Dictionary of Psychological and Psychoanalytical Terms.*

The diverse forms people have assigned to their gods indicate the different characteristics that have been attributed to them and the different type of influence each has been expected to exert. (Left: Diana by Jean Goujon, from the Château of Anet, before 1554. The Louvre, Paris. Photo: Bulloz. Right: Siva as King of Dancers, from south India, 12th or 13th century. Museum of Asiatic Art, Amsterdam. Photo: Elisofon.)

with "explanations." Elaborate systems were devised, centered around one or more deities who were believed to be the origin and cause of everything—natural or supernatural. In many instances these deities were really spirits in more glorified form. But although men begged the aid of the spirits, often with elaborate rituals, they did not worship them in the way they worshipped their gods.

Although it is not our intention here to digress into a history of the development of the religions of the world, we should like to glance at a few characteristics of religions, characteristics that have influenced man's efforts to adjust to his world. Actually, religious beliefs and practices are as diverse as the people who practice them, and their characteristics reflect this diversity.

The characteristics attributed to the gods, and the methods designed to win their favor, vary from religion to religion. Almost all religions advocate prayers and rituals. But other behavioral standards depend on the personalities of the gods in whose honor the religion was founded. Some gods were models of virtue and expected their subjects to be virtuous too. Others were fun-loving and could look the other way or even join in when their subjects were making merry. Some gods spent a great deal of time in meditation and liked their subjects to do the same. Others seemed almost constantly involved in heroic love affairs, and this too was reflected in the behavior of their subjects. Some gods looked like human beings and some looked like various combinations of animals. Some were beautiful and some grotesque. Some mingled with the people; some remained aloof.

In societies where religion was (or is) the center of existence, these characteristics have exerted great influence on the way the people have interacted with each other and with their environments. To different extents men have tried to obey or imitate their gods. Sometimes they were imitating men who had actually lived on earth and had set real examples. Sometimes they were imitating imaginary people who were really projections of the personalities of those who worshipped them. But however they originated, these examples to be imitated, or these dictums to be obeyed, helped man to feel secure and adequate by setting standards and limits for his behavior.

Furthermore, because many of these religions were built around the lives of real people, they could claim more of a factual basis than systems founded on assumptions regarding spirits. Thus, religions are more acceptable to intelligent men. Many men have made a satisfactory adjustment to life on the basis of their religious beliefs.

Religious beliefs do not lend themselves to scientific investigation and cannot, therefore, be scientifically validated. It is interesting to note, however, that many religious therapists no longer counsel merely on the basis of their religious principles. They have introduced into religious therapy elements that originated with psychology.

Astrology and Related Pseudo-Sciences

The *theory* of *astrology* emerged during the Middle Ages as a single, elaborate system derived from the *science* of *astronomy*. The medieval astrologer divided a globe of the universe into twelve sections, each representing a specific "house of heaven." The sun, the moon, and all of the stars passed through each of these houses every twenty-four hours; and it was—and still is—believed that an individual's character, personality, and future were determined by the position of the sun, moon, and stars at the moment of his birth. It would seem to follow that all people born in the same part of the world at the same time should share identical futures, but the discrepancy between this idea and simple observed facts did not bother the medieval astrologer any more than it bothers his modern counterparts. When it was discovered that the earth was not the center of the universe, however, popular faith in astrology was somewhat shaken.

To keep in step with changing times, astrologers (they call themselves astrolo*gists*), many of whom sincerely believe in their systems, have begun to describe them in recognized neurological, physiological, or psychological terms. The use of such "scientific" terminology, however incorrect, serves to impress the unwary, who confidently consult such "specialists" as *bioastrologists, biopsychophysic astrologists, glandular astrologists, natal astrologists,* and *radix astrologists.* It is estimated that there are at least 25,000 astrologers working full or part time to supply the demands of the millions of people who seek their advice on adjustment problems. *Fortune tellers,* under which heading astrologers can be included, are estimated to number about 80,000 in the United States. The Better Business Bureau has estimated that Americans spend over $200,000,000 annually for astrological services. There are over 20 astrological associations; at least five leading astrology magazines, with a total circulation of approximately 1,000,000; and about 2,500 daily and weekly newspapers carrying astrological features.

H. F. Pringle, who made rather extensive investigations years ago, found such a tremendous amount of evidence against astrology and such complete rejection of it by men of science that he felt it only fair to give the Astrologers Guild a chance to defend itself. He asked the president of the Guild to choose four of his most able astrologers and to send them to the office of Good Housekeeping, the magazine for which Pringle did the article, where they would be placed in separate rooms and asked to give astrological readings for the same two subjects. All records were to be published verbatim no matter how they came out. Although the president of the Guild seemed to think that this was a good plan, no astrologers were ever sent to participate in the experiment in spite of repeated requests. Nor did any others throughout the country volunteer.

A group of scientists were questioned some years ago concerning their views about astrology. The following excerpt clearly indicates the general opinion held by men of science:

> Psychologists find no evidence that astrology is of any value whatsoever as an indicator of past, present or future trends . . . (or that) social events can be foretold by divinations of the stars. . . . A considerable section of the American public (has faith) in a magical practice that has no shred of justification in scientific fact. The principal reason why people turn to astrology and to kindred superstitions is that they lack in their own lives the resources necessary to solve personal problems confronting them. . . . They yield to the pleasant suggestion that a golden key (to their difficulties) is at hand. . . . Faith in astrology or in any other occult practice is harmful in so far as it encourages an unwholesome flight from the persistent problems of life . . . it does no good to turn to magic and mystery in order to escape misery . . . men's destinies are shaped by their own actions in this world. . . . Our fates rest not in the stars, but in ourselves.[3]

[3] B. J. Bok and M. W. Mayall, "Scientists Look at Astrology," *The Scientific Monthly*, LII (1941), 244. By permission of *The Scientific Monthly*.

Astrology, used as a psychological crutch by persons in need of support, is an opiate; and there are no harmless opiates. It is an escapist device that can weaken a person's ability to adjust to the continuous demands and problems of daily living.

Another pseudo-science is *phrenology*. Phrenology holds that the protrusions or bumps on a person's head may be taken as indicators of his personality or character. According to this "bumpology," the shape of a person's head might indicate such characteristics as combativeness, congeniality, jealousy, discretion, envy, ambition, honesty, and so forth.

There is no scientific evidence that the mind consists of a large number of different emotional, esthetic, or intellectual faculties and traits localized in specific areas of the cortex, or that the degree of development of the cortex in any way reflects the strength of the trait, or that the development of the cortex can in any way be determined from the outer surface of the skull. The cerebral localization found from a careful study of the cortex is of an entirely different kind.

It should be noted, further, that most of these terms do not refer to actual *behavior*, but rather to *evaluations* or *judgments* made about one person's behavior by another person. For example, to characterize a person as "ambitious" tells us nothing about his specific behavior but only presents an evaluation of his behavior in the opinion of the person using the term. It may, in fact, tell us more about the person who uses the term than about the one to whom it is applied.

Another pseudo-science similar to phrenology is *physiognomy*. While phrenology is concerned with the bumps on the head, physiognomy uses the shape of the face and its parts as an indicator of psychological traits. Here the assumption is made that psychological traits are reflected in the face. Thus we find claims that a certain kind of chin denotes strength or weakness, that the set of the eyes indicates honesty or deceit, or that the lips reveal sensitivity or grossness. We

Figure 1. Localization of functions in the brain: science vs. phrenology. Top: scientifically established localization of functions. Bottom: phrenologist's map of the brain. (Top drawing is adapted from Clifford T. Morgan, Physiological Psychology. *New York: McGraw-Hill, 1943, p. 16. By permission of McGraw-Hill Book Co., Inc. Drawing at bottom is adapted from Spurzheim.)*

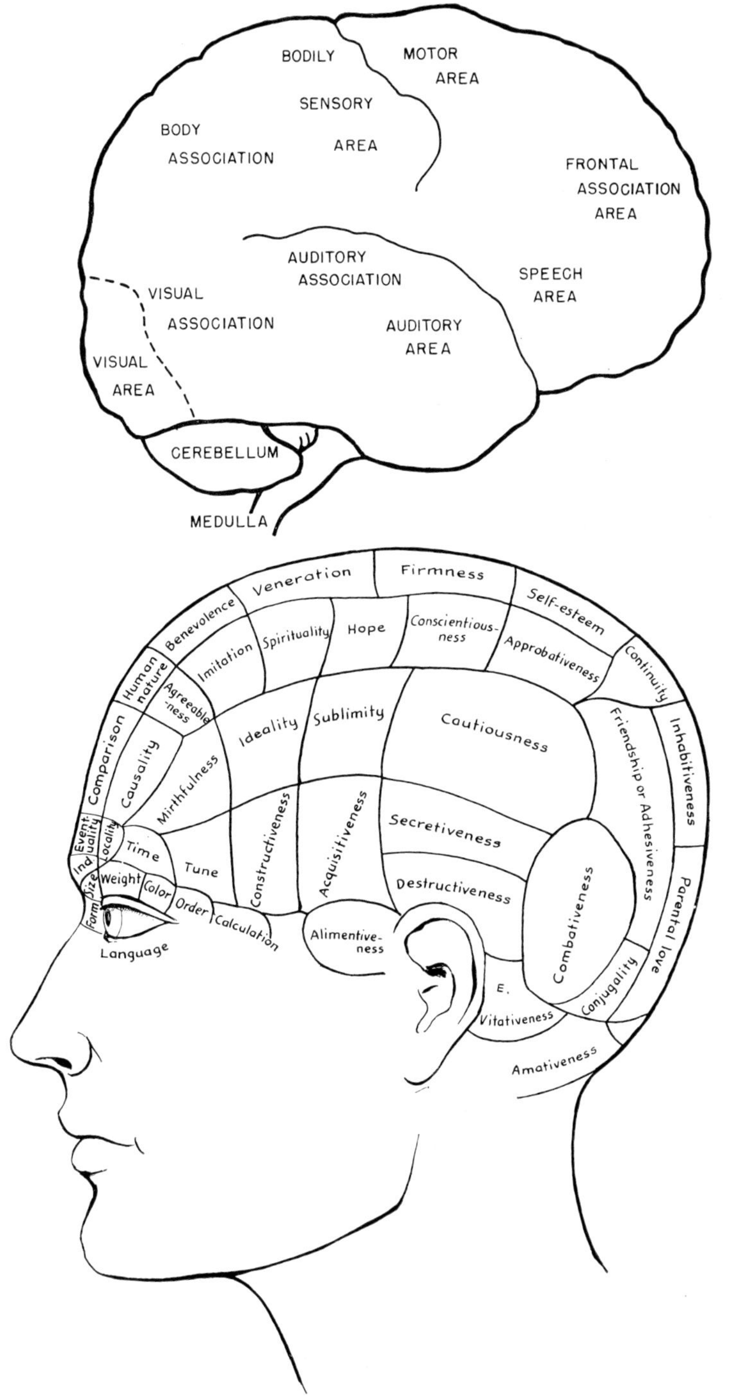

BODILY
MOTOR
AREA
SENSORY
AREA
BODY
ASSOCIATION
FRONTAL
ASSOCIATION
AREA
AUDITORY
ASSOCIATION
SPEECH
AREA
VISUAL
ASSOCIATION
AUDITORY
AREA
VISUAL
AREA
CEREBELLUM
MEDULLA
Veneration
Firmness
Self-esteem
Benevolence
Spirituality
Hope
Conscientious-
ness
Approbativeness
Continuity
Human
nature
Imitation
Agreeable
-ness
Ideality
Sublimity
Cautiousness
Friendship or Adhesiveness
Inhabitiveness
Comparison
Causality
Mirthfulness
Constructiveness
Acquisitiveness
Secretiveness
Event-
uality
Locality
Time
Tune
Ind.
Size
Weight
Color
Order
Destructiveness
Combativeness
Parental love
Form
Calculation
Alimentive-
ness
Language
E.
Vitativeness
Conjugality
Amativeness

are aware, of course, that a sorrowful face may appear different from a joyful one, but this difference stems from behavior, not from personality or character.

The claims of palmists, graphologists, or mediums and occultists of various kinds are equally unreliable.

What about the predictions these persons make? "But," you often hear someone say, "astrology (or phrenology) is accurate; the astrologist (or phrenologist) *can* predict the future." A mistaken sense of the predictive accuracy of these systems arises from the following techniques, employed by their practitioners in order to imbue their pronouncements with the appearance of authenticity and accuracy: (1) They employ broad generalizations that are true of everyone to some extent. (2) They flatter their visitors until they are ready to believe anything. (3) They give contradictory information in the same statement. For example, the astrologist might say, "You are generous but careful to spend wisely." Obviously most of us like to think we spend wisely, and where this is not the case, we like to think we are generous. (4) These persons have developed the "fishing" technique into a fine art. With gentle and unobtrusive probing, prying, and observing, they are able to get twice as much information from a client as they give back. (5) They draw analogies between superficial or nonrelated resemblances. For example, a graphologist will say that the person who makes an open "L" is "generous" while the person who makes a tight "L" is stingy. Or that the open "L" means "honesty," equating "honesty" with "openness."

None of these pseudo-sciences has been scientifically validated, and those who practice them, no matter how sincere and well-intentioned they may be, are asking their believers to base their behavior and adjustment on sheer guesswork. A person with severe adjustment problems who tries to follow the pseudo-scientist's advice may succeed only in intensifying his difficulties.

Popular Superstitions

Superstition may be defined as a belief or theory that omens, signs, charms, or certain types of activity can produce magical effects—can, that is, help us to adjust by mysteri-

Superstition: Ground Hog Day. If the animal, emerging from its hole on February 2, sees a shadow, then back it scrambles, legend says, for another six weeks of sleep which connotes six more weeks of winter weather. In this picture, taken during the 30's, the Slumbering Ground Hog Lodge of Quarryville, Pennsylvania, gathers on Ground Hog Day to see that nothing frightens the little creature into prolonging the cold. (Photograph by Willard R. Culver.)

ously satisfying our needs and solving our problems by means of some magical power that requires no effort on our own part. The examples of superstitious beliefs in our own behavior are almost endless. The following are but a few.[4]

Today, instead of blaming an occurrence on a spirit, we attribute it to "good or bad luck." Some of us attempt to court "Lady Luck" by wearing special charms, just as did primitive man. We still

[4] For a compilation of superstitions see Claudia de Lys, *A Treasury of American Superstitions* (New York: The Philosophical Library, 1948).

have "wishbones," carry around a rabbit's foot, nail horseshoes above doors, and give mystic credence to the "power" of a certain number. Thirteen has been considered an unlucky number since Jesus sat down with his disciples and was betrayed—and is still considered unlucky by many. This is carried so far that in many hotels one finds no thirteenth floor, the number going from twelve to fourteen. The mystic 3 also gets a great deal of attention. Many games are built around the number (3 strikes, you're out), many religious practices employ it, and many believe that a drowning man who goes down for the third time does so for the last time. Similarly, seven years of bad luck are believed to follow the breaking of a mirror (because it was once believed that the "soul" was reflected there).

Before facing a problem situation we sometimes knock on wood or cross our fingers to make sure we get through it all right. At weddings an unmarried girl tries to catch the bride's bouquet so that she will be the next to marry. By contrast, the girl who finds a thimble in her piece of wedding cake knows that she will never find a husband. She can still take heart, however, because since she is unlucky in love she will be lucky at cards. If a person is grouchy he must have gotten up on the wrong side of the bed. If we walk under a ladder something terrible may happen to us. If we spill salt we must toss some over our left shoulder to prevent bad luck.

Most of us profess to be merely amused by such superstitions. But we practice many of them just the same—"just in case."

Superstitions have never been scientifically validated. Many of them are remnants of earlier religious beliefs, beliefs that were abandoned as civilization progressed. Those who rely on superstitions to see them through their adjustment problems are in danger of losing contact with reality.

Wishful Thinking

Wishful thinking is not far removed from superstition as a device for attempting to satisfy needs or solve problems. To believe what we wish to believe rather than to consider the facts is like expecting a good luck charm to help us to get a job.

Even in the absence of a recognizable superstition, many of us indulge in this tendency to believe what we want to believe regardless of evidence to the contrary.

To mention wishful thinking as a theory of adjustment may seem a trifle far-fetched. Yet, basically, it does function in place of a theory of adjustment for those who prefer to ignore the facts, who would rather not be bothered to learn the difference between potentially useful and potentially harmful methods. To presume that we will always take the right step without bothering to learn what the right step may be is to think wishfully that our own infallibility will see us through. Such people arrive at conclusions on the basis of their own feelings and avoid facing facts for fear the facts will disturb those conclusions. Then they tend to reinforce such conclusions by assertion rather than by verification. It is an interesting psychological phenomenon that the person who is least secure about the conclusions he has accepted ready-made (or on the basis of his wishful thinking) is the one who proclaims them the most vociferously and with the least tolerance for the conflicting opinions of others. This process of wishfully arriving at an opinion that pleases us and then persisting in believing it is one that asks for no scientific validation, but neither does it facilitate satisfactory adjustment.

We may conclude this discussion of alternative approaches to adjustment by saying that we cannot pride ourselves on our modern enlightenment. Although superstition recedes before the spread of knowledge, it does so very slowly. Change is a constant condition of living, but many of us try to insulate ourselves against it. When a new idea contradicts one of our sacred or valued beliefs, we resist it with all the power at our command.

Yet intelligent living and the solving of personal and social problems cannot take place in psychological rigidity. We must reason our way through problems if we are to live effectively. Sometimes our pet philosophies and most cherished beliefs may be at variance with reality. What may seem obvious is not always necessarily accurate. In the appreciation of change lies the hope of progress. In the appreciation of the need to learn *continuously*, regardless of age, lies the source of good mental health.

For Additional Reading

Alexander, Franz, *The Western Mind in Transition: An Eyewitness Story*. New York: Random House, 1960.

Allport, Gordon W., *The Individual and His Religion*. New York: Macmillan, 1950.

Bok, B. J. and M. W. Mayall, "Scientists Look at Astrology," *Scientific Monthly*, LII (1941), 233-244.

Castiglioni, Arturo, *Adventures of the Mind*. New York: Knopf, 1946.

Chase, Stuart, *The Proper Study of Mankind: An Inquiry into the Science of Human Relations* (rev. ed.). New York: Harper and Row, 1963.

Church, Joseph, *Language and the Discovery of Reality. A Developmental Psychology of Cognition*. New York: Random House, 1961.

Cohen, M. R., *Reason and Nature*. Glencoe, Ill.: Free Press, 1953.

———, and E. Nagel, *An Introduction to Logic and Scientific Method*. New York: Harcourt, Brace, 1934.

Coleman, James, *Personality Dynamics and Effective Behavior*. Chicago: Scott, Foresman, 1960.

Dobzhansky, Theodosius, *Mankind Evolving: The Evolution of the Human Species*. New Haven: Yale University Press, 1962.

Fielding, William J., *Strange Superstitions and Magical Practices*. Philadelphia: Blakiston, 1945.

Fromm, Erich, *Escape from Freedom*. New York: Farrar and Rinehart, 1941.

Halbwachs, Maurice, *Sources of Religious Sentiment*. New York: Free Press of Glencoe, 1962.

Jourard, Sidney M., *Personality Adjustment. An Approach Through the Study of Healthy Personality*. New York: Macmillan, 1958.

Kantor, J. R., "Perspectives in Psychology: History of Science as Scientific Method," *Psychological Record*, X (1960), 187-189.

Lazarus, Richard S., *Personality and Adjustment*. Englewood Cliffs, N. J.: Prentice-Hall, 1963.

Lehner, George F. J., *Explorations in Personal Adjustment: A Workbook* (rev. ed.). Englewood Cliffs, N. J.: Prentice-Hall, 1957.

Lewis, Donald J., *Scientific Principles of Psychology*. Englewood Cliffs, N. J.: Prentice-Hall, 1963.

Mathews, W. Mason, "Successful Adjustment: A Frame of Reference," *American Journal of Orthopsychiatry*, XXX (1960), 667-675.

McClelland, David C., "Toward a Science of Personality Psychology," in *Perspectives in Personality Theory*, eds. Henry P. David and Helmut von Bracken. New York: Basic Books, 1961, pp. 355-382.

Patton, Robert *et al.*, *Current Trends in Psychological Theory: A Bicentennial Program*. Pittsburgh: University of Pittsburgh Press, 1961.

Popper, Karl R., *The Logic of Scientific Discovery*. New York: Basic Books, 1959.

Postman, Leo, *Psychology in the Making: Histories of Selected Research Problems*. New York: Knopf, 1962.

Reichenbach, Hans, *Experience and Prediction—An Analysis of the Foundations and the Structure of Knowledge*. Chicago: University of Chicago Press, 1949.

Rhine, J. B. and J. G. Pratt, *Parapsychology: Frontier Science of the Mind*. Springfield, Ill.: Thomas, 1957.

Rokeach, Milton, *The Open and Closed Mind. Investigations into the Nature of Belief Systems and Personality Systems*. New York: Basic Books, 1960.

Sarnoff, Irving, *Personality Dynamics and Development*. New York: Wiley, 1962.

Seligmann, Kurt, *The Mirror of Magic*. New York: Pantheon, 1948.

Selltiz, Claire, Marie Jahoda, Morton Deutsch, and Stuart W. Cook, *Research Methods in Social Relations* (rev. ed.). New York: Holt, 1960.

Shaffer, Laurance F. and Edward J. Shoben, Jr., *The Psychology of Adjustment* (2nd ed.). New York: Houghton Mifflin, 1956.

Shaw, Franklin J. and Robert S. Ort, *Personal Adjustment in the American Culture*. New York: Harper, 1953.

Singer, Charles, *A Short History of Scientific Ideas to 1900*. Cambridge: Oxford University Press, 1959.

Smith, Henry Clay, *Personality Adjustment*. New York: McGraw-Hill, 1961.

Smith, M. B., J. S. Bruner, and R. W. White, *Opinions and Personality*. New York: Wiley, 1956.

Steiner, Lee R., *Where Do People Take Their Troubles?* Boston: Houghton Mifflin, 1945.

Ward, Henshaw, *Thobbing—a Seat at the Circus of Intellect*. Indianapolis: Bobbs-Merrill, 1926.

Interpersonal Relationships

2

From the time we are born
we are involved
in *interpersonal relationships.*
At every stage
our growth is marked by direct and intimate
association with others.
At birth, and for many years thereafter,
these associations are characterized by dependence.
We rely on others,
usually our families,
for food, clothing, shelter, and other necessities.

And although we eventually outgrow this dependence, we continue, throughout our lives, to be involved in *interpersonal relationships.*

In this chapter we shall discuss the general nature of these interpersonal relationships and their effects on our growth and development. Since we form many of these relationships as members of groups, we shall devote a portion of the chapter to a consideration of groups —how they function and the kinds of needs they satisfy.

The Effect of Early Family Experiences

A child's interpersonal relationships begin in his family. Early family experiences influence the behavior patterns he acquires, the goals he seeks, and the kind of adjustment he achieves. True, experimental evidence presents an inconsistent and sometimes conflicting picture of how much and in what ways these early experiences influence later behavior; but it seems reasonably clear that the nature of a child's early contacts with others, particularly with the family, does determine to what extent he will be, for example, shy or bold, cooperative or individualistic, boastful or modest, sympathetic or indifferent.

At first the small child is apparently nonsocial. In the beginning he does not distinguish himself from others; his awareness of the dis-

The child's interpersonal experiences begin in the family. Unqualified acceptance from the family and, particularly, a warm, affectional relationship with the mother give the child a feeling of security that provides a firm foundation for the establishment of satisfactory interpersonal relationships outside the family. (From Monkmeyer, by Max Tharpe, Lowber Tiers, and Sybil Shelton.)

tinction between himself and others must be learned. In time, however, he begins to develop both self-awareness and social awareness. He begins to perceive, remember, act, and feel with reference to others. He learns that other people are not only physically separate from himself, but that they have feelings, needs, and thoughts different from his own. As he grows older he begins to develop understanding and sympathy and greater friendliness, concern, and affection. His social horizon expands as playmates, and then schoolmates and teachers, supplement his early family contacts. Still later, as he grows into adolescence and adulthood, his circle of acquaintances widens to include co-workers and employers, people in various organizations he may join, and new friends. Dating, courtship, and then marriage become important areas of social interaction, involving special adjustment. Figure 1 on page 40 illustrates this widening range of experience.

How well the growing child manages the gradual expansion of his social contacts depends, as we have already suggested, on his early relationship with his parents. From them he learns fundamental emotional patterns and attitudes that govern his later dealings with people and social institutions. His reaction toward parental authority, for example, will influence his adjustment to other authority figures, such as police, teachers, and employers. And whether or not he feels he "belongs" in his family will largely determine whether or not he feels at home in other groups.

Possibly the most important contribution a family can make

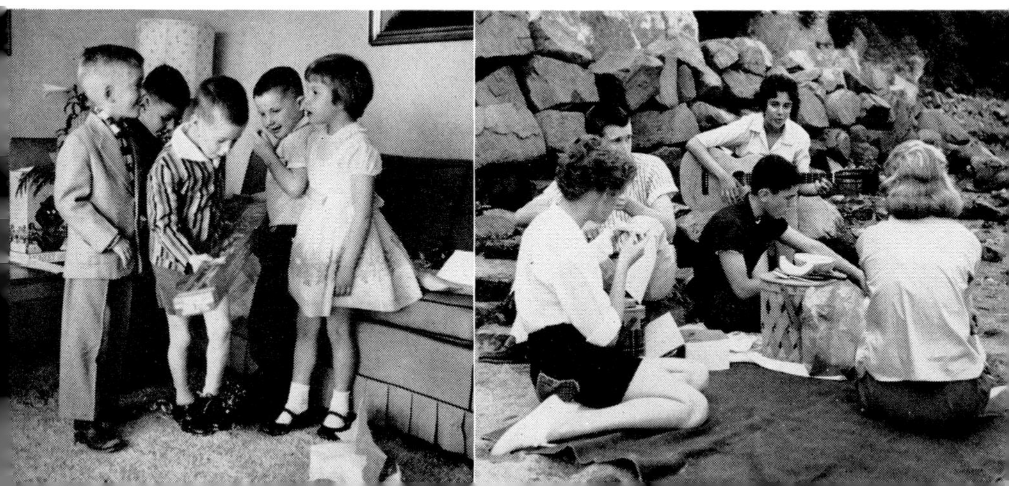

to the child's ability to interact satisfactorily with others is to satisfy his need for love and affection, that is, his need for an *unqualified acceptance* that makes him feel emotionally secure. Unqualified acceptance means that the child knows that love and affection will be forthcoming regardless of his behavior; he knows that even if he disobeys his parents he will not lose their love.

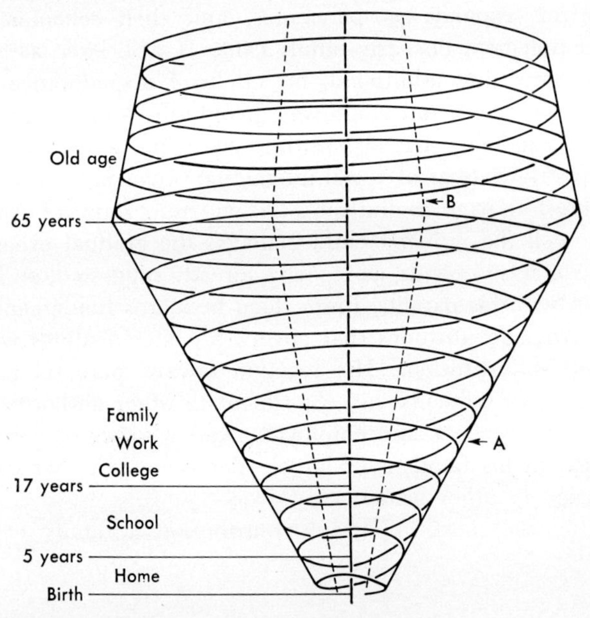

Figure 1. The widening range of experience in normal development. As the child becomes an adolescent and then an adult, his range of experience and contact with others widens. For some people the increasing range may be a very wide one (A). For others, the increasing range may be relatively narrow (B).

The way a child's need for affection is handled may have a decisive influence on how he seeks or expresses affection as an adult. Particularly important is the affectional relationship between a child and his mother. If this relationship is warm and emotionally satisfying, he is likely to form the same kind of relationships with others; if it is cool and distant, he will probably relate to others the same way. Out of the first affections between mother and child come the foundations for later attachments to playmates, colleagues, wives, children.

Lack of love and affection can give a child a sense of insecurity that can either make him fear mingling with others or compel him to seek companionship constantly in order to feed his love-hunger. An unloved child can turn into a selfish adult, craving love and attention but unable to give anything of himself in return. Such an adult, because he cannot give of himself, antagonizes others and so frustrates his own need for acceptance.

Although unqualified acceptance is most often found in families, it can also mark very close friendships. The affection of a close friend or relative is important to us because it engenders trust, and this trust enables us to accept from him criticisms we may badly need but which we would not be able to accept from anyone else. The same kind of trust may mark a business partnership or a partnership of creative artists. The partners may disagree at times, but their relationship is not threatened.

It seems safe to say that satisfactory adult human relationships start in infancy and early childhood. Psychologists recognize this fact and emphasize the great importance of child-rearing in mental health. Indeed, childhood might be called the "golden age" for promoting mental health, a time when the foundation is laid on which we build the complex structure of our personalities.

Fundamentals of Interaction

Basic to all social relationships is interaction between two or more people. Our behavior influences someone else's, and his in turn influences ours. This interaction leads to continuous modification. What we say and do modifies what the other person says and does, and his response modifies what we say and do. A process of mutual stimulation takes place.

We may highlight the importance of interaction for human growth if we consider what happens when such interaction is absent or drastically reduced. Cases of complete isolation from human contact are rare, and those that have been reported are often poorly documented. We can observe the effects of isolation after contact has been reestablished, but we have to infer what happened during the period of isolation.

We may distinguish two conditions that bring about such isolation. The first is where a child is removed from the social environment altogether, as happened with the so-called wolf-children of India and with the wild boy of Aveyron, France.[1] The second condition is one of sensory deprivation—blindness or deafness, for example. These afflictions make it extremely difficult, perhaps impossible, to establish relationships. We may also speak of sensory deprivation when a child is forcibly isolated from the outside world, perhaps locked in an empty room for years with no human contacts beyond those necessary to keep him alive. In almost all such instances of isolation, whether from sensory deprivation or actual removal from the social environment, both physical and mental development are greatly retarded.

When society imposes isolation on a person, it usually does so as a punishment—in its child-training practices, for example, and in its treatment of prisoners. The child is told to go to his room alone and stay there until he can behave in a more acceptable manner. The obstreperous prisoner is placed in solitary confinement. Social ostracism is an attempt to punish a person by cutting off his social relationships.

Adequate interaction is essential to our well-being and development. We can identify five elements that contribute to such interaction. They are (1) communication, (2) feedback, (3) social expectations, (4) role behavior, and (5) reciprocal gratification.

Communication

Interpersonal relationships depend on communication. In the absence of communication, especially communication by way of language symbols, social and cultural life would be impossible. Also impossible would be the socialization of children and the transmission of social norms and of the cultural heritage.

[1] For a description of such cases of social isolation, see M. F. Ashley Montague, *The Direction of Human Development: Biological and Social Bases* (New York: Harper, 1955).

By communication we mean the transmission of stimuli by one or more persons and the reception of and reaction to these stimuli by one or more others. Stimuli may be transmitted by gestures, words, or other symbols. Definitions of communication may differ in detail, but they all emphasize the interaction between communicator and recipient, between sender and receiver. The marvel of language is that through it we can convey concepts regarding objects, events, or situations which are distant either geographically or in time. In his ability to utilize language in this manner man is unique.

A few specific situations will illustrate for us the importance of communication. A college student's success or failure depends largely on how well he can communicate with others. It is not enough that he learn an assignment well; he must also be able to speak or write about it, to communicate his knowledge to the instructor. Furthermore, he must be able to communicate his knowledge in a variety of situations. Sometimes a student is quite capable of coaching a fellow student but cannot get the same information across when called upon to recite in class.

The importance of communication is further recognized by the person who finds himself in a country whose language is not familiar to him. He will be compelled to deal mainly with those who speak his own language, a very limited and perhaps nonrepresentative group of the country in which he finds himself. To some extent, he may be helped by observing carefully the dress, customs, and habits of the native inhabitants, but he will still be hampered by his inability to speak with them in their own idiom. With verbal communication impaired, the opportunities for interacting are seriously limited.

But even people who speak the same language sometimes have difficulty communicating. The same words often mean different things to different people; the technique of language permits many different kinds of misunderstandings between the communicator and his recipient. We all know that the same words may be interpreted quite differently by different persons because these persons have different experiences as the basis for interpreting these words. Often people who work together or belong to the same club or religious group speak a characteristic language that tends to isolate others who lack the background of common experiences shared by those who belong to the group.

Language, of course, is our principal communication technique, but other, non-verbal means are sometimes employed to express moods and attitudes. The shrug of resignation, the bowed head of despair or defeat, and the frown of anger are sometimes even more expressive than words. Dance, sculpture, and painting are highly symbolic examples of communication. They often convey very subtle cultural meanings.

People frequently communicate in order to influence the behavior of others. Advertising, for example, is a technique of mass communication by which thousands, even millions, of people may be reached. In recent years advertising and the related technique, propaganda, have been refined into extremely effective tools for inducing behavioral and social changes. Both advertising and propaganda make a deliberate effort to control attitudes. They may try either to induce change or to prevent it, either to persuade us to continue smoking a certain cigarette, for example, or to tempt us to switch brands. Mass media such as television, radio, motion pictures, magazines, and newspapers have greatly extended the scope of advertising and propaganda.

In our highly literate society communication plays a tremendously important role. Since speaking, reading, and writing are our most important tools for interacting with others, it is important to learn to use them well. Interference with their use will hinder effective, satisfying social interaction. Indeed, such interference often may lead to social isolation. Disturbance in ability to communicate with others is usually one of the first symptoms of neuroses.

Feedback

Feedback is closely related to communication. We receive feedback when we perceive—by noting how they behave toward us—the effect we have on other people. Such feedback includes gestures, facial expressions, and conversational clues, as well as the frequency with which people seem to seek us out or avoid us. Feedback, then, is what we learn about ourselves through clues provided by others.

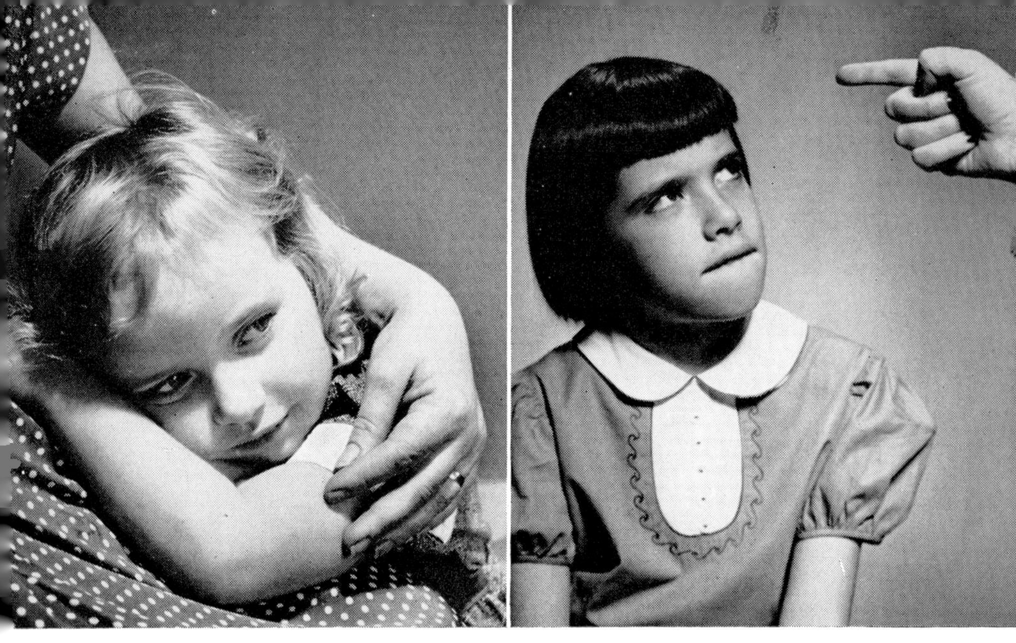

The faces of these two girls mirror the effects of two contrasting types of feedback. One is reacting to gestures of approval, the other to gestures of disapproval. (From Monkmeyer, by Eva Luoma, and Lew Merrim.)

There are two kinds of feedback, *positive* and *negative.* Positive feedback reinforces and encourages us. If a little girl is taking piano lessons, for example, and her parents tell her often how very much they enjoy hearing her play, she will feel happy and confident and will probably practice even more intensively. Positive feedback is *rewarding* and *reinforcing.*

Negative feedback tends to discourage effort. If the parents of the little girl who is studying piano criticize every mistake she makes, or never bother to comment about her playing at all, she will feel depressed and discouraged and will probably give up trying. Negative feedback has a *punishing* effect.

It is essential for us to obtain feedback in order to correct errors in our behavior that prevent us from functioning at our highest level of efficiency. Our personal effectiveness and the ease with which we can correct, modify, or change our behavior results from our willingness to pay attention to the signals others are sending and to take the necessary corrective measures. Many of us, however, seem reluctant to heed the signals we receive.

Let us look at an example. Day after day, Jill, a newlywed, spends hours preparing a delicious dinner for Jerry, her husband. Jerry comes home full of news about a business project he is involved in, and while he eats dinner he brings her up to date on all the details. Jill is more interested, momentarily, in his reaction to her dinner than she is in his business. Whenever she gets a chance she asks him if the meat is all right or if the salad dressing suits him or if some other detail comes up to his expectations. He simply comments that everything is fine and goes on talking about his business.

As the weeks go by, Jill becomes more and more depressed because Jerry seems to appreciate her efforts so little. Jerry, on his part, begins to come home later and later in the evening, because Jill seems to show so little interest in what he is doing. Both want to be complimented and told they are doing a good job. But because this feedback is lacking, neither is fully satisfied with the relationship.

Furthermore, not only are they failing to *receive* any positive feedback, they are also failing to *heed* the negative feedback they *are* receiving. They are ignoring the signals that indicate that each is falling short of expectations, failing to satisfy the other's needs.

In order to gain the benefits of feedback we must first of all desire it. In some people the desire for feedback is so small that no effort, direct or indirect, is made to get it. In others the desire is so intense that frequently feedback is looked for from situations or people that cannot provide it.

Secondly, it may frequently be necessary to request feedback. Requesting it increases the chances of getting it, but the manner in which this request is made may be important in determining both how much and what kind will be received. If we want satisfactory feedback we should tell the person from whom we wish to receive it what kind of information we want and when and why we want it.

Having invited feedback, we must be willing to accept it graciously, even if it happens to be unexpected criticism. If we react by trying to defend the behavior that has led to critical comment we may discourage any future feedback.

It is important to remember that everyone wants feedback even though many people never communicate this desire. Awareness of this fact should encourage us to comment favorably when we notice and approve something that someone does. Even critical comments can be helpful if they are made in a friendly manner.

Social Expectations

Also fundamental to interpersonal relations are impressions people make on us during the process of social interaction. These impressions give rise to social expectations. During our first exploratory meetings with people we arrive at certain conclusions about their attitudes and behavior patterns. We come to expect them to think and act in certain characteristic ways. Our expectations are subjective impressions and are not necessarily accurate. Nevertheless they affect our relationships. One acquaintance may seem to us to be habitually gloomy, and we avoid him because we expect to be depressed. Another may be congenial and charming and we seek him out because we expect to be amused. With some people we feel at ease, and so we see them frequently; with others we expect to feel tense, and so we see them only when we must. We expect some people to be aloof, others to be intimate, some to be formal and others to be casual.

Our expectations are not always realized, of course. People often surprise or disappoint us. If we are disappointed it may be because we expected too much. If we are surprised it may be because we received more than we expected. In either case we must revise our original estimate and alter our expectations.

Once we form an estimate of someone it is frequently difficult to change it. If someone has been inconsiderate in the past, we assume he will be inconsiderate in the future, and this belief may persist even in the face of evidence to the contrary. Sisters and brothers who were hostile and jealous of one another in childhood often carry these attitudes over into their adult lives. It often requires great effort to rid oneself of such an emotional bias.

Role Behavior

The term *role* refers to the individual's function in a group or characteristic contribution to it. Our expectations regarding another person's behavior are usually based on the role he plays in a given situation. If we observe a group of our friends, for example, we may note that one usually plays the role of the *leader,* is usually trying to direct the others. Another may play the role of the *clown,* always trying to make people laugh, while a third may play the role of the *skeptic,* questioning the judgment of the others. Still another may usually play the role of the *do-gooder,* always trying to be helpful. The list of roles people play or try to play is almost endless.

Most of us play a variety of roles every day. Society expects of us, and we expect of ourselves, certain kinds of behavior because of our age, sex, occupation, and social position. Wives, husbands, mothers, fathers, daughters, sons each have their characteristic roles. So do co-workers, supervisors, and committee chairmen. Some of these roles we may choose freely and enjoy. Others may be forced on us and resented.

Each role carries with it certain general obligations which apply to anyone assuming it. A student, for example, is expected to attend lectures, read the course material, prepare papers, take examinations. But within this framework of *expectations* and *obligations* a considerable variation of role *performance* is possible, depending on the individual personality.

A person may unconsciously experiment with a number of different roles, discarding some and retaining others in accordance with his own needs or those of the group, or in accordance with changes in his interests, work, place of residence, or friends.

Our lives are enriched if we can function adequately in several roles. But we must not assume that someone who plays many roles is better adjusted than someone who plays few. Playing too many roles may bring conflict and confusion simply because we do not have time to play any of them well. The final criterion of adequate adjustment is the *satisfaction* a person gets from each role he plays.

Dissatisfaction with roles can arise in a number of ways. A person may be forced to play a role he dislikes because others expect him to play it. He may be afraid to play a role entailing responsibility and may become nervous and panicky if called upon to do so. He may not know how to play a role, because training or background may not have fitted him for the task confronting him. And, his personality may be so rigid or compulsive that it prevents his playing certain roles. He may, for example, treasure his own dignity so highly that he is lost at the company barbecue, where he is required to play the role of a relaxed, casual guest.

At times the behavior called for by one role may be quite different from that required by another, and this may create conflict in the individual. The contradictory demands of a culture may also create role-playing problems. Again, people going through a period of transition in which old behavior patterns must be discarded in favor of new ones often experience conflict. Anyone who has read George Bernard Shaw's *Pygmalion,* for example, will remember the anguish that attended the slum girl's efforts to learn the manners and attitudes of upper-class English society. The situation described in the play is the same as that confronting the immigrant, who must adapt to a new and alien culture. It also confronts, although to a lesser extent, the child of the immigrant, who lives both in the Old World culture at home and in the New World culture in school and elsewhere. Conflict in roles between the home and the new country can cause many emotional problems.

Conflict also occurs when a person is forced to choose between the roles of good friend and good citizen—when, for example, someone who has engaged in questionable business dealings asks a friend to appear in court as a character witness for him. Such situations compel us to make decisions and often produce conflicts.

We may meet these conflicts in a variety of ways. We may repress some of our emotional reactions, rationalize our behavior, or attempt to isolate ourselves. These and other mechanisms people may resort to in order to escape from conflict situations they cannot satisfactorily resolve are discussed in Chapter 5.

But we face any of these situations, play any of these roles, with less anxiety if we have a clear understanding of what is expected of us. This desire for certainty is partly responsible for the behavior patterns we call *etiquette* or *good manners.* These patterns help us to know how to function in certain roles. Once we have learned them they spare us embarrassment and the trouble of making decisions about a number of minor points of social behavior.

Anyone can occasionally find himself caught up in a role he does not know how to play, but such situations are the exception rather than the rule. Those who are never sure of themselves or their roles are maladjusted and would be wise to seek professional help for their problems.

Reciprocal Gratification

Interpersonal relationships are most satisfying when they provide a *balanced mutual satisfaction* of the needs of everyone involved. Anyone who approaches others with the idea of trying to get all he can violates this principle of reciprocity, as does anyone who seems always to be giving, who creates in others a sense of obligation because they cannot respond in kind. When we take too much or give too much we put others on their guard against us and damage our chances of interacting successfully.

Reciprocal gratification cannot be measured precisely. In business and politics we may trade work and favors—if you help me paint my house I'll help you put in your lawn; if you support me in this action I'll see to it that you get that contract. But the more personal and intimate social interactions do not lend themselves to bargaining for two main reasons. First, in a good friendship we are so concerned about the needs and happiness of our friend that we share his joy and sorrow. By helping to satisfy his needs we satisfy our own. The outstanding characteristic of friendship is that it is other-oriented, rather than self-oriented. Secondly, where friendship is involved, a community of interests and needs is established, and whatever is given to one is given to the other. In this sense, psychologically speaking, we do receive by giving. If this kind of friendship develops between a man and a woman it can lead to the satisfaction of an even larger need—the need for a mate, for a husband or a wife. In marriage, ideally, we achieve a high degree of reciprocal gratification.

Groups

Many of our relationships are formed as members of groups, and many of the needs we satisfy through interpersonal relationships are satisfied in a context of group membership. Therefore, we shall devote the remainder of this chapter to a discussion of groups. Our use of the term generally refers to what might be further designated as a direct-contact group, that is, "two or more persons in such close physical proximity that each member may respond to sensory stimuli or signals emitted by each of the others, whether intentionally or not." [2]

[2] English and English, *Dictionary of Psychological and Psychoanalytical Terms.*

To be accepted by the group of our choice is important to psychological well-being. The girl in the top photograph shows the effect of being excluded, while the girl in the bottom photograph shows the effect of belonging. (From Monkmeyer, both by Sybil Shelton.)

How We Attain Group Membership

We attain group membership in four ways: by birth, by choice, by invitation, and by mutual consent. A child belongs automatically to certain groups because he is born into them—into a family, a minority group, a church or religious organization. From the family he extends his contacts to the peer group, where he may choose and be chosen by playmates, or where he may belong to a group assembled through mutual consent. Adults join many kinds of groups. To join some they must simply indicate willingness to belong. To join others they must wait to be invited. Through mutual consent an adult may belong to certain neighborhood groups or to groups made up of his co-workers.

Not everyone places the same value on group membership. Some people, in fact, prefer to be alone than to be involved in group activities. They may have interests they can pursue more satisfactorily by themselves, or they may fear to meet or mingle with others. At the other extreme are those who constantly seek companionship, as if in so doing they hope to escape from themselves. These people crave acceptance from others but often give little of themselves in return, with the result that they antagonize others and make the group membership they desire more difficult to attain.

Some people have trouble deciding which groups they really want to belong to. This is often true of those who are going through a period of transition, perhaps from one culture to another or from one stage in life to another. The adolescent, for example, is no longer a member of the children's group but is not yet fully accepted in the adult group. This creates conflict and a confusion of values, some values belonging to the child group, others to the adult group. It is because of this conflict that we find fluctuation in behavior so common in adolescents, fluctuations such as swings from timidity and shyness to aggressiveness and hostility.

A person who has a certain group membership thrust on him by birth has another problem. He may resent his enforced membership so intensely that he rebels against it. If he is frustrated, perhaps by prejudice, from reaching the goals he considers worthwhile, his frustration may express itself in self-hatred, in hatred for his family, or in hatred for the group—either the group to which he belongs, or the group from which he is excluded, or both. Sociologists and psychologists would describe him as a "marginal man." A marginal man, illustrated in Figure 2, is one who is uncertain where he belongs or

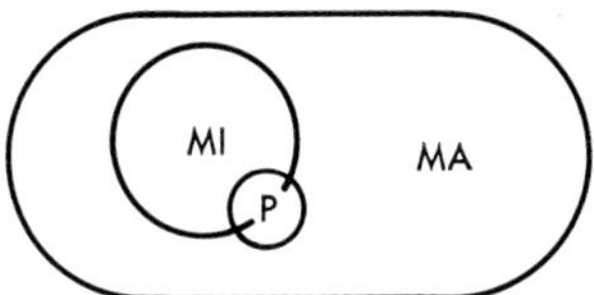

Figure 2. The marginal man is the person, P, *standing on the boundary line between the minority group,* MI, *and the majority group,* MA. *(Adapted from Kurt Lewin,* Resolving Social Conflicts. *New York: Harper, 1948, p. 181. By permission of Harper and Row, Publishers, Inc.)*

one who is prevented from choosing the group to which he would like to belong. The term usually refers to members of minority groups, but it can also refer to those who are going through a period of transition.

How Groups Operate

Before we begin this discussion let us further define what we mean by a group. When we speak of a group we are not referring to a mere aggregate of people, such as a crowd around a bargain counter or the spectators at a parade. A group must have some structure and its membership some interdependence and shared goals and expectations. These characteristics may not be very marked, but unless they exist to some degree, there is no group.

In our present discussion we shall be concerned primarily with small face-to-face groups, numbering two to perhaps two dozen, although the upper limit is indefinite. Examples would be families, seminars, bridge clubs, work groups within a factory, neighborhood clubs, cliques, or gangs. These are the kinds of groups in which we actively participate, maybe daily, maybe once a week or a month, as distinguished from groups in which we merely hold a nominal membership. The members of such groups know one another, if not well at least well enough to recognize one another as members of the same group. And their relationships can sometimes be very close. Some of these groups may be short-lived. They may arise to serve a specific, limited purpose, their members perhaps meeting only a few times. Once such a group has accomplished or given up its purposes it dissolves again. Other groups may last a lifetime—a family, for example, or a friendship group.

Groups have some *purpose* for existing, some *goal* toward which the activities of the members are directed. Sometimes the goals are explicitly stated, sometimes implicitly understood. For some groups there are specific, limited objectives. A neighborhood club may be formed to make the neighborhood more attractive by planting trees along the street. For other groups the goals may be vague. Teenagers may form a club simply to have a good time, with no special activity planned.

Members are expected to accept the group's objectives and to share in the tasks necessary to accomplish them. Commitment to the objectives and willingness to work may vary greatly among the members but must exist to some degree. Otherwise membership becomes pointless and possibly even disruptive. To the extent that these *expectations* are genuinely shared and accepted by members of the group they make for cohesiveness.

Group expectations are enforced through a system of rewards and punishments, the most severe form of punishment being expulsion. Other punishments are temporary suspension, exclusion from holding office, fines, public reprimand, or perhaps just a private word of warning. But the group also offers rewards to its members. The most fundamental of these is the continued personal satisfaction of simply belonging to a group. More dramatic rewards include public commendation and recognition, special awards, or election to office.

The common understandings that are the necessary bases for group functioning can come about only through adequate *communication* among the members. If communication is inadequate, if it fails, for example, to convey the fact that a member is dissatisfied with the particular behavior expected of him, the functioning of the group will be disrupted.

There are, of course, many other conditions that can lead to the disruption of the group. And the fact that the behavior of one or more members can bring it about points up another basic characteristic of the group—the *interdependence* of its members. The interdependence of the group members results from the fact that different members assume different functions and roles, and that all of them are necessary for the operation of the group. In the family, for example, it is apparent that husband and wife carry out different functions and that they behave differently, as father and mother, in relation to their children.

Many different criteria may be used in assigning different roles to members of a group, including age, sex, social position, special abilities, or general competence. Roles may also be decided in terms of dominance or submission. Some members will gradually assume dominant roles as they lead discussions and influence the group to take this or that step. The submissive members accept the decisions of the others and do their jobs without making suggestions or asking questions. The roles members play may also be influenced by the activity the group is engaged in. If a committee is trying to raise money for a project, the member with the most fund-raising experience will probably assume the leadership. Someone with theater experience will direct a dramatic presentation that is planned.

The location of power is an important aspect of group functioning. Power may be unevenly divided, as is true in authoritarian groups, where it is concentrated in the hands of a few individuals who make all the decisions. Although individuals may usurp power, it may also be offered to them. They may even be drafted by other members whose emotional insecurity compels them to shun independence and submit to authority in order to avoid facing problems and making decisions.

The relationship between the leader and the group member is a social interaction. The actions of the leader influence the behavior of the group, and his behavior is in turn modified and influenced by the demands of the members. Many attempts have been made to list the requisites of good leadership, but this is difficult to do because what is a good leader differs according to the situation. In a broad sense, the best leader would appear to be the one most capable of satisfying the needs of the members and of accomplishing the objectives of the group.

This network of interpersonal relationships within the group, consisting of the functions of its different members and its distribution of power, is usually referred to as the *structure* of the group. Some-

Groups may fulfill a variety of needs. The boys in the top photograph are satisfying the need to increase their knowledge, while those in the lower photograph are satisfying the need to relax. (From Monkmeyer, both by Sybil Shelton.)

times the group is highly formalized; sometimes it is very loose and informal. The formal group is usually presided over by an officer or by a number of officers, with meetings conducted more or less according to parliamentary procedures. An informal group is more casual and may consist of an association of people bound together by common ideas and aims but without any formalized stratification of their functions.

The formal structure of a group and its psychological structure are not necessarily the same. For example, the chairman may have less influence on the behavior of the members than someone who holds no official position. Likewise, someone who is very popular with the members may not be elected to a position of responsibility. We see, then, an interaction of organizational and personal factors influencing the operation of the group. At the first few meetings of a group the position of different members may be in a state of flux, but as the group continues, each person's position becomes more definite, and certain status levels may be established.

How Groups Serve the Individual

Each group is faced with two major problems. One is that of *dealing with a task,* of doing what is necessary to achieve the aim it has set for itself. Common interests provide the basis for such activities. The second major problem is that of *working out the social and emotional relationships* among the members. Activities related to this problem express the needs of the individual members. Needs for affectional bonds, for acceptance and support, for recognition and prestige, for creative expression and achievement are among the motivating factors that direct us toward certain groups.

As adults we satisfy these needs by joining civic clubs, bridge clubs, garden clubs, bowling clubs—any kind of group that offers a chance to interact with others. We do so in the hope that what is important to us will also be important to other members. We also realize that we shall be expected to contribute in some way to group needs and goals and that this effort will help to satisfy our need to be creative. Thus the group and the individual provide reciprocal support for one another.

The more groups we join the more their functions tend to overlap, as is illustrated in Figure 3. Each group satisfies, at the center, our need to belong, to be accepted. But each reaches out to encompass one or more different interests. Thus, our interest in children attracts us to the PTA or the Little League, or both; our interest in sports draws us to a beach or country club, or both; our interest in art and music leads us to one or more cultural associations. All such groups serve both common and specialized functions in satisfying our needs.

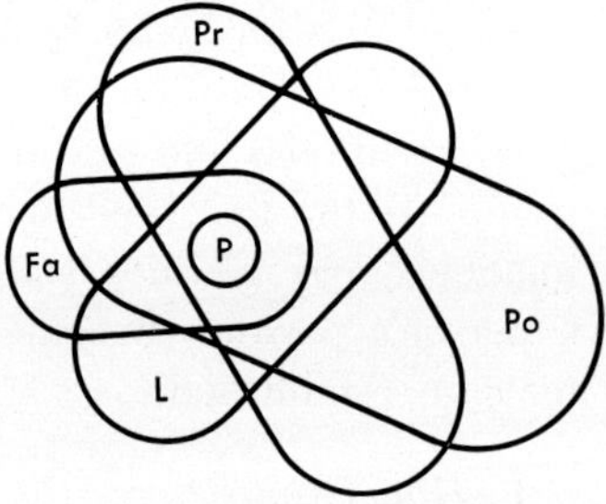

Figure 3. The person as a member of several overlapping groups. P—*person,* Fa—*family,* Pr—*professional group,* L—*luncheon club,* Po—*political party. (From Kurt Lewin,* Resolving Social Conflicts, *p. 85. By permission of Harper and Row, Publishers, Inc.)*

By observing a specific group we may gain insight into some of the various needs that prompted its individual members to join. In analyzing these needs, however, let us remember that we make *inferences* about the needs from the behavior observed and that the same behavior may express different motivation for different individuals.

The particular group we shall consider consists of 15 people who have been brought together through a common concern about problems of war and peace. The group has been in existence for only a short time and has no formal structure except that a discussion leader is chosen for each meeting and that its members are pacifists. The group has no affiliation with other groups.

Why did the members form this group? In general, the members feel themselves to be a minority group because of their pacifist beliefs. They are considered odd by many of the people with whom they work, and even by some members of their own families. Some of them feel isolated in their normal daily activities and seek out others of like mind to reinforce their need for *acceptance.* Among those who share their ideas they need not be continually on guard or continually find it necessary to defend their beliefs.

Closely tied in with the need for acceptance, then, is the need for *support.* One person, for example, comments that he wishes some members of the group would go with him to another meeting that he attends regularly. He is the only pacifist in that group and he needs support to counter antipacifist arguments. Actually, what he wants is not so much help in numbers, but emotional support, the feeling that he will not be alone when he takes a stand.

Others have joined the group hoping to improve their ability to discuss and debate current problems. The question frequently heard at the meetings is: What do you *say* to people, how do you answer their arguments?

Still others have joined because they are confused by the pace of modern living, by the variety of conflicting demands they are called upon to face daily. Within the confines of their small group they exchange ideas with others, gain new perspectives on their problems, become stimulated to work through their uncertainties. For them the group has a *problem-solving* function.

But a person desiring *prestige* and *status* would hardly turn to a small, inconspicuous group such as this. If eligible, he would probably seek admission to a professional organization or honorary society—in part because membership would require a certain amount of competence and certain qualifications, and in part because prominent people might belong. Both these considerations make for a certain degree of exclusiveness that adds to the prestige value of belonging.

Professional and similar organizations also frequently satisfy the individual's need for *recognition.* He may deliver a paper or address a convention, he may become a member of the governing board, he may get his work published in a professional journal, he may win an award from grateful, appreciative colleagues. Everyone must have a sense of personal worth, and in large part this comes from being recognized by others. For some, the greatest punishment is to be ignored.

Each group must satisfy some of its members' needs. If members are not satisfied they are likely to cease participating in group activities and even to leave the group if possible. If they cannot leave, they may become unproductive members, or they may initiate activities aimed at bringing about changes in the group. However diverse the needs of the various members may be, they must, to some extent, be combined with the needs of the group if the group is to survive or succeed. Group functioning will be disrupted if a member persistently tries to inject his personal needs or problems—his marital difficulties, for example—into group-oriented discussions.

In the satisfactorily integrated group, the interests and needs of the members are channeled into activities that are relevant either to the group's particular objectives, to its social-emotional functions, or both.

For Additional Reading

Allport, Gordon W., *Personality and Social Encounter: Selected Essays*. Boston: Beacon, 1960.

——, "The Psychology of Participation," *Psychological Review*, LIII (1945), 117-132.

Asch, Solomon, *Social Psychology*. Englewood Cliffs, N. J.: Prentice-Hall, 1953.

Bowlby, John, *Maternal Care and Mental Health*. New York: Columbia University Press, 1951.

Brown, Roger, *Words and Things*. Glencoe, Ill.: Free Press, 1958.

Chisholm, George B., "Social Responsibility," *Journal of Social Issues*, Supplement Series No. 1 (December 1948), 6-13.

"Communication and Information," *International Social Science Journal*, XIV, No. 2 (1962).

Dalton, Robert H., *Personality and Social Interaction*. Boston: Heath, 1961.

Hare, A. Paul, *Handbook of Small Group Research*. New York: Free Press of Glencoe, 1962.

———, Edgar F. Borgotta, and Robert F. Bales, *Small Groups: Studies in Social Interaction.* New York: Knopf, 1955.

Hartley, Eugene L. and Ruth E. Hartley, *Fundamentals of Social Psychology.* New York: Knopf, 1952.

Hayakawa, S. I., *Language in Thought and Action.* New York: Harcourt, Brace, 1949.

Homans, George C., *The Human Group.* New York: Harcourt, Brace, 1950.

———, *Sentiments and Activities. Essays in Social Science.* New York: Free Press of Glencoe, 1962.

Hovland, Carl I., "Social Communication," *Reader in Public Opinion and Communication,* eds. Bernard Berelson and Morris Janowitz. Glencoe, Ill.: Free Press, 1953.

Jahoda, Marie, "Conformity and Independence: A Psychological Analysis," *Human Relations,* XII, No. 2 (1959), 99-120.

Kardiner, Abram, *The Psychological Frontiers of Society.* New York: Columbia University Press, 1945.

Katz, Daniel, "Psychological Barriers to Communication," in W. H. Yeager and W. E. Utterback, "Communication and Social Action," *Annals of the American Academy of Political and Social Science,* CCL (March 1947), 17-25.

———, D. Cartwright, S. Eldersveld, and A. McClung Lee, *Public Opinion and Propaganda.* New York: Dryden, 1954.

Kelman, H. C., *Social Influence and Personal Belief.* New York: Wiley, 1962.

Kluckhohn, Clyde and Henry A. Murray, eds., *Personality in Nature, Society, and Culture* (2nd ed.). New York: Knopf, 1953.

Kluckhohn, Richard, ed., *Culture and Behavior. The Collected Essays of Clyde Kluckhohn.* Glencoe, Ill.: Free Press, 1961.

Krech, David, Richard S. Crutchfield, and Egerton L. Ballachey, *Individual in Society.* New York: McGraw-Hill, 1962.

Lane, Robert E., *Political Life: Why People Get Involved In Politics.* Glencoe, Ill.: Free Press, 1959.

Lewin, Kurt, *Field Theory in Social Science,* ed. Dorwin Cartwright. New York: Harper, 1951.

Lifton, Walter M., *Working With Groups. Group Processes and Individual Growth.* New York: Wiley, 1961.

Lindzey, Gardner, ed., *Handbook of Social Psychology.* Cambridge, Mass.: Addison-Wesley, 1954.

Lippitt, Ronald, *Training in Community Relations*. New York: Harper, 1949.

——, Jeanne Watson, and Bruce Westley, *The Dynamics of Planned Change*. New York: Harcourt, Brace, 1958.

Maccoby, Eleanor E., Theodore M. Newcomb, and Eugene L. Hartley, eds., *Readings in Social Psychology* (3rd ed.). New York: Harper, 1958.

Maier, Norman R. F., *Principles of Human Relations*. New York: Wiley, 1952.

Marrow, Alfred J., *Living Without Hate. Scientific Approaches to Human Relations*. New York: Harper, 1951.

——, *Changing Patterns of Prejudice*. Philadelphia: Chilton, 1962.

Miller, James G., *Experiments in Social Process—A Symposium on Social Psychology*. New York: McGraw-Hill, 1950.

Montagu, M. F. Ashley, *The Direction of Human Behavior*. New York: Harper, 1955.

Moustakas, Clark E., *Loneliness*. Englewood Cliffs, N. J.: Prentice-Hall, 1961.

Murphy, Gardner, "Social Motivation," in *Handbook of Social Psychology*, Vol. 2, ed. Gardner Lindzey. Cambridge, Mass.: Addison-Wesley, 1954, pp. 601-633.

Parsons, Talcott and Edward A. Shils, eds., *Toward a General Theory of Social Action*. Cambridge, Mass.: Harvard University Press, 1951.

Ruesch, Jurgen and G. Bateson, *Communication, the Social Matrix of Psychiatry*. New York: Norton, 1951.

——, and Weldon Kees, *Nonverbal Communication*. Berkeley and Los Angeles: University of California Press, 1956.

Sarbin, Theodore R., "Role Theory," in *Handbook of Social Psychology*, Vol. 1, ed. Gardner Lindzey. Cambridge, Mass.: Addison-Wesley, 1954, pp. 223-258.

Schachter, Stanley, *The Psychology of Affiliation*. Stanford, Calif.: Stanford University Press, 1959.

Shibutani, Tamotsu, *Society and Personality*. Englewood Cliffs, N. J.: Prentice-Hall, 1961.

Smelser, Neil J. and William T. Smelser, *Personality and Social Systems*. New York: Wiley, 1963.

Solomon, Philip *et al.*, *Sensory Deprivation*. Cambridge: Harvard University Press, 1961.

Stouffer, Samuel A., *Social Research to Test Ideas.* New York: Free Press of Glencoe, 1962.

Tagiuri, Renato and Luigi Petrullo, eds., *Person Perception and Interpersonal Behavior.* Stanford, Calif.: Stanford University Press, 1958.

Thibault, John W. and Harold W. Kelley, *The Social Psychology of Groups.* New York: Wiley, 1959.

Verba, Sidney, *Small Groups and Political Behavior: A Study of Leadership.* Princeton, N. J.: Princeton University Press, 1961.

Motivation

3

What moves a person to action?

What initiates his behavior

and keeps it going in a certain direction?

In short,

why does he do what he does?

These are the central questions in

the study of *motivation*.

Behavior is motivated by innumerable factors—

Some apparent, some suspected,

some verified,

some as yet undiscovered.

We have theories about many of these factors, but new research is constantly modifying our interpretations.

To consider a simple problem in behavior, we might ask ourselves why we smile when we pass a friend on the street. We smile, we might say first of all, because we like our friend and want to show him we are happy to see him. But what motivated us to become acquainted with him in the first place? What caused us to like him? And suppose we do not like him. Is it not possible that we still might smile at him? Why would we do so?

The Process of Motivated Behavior

To answer the questions raised in the preceding paragraph we must attempt to understand the process of motivated behavior. We may distinguish four phases in this process:

1. A need is aroused in an organism.
2. Behavior directed toward satisfying the need is set in motion.
3. The need is satisfied.
4. The organism relaxes.

During the period between arousal and satisfaction of need, the organism is in a state of *tension,* a condition of unrest or uneasiness. After the need is satisfied the organism can relax, because *equilibrium* has been restored, equilibrium being defined as a condition in which no pressures (needs) are compelling the organism to become active. *Motivation, then, is a stimulating condition, either external or internal or both, by which a process of behavior is initiated and continued until a state of equilibrium is restored.*

With recurring needs like hunger and thirst the organism generally regains the same state *after* satisfaction of the need that characterized it *before* the need appeared. But with certain other needs the completion of a motivated act brings the individual into a *new* state of equilibrium. In this situation new needs, new perceptions and new goals appear.

Suppose, for example, that you are motivated to experiment with photography. You buy a camera. You have some notion of what you would like to achieve and you set out to achieve it. Regardless of whether you succeed or not, your situation after making the effort is not the same as your situation when you started out. You know more about the creative possibilities of photography and more about its technical requirements. You have also found your efforts either pleasant and satisfying or frustrating and irritating. If the experience has been satisfying you may go on to further experimentation, setting higher and higher standards for yourself. But if you have been disappointed, you may decide not to attempt this means of satisfying the need for self-expression again. Whichever happens, your position with reference to the medium of photography as a means of self-expression will have altered since the day you first bought the camera. You will be at a different level of equilibrium. This emergence of new levels of equilibrium is the basis for human growth.

Our behavior may be motivated both consciously—when we are aware of what leads us to act—and unconsciously. What sort of be-

The manner in which this girl is using her hands and the position of her feet indicate the effect of unconscious motivation. (From Monkmeyer, by Sybil Shelton.)

havior can be assumed to be unconsciously motivated? The following criteria have been suggested: (1) behavior leading to consequences which the person denies intending to produce; (2) behavior showing signs of emotional tension which he claims he does not feel; (3) behavior showing inconsistencies from one time to another, for example, kindness at one time and brutality at another; (4) dreams and fantasies whose content is surprising and shocking to the person; (5) errors of commission, e.g., slips of speech and writing, or errors of omission, e.g., forgetting dates and names; (6) accidents and accident-proneness; and (7) performance on various projective tests.[1]

To get a slight idea of the effects of unconscious motivation, try to explain to yourself why you light a cigarette or reach for a piece of candy when you are reading a book or concentrating intensely on a work project. Why do you tap your fingers on the arm of your chair? Why do you fiddle with your hair? Why do you toss your head or gesture with your hands while you are talking? Why, when you go to a movie, do you laugh at cartoons that show characters being smashed flat by falling boulders, diving into empty swimming pools, or falling off cliffs? Is it because these situations are really funny? Many factors contribute to unconscious motivation, just as they do to conscious motivation. We shall not elaborate on them here, but the student should at least be aware that he is unconsciously motivated to behave in a variety of ways.

As we have already indicated, behavior can be motivated by a wide variety of stimuli. Any aspect of the interaction between ourselves and our environment can initiate behavior. Let us now consider more closely how personal needs motivate behavior.

Personal Needs

Before we can discuss how needs motivate behavior we must understand what we mean by a need. The term is difficult to define, though many attempts to do so have been made by psychologists and others. Part of the difficulty stems from the fact that a need cannot be seen. We can only infer that a certain type of need must have activated

[1] Sidney M. Jourard, *Personal Adjustment—An Approach through the Study of Healthy Personality* (New York: Macmillan, 1958), p. 47.

the organism. We base this inference on observation of conditions before the need was aroused and of behavior after it was aroused. Thus we say that a person is hungry because we know he has been deprived of food for many hours and because we see that he starts to eat as soon as food becomes available. This leads one psychologist to say that a need or want could simply be redefined as "a condition resulting from deprivation and characterized by a special probability of response." [2]

But for the present discussion need is defined as a *personally felt lack of something* (e.g., food or attention) *which induces the organism to act in order that a state of satisfaction may result.* This definition is similar to the one that describes a need as "the lack of something which, if present, would tend to further the welfare of the organism or of the species, or to facilitate its usual behavior." [3]

When we say that the desire to satisfy our needs motivates our behavior we mean that it directs us toward behavior that promises to satisfy the need. The satisfaction of a need, then, becomes a goal; and our behavior becomes *goal-directed.* At the same time our behavior becomes *selective.* Our needs sensitize us to specific aspects of our environments, to those persons or objects that can help us to satisfy the needs. Until the need is satisfied, these become the persons or objects we select to interact with.

A need for food, for example, may send us to the grocery store. But first we may need to stop at the bank to draw out money. If we have no money, the same need may motivate us to look for a job. In each instance, our behavior is (1) motivated by a need—food; (2) directed toward a goal—the satisfaction of that need; and (3) selective in that we choose to interact with those parts of the environment that will help us to satisfy our need. Needs, then, result in goal-directed, selective behavior.

In observing need-motivated behavior we may note the following processes:

1. *Behavior motivated by an identifiable need toward an identifiable means of need-reduction or need-satisfaction.* Thus, we know we

[2] B. F. Skinner, *Science and Human Behavior* (New York: Macmillan, 1953), p. 144.

[3] English and English, *Dictionary of Psychological and Psychoanalytical Terms.*

need food because we are hungry; we know we must eat in order to reduce or satisfy the hunger; we eat; we are no longer hungry. After a while the hunger will reappear and initiate the same behavior sequence again.

2. *Behavior motivated by an identifiable need toward an unidentifiable means of need-reduction or need-satisfaction.* For example, many young mothers today recognize many needs—such as the need for more rest, or for status, or for certain areas of creativity—that they cannot fulfill because of their time-consuming responsibilities to their families and their homes. They may consciously convince themselves that the satisfaction of these needs can be indefinitely postponed, but the needs will affect their behavior just the same. All of us are aware, for example, of how fatigue—a recognized but unsatisfied need for rest—affects whatever we may be trying to accomplish.

3. *Behavior motivated by an unidentifiable need toward an identifiable means of need-reduction or need-satisfaction.* We do many things because we feel impelled to do them without understanding why, as in the previously mentioned examples of the effects of unconscious motivation. The persistence of our determination to do them is seldom diminished by our inability to identify the motivational need. This is vividly illustrated in the case of the alcoholic, whose determination to take a drink does not depend on his ability to explain why he wants one.

4. *Behavior motivated by an unidentifiable need toward an unidentifiable means of need-reduction or need-satisfaction.* An example is the child whose need for love has not been satisfied. Unable to identify his need, aware only of a restlessness that drives him into various forms of trial-and-error behavior, the child can take no effective steps toward reducing or satisfying his need. Nevertheless, his need motivates his behavior.

Recognition of both *need* and *method of need-reduction or need-satisfaction* is essential to effective behavior. We must, that is, be aware of our needs and understand the sequence of behavior that leads from need to need-reduction or satisfaction if we are to cope with our needs adequately and achieve satisfactory adjustment. Our efforts to satisfy our needs may lead us to either adjustive or maladjustive behavior; and —as we have already pointed out and shall continue to emphasize—

sometimes behavior that seems adjustive from our own point of view may be maladjustive from a social point of view. The difference is that maladjustive behavior does not really resolve the need. It is merely a temporary expedient and actually may impede complete satisfaction.

We mentioned earlier that needs motivate selective behavior, that each need sensitizes us to the persons or objects we associate with the satisfaction of that particular need. A number of experiments have been conducted to show how needs influence such perceptions when the environmental stimuli are not clearly defined. In one of these studies [4] a group of college students was asked to interpret meaningless drawings, ambiguous drawings of food articles, and drawings of various household articles. Each subject was tested once a week at periods ranging from one, three, six, and nine hours after eating (see Figure 1). The results show that the students who went without food for the

[4] R. Levine, I. Chein, and G. Murphy, "The Relation of Intensity of a Need to the Amount of Perceptual Distortion," *Journal of Psychology,* XIII (1942), 283-293.

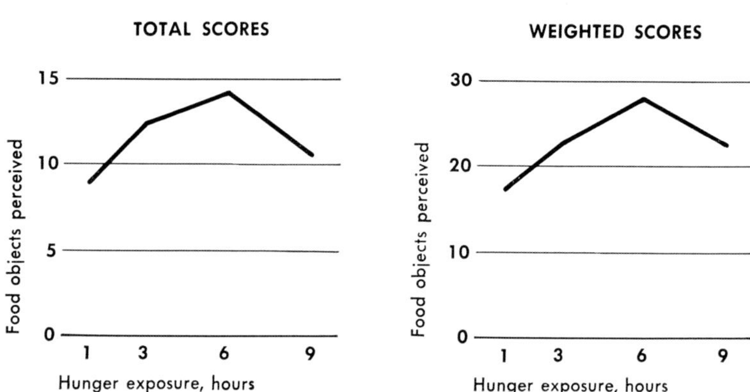

Figure 1. Effect of hunger on perception. The average number of ambiguous objects that college students perceived as food objects increased with the number of hours since they last ate, up to six hours. When the scores were weighted for the different time intervals in terms of "strong" and "weak" food responses, the relationships among the scores for the different time intervals were essentially the same. (Adapted from R. Levine, I. Chein, and G. Murphy, "The Relation of Intensity of a Need to the Amount of Perceptual Distortion," The Journal of Psychology, *XIII (1942), 291. By permission of* The Journal of Psychology.*)*

longest time tended to perceive the largest number of food responses in the ambiguous figures, although beyond a certain length of deprivation a decrease occurred in the number of food responses perceived. Two different processes seem to operate that account for the results: (1) an *autistic,* or wish-fulfilling, process which leads to an increased number of perceived food objects as the period of deprivation increases, and (2) a *reality* process in which reactions based on the factual situation predominate and which makes it increasingly necessary to find some means of satisfying the hunger. As the period of deprivation increases, the reality process takes precedence over the autistic process, since the pictures do not really satisfy the need for food.

Man differs from other organisms in that he must satisfy psychological as well as physiological needs. These needs are closely *interrelated.* The satisfaction or frustration of a child's physiological needs, for example, will affect his psychological development as well as his physical growth. And if the child's psychological needs are left unsatisfied his physical development will be impaired even if his physiological needs are satisfied. This interrelation must be kept in mind when we consider physiological and psychological needs. It is often difficult to distinguish one from the other.

Physiological Needs

Hunger, thirst, excretory needs; needs for sleep and sexual gratification; needs to adapt to differences in temperature; needs for a sufficient amount of oxygen—all these are among the physiological needs we might call *life-perpetuating.* Although we can postpone satisfaction of these needs for a time, they must eventually be satisfied if we are to survive. When they arise they are ordinarily accompanied by a feeling of discomfort or pain which the organism strives to reduce or eliminate. For example, we are hungry; we eat; we are no longer hungry. After a certain length of time the hunger reappears and the sequence is repeated.

At first sight it may appear fairly easy to determine the physiological need motivating a given kind of behavior. We watch a child greedily devour a sandwich, for example, and we say he must have been very hungry. We assume the act of eating to have been motivated by the pain associated with the physiological state of hunger. But what if we eat a large piece of apple pie on top of a big meal? Are we hungry? Probably not. More likely we eat it because it tastes good. Thus different causative factors, here pain and pleasure, can produce similar responses.

Eating, then, not only relieves pain; it also produces pleasure. Anticipated pleasure is as important a motivational factor as is pain. Children run and jump because they get pleasure from doing so. We seek pleasurable sights, sounds, smells, and tastes because we enjoy them. Actually, we *need* them—our physical as well as our psychological well-being would be affected if we were deprived of them for long. Any theory of motivation has to take into account the seeking out of comforts and pleasures as well as the avoidance of discomfort and pain.

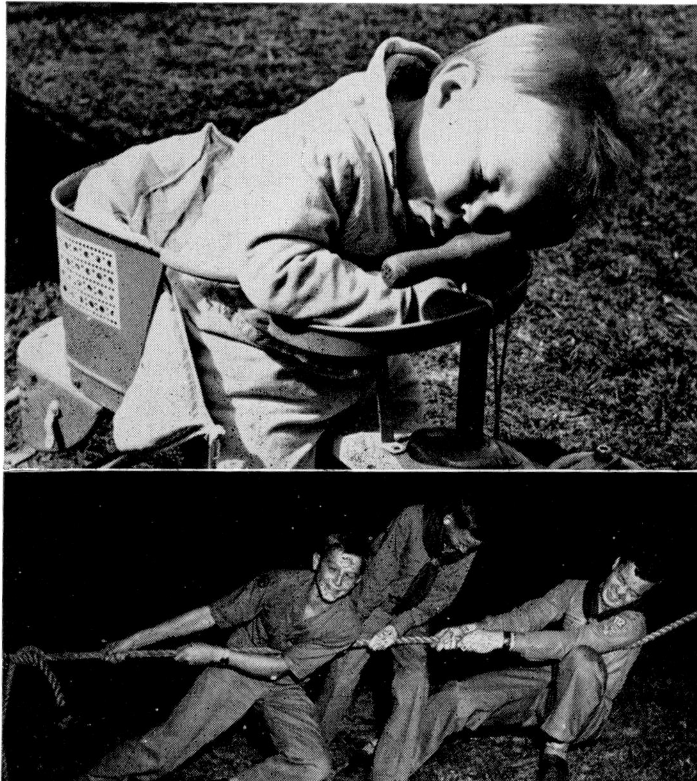

The need to sleep and the need to exercise our muscles are among the compelling, life-perpetuating physiological needs. (Top: a Lehner-Kube photograph. Bottom: Standard Oil Co. of N.J.)

Psychological Needs

The need to give and receive love and affection, the need to belong, the need for acceptance, recognition, and self-fulfillment are among the *psychological* needs. We might refer to these as *morale-maintaining* needs. Although the satisfaction of these needs may not be essential to sheer physical survival, allowing them to remain unfulfilled can seriously injure our self-concept as well as our morale.

Whether these needs are satisfied or not they will affect our behavior. For example, if we are confident that our parents love us we may be able to develop the self-assurance necessary to make friends easily and enjoy a wide variety of activities. But if we feel that no one loves us we may try to avoid social contacts. Or, without even realizing what we are doing or why, we may try to strike back at the world by driving our car recklessly or by bullying people. Such acts threaten the safety, comfort, and pleasure of others; and moreover they threaten our own well-being because they lessen our chances to

The need to be creative and the need to give and receive love and affection are among the psychological needs that assert themselves early in life. (Lehner-Kube photographs.)

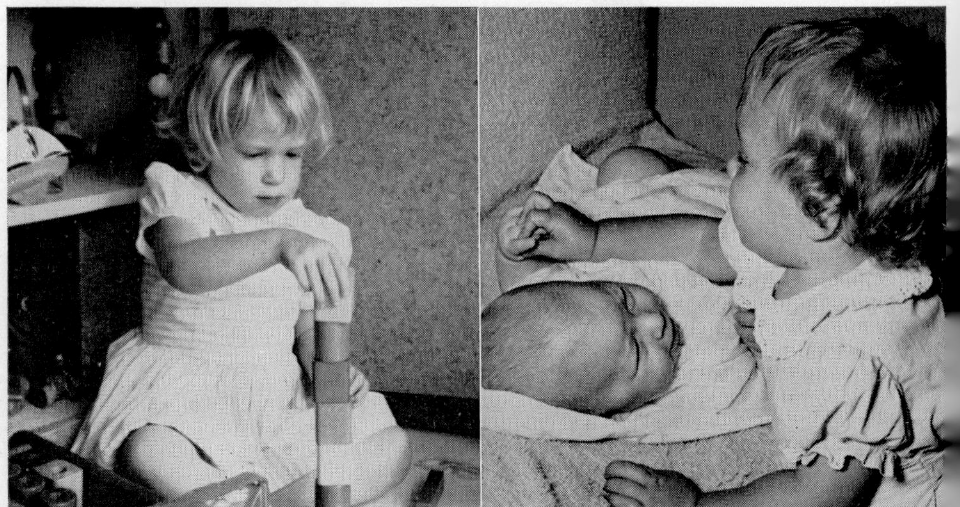

establish warm, friendly relationships or to find love. Yet ironically all of these acts can be motivated by a need for love.

But obviously these acts are not *necessarily* motivated by a need for love, any more than eating is necessarily motivated by hunger. It is very difficult to identify the psychological needs that motivate behavior; we find that it is much easier to identify their *effects*. If a boy asks a girl for a date and she accepts they may both experience a sensation of elation that is not too hard to describe. But the specific needs that motivated the act that led to the elation cannot be easily identified. A boy could want a date with a girl for many reasons, all of them arising from different, though possibly related, needs. He might need companionship; he might need affection. He might need to impress his friends; he might need relaxation. He might need encouragement; he might need help with his homework. Any one or a combination of all of these needs could constitute his motivation. A similar complexity of needs could motivate the girl to accept.

Need Interrelationships

We have already noted that our needs are closely interrelated. At times, they may be mutually supportive. We may discern one dominating need, but there may be others, perhaps less strong, which give further impetus to an action. Thus we may choose an occupation not only because we need to earn a living but also because it gives us status among our friends and acquaintances, because we enjoy the work, and because we like the contact with our fellow workers.

But needs may also *conflict*, and when they do a hierarchical organization of needs becomes necessary. Some will have to take precedence while others must be held in abeyance for the time being. Sometimes a conflict can be resolved quite easily, but at other times it may be a source of severe frustration and conflict.

If our survival is at stake, needs related to survival will usually take precedence over others. If we are faced with starvation, our need for food will be so great that other needs will have no chance to assert themselves. Even if we know that we will not starve, we may when we get very hungry become so preoccupied with food that nothing else is likely to hold our attention.

Once we are free from the pressure of hunger and thirst and other such urgent needs—and from the constant worry about how to satisfy them—other needs become important. Once this criterion of survival is ruled out, how is the conflict between competing needs resolved? One recently developed theory[5] puts forth the view that our needs may be arranged in a *hierarchy* of demand potency. Such an arrangement indicates that after a person has satisfied his physiological needs he can then proceed to satisfy his other needs in order of demand. The hierarchy from most potent to least potent needs is as follows:

1. The physiological needs—hunger, thirst, sex, and the other basic life-perpetuating needs. When these are satisfied there emerge:
2. The safety needs—needs for protection against danger and deprivation, needs for security and stability in a familiar setting. When these are satisfied there emerge:
3. The belongingness and love needs—the need to be accepted by others, the needs to give and to receive affection and love. When these are satisfied there emerge:
4. The esteem needs—the ego needs—the needs for competence, mastery of knowledge, self-confidence, and for recognition and appreciation. When these are satisfied there emerges:
5. The need for self-actualization—the need for self-fulfillment, for self-expression, for realizing our potentialities, for continued self-development, for creativity.

In our attempt to resolve conflicting needs, values and ideals play an important part. We may, for example, greatly desire an education; we may also be strongly motivated to establish a family. Unless we have enough money to do both, we have to make a choice; and the choice made will depend, at least in part, on whether having family ties or achieving individual success constitutes a more important value. Values and ideals act as frameworks within which conflicting needs are resolved.

Need-Satisfaction in Child Development

If a child is to survive, someone has to attend to his needs. In our culture this person is usually the mother, and we refer to her attendance to his needs as *mothering*. The mother

[5] A. H. Maslow, *Motivation and Personality* (New York: Harper, 1954).

feeds the baby, bathes him, holds him, loves him, and tries to protect him. In doing so she attends to both his physiological and his psychological needs—his physiological needs for food and drink, cleanliness and protection, and his psychological needs for love and attention. The child's emotional reactions to the quality of mothering he receives affect his psychological development.

Everyone who has spent much time around a baby knows that his personality begins to develop rapidly, as is evident by the way he reacts to the satisfaction or frustration of his needs. From the way he is treated he begins to form his impression of the world and to select his methods of satisfying his needs and solving his problems. At first his choice is limited. Crying is his principal means of communication, supplemented by smiling and gurgling. When his needs are satisfied he lies or sits in his crib or pen smiling contentedly. He feels loved. He feels important. He is psychologically content.

But when his needs are not satisfied he cries, and if this brings no relief he may begin to screech at the top of his lungs. He is trying to say that he expects to be fed or fondled or changed. If his demands are not heeded soon enough he feels frustrated and begins to learn what *rejection* feels like; and if he feels rejected too often he begins to doubt that anyone loves him. As he grows older this doubt can develop into a conviction that he must not be worth loving, which, in turn, can cause him to develop feelings of inferiority, to become overly aggressive, or to develop other forms of maladjustive behavior.

This brief developmental picture suggests the far-reaching effects of people's emotional reactions to the manner in which their infantile needs were met. We can get a more vivid picture from the following account of a once deadly illness. Four decades ago a disease known as *marasmus* was responsible for about half of the deaths of babies under a year old. Marasmus, meaning "wasting away," was found in well-to-do homes as often as among poor families. The careful study of this condition, undertaken by physicians and social workers, showed that in almost every case of the disease the infants had received very little attention from the mother, attention such as being held, fondled, talked to, and played with. The afflicted babies were wasting away as though starved by lack of adequate psychological care. This emotional hunger gradually affected their physical health, first the elimination process and then breathing and the circulatory system. A similar illustration of the effect of mothering can be seen in Figure 2, which compares infant development in a nursery and a foundling home.

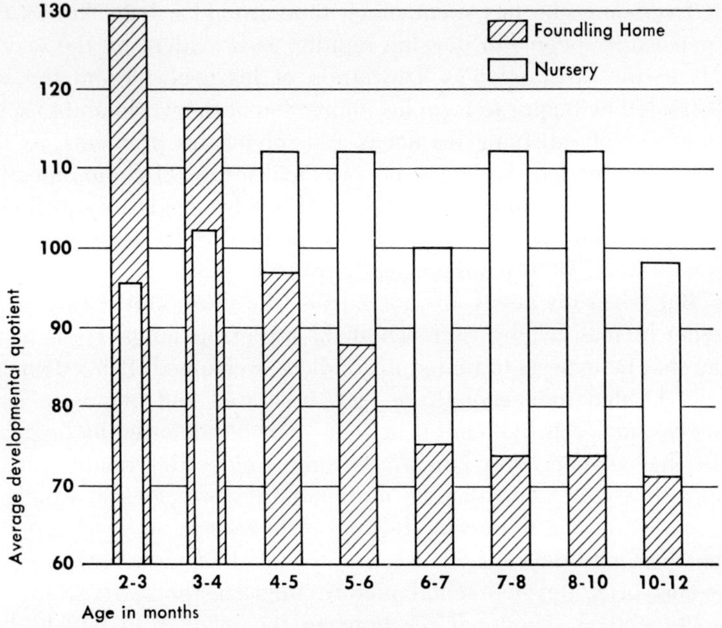

Figure 2. Comparison of development in "Nursery" and "Foundling home." The two institutions were similar in all respects except one—the amount of emotional interchange offered to the children. In the nursery, the children were raised by their own mothers, in the foundling home by overworked nursing personnel from the third month on, with one nurse taking care of from eight to twelve children. The developmental quotient represents the total of the development of six sectors of personality—mastery of perception, of bodily functions, of social relations, of memory and imitation, of manipulative ability, and of intelligence. The response to the mothering in the nursery and to the lack of mothering in the foundling home expresses itself in striking differences in the developmental quotient. (Adapted from Rene A. Spitz, "The Role of Ecological Factors in Emotional Development in Infancy," Child Development, *XX (1949), 148. By permission of the author and the Society for Research in Child Development.)*

It is evident that both the satisfaction of physiological needs and adequate mothering are essential to the healthy development of the child. Mothering seems to give the child certain types of sensory experiences which enhance the satisfaction he gets from attendance to his physiological needs. Muscular tension disappears when the child is sucking; his breathing is improved when he is held or fondled; he is soothed when the mother speaks or sings softly to him. Through such mothering the mother also facilitates the process by which the child's emotional, sensory, and perceptive processes are developed and integrated. The mother's prolonged care for the child is also the basis for its socialization, the process by which a biological organism becomes a social being.

If such mothering is interrupted or withdrawn, the child's well-being is affected. If there is a sudden change he may have difficulty adjusting to it because the behavior he has previously learned is inadequate to meet the new situation. If the mother vacillates between tender care and neglect, the child may show disturbed physiological functioning, such as increasing muscular tension and disturbed breathing.

The care and love with which a mother attends to her child's needs may take many forms and express itself in a great variety of nursing, weaning, and toilet-training techniques. Numerous studies [6] have been made examining the relationships between particular child-care techniques and the personality characteristics of children reared under them. Others have tried to trace the characteristics of adult personalities to the training disciplines they were exposed to as children. The evidence is contradictory. Some studies, for example, showed that children who were breast-fed for long periods presented signs of overprotection and that children who were breast-fed for short periods showed symptoms of rejection. Other studies found no such correlation, however. Also, some authorities believe that pessimistic or sadistic characteristics in the adult are linked to early weaning, self-assurance and optimism to late weaning. But no empirical studies appear to prove this claim.

In part, the contradictory results from such studies are due to

[6] For an extensive survey of such studies see Harold Orlansky, "Infant Care and Personality," *Psychological Bulletin*, XLVI (1949), 1-48.

the fact that the child-rearing techniques are studied as *isolated* segments of the child's life, without taking into account the total relevant situation. A given discipline conveys different meanings and has different effects on a child according to the feelings and attitudes with which the parents enforce it and according to the child's particular capacities and stage of development. The inconclusive nature of studies attempting to link adult characteristics with particular child-care techniques seems to indicate that we have probably exaggerated the rigidity with which character structure in the adult is determined during the first year or two. The normal infant has a wide range of experiences subsequent to his first year; and since his personality is relatively plastic and susceptible to change, a later set of influences may offset or even nullify earlier ones. Maladjusted behavior, such as temper tantrums and excessive hostility toward other children, often disappears when the child is transferred to a social situation that gives him the opportunity to satisfy needs that were previously frustrated.

Although infancy is his period of greatest helplessness, the child depends on others for many years beyond infancy. From others he gradually learns certain skills by which to satisfy physiological needs, but these skills are only a small fraction of the total he must acquire. Others will initiate him into a highly complex world of physical objects, of social relationships, and of group behavior. The young child born into our society has to struggle with complicated and cumulative customs of thousands of years in order to fit and conform to the social requirements that face him. The social group imposes on him a heavy task of learning many things, a task for which parents and teachers must provide endless patience and sympathetic understanding. A small child, for example, may make many errors concerning private property, for which parents and others frequently punish him, sometimes even accusing him of being a "thief" or a "liar." Out of these experiences in learning what is demanded of him, a child acquires attitudes and feelings not only about the problems that confront him, but also about ways in which to handle these problems. Thus he may come to approach problems and learning situations with timidity or anxiety, or he may become intensely concerned with getting the better of everyone in all situations.

As the child grows older, his psychological needs become more evident. The development of speech, both in terms of understanding other people and of communicating his needs to them, enables him to satisfy some of his needs at the symbolic level, through encouragement, praise, sympathy, and instruction. He learns to differentiate other persons more clearly and, as his social horizon broadens, he comes to expect certain things of them, just as he does of his mother. He learns to regard others, as he does his mother, as sources of gratification or frustration, to anticipate their presence with pleasure, fear, or anxiety.

If his relationship with his parents has been warm and affectionate, he may expect his contacts with others to be likewise. If he has been rejected or dominated by his parents, he may expect others to ignore him or to order him about. The parent-child relationship is highly important, but it does not inalterably fix the child's personality. Human personality and behavior are flexible and can be modified. A child who has been rejected by his parents may receive love and attention from a grandmother, or perhaps a teacher. The child who can differentiate among persons does not automatically become a "problem" when certain people reject or ignore him. His personality is determined not only by his early associations with his parents, but also by his continuing experiences with others. Some of these will reinforce his early experiences, others will modify or perhaps negate them.

We must consider one further aspect of the developmental process in order to understand the importance of a child's relationships with others—the self-concept. The self-concept develops out of the child's social interaction with others, with parents and friends. Parents can help the child to build a sound and satisfying self-concept. By giving him a feeling of belonging, by accepting him, parents give their child the self-confidence and security he needs to adjust to others and to meet new situations easily.

Psychological needs have a biological-social basis. They grow out of the early experiences of the child and are characterized by certain feelings and attitudes that are conditioned by the satisfaction or frustration of physiological needs. They develop in a context of interpersonal relationships, first with a mother or a mother-substitute and later with other people. The satisfaction or frustration of such psychological needs is an important factor in the personality development of the child. Although early experiences are important, subsequent ones may greatly change or reinforce the earlier ones. In understanding the effects of such experiences, we must take into account not so much specific disciplines, but primarily parental attitudes and the meaning that a given culture attaches to certain forms of behavior, as well as individual differences among children.

The Social Framework

We have seen that our needs motivate us to try to attain certain goals. Social standards and environmental conditions provide a framework within which we select goals and try to attain them. These standards and conditions channel our activities and help define our goals. We shall discuss our interaction with the environment in which we live in terms of (1) life-space and (2) sociocultural norms.

Life-Space

The term *life-space* refers to the situation in which we live, to our environment. But we say life-space to distinguish that part of the environment which we experience directly and which affects our behavior. Our perception of and relation to that environment, and our selection of aspects to react to, are all included in our use of the term. From our physical and social surroundings we each select, consciously or unconsciously, the particular elements we prefer to relate to.

Thus, in the life-space of an athlete the "world of sports" is of major importance. In the life-space of a stock-broker, however, the "world of finance" will carry considerably more weight. Both "worlds" might be considered part of the environment of the stock-broker, for example, but only the one he is especially interested in might be considered part of his life-space. Our life-space, then, can be called *our environment as we define it, as we perceive and experience it.*

To give another example, different guests will experience the same social gathering in different ways. To one it may be an opportunity to make business contacts. To another it may be a chance to attract attention, to be the life of the party. To a third, who is extremely shy, it may be a painful ordeal. What each perceives in the situation is influenced not only by the physical characteristics of the situation, but also by his own needs, goals, and past experiences. The result is that he *perceives selectively and behaves accordingly.*

Different reactions to similar environments can also be seen in the differences in behavior shown by children of the same family. Parents are frequently puzzled that their children are so unlike one another even though they have grown up together, lived in the same house, participated in the same activities, and heard the same discussions. But there are other factors operating that create differences in the seemingly similar life-spaces and that expose different children to different experiences. These factors include changes in the ages and possibly in the socioeconomic conditions of the parents between the births of the children; differences in amount of social stimulation which they have received from earliest childhood (for example, the third born would have the attention not only of the parents, but also of the older children); and constitutional differences among the children, such as differing sensitivity to various kinds of stimuli. In addition, each child perceives the environment in his own special way. Each has his own interests, and where one child may fill his room with airplanes, another may fill his with boats. A third may be most interested in objects and activities related to the care and training of horses.

The life-space opens up fields of action for the individual that he would have been unlikely to envision on his own in isolation from his environment.

Sociocultural Norms

When we speak of society we refer to the organization or structure of the network of social groups within which a person lives—his family, schools, clubs, business firms, for example. When we speak of culture we refer to the customs, roles, and general characteristics of a particular social structure. *Sociocultural* includes both the social structure and the cultural characteristics.

Whatever the nature of the needs we seek to satisfy, their expression and satisfaction is socially determined. Therefore, to understand what a person will do, how he will do it, and why he will do

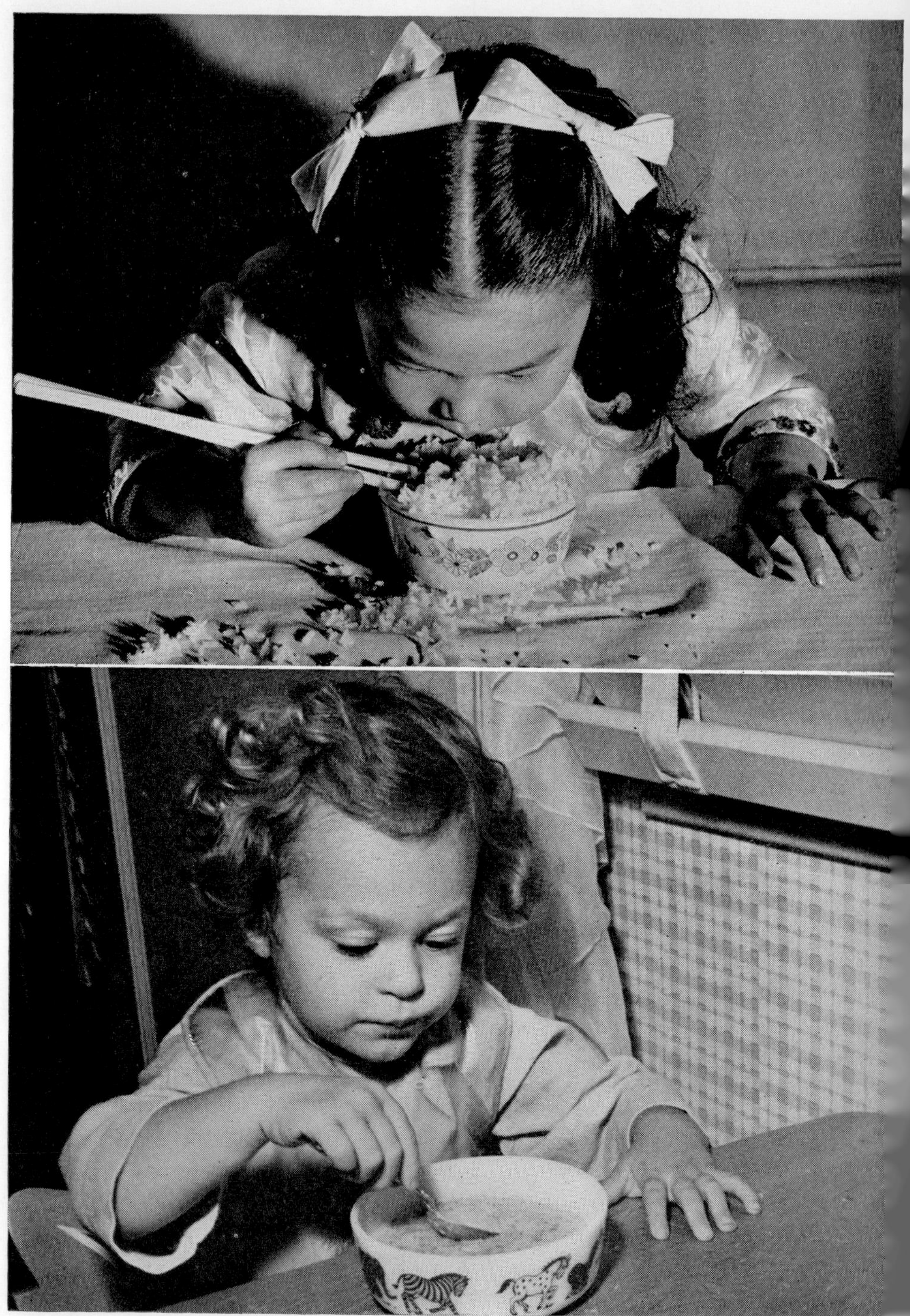

Behavior patterns are culturally determined. The Chinese child learns to eat rice with chopsticks; the American child learns to eat cereal with a spoon. (Top: from Monkmeyer. Bottom: a Lehner-Kube photograph.)

it, we need to know something not only about his needs but also about the sociocultural background in which he has learned to satisfy them.

Knowledge of the physiological state alone is not a reliable criterion for predicting behavior. The manner in which the same physiological need is satisfied and the objects chosen for need-satisfaction are different for different people. You, for example, have certain food preferences, but the foods you enjoy may be unpalatable to someone else. Some people eat with chopsticks, some with forks, and some with their fingers, depending on their cultural backgrounds. Techniques used for satisfying needs are *culture-bound*—they are learned in a particular culture.

We call the values and standards of behavior which are characteristic of a particular sociocultural environment the *sociocultural norms* or *social norms*. In the process of growing up we learn to internalize these norms. Although social norms vary for different societies, the process of learning them shows certain uniform characteristics. At first, the social norms are stimuli external to us. Some may remain so throughout our lives. Others, however, become internalized. That is, they become part of our mode of life and are no longer felt as a compulsion imposed from outside. If they are thus learned, we may express them in our behavior without being aware of them. We can see this process of internalization by looking at the way a child learns to say "thank you." At first, he will say the words only when his parents ask him to; a bit later he will say them only if his parents are present; but eventually he will do so on his own without any parental pressure.

The person who rejects or departs from the social norms, perhaps on the basis of a self-conscious, intellectual rebellion against them, may still experience feelings of guilt about his rebellious behavior. His earlier feelings regarding the acceptance of social norms may persist even though he consciously rejects the norms.

In a complex society such as ours, it is not easy to describe the content of the social norms. They are not always explicitly stated or formally codified. But norms always imply expectations and obligations. Some norms, such as fashions and fads, are temporary and merely incidental to the functioning of society. High-school students are particularly susceptible to such passing fancies, with college students not far behind. Other norms are more enduring. Religion, for example, has kept some of its basic tenets throughout human history because it answers questions that man has felt a need to answer—questions about the nature of God, the nature and destiny of man, and the nature of the universe.

Sometimes norms are inconsistent and create conflict for the individual. For instance, we are taught Christian concepts of brotherly love, charity, and fellowship; but we find these ideals clashing head-on with an emphasis on intense individual competition. In school, at play, at work, in sports, we are continually encouraged to get ahead of somebody else, to do better than the other fellow, to win. As a result we may become hostile toward others and overanxious if we feel that we are failing or falling behind.

A conflict also arises when, within a society, needs and desires are created, but no means of satisfying them is provided. Such a gap between what people want and what they can reasonably expect to have makes for discontent and restlessness. If this gap becomes too great, the social norms which regulate need-satisfying behavior will break down.

In general, social norms are means of social control by which the society directs and regulates the behavior of its members. Some norms are rigidly enforced, and transgressions against them are severely punished. Others are more flexible and permissive. Within the range of permissible behavior established by the norms, there is scope for individual expression. There is some leeway in choosing our own way of doing things without having to risk social disapproval or punishment.

Factors in Goal Attainment

Our behavior is motivated by our needs and channeled by our social environment in the direction of certain goals. What determines whether or not we shall attain our goals? We shall now consider social influences, learning, and various personal factors that influence goal attainment.

Social Influences

Social interaction may facilitate or hinder the attainment of goals. As we work toward a goal we are at times beset by doubts about our ability to reach the goal or about whether the goal itself is worth all the effort we expend in reaching it. At such times, the confidence and support of others, of parents, friends, teachers, and co-workers, may be crucial in helping us over the hump. A friend's faith in our ability to solve a problem, overcome a handicap, or create something worthwhile, may inspire us to carry through a project we might otherwise have abandoned. A teacher's encouragement may urge us on to renew our efforts after a temporary setback.

It may also happen, of course, that instead of encouraging us a teacher advises us to give up. And a friend may doubt the worth of what we are doing, or a family make so many demands that we have little time or energy left to pursue our goals. If we come to consider such doubts and demands as legitimate, we may give up trying to reach our goal. But even if we persist, our self-confidence may be undermined and the attainment of our goal made more difficult.

Learning

The child is born with certain needs that impel him to action but that do not, at first, guide his behavior in any one direction or toward any one goal. He has to *learn* the appropriate response, the response that will lead to need-satisfaction. And he has to learn what objects will help him to satisfy his needs. The child cries when he is hungry; he soon *learns* that the crying brings his mother to his side, that his mother brings him milk, and that after he has had his milk he no longer feels hungry.

As the child develops he learns new responses and discovers a variety of ways to satisfy his needs. He also learns new skills which will enable him to achieve his goals more effectively. As the learning process continues to reveal new behavioral methods, as he adds to his repertoire of responses and skills, he abandons those he has found to be unacceptable. Even if they may have seemed to satisfy his needs, he abandons them because he finds the social norms becoming increasingly insistent about the manner in which those needs are to be fulfilled.

This process of learning in response to a need continues throughout our lives. A need drives us to learn about persons and objects that can satisfy it and about behavior that can facilitate the process. Through learning we acquire the intellectual competence, manipulative skills, and social skills essential to the attainment of our goals.

But learning does even more: through it we discover new goals, and through it we may acquire new needs. Let us look at an example of goal-oriented behavior. Suppose you have never painted a picture but you are curious to try (goal number one, motivated by need for self-fulfillment). You accompany a friend to an art class and experiment with some of the materials. In the process of experimenting you discover that you enjoy using certain materials and you decide to learn more about them (goal number two, with your need for self-fulfillment directed along more definite lines by what you have learned by attempting to satisfy goal number one). You want to learn more because you have already learned that these materials exist and that you enjoy using them. We can see here that something motivates us to learn and what we learn then increases our motivation and redefines our goals. Each step in the learning process helps us to set up new goals—goals which can only be reached by further learning.

Let us change the situation to illustrate the emergence of a new goal and a new need. Suppose you first accompany your friend to an art class because you enjoy her company. You watch how she handles the materials, how skillful she is in expressing her feelings and thoughts in a painting, how she seems to enjoy herself. You become curious, then interested, and finally eager to know whether you would also find these activities satisfying. You try them out and find they give you pleasure. Next time you accompany your friend again to the art class, not only because you want her companionship but also because a new need for self-expression has been aroused in you.

We see, then, that motivated behavior often starts when certain objects directly excite our interest and our desire to explore them, and that through them new needs and new goals may be learned.

The learning process we undertake in order to attain a goal is called *purposive* learning. We choose to learn certain things because we believe they will facilitate our attainment of the goal. Purposive learning determines our choices of college courses. Purposive learning sends one boy to a trade school and another to a business school. No matter what goal we hope to attain, some sort of previous learning must have taken place before we can attain it.

Psychologists recognize two ways of learning, *conditioning* and *trial and error.* When we learn by conditioning, we associate certain meanings, qualities or characteristics with certain objects or situations and react to those objects or situations according to our associations. Because he fears noise, a small child may learn to be afraid of the gardener who brings a noisy power lawnmower into his peaceful play yard. A man who has been in a train wreck may react to the experience by learning to fear trains and determining never to ride on one again, even though he may not have been injured. The fears these situations arouse—fears not easily dispelled—teach the individual to try to avoid the situations. Just as we learn what we like, we learn also what we dislike. Just as we learn what to try, we learn what to avoid.

In trial-and-error learning, we try different methods of satisfying a need or solving a problem until we hit on one that seems to succeed. This is the one we will probably try first the next time we are faced with a similar need or problem. Thus trial-and-error learning establishes patterns for future behavior.

Learning helps us both to choose and to reach our goals, but it can also prevent us from reaching our goals. If Freddie throws a temper tantrum in a store and his mother quiets him by buying him a new toy he wanted, he has learned a form of maladjustive behavior that he will no doubt try again. But if he expects this learned behavior to help him reach his goals as an adult, he is likely to encounter difficulties.

Maladjusted, neurotic, and psychotic individuals have in one way or another failed to learn acceptable methods for meeting the demands of their environment. Their symptoms are the evidence of their maladjustive reactions. The neurotic, therefore, is one who has "mislearned" and must be helped to relearn if he is to make a satisfactory adjustment. This process of relearning, involving primarily attitudes and feelings, is what we call *psychotherapy*. Learning, neurotic behavior, and psychotherapy will all be discussed further in later chapters.

Personal Factors

Goal attainment is also influenced by such personal factors as interest, ability, and emotional control. Let us briefly consider them.

INTEREST Whether or not we attain a goal depends upon the extent of our interest in it. If interest is strong we may persist in the pursuit of the goal regardless of difficulties. If interest is weak we are easily diverted or satisfied with a goal that calls for less effort. While interests reflect needs, they are not the same as needs but rather preferences for certain ways of obtaining need-satisfaction and for certain goal-objects. Two people, for example, may be equally hungry, but although one may be content with an ordinary meal as long as it satisfies his hunger, another may be greatly interested in the kinds of food he gets and prefers to satisfy his hunger with gourmet dishes. Having developed such likes and preferences, he is willing to spend time and effort to get satisfaction by these preferred means.

ABILITY To attain a goal we must have the necessary ability and skills. By ability we mean the capacity to perform a given activity well. In addition to our general physical or intellectual abilities, we may have special abilities, usually called talents, in such areas as music, mathematics, and certain sports. Our abilities influence our choices of goals because we take pleasure in being able to do something well and tend to concentrate our interests in these areas. Ability, then, is an important determining factor in goal attainment.

EMOTIONAL CONTROL Popularly known as self-control, emotional control enables us to experience strong feelings without permitting them to divert our behavior into inappropriate channels. It involves the ability to keep one's head in stress situations, to perform a job or to behave appropriately regardless of the inner turmoil one may be experiencing. Emotional control enables us to tolerate frustrating interruptions or barriers that block immediate progress toward a goal.

OTHER PERSONALITY CHARACTERISTICS Certain other personality characteristics affect the attainment of our goals. These include the skills we have developed for interacting with others and the kinds of feelings aroused in us as a result of interaction with others. Many personality tests have been devised to measure such traits. These measure such factors as extraversion and introversion, dominance and submissiveness, tolerance and intolerance, emotional responsiveness and unresponsiveness, and authoritarian versus democratic interactions. The degree to which these characteristics are found in our personalities, and the manner in which we use them, will influence our goal attainment. A shy, submissive person, for example, will face different problems in trying to reach a goal than will someone who easily asserts himself.

For Additional Reading

Aberle, David, "Culture and Socialization," in *Psychological Anthropology. Approaches to Culture and Personality*, ed. Francis L. K. Hsu. Homewood, Ill.: Dorsey, 1961, pp. 381-399.

Allinsmith, Wesley and Judy F. Rosenblith, eds., *The Causes of Behavior: Readings in Child Development and Educational Psychology*. Boston: Allyn and Bacon, 1962.

Allport, Gordon W., *Becoming*. New Haven: Yale University Press, 1955.

Asch, Solomon E., *Social Psychology*. Englewood Cliffs, N. J.: Prentice-Hall, 1952.

Atkinson, John W., *Motives in Fantasy, Action, and Society: A Method of Assessment and Study*. Princeton, N. J.: Van Nostrand, 1958.

Bredemeier, Harry C. and Jackson Toby, *Social Problems in America: Costs and Casualties in an Acquisitive Society*. New York and London: Wiley, 1960.

Bühler, Charlotte, "Theoretical Observations about Life's Basic Tendencies," *American Journal of Psychotherapy*, XVI, No. 3 (July 1959), 561-581.

Cofer, Charles N., "Motivations," in *Annual Review of Psychology,* eds. Paul R. Farnsworth and Quinn McNemar, X (1959), 173-202.

Foss, Brian, ed., *Determinants of Infant Behavior.* New York: Wiley, 1961.

Frank, Lawrence K., "The Fundamental Needs of the Child," in *Outside Readings in Psychology,* eds. E. Hartley, H. G. Birch, and R. Hartley. New York: Thomas Y. Crowell, 1950.

Hall, Calvin S. and Gardner Lindzey, *Theories of Personality.* New York: Wiley, 1957.

Harlow, Harry F., "The Nature of Love," *The American Psychologist,* XIII (December 1958), 673-685.

Harris, Dale B., ed., *The Concept of Development. An Issue in the Study of Human Behavior.* Minneapolis: University of Minnesota Press, 1957.

Honigmann, John H., *Culture and Personality.* New York: Harper, 1954.

Irwin, F. W., "Motivation and Performance," in *Annual Review of Psychology,* eds. P. R. Farnsworth *et al.,* XII (1961), 217-242.

Lewin, Kurt, *A Dynamic Theory of Personality.* New York: McGraw-Hill, 1935.

Lindzey, Gardner, ed., *Assessment of Human Motives.* New York: Rinehart, 1958.

Maslow, A. H., *Motivation and Personality.* New York: Harper, 1954.

McClelland, D. C., ed., *Studies in Motivation.* New York: Appleton-Century-Crofts, 1955.

———, *et al., The Achievement Motive.* New York: Appleton-Century-Crofts, 1953.

Murphy, Gardner, *Human Potentialities.* New York: Basic Books, 1958.

———, "Social Motivation," in *Handbook of Social Psychology,* Vol. 2, ed. Gardner Lindzey. Cambridge, Mass.: Addison-Wesley, 1954, pp. 601-633.

Murphy, Lois B. *et al., The Widening World of Childhood.* New York: Basic Books, 1962.

Nebraska Symposium on Motivation. Lincoln: University of Nebraska Press, 1962.

Nuttin, Joseph, "Personality Dynamics," in *Perspectives in Personality Theory,* eds. Henry P. David and Helmut von Bracken. New York: Basic Books, 1961, pp. 183-196.

Orlansky, Harold, "Infant Care and Personality," *Psychological Bulletin,* XLVI (1949), 1-48.

Peck, Robert F. and Robert J. Havighurst, *The Psychology of Character Development.* New York: Wiley, 1960.

Rethlingshafer, Dorothy, *Motivation as Related to Personality.* New York: McGraw-Hill, 1963.

Ribble, Margaret A., "Infantile Experiences in Relation to Personality Development," in *Personality and the Behavior Disorders,* Vol. 2, ed. J. McV. Hunt. New York: Ronald, 1944, pp. 621-651.

Rohrer, J. M. and Muzafer Sherif, eds., *Social Psychology at the Crossroads.* New York: Harper, 1951.

Rotter, Julian B., *Social Learning and Clinical Psychology.* Englewood Cliffs, N. J.: Prentice-Hall, 1954.

Schachtel, Ernest G., *Metamorphosis.* New York: Basic Books, 1959.

Sherif, Muzafer, *The Psychology of Social Norms.* New York: Harper, 1936.

Skinner, B. F., *Science and Human Behavior.* New York: Macmillan, 1953.

Stacey, Chalmers L. and Manfred F. DeMartino, eds., *Understanding Human Motivation* (rev. ed.). Cleveland, Ohio: Allen, 1963.

White, Robert W., "Motivation Reconsidered: The Concept of Competence," *Psychological Review,* LXVI, No. 5 (September 1959), 297-333.

Whiting, John W. M., "Socialization Process and Personality," in *Psychological Anthropology. Approaches to Culture and Personality,* ed. Francis L. K. Hsu. Homewood, Ill.: Dorsey, 1961, pp. 355-380.

Young, Paul Thomas, *Motivation and Emotion. A Survey of the Determinants of Human and Animal Activity.* New York: Wiley, 1961.

SOURCES OF FRUSTRATION

Environmental Conditions

Personal Factors

EFFECTS OF FRUSTRATION

Individual Differences

Disruptive Effects

Constructive Effects

FRUSTRATION TOLERANCE

Contributory Factors

Increasing Frustration Tolerance

Frustration

4

When we cannot satisfy a need

or solve a problem

because an obstacle is blocking our efforts,

we experience feelings of *frustration*

that disturb us,

distract us from our other responsibilities,

and interfere with our capacity

to remain rational.

If our inability to overcome the obstacle

continues,

further problems and conflicts arise.

Handling *frustration* is an important aspect of personal adjustment. Sources of frustration, effects of frustration, and tolerance for frustration will all be discussed in this chapter.

Sources of Frustration

The frustrating obstacles that prevent us from satisfying our needs or solving our problems may be either (1) external or *environmental* conditions, or (2) internal or *personal* factors, or a combination of both. Let us briefly consider these two types of factors.

Environmental Conditions

These include any obstacles we may encounter in our physical environment. If we need to prepare an early breakfast, and we discover that we are out of eggs and bread, and the stores are still closed, we are caught in a frustrating situation. If we have an important appointment and find that the car will not start or that the road has been washed out, we are again frustrated. The man in prison finds the bars frustrating; so may the child in his playpen. Both are blocked by physical restraints.

In attempting to achieve our goals we may also find ourselves in conflict with environmental obstacles raised by sociocultural mores. We Americans, for example, place great stress on getting ahead, on beating the other fellow. But we also stress cooperation and consideration for our fellow man. Thus there emerges a frustrating conflict between competition and cooperation.

Personal Factors

Internal conflicts may arise as a result of personal factors that make it necessary for us to choose between conflicting needs and goals, or conflicting approaches to a goal.

We may, for example, need to study and yet, at the same time—because we are lonely and have few friends—need to become better acquainted with the fellow-student who drops by. In such a situation we are frustrated by incompatible personal needs.

We may have a goal to bolster our finances by taking a summer job and at the same time have a goal to make a bicycle tour of the

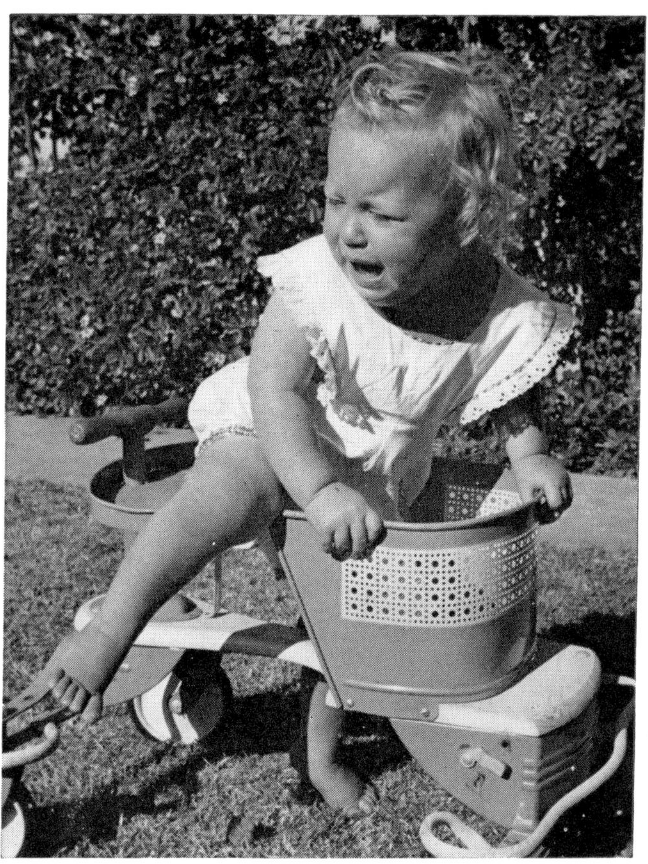

This child is frustrated because of an environmental barrier. She cannot extricate herself from the walker. (A Lehner-Kube photograph.)

country with a group of friends. In such a situation we are frustrated by incompatible personal goals.

We may wish to achieve financial security as soon as possible. We can spend four years at a university learning a profession that would help us get a good job or we can accept a friend's offer to get in on the ground floor of a "deal" that promises rich financial rewards immediately. In such a situation we are frustrated by having to choose between incompatible approaches toward a goal.

The essence of these frustrating conflicts is that no one can go in two different directions at once. Each conflict must be resolved before any action can be taken.

Personal factors can serve as frustrating barriers even when they exist only in our imagination. Such barriers may prevent us from attempting to acquire new skills because we imagine we would be clumsy and inept. We may, for example, forego tennis or skating or dancing for this reason, while at the same time envying those who are able to enjoy these activities.

Physical limitations may also serve as sources of frustration. An athlete may suffer a frustrating injury that forces him to the sidelines. A girl may be frustrated because she thinks she is too short to look chic.

Certain personality or behavior characteristics may frustrate our efforts to make friends. If I am hypercritical of others, for example, or ill-tempered, I may receive few social invitations. My desire to be accepted by others will then be frustrated, and I may not even realize why. My reaction to this frustration may be anxiety, loneliness, or anger. Or I may eventually take a good look at myself and realize that if I change my behavior my social relationships will improve.

Internal conflict situations are generally classified into three types according to the contradictory nature of the goals or alternatives. These are:

1. The *approach-approach* conflict, in which a person must resolve a conflict between two equally desirable goals—between two excellent job opportunities, for example. Such a conflict might be diagrammed this way:

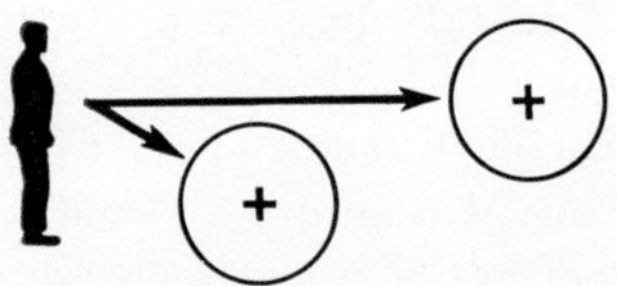

2. The *avoidance-avoidance* conflict, in which a person must make a choice between two equally undesirable goals—must decide, for example, whether to sell his car or move to a cheaper room in order to avoid going further into debt. Such a conflict might be diagrammed this way:

3. The *approach-avoidance* conflict, in which a person is both attracted and repelled by the same goal—as might be the case when a young man wishes to marry a girl who is extremely beautiful (encouraging the approach reaction) but who is also aggressive and demanding (encouraging the avoidance reaction). These mixed feelings of positive and negative factors, of approach to and avoidance of the same object, we also speak of as *ambivalent* feelings. Such a conflict might be diagrammed this way:

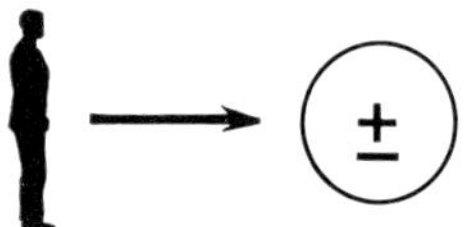

The need to make a choice in any of these three types of conflict can block our progress toward our goal and thus create a frustrating situation. We cannot proceed until we make one choice or the other or until we devise a satisfactory compromise.

This frustrating internal turmoil and conflict that often attends the making of choices is described in an interesting way by William James[1] (1842-1910), the famous American psychologist.

> I am often confronted by the necessity of standing by one of my empirical selfs and relinquishing the rest. Not that I would not, if I could, be both handsome and fat and well-dressed, and a great athlete, and make a million a year, be a wit, a bon-vivant, a lady-killer as well as a philosopher; a philanthropist, statesman, warrior, and African explorer, as well as a "tone-poet" and saint. But the thing is simply impossible. The millionaire's work would run counter to the saint's; the bon-vivant and the philanthropist would trip each other up; the philosopher and the lady-killer could not well keep house in the same tenement of clay. Such different characters may conceivably at the outset of life be alike possible *to a man*. But to make any one of them actual, the rest must more or less be suppressed. So the seeker of his truest, strongest, deepest self must review the list carefully, and pick out the one on which to stake his salvation. All other selves thereupon become unreal, but the fortunes of this self are real. Its failures are real failures, its triumphs real triumphs, carrying shame and gladness with them. This is as strong an example as there is of that selective

[1] William James, *The Principles of Psychology* (New York: Holt, 1890). Reissued in 1950 by Dover Publications. By permission of Holt, Rinehart and Winston, Inc.

> industry of the mind on which I insisted some pages back. Our thought, incessantly deciding, among many things of a kind, which ones for it shall be realities, here chooses one of many possible selves or characters, and forthwith reckons it no shame to fail in any of those not adopted expressly as its own.

Effects of Frustration

Individual Differences

The effects frustration produces are determined by the personalities of the individuals encountering it. Various reactions are possible. Let us consider briefly how individuals differ in this respect. Frustration affects people in different ways. What upsets one may not bother another. Consider, for example, two people trying to solve a mathematical problem. One may throw down his pencil in disgust after a few minutes, frustrated by his failure to solve the problem quickly. The other may continue puzzling over the problem for hours, or even days, until he has solved it.

Although we have described these contrasting approaches as applying only to a temporary situation—solving a mathematical problem—the same reactions may characterize the individual's approach to any situation in which he finds himself and may determine the extent of frustration he will continue to encounter. If he has failed to solve one problem, the next problem may be doubly difficult and increasingly frustrating, and this may magnify the emotional intensity of his reaction. Eventually he may resort to such generalizations as, "I am no good at mathematics," which may, in time, lead to the even broader generalization, "I am no good." In adopting this attitude he denies himself the chance to develop the skills necessary to deal with his problems. Conversely, the person who sticks with the problem until he solves it may acquire increasing confidence and skill that can facilitate his handling of future problems. Thus our ability to solve problems is rooted in our ability to handle frustration. This will be discussed further under the heading *Frustration Tolerance.*

What we have said about solving problems may also apply to interpersonal relationships. A person who does not get along well with other people, for example, may perceive withdrawing from all

Children entering school experience approach-avoidance feelings. They are eager, curious, and at the same time a little afraid. (From Monkmeyer, by Elizabeth Hibbs.)

social contacts as the easiest way out of his frustrating predicament. But obviously he cannot learn how to get along with people by staying away from them.

In addition to differences in the amount of native or acquired competence they bring to their problems, people also differ in the flexibility of their approaches. Some people become so accustomed to trying to solve all their problems by one method that has been useful in certain situations that they become incapable of considering other possibilities. This habit can boomerang, however, because when a problem they cannot solve by the familiar method arises, they become frustrated and develop feelings of anxiety and inadequacy. Such people have lost their flexibility. The following well-known problem illustrates this tendency.

Without lifting the pencil from the paper it is possible to draw four straight lines that will pass through all the nine dots in the figure. Try to think this out without drawing the lines. Then, if necessary, make a copy of the figure and try drawing the actual lines.

Our natural inclination is to try to draw a square figure. But to solve the problem we must abandon this approach and seek another solution. After attempting to solve the problem, check the answer on page 114.

People also differ in ability to remain problem-oriented. A person who needs to give the impression that he is competent and well-informed, for example, may find it difficult to ask questions or even to subject himself to new situations that might require him to learn something he does not already know. Thus he reacts to frustration in an ego-defensive rather than problem-solving manner. He would rather maintain the illusion of self-sufficiency than solve the problem. This behavior will be discussed further in Chapter 5.

We may say, then, that people encountering frustration differ according to (1) their emotional reactions, (2) the persistence with which they deal with the frustrating situation, (3) the flexibility or competence they bring to the situation, and (4) the degree to which they remain problem-oriented or become ego-defensive. Keeping these individual differences in mind, let us now consider some of the varying effects of frustration. We have classified them under (1) *disruptive effects* and (2) *constructive effects.*

Disruptive Effects

The disruptive effects of frustration are those that are maladjustive or harmful to the organism. We shall consider them under the following headings: *Tension, Hostility and Aggression, Displaced Aggression, Reduced Aspiration,* and *Apathy and Efforts to Escape.*

TENSION The amount of tension that will be aroused by a frustrating barrier depends on: (1) the urgency or strength of the need or desire we seek to satisfy; (2) the size of the barrier; and (3) the persistence of the barrier.

Concerning the first point, when we need something very much and are frustrated in our efforts to get it, we react more intensely than we do when a less urgent need is frustrated. For example, we react more intensely if we run out of gas on the way to an important job interview than we would if we were going to the drugstore for tooth paste.

Concerning the second point, we may react more intensely to a large, apparently insurmountable barrier than to a small one we think we can get over easily. Therefore, if we know of an excellent job opportunity in a distant city, but we have no money for transportation costs, we may react more intensely than we would to the frustration of having to get a few letters of recommendation before we could apply for the job.

As for the third point, the persistence of the barrier, we all learn as we grow up that we cannot satisfy all of our needs immediately. Some of them can be satisfied only in the future, and often only after prolonged effort. We learn, therefore, to anticipate and deal with reasonable delays, with barriers that take time to surmount. But if the satisfaction of a particular need is persistently frustrated, if we cannot seem to overcome a barrier no matter how hard we try, this prolonged frustration may make us extremely tense.

HOSTILITY AND AGGRESSION A frequent reaction to frustration is to become hostile and aggressive toward whatever is frustrating us. We have all seen both children and adults exclaiming or gesticulating angrily because their desires were frustrated.

If we define *aggression* as an actual attempt to inflict mental anguish or bodily harm, and define *hostility* as a desire to commit aggression, we may note that one of the principal factors determining whether or not aggression will be committed is the amount of punishment or disapproval the frustrated person fears will result from such behavior. The standards of our society brand aggression unacceptable in most situations, and anyone who chooses to violate these standards runs the risk not only of being punished but also of burdening himself with feelings of guilt.

A child chafing under strict home discipline, for example, may feel hostility and want to strike out at his parents, but he does not dare because sociocultural standards forbid such behavior. The child realizes that the punishment that might follow such an act would be painful even if it merely involved self-inflicted feelings of guilt. Similarly, an employee whose boss frustrates him with unreasonable and impossible demands will react with hostility he cannot express. Even if he expresses this hostility only through an *imagined* act of aggression against his boss, he may feel guilty for entertaining such thoughts.

Actual aggression can lead to further problems. We all know that if we attack someone, either physically or verbally, the most immediate reaction is usually counterattack. Aggression rarely solves a problem and often intensifies it. Most of us know how it feels to say or do something in anger and then regret it for hours or days or even longer. The need to release aggression constructively is a serious problem for many people, and often constitutes a major source of concern for those seeking psychotherapy.

In considering frustration and aggression, however, we must keep in mind that although frustration is an important stimulus to aggression, it does not *always* lead to aggression. Nor is all hostility or aggression necessarily due to frustration.

DISPLACED AGGRESSION A special aspect of aggression still needs to be considered. When frustration arouses hostility that cannot be directly expressed, it may lead to what is known as *displaced* aggression. Thus the child who feels hostile toward his parents may break a toy, kick the dog, or attack a brother or sister. Such aggression is not directed toward the *source* of frustration but rather toward an innocent *substitute*. This is the basis of the *scapegoating* phenomenon, in which an innocent person must face a fury he did nothing to arouse.

Because of our sociocultural taboos against the expression of aggression, a frequent consequence of expressing it—and especially of displacing it—is the development of generalized feelings of anxiety and guilt. It is a common clinical observation that frustration, hostility, aggression, and anxiety go hand in hand.

REDUCED ASPIRATION If we are frustrated in reaching an important goal, we may react by giving up this goal and substituting another. We may, that is, condition ourselves to be satisfied with less. A student may have planned, for example, to read every book by an author on whom he expects to write a term paper. But when he discovers that some of the books are difficult to understand, or that the project will require more time than he cares to devote to it, he may decide that three or four books will suffice. Similarly, a man who has aspired to become the president of his company may decide to be satisfied with a lesser job as frustrations continue to come between him and his original goal.

Reduced aspiration, then, means the acceptance of lesser goals. And where a person has the ability to do greater things, accepting lesser goals can prevent him from fulfilling his potentialities. In this

The disruptive effects frustration can produce include tension, *as demonstrated by the expression and gestures of the girl in the left-hand photo; and* apathy, *as demonstrated by the attitude of the child in the right-hand photo who has lost interest in her toys. (From Monkmeyer, by Lew Merrim, and Sybil Shelton.)*

way, to use Thoreau's expression, many men come to "lead lives of quiet desperation."

APATHY AND EFFORTS TO ESCAPE When blocked by a frustrating barrier, some people simply lose interest in their goals. They become apathetic and listless and adopt an "I-don't-care" attitude. Frequently they direct their efforts toward escaping from the project. They do not want to be bothered. They do not want to try. They just want to be left alone.

All of the reactions to frustration we have mentioned may involve the utilization of one or more defense mechanisms. These will be discussed in detail in Chapter 5, and all we need say now is that the purpose of these mechanisms is to protect us against the feelings of failure that come from frustration.

Constructive Effects

The constructive effects of frustration are those that help the organism to learn better ways of solving problems. We shall discuss them briefly under the following headings: *Catharsis, New Skills,* and *Improved Solutions.*

CATHARSIS Although hostility was discussed as a disruptive reaction to frustration, it should be pointed out that the *expression* of hostility may serve to release a frustrated person's pent-up feelings and so reduce actual aggressive behavior. This release of feelings is a beneficial response we call *catharsis.* After catharsis a frustrated person will often see his situation more clearly than he possibly could while blinded by hostility or tension.

Psychologists do not recommend that we keep our feelings of hostility bottled up inside of us. The important point to remember, however, is that when we express them we do so in a manner that will hurt no one and that will not lead to future feelings of guilt. Often a person who is frustrating us *needs* to be told—in a rational manner—that his expectations are unreasonable. Often the tension we feel as a result of some environmental or personal barrier *needs* to be released in a harmless manner. Striking a pillow, for example, rarely hurts the pillow, but it may help our feelings. There are many acceptable ways of releasing hostility and tension and of achieving catharsis. If we are able to reduce our hostility and proceed with renewed vigor toward our goal, our frustrating experience may have had a constructive effect.

NEW SKILLS When we are frustrated in satisfying a need or desire we may react by mobilizing skills and energies we might otherwise never have used. A businessman who is frustrated by stage fright whenever he must address a conference, for example, may devote special efforts to overcome this handicap and consequently may become an outstanding public speaker. Similarly, someone with a slight physical defect may undergo special training to compensate for it and so develop into a competent athlete.

It follows, therefore, that when we increase our efforts to resolve a frustrating situation, the additional skills we develop may open up for us new areas to explore, areas we might not otherwise have considered ourselves capable of entering. Thus our frustrating experience will have produced constructive results.

IMPROVED SOLUTIONS A frequent consequence of frustration is a reassessment of the methods we have been using in our efforts to reach our goals. When our present methods fail, a further examination of the problem may reveal new and better ways of handling it. Ideas that lead to new inventions grow out of frustration for if the previous methods had not frustrated us we might not have sought and discovered better ones. Improved solutions, therefore, may be a constructive effect of frustration.

Frustration Tolerance

Our reactions to frustration depend to a great extent on how well we have developed *frustration tolerance*—the ability to endure blocking and delay of satisfaction without turning to disruptive, maladjustive behavior. As small children all of us have a very low tolerance for frustration. The slightest blocking of our wishes may produce violent expressions of anger. As we grow and develop, however, we encounter many varieties of frustrating experiences; and as we learn how to work our way through or around them, we slowly increase our frustration tolerance.

Contributory Factors

Individuals differ in their ability to tolerate frustration. What makes for these differences? Why are some people always in a stew about something, always upset about

When a small girl wants to play she may have little tolerance for the frustrating nuisance of letting mother dress her. In such a situation, a mother who can calmly deal with this barrier to her own objective is displaying, by contrast, a high degree of frustration tolerance. (A Lehner-Kube photograph.)

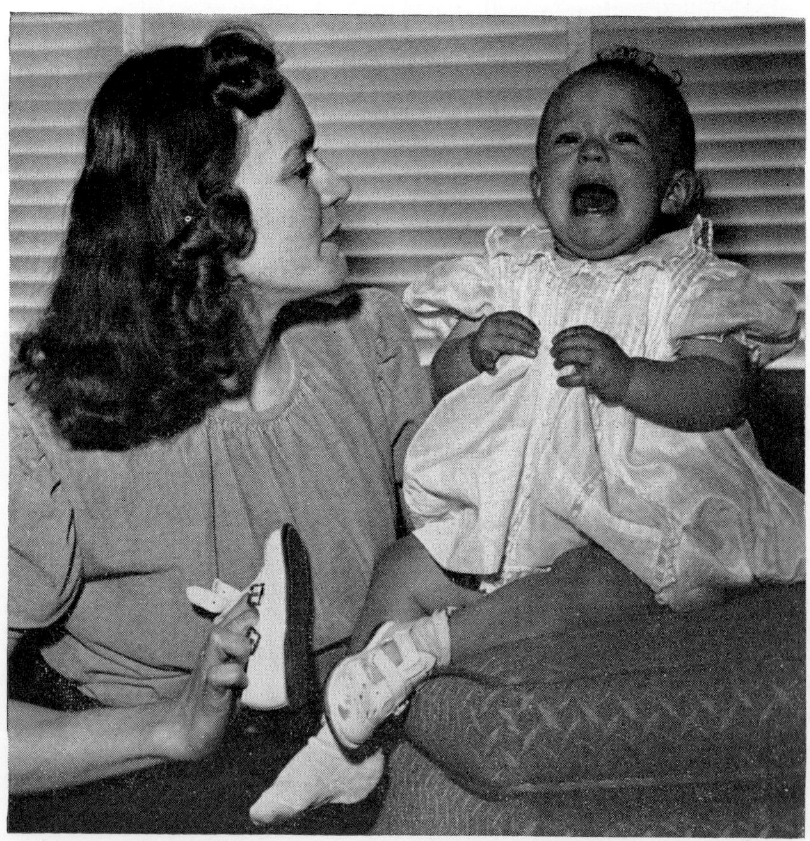

one little thing or another, while others may take major difficulties calmly? We shall discuss the factors responsible for these variations in frustration tolerance under the headings: (1) *The Significance of the Goal,* (2) *The Cause of the Frustration,* and (3) *Temporary Personal Factors.*

THE SIGNIFICANCE OF THE GOAL In order to understand an individual's frustration tolerance better, we need to consider his relationship to the frustrating situation. The same event may have different meanings for different people. For one student, for example, to fail an examination may be merely annoying. For another, who is struggling to maintain a scholarship, failure may mean loss of the financial support that enables him to remain in college. Frustration of his efforts to pass his courses may produce considerable emotional strain, and the effect on his future adjustment may be far-reaching.

Related to meaning is the fact that different persons *interpret* frustration in different ways. Thus one student who fails may interpret this as merely a temporary setback, while another may interpret it as a sign that his mental ability is inferior. The former may view his failure as a sign that he needs to study harder, a frustration that he does not find too difficult to tolerate. The latter may view his failure as a threat to his ego, and, as such, it may call for more frustration tolerance than he has as yet developed.

These differentiations in the meaning of a frustrating situation form the basis for individual differences in frustration tolerance. Obviously it is easier to tolerate what seems to be a minor frustration than what seems to be a major one, but whether or not the frustration is major or minor seems often to depend more on perception than on actual fact. This has been stressed by a number of psychologists, who speak of *need-persistive* and *ego-defensive* reactions to frustration. In need-persistive reactions our interest is centered on the obstacles to be overcome. We are, that is, problem- or goal-oriented. In this type of reaction relatively little tension is aroused beyond that related to overcoming the obstacle. Frustration tolerance can, therefore, remain fairly high. In ego-defensive reactions, however, we tend to perceive the frustrating obstacle as a personal threat, which makes it difficult to tolerate and which causes us to react defensively and become overanxious.

Need-persistive reactions are more limited in scope than ego-defensive reactions. In the former, only a segmental need—a need for a passing grade, for example—is frustrated. In the latter, the total personality may be involved. Not only feelings of intellectual competence but also feelings of social confidence or emotional security may be affected.

The significance to us of the goal we are seeking may be either *intrinsic* or *symbolic*. Thus one child whose mother refuses him an ice cream cone may regard the refusal as a case of simple denial. But another may interpret such a refusal as a sign that his mother no longer loves him. For him the ice cream cone has a symbolic value as well as an intrinsic one, and the blocking of his desire becomes a major frustration and extremely difficult to tolerate. Whether or not these two kinds of frustrations should even be called by the same name has been questioned,[2] since their effects on behavior are quite different. It is only when the goal object is endowed with psychological significance, when it represents a level of prestige, when it is urgently important to the feelings of the individual, that being deprived of it will have the disruptive emotional effect ordinarily attributed to frustration. In order to understand an individual's frustration tolerance, therefore, we must know whether his goal holds intrinsic value or symbolic significance.

THE CAUSE OF THE FRUSTRATION Also significant to frustration tolerance are our perceptions of causative factors. A frustrating situation that we feel was caused by some external force over which we had little or no control will differ in significance from one that we feel was brought about by our own actions. If the cause of a frustrating event can be assigned to an external force for which we are not responsible, we are less likely to feel guilty about it and can therefore tolerate the frustration more easily. If we are late for an appointment, for example, we can better tolerate our frustration if we can attribute our tardiness to flooded roads rather than to the fact that we overslept or miscalculated the amount of time we would need to get there.

Our degree of frustration tolerance, therefore, may depend on

[2] A. H. Maslow, "Deprivation, Threat and Frustration," *Psychological Review*, XLVIII (1941), 364-366.

what we blame or whom we hold responsible. It may depend, that is, on whether we blame ourselves, or another person, or no one in particular. One study of this phenomenon[3] distinguishes between *extrapunitive* (blaming others), *intrapunitive* (blaming self), and *impunitive* (blaming no one) reactions. The extrapunitive person tends to blame factors outside of himself and to avoid accepting responsibility himself. If he breaks a vase it was slippery or his wife put it too close to the edge of the table. The extrapunitive person's characteristic emotional reaction to frustration is hostility directed toward someone else. The intrapunitive person, however, tends to blame himself. If he breaks a vase he feels humiliated, apologizes for his clumsiness, and offers to pay for the damage. The impunitive person has still a different attitude. He treats the situation impersonally, blaming neither himself nor others. He feels, "It couldn't be helped," or "That's life."

In any given situation it may appear realistic for a person to blame himself for breaking a vase because he was careless, or to blame somebody else because the other person was actually at fault, or to blame nobody because it really appeared to be nobody's fault. But if a person consistently blames himself, or someone else, or if he consistently refuses to consider the question of blame at all—if one of these tendencies always dominates his reactions—we may suspect that a maladjusted attitude is blocking his ability to solve his problems.

It might be well to try occasionally to observe our own reactions in this respect. The *Rosenzweig Picture-Frustration Test* (Figure 1) is a projective technique by which an assessment of these tendencies is possible. If we tend always to blame the other person when something goes wrong, we are not likely to attempt to alter our own behavior. If we always blame ourselves, we are likely to become burdened with ineffectual feelings of remorse and guilt.

TEMPORARY PERSONAL FACTORS Frustration tolerance varies not only among different individuals but may also vary for a given individual at different times. A person's frustration tolerance may be much lower when he is fatigued, for example, than when he is rested. It

[3] S. Rosenzweig, "Need-Persistive and Ego-Defensive Reactions to Frustration as Demonstrated by an Experiment on Repression," *Psychological Review*, XLVIII (1941), 347-349.

should be noted, however, that fatigue itself may sometimes be a symptom of low frustration tolerance, since the emotional tension generated by frustration often produces fatigue. A person trying to do his job, for example, may be more fatigued by the strain of competing with his fellow workers or of trying to please his superiors than by the actual effort the job requires. Low tolerance for these frustrating factors may lead to fatigue. Often it is not so much the work we do as how we feel about it that makes us tired. Illness may play a similar role. A person's lowered energy and discomfort may reduce his tolerance for frustration.

Someone who is relatively free from worries can tolerate a frustrating experience better than someone who is disturbed by other problems. When too many upsetting events occur simultaneously, one

Figure 1. Rosenzweig Picture-Frustration Test. Two items from a series of situations that the test covers. The subjects are instructed to write in the blank box the very first answer that comes to mind. (Reproduced, by permission, from the Rosenzweig Picture-Frustration Study, copyright, 1948.)

more frustrating experience may be "simply the last straw," reducing tolerance to a minimum.

Increasing Frustration Tolerance

If effective behavior and personal welfare depend on the ability to endure frustrating situations without becoming unduly disturbed, then a question arises as to how we can increase our tolerance for frustration and thereby avoid behavioral disturbances.

While considerable research material deals with the sources and effects of frustration and with individual variability in frustration tolerance, very little is known about the factors which might help to increase personal frustration tolerance. Yet the question is a critical one, since susceptibility to maladjustive behavior is related to the ability to tolerate frustration.

The following suggestions are made in the hope that they will point to ways of increasing frustration tolerance, thus minimizing the disruptive effects of frustration and maximizing the constructive effects.

1. Develop increased awareness of the relationship between ourselves and the problem or situation by analyzing (1) what we are doing, and (2) the effects of what we are doing on (a) the hoped-for solution and (b) our feelings. This may help us avoid being exclusively a participant or an observer and help us play the dual role of participant-observer, thus maximizing the feedback we receive from two critical sources—the situation and our feelings about it.

2. Focus on and maintain a *procedure* orientation rather than a *solution* orientation. This permits (1) a careful appraisal of the degree and relevance of personal skills we can bring to the situation and (2) an appraisal of the time required to effect a satisfactory solution. With reference to the latter, extending the amount of time allowed for satisfying the need or solving the problem may noticeably alter frustration tolerance. For example, if we expect to complete in a single day a task that cannot possibly be satisfactorily completed in less than a week, our unrealistic time expectations increase our frustration and decrease our tolerance.

3. Develop flexibility in reinterpreting or re-evaluating the personal significance of the frustration. Such reinterpretation may be achieved by pausing now and then to consider the inconsequentiality of seemingly consequential things, or the relative unimportance of goals to which we may be attaching too much significance.

4. Develop flexibility in considering various possible approaches to the goal. This may help us to discover alternative means of achieving it.

5. Develop the ability to distinguish between *instrumental acts*, which might overcome the frustration, and *feeling reactions*, which may obstruct our view. The latter cause us to concentrate our attention on how badly we may feel; the former keep our attention focused on the question, "What can I do about it?"

Solution to problem on page 102.

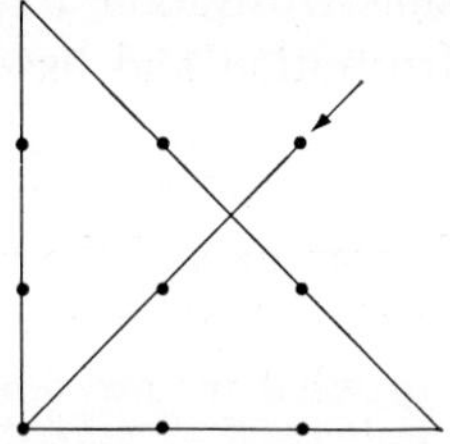

For Additional Reading

Allport, Gordon W., J. S. Bruner, and E. M. Jandorf, "Personality Under Social Catastrophe. Ninety Life-Histories of the Nazi Revolution," in *Personality in Nature, Society, and Culture* (2nd rev. ed.), eds. Clyde Kluckhohn and Henry A. Murray. New York: Knopf, 1953, 436-455.

Berlyne, D. E., *Conflict, Arousal, and Curiosity*. New York: McGraw-Hill, 1960.

Bettelheim, Bruno, *The Informed Heart: Autonomy in a Mass Age*. Glencoe, Ill.: Free Press, 1960.

Brown, Judson S., "Principles of Intrapersonal Conflict," *Journal of Conflict Resolution,* I, No. 2 (June 1957), 135-154.

Buss, Arnold H., *The Psychology of Aggression.* New York: Wiley, 1961.

Cameron, Norman, *The Psychology of Behavior Disorders.* Boston: Houghton Mifflin, 1947.

Dollard, J., L. W. Doob, N. Miller, O. H. Mowrer, and Robert R. Sears, *Frustration and Aggression.* New Haven: Yale University Press, 1939.

Krech, David, Richard S. Crutchfield, and Egerton L. Ballachey, *Individual in Society.* New York: McGraw-Hill, 1962.

Lewin, Kurt, *A Dynamic Theory of Personality. Selected Papers.* New York and London: McGraw-Hill, 1935.

Maier, Norman R. F., *Frustration—The Study of Behavior Without a Goal.* Ann Arbor: University of Michigan Press, 1961.

Maslow, A. H., "Deprivation, Threat and Frustration," *Psychological Review,* XLVIII (1941), 364-366.

May, Rollo, *The Meaning of Anxiety.* New York: Ronald, 1950.

Miller, N. E., "Experimental Studies in Conflict," in *Personality and the Behavior Disorders,* Vol. 1, ed. J. McV. Hunt. New York: Ronald, 1944, 431-465.

Morlan, George K., "A Note on the Frustration-Aggression Theories of Dollard and his Associates," *Psychological Review,* LVI (1949), 1-8.

Redl, Fritz and David Wineman, *The Aggressive Child.* Glencoe, Ill.: Free Press, 1957.

Rosenzweig, Saul, "An Outline of Frustration Theory," in *Personality and the Behavior Disorders,* Vol. 1, ed. J. McV. Hunt. New York: Ronald, 1944, 379-388.

———, "Need-Persistive and Ego-Defensive Reactions to Frustration as Demonstrated by an Experiment on Repression," *Psychological Review,* XLVIII (1941), 347-349.

———, "Types of Reaction to Frustration," *Journal of Abnormal and Social Psychology,* XXIX (1934), 298-300.

Sargent, S. S., "Reaction to Frustration—a Critique and Hypothesis," *Psychological Review,* LV (1948), 108-113.

Whiting, J. W. M. and I. L. Child, *Child Training and Personality.* New Haven: Yale University Press, 1953.

Yates, A. J., *Frustration and Conflict.* New York: Wiley, 1962.

PART TWO

Misdirected Adjustment

Defense Mechanisms

5

Impaired self-esteem

and feelings of *guilt* and *anxiety*

may accompany our feelings

of frustration

when we cannot satisfy a need

or solve a problem.

Self-esteem is impaired because we fell short

of our own expectations.

Guilt feelings arise because we assume

we have also disappointed

our families, friends, or employers.

Anxiety results because we anticipate punishment for our shortcomings. To overcome such disturbing reactions we may resort to *defense-motivated* behavior.

Let us consider what this process involves.

The Defense-Motivated Process

The process by which we attempt to defend ourselves against impaired self-esteem or feelings of guilt and anxiety may involve either of two approaches:

(1) *Task-oriented* behavior, in which we renew our efforts to remove the frustrating obstacle and solve the problem; or

(2) *Defense-oriented* behavior, in which we produce, consciously or unconsciously, some sort of explanation for our failure, both for ourselves and for others.

Either type of behavior involves the application of one or more *defense mechanisms,* since either type is an attempt on the part of

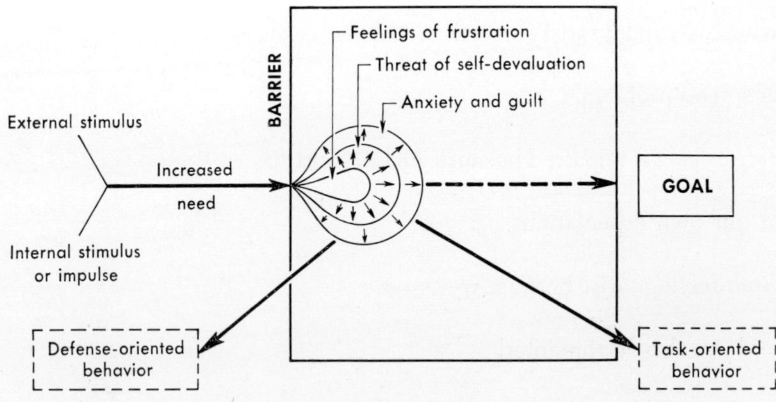

Figure 1. The defense-motivated process. When a frustrating barrier prevents him from reaching his original goal, the individual's aim may be diverted to task-oriented or defense-oriented behavior.

the individual to defend himself against the possibility of failure or the feelings failure produces. A defense mechanism is a means of *denying reality*—failure or frustration or the unpleasantness they produce—by overlooking or ignoring it and replacing it with something else. Task-oriented defense mechanisms, even though they are motivated by the desire to *avoid failure,* sometimes go so far as to *achieve success.* Thus, even though we classify them as defense mechanisms—because they are prompted by defensive motives—they may serve to reinforce behavior patterns that lead to satisfactory adjustment. The defense mechanisms that lead to *mal*adjustment are those which, by their very nature, can seldom lead to success and can serve mainly as *ego-sparing* or *anxiety-relieving* alibis that attempt to explain away failure.

Figure 1 shows how a person who is blocked in the satisfaction of his needs responds with feelings of frustration, self-devaluation, guilt, and anxiety, which divert his aim toward either task-oriented or defense-oriented goals, depending on which defense mechanism he selects.

But, as Figure 2 shows, this diversion of the original aim may occasionally lead to choices that combine both task-oriented and

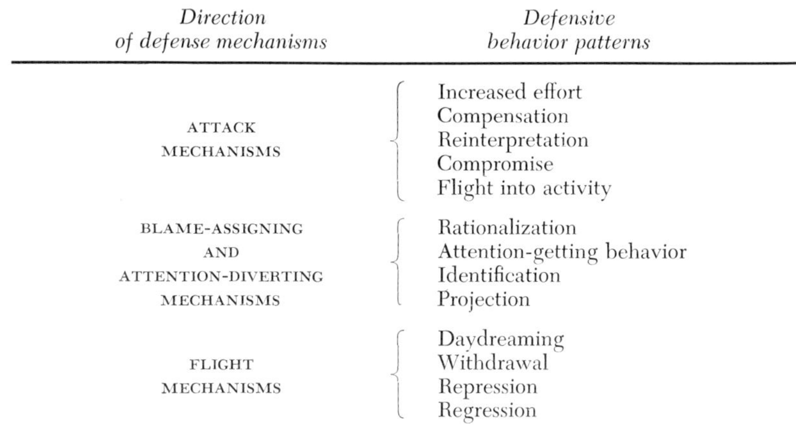

Direction of defense mechanisms	*Defensive behavior patterns*
ATTACK MECHANISMS	Increased effort Compensation Reinterpretation Compromise Flight into activity
BLAME-ASSIGNING AND ATTENTION-DIVERTING MECHANISMS	Rationalization Attention-getting behavior Identification Projection
FLIGHT MECHANISMS	Daydreaming Withdrawal Repression Regression

Figure 2. Types of defense mechanisms.

defense-oriented elements. Here the different types of mechanisms are grouped into three categories: (1) *attack,* (2) *blame-assigning* or *attention-diverting,* and (3) *flight.* The mechanisms in the first group may frequently serve task-oriented functions. Although those in the second may occasionally appear as elements of task-oriented behavior, all but one of them fall more generally under the heading of defense-oriented behavior. Those in the third group represent almost exclusively attempts to resort to the defense-oriented mechanism of running away in order to avoid conflict and failure. The behavior the frustrated person selects may combine several of these elements.

When dealing with the defense mechanisms, as with most aspects of human behavior, it is often necessary to qualify our comments with such expressions as "to a certain extent," or "depending upon the degree." The various behavioral gradations that occur result from the amount of emphasis each behavior pattern receives as it is combined with others in the total personality structure. Whether the defense mechanisms serve an adjustive or a maladjustive function is mainly a matter of degree. There is no clear line of demarcation between satisfactory adjustment and maladjustment. Even the best adjusted individual probably uses most of the defense mechanisms every now and then. But he does not make any of them a way of life. He does not overemphasize their use.

Keeping this in mind, let us now consider the different defense mechanisms and how they function in the adjustment process.

Attack Mechanisms

The task-oriented or *attack* mechanisms are classified as defense mechanisms because they are prompted by defense motives. They do involve an effort to solve a problem rather than merely to be defensive about it, but the person's motive in trying to solve the problem is to *defend* himself against feelings of inadequacy, guilt, and anxiety. The task-oriented mechanisms we shall consider are *increased effort, compensation, reinterpretation and compromise,* and *flight into activity.*

The boy lifting the barbells might be employing the attack-mechanism of increased effort or of compensation or both. Or he might be resorting to attention-getting behavior, one of the defense-oriented mechanisms. Many factors must always be brought to light before the mechanisms being utilized can be determined. (From Monkmeyer, by David Strickler.)

Increased Effort

To reword slightly a proverb we have all heard, the best defense is a good attack. In an attempt to deny frustration and failure, therefore, we may be stimulated to work harder and harder to overcome the barriers between ourselves and our goals. Our increased efforts may be characterized by any one or a combination of the following approaches:

1. Increased intensity of effort—putting out more energy than before;
2. Increased duration of effort—prolonged assault on the problem;
3. Increased utilization of problem-solving procedures—trying different approaches to the problem;
4. Increased personal courage to do what needs to be done to overcome the barrier.

Compensation

Compensation is an attack mechanism by which we try to offset a deficiency in one area by substituting a skill in another. If, for example, we wish to ask someone to participate in a project but do not feel adequate to the task of approaching him personally, we may compensate for this deficiency by writing him a skillfully worded letter, and thus defend ourselves against anticipated failure. A person who has a physical defect that prevents him from satisfying his needs in one way may try to overcome his frustration by emphasizing or developing other traits and abilities in which he *can* excel. Such compensatory activities often lead to productive and socially rewarded achievements. The crippled, unsightly Toulouse-Lautrec compensated for his shortcomings by perfecting his talent for painting and so achieved acceptance, fame, and a wide circle of friends. Similarly, a sickly boy who cannot compete successfully in athletics may compensate by developing his intellectual capacities. Even if his level of intelligence is low he may nevertheless gain the admiration of his teachers by being attentive and cooperative.

Another kind of compensatory activity is utilized by people who develop unusual hobbies or skills in which they find it easy to excel because no one else is trying to compete with them. They avoid feeling threatened by having the whole field to themselves. Someone, for example, may develop the ability to tear telephone directories in half. Although the value of such an ability is questionable, it makes its possessor in one way unusual and gives a means of entertaining his friends and compensating for his lack of social skills.

Parents who try to satisfy their ambitions through their children are also utilizing the mechanism of compensation. A father whose youthful dreams of a medical career were frustrated by lack of money may try to compensate by sending his son to medical school. A mother whose husband did not measure up to her expectations may try to compensate by arranging what she considers a brilliant marriage for her daughter. Although such compensatory activity sometimes satisfies the parents, it may often frustrate the children.

Persistent compensation can be maladjustive. We may fail to develop needed skills if we constantly substitute others that are easier for us. Someone who always wrote letters, for example, would be unlikely to develop the skills necessary for relating with people face-to-face. He would be diverting attention away from an area that needed to be explored.

Reinterpretation and Compromise

The attack mechanisms of reinterpretation and compromise offer additional task-oriented means for solving problems and thereby defending against failure. Reinterpretation involves seeing the goal and the possible ways of attaining it in a new light, or making adjustments or concessions which permit satisfying certain needs or attaining certain goals in a manner somewhat different from that originally anticipated. Compromise involves such behavior as: (1) finding substitute goals when the original goal cannot be attained; (2) lowering the level of aspiration by bringing expectations in line with what may be more easily attained; and (3) changing time perspective, that is, allowing oneself more time to achieve the goal.

Flight into Activity

When increased and persistent effort no longer serves as a means of solving problems but becomes an end in itself, effort for effort's sake, neither productive nor rewarding—then this behavior, although task-oriented, becomes merely a defense against feelings of anxiety, inadequacy, or guilt. Such behavior, which we call *flight into activity,* is unrealistic and maladjustive and invites new frustrations. An extreme example of such flight into increased activity may be seen in the following case:

Bert F., 19, was determined to become a great chemist. Through intensive effort he had done passing work in high school, but when he entered college it soon became clear that he lacked the ability to achieve his goal. Eventually he flunked out of college. Withdrawing from all social contacts, he secluded himself in his room and spent his time frantically studying chemistry, working out involved and often fantastic formulas that absorbed him completely although they bore little or no relationship to established chemical knowledge. His father finally persuaded him to obtain professional help, and eventually he was able to learn more adjustive ways of dealing with his frustrations.

Blame-Assigning or Attention-Diverting Mechanisms

In contrast to the task-oriented mechanisms which seek to solve the problem, the defense-oriented mechanisms serve a mainly defensive function. Among the characteristics common to all of the defense-oriented mechanisms we may note that they reflect a high degree of *emotionality.* In addition, the person utilizing them tends to *overreact.* His response is out of proportion to the stimulus, and his behavior would be perceived as irrational by an impartial observer. It may be subjectively important to him, but it is likely to appear irrelevant or inappropriate to others.

A person who cannot bear to admit he has made mistakes may resort to the *blame-assigning* mechanisms. He may search for a scapegoat on whom he can blame his own shortcomings. Or if he cannot blame them on a person he will try to find a condition or a situation to blame them on. He could not do his homework because his roommate was playing the radio or because the janitor had let the building get too warm or because he had just received a disturbing letter from his mother. Such a person is unconsciously resorting to defense-oriented behavior. He is exonerating himself by finding someone or something else to blame.

A similar phenomenon is at work in the *attention-diverting* mechanisms. The person, consciously or unconsciously, attempts to divert attention away from his shortcomings and failures by focusing it on something else. He may try to get the teacher involved in a complicated discussion during class in the hope that she will not discover that he has neglected to complete his homework.

Blame-assigning and attention-diverting mechanisms include *rationalization, attention-getting behavior, identification,* and *projection.*

Rationalization

Rationalization is the process by which we fool ourselves with our own alibis when we encounter failure, frustration, or threats to our self-esteem. It helps us to replace the real reasons with ego-sparing reasons to explain why we cannot solve a problem.

Perhaps the best known defense by rationalization is the *sour grapes* reaction, from the story of the frustrated fox who justified his failure to obtain the grapes by calling them sour. In this way he converted the *unattainable* into the *undesirable*. This same mechanism is illustrated in the behavior of a young man who misses out on a job he wanted very much and tried very hard to get. When he learns that someone else has been hired, he begins to belittle the job in order to defend himself against his feelings of failure. He insists that he really did not want the job in the first place—that it did not pay enough, that it required too much work.

The reverse of the sour-grapes mechanism is what is sometimes called the *sweet lemon* reaction. Instead of trying to convince himself and others that he did not really want what he failed to get, someone using this mechanism is concerned with convincing himself that he likes what he has to put up with. This reaction is illustrated by those who insist that life suits them fine just the way it is, even though they may be living in squalor. Similarly, the man who is never promoted, whose job seems to be leading nowhere, is rationalizing in this manner when he says he likes what he is doing and does not want to do anything else.

Another form of rationalization is to blame circumstances or other people for frustrations or failures for which we alone are responsible. We kick the chair that caused us to stumble; we blame the tools for our poor workmanship; we blame the tennis racket for our poor play. We neglect to prepare for an exam and try to explain away our failure by saying that the instructor has a grudge against us. If our business fails we absolve ourselves by accusing our competitors of shady dealings. Some of us blame our failures on some almighty power ("it's the Lord's will") or on impersonal forces ("that's fate"). If we consistently blame others for whatever goes wrong in our lives we may become dissociated from reality and develop delusions of persecution.

To a certain extent rationalization can be useful, because it helps us to maintain our self-respect and self-confidence. Like the other defense mechanisms, it is dangerous only if used so persistently or so exclusively that it interferes with normal development. Failures and disappointments are inevitable, and if we had no means of protecting ourselves against them it would be difficult to carry on at all. But if we persistently refuse to accept responsibility for our failures we may never be able to overcome them. And if we persistently blame others we may lose contact with reality.

Attention-Getting Behavior

A person who feels threatened and unsure of himself, who consciously or unconsciously anticipates failure, may try to reassure himself—and *divert* his attention away from what he ought to be doing—by getting people to notice him. In resorting to this behavior he may be unconsciously equating *attention* and *acceptance.* He may feel that when people notice him it means that they like him, when actually they may be resenting him, privately ridiculing him, or merely patiently tolerating him.

The child who refuses to eat, for example, becomes the center of attention while his parents plead with him, coax him, or even punish him. This serves to reinforce his feeling of importance. Another child may disobey his parents' instructions because he would rather be punished than ignored. If he adopts this as his characteristic method of behaving, he may never learn to achieve his goals through socially acceptable means. By the time he has grown up he may have learned to repudiate society and scoff at the law. Although he is likely to be punished, the amount of attention he will receive may seem worth the price to him.

Feigning discomfort is another example of attention-getting behavior. The child who feels that his sick brother is getting too much attention may start complaining about imagined ills of his own. The three-year-old, nicely toilet trained for several months, may with the arrival of a new baby, suddenly regress to wetting himself as a means of getting some of the attention he now sees focused on the new arrival. A neglected wife or mother or old person may conjure up all manner of ailments and behavior disturbances in an effort (frequently unconscious) to get attention.

Identification

Identification is a process whereby someone who has been unable to achieve his own goals enhances his self-esteem by identifying himself with others and trying to share their achievements or fame. One of the most common forms of identification is hero-worship, exemplified by the frustrated adolescent boy who basks in the reflected glory of his football idol's accomplishments while neglecting his own responsibilities. Adults often identify themselves with recognized prestige groups. Membership in various clubs and organizations often reflects this need to bask in reflected glory. Such identification diverts their attention away from their own inadequacies.

We identify, then, not only with people, but also with groups.

The child who practices adult roles is identifying *with his parents. Such identification serves a constructive function in his socialization process. Many traits, ranging in importance from mannerisms to moral and social attitudes, are learned by children in this way. (Left: a Lehner-Kube photograph. Right: courtesy Pacific Oaks College.)*

We join a club and it becomes *our* club. We speak of *our* school, *our* team, *our* party, *our* country. The achievements of *our* group become *our* achievements, and we become upset when any slurring remark or attack is made against the group with which we are identifying.

While identification may lead to maladjustive behavior, it may also serve a constructive function, particularly in the socialization of the child. By identifying with his mother and father the child not only enhances his own self-esteem and feelings of worth, as we see when a child boasts about his father or mother, but through this process he also learns acceptable attitudes, standards, and behavior patterns. We often see children emulating their parents in games of make-believe, or we hear them boasting about what their fathers or big brothers can do, thereby raising their own status by sharing in the family prestige.

Whether or not the process of identification serves a constructive function in the development of personal adjustment depends on several factors. In his adjustment to society, it will make a great difference whether a growing child identifies with a gangster or a priest, a Hitler or a Ghandi. The hero or model chosen influences the direction in which he will be motivated to apply his own ability and training. The extent, as well as the direction, of identification also affects adjustment. Occasional identification may help to steer us in the right direction, but if we persistently do this we may never develop our own resources and become individuals in our own right.

Projection

Projection is the process of unconsciously assigning to others characteristics and qualities we cannot tolerate in ourselves. Most of us have at times had certain ideas or feelings we were unwilling to recognize or accept. Hostility toward parents or children, jealousy of husband or wife, envy of a friend's success—probably all these have been felt at one time or another by almost everyone. If a person regards such thoughts and feelings as signs of personal depravity and feels guilty about them, he may try to defend himself against them by unconsciously projecting them onto other people—thus externalizing his inner world.

For example, the student who is tempted to cheat, but who finds the thought intolerable, may decide that other students are cheating and begin to see evidence of "cheating behavior" in all of their actions.

Projection of unacceptable impulses and characteristics onto other individuals or groups can have serious consequences for the victims of this projection. Once someone has succeeded in making this transfer he then feels free to attack the targets of his projection for what are now *their* faults. For this reason some people feel justified in withholding privileges from minority groups or in denying them equal opportunities. Projecting gives a person the satisfaction of feeling virtuous by attacking the evils or weaknesses he has unloaded onto others. By placing himself in a position of righteousness, of moral vigilance, he further helps to allay any doubts he may have about himself. Such projection is often characteristic of anti-Semitism and other forms of prejudice.

Projection is characteristic of some of the extreme forms of personality disturbances. The persecution-delusions of the paranoiac (see Chapter 7) stem from his tendency to project his hostile impulses.

The term projection may also be used in another sense than that of ascribing to others one's own undesirable characteristics. In this second sense we perceive stimuli (e.g., an inkblot) or situations (e.g., seeing people talking together without hearing their words) in accordance with our personal interests, desires, or fears and then "read into" reality our own subjective state. Generally the more ambiguous the stimulus or situation the more readily we can read our own feelings into it. The tendency to *project* in this manner has given rise to the so-called *projective tests* (see Chapter 14), which are based on the assumption that the individual projects his own feelings, attitudes, and values into his responses to inherently meaningless or unstructured material.

Apart from such projective tests, the process of projection may also operate in our interpretations of another person's motivation or impressions. We draw our conclusions about his reactions to an experience by projecting onto him our own motivations and feelings. This tendency corresponds to the creative artist's projection of himself into that which he creates. He externalizes his emotions, desires, and needs by projecting them into the characters of the play, novel, or painting.

Flight Mechanisms

Flight mechanisms are the defense-oriented methods we employ when we try to avoid or run away from situations we feel to be insurmountable, unsolvable, or emotionally intolerable. We are utilizing flight mechanisms when we give up our efforts, thus abandoning our goals. We may seek new goals to replace those we are abandoning, or we may indicate by our behavior that we would rather not attempt to achieve any goals at all.

Flight behavior may often be a last resort for a person whose attack, blame-assigning, or attention-diverting mechanisms have produced no satisfactory solution to a problem. A person who resorts exclusively to flight mechanisms is extremely maladjusted. The various forms these flight mechanisms can assume include *daydreaming, withdrawal, repression,* and *regression.*

Daydreaming

Through *daydreaming* (often called *fantasy*) we unconsciously withdraw from reality into a private "dream world" that protects us from the threat and anxiety of unsolved problems and disturbing situations. An escape into such fantasy is an effort to find satisfactions that are denied us in real life. In daydreams we can sweep away the obstacles that frustrate us and manipulate objects and people as we please. We can see ourselves as conquering heroes. We can be the life of the party, the adored lover, the successful and respected businessman, the brilliant lawyer who helps the poor and oppressed, the artist whose paintings receive world-wide acclaim. Figure 3 shows the kinds of daydreams normal people engage in.

The following case illustrates how we can daydream to divert our attention from reality. L. W. wanted to write a famous novel. Writing a novel means plugging away hour by hour, day by day, for weeks, months, and sometimes years. It takes self-discipline and perseverance. L. W. lacked these qualities and did not get his novel written. Failing to attain the satisfaction of completing the job, he resorted to daydreaming, where he imagined himself as having already finished. Daydreaming was easier than writing, and for L. W. this retreat into fantasy became an opiate, a mental crutch that enabled him to see himself as a success when he was really a failure.

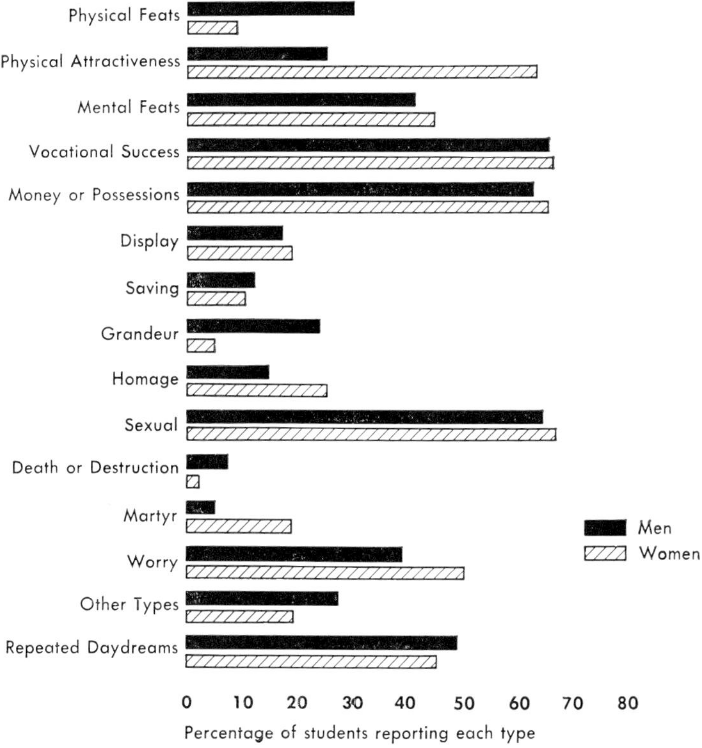

Figure 3. Daydreaming among normal people. Responses to a questionnaire, answered by 64 men, mostly students of engineering, and 131 women, about evenly divided in the practical arts and the fine arts, concerning the kind of daydreams that they have frequently. (Based on data from L. F. Shaffer, The Psychology of Adjustment, *rev. ed. Boston: Houghton Mifflin, 1956.)*

There are also ready-made daydreams we may escape into when we want to avoid our problems. The student who is baffled by or bored with his assignments can go to the movies or watch television, both of which offer excitement and make no demands. But by doing so he may fall further and further behind in his work, thereby intensifying his motivation to retreat into fantasy and consequently setting up a self-perpetuating condition. A danger in this situation is that the daydreams may become more satisfying than everyday experiences and lead to a loss of contact with the real world. When this happens, a person may develop psychotic symptoms of hallucination (see Chapter 7). This phenomenon is illustrated in the play, "Harvey," in which an imaginary rabbit plays a principal part.

Whether daydreaming is adjustive or maladjustive depends on its intensity and extent. Often it affords a necessary opportunity to relax, to withdraw temporarily from the bustle of everyday living and to gain a new perspective from which to attack our problems. Sometimes daydreams provide a basis for careful, useful plans. To-

Daydreaming, as illustrated in the first picture, and withdrawal, as illustrated in the second, are frequently utilized by persons who wish to defend themselves against reality. (From Monkmeyer, by Lew Merrim, and Nancy Hays.)

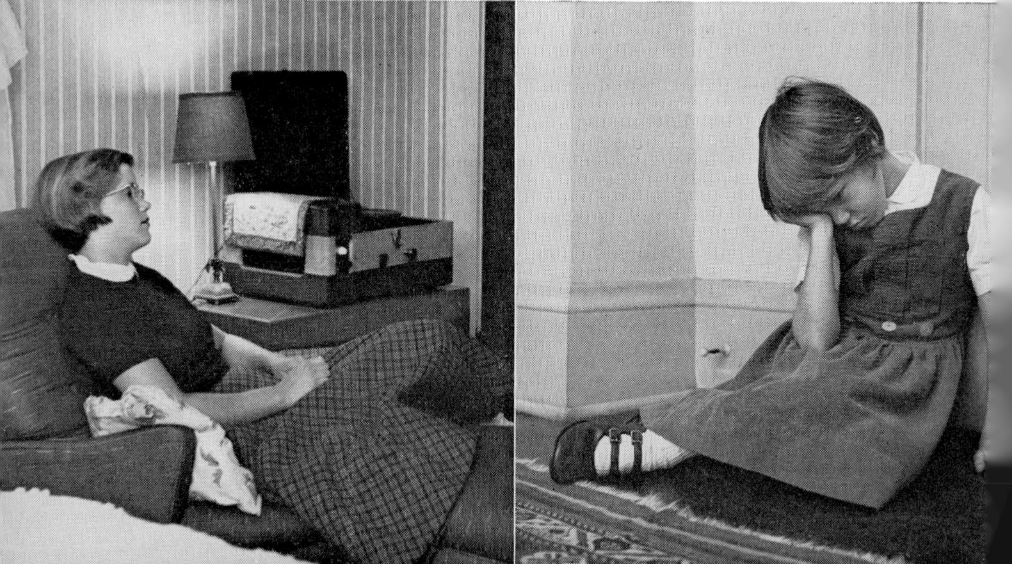

day's daydreams can become tomorrow's accomplishments, provided we use fantasy, not as a form of retreat, but rather as a means of regaining our energy and planning a new attack.

Withdrawal

Daydreaming is a form of intellectual withdrawal, but not all withdrawal involves daydreaming. In *withdrawal* we defend ourselves against anxiety by removing ourselves *physically* from the disturbing situation, thus terminating constructive efforts to deal with it. People who withdraw constantly are often anxious and fearful, and their withdrawal may also be accompanied by feelings of hopelessness and apathy that, in extreme cases, lead to seclusion and isolation. The student who withdraws to his room because he is failing in school, the husband who withdraws to his office because he cannot meet the obligations of family life, are examples.

Withdrawal may indicate that these people have no confidence in themselves. Yet they may, at times, appear to be reserved and formal, or indifferent and self-sufficient because they have cultivated a cloak of aloofness with which to conceal their deep-seated feelings of inadequacy. They may keep others at a distance for fear that the others may come to share their own low opinion of themselves. The acquaintances of such people, therefore, can never feel they really know them.

Other people may withdraw by becoming submissive and shy. They may shun people who threaten their security and avoid tasks they feel they cannot accomplish. Frequently the problems of the shy, retiring individual escape detection; his maladjustive behavior goes unnoticed. A parent or teacher is more likely to notice—and take steps to correct—behavior that indicates hostility and aggression, while ignoring the quieter children. Yet if a tendency to withdraw becomes pronounced it may indicate serious maladjustment.

Those people who have felt threatened and insecure at some time —at home, in school, at a social gathering—may persistently fear the possibility of having to face such a situation again. They generalize from one situation to others and respond to anticipated, threatening situations by avoiding them.

Sometimes a *traumatic* experience, that is, an unexpected incident which comes as a shock, may bring about withdrawal. If a woman is suddenly deserted by the man she expected to marry, the event is likely to be traumatic. If her friends also know of it, the element of wounded pride is added. She may withdraw from all social engagements, not only in order to be alone with her grief, but also to avoid having to face the pity of her friends. Her disappointments may make her bitter, and although she may reject sympathy by insisting that she has forgotten the man and does not wish to hear him mentioned again, the hurt persists. Her withdrawal tendencies may also lead to the utilization of other defense mechanisms. Her reluctance to face her friends, for example, may be rationalized into a claim that social gatherings are a waste of time, that she would rather spend her time at home reading. Or she may resort to daydreaming, in which she might indulge in the satisfaction of imagining that the man begs her to take him back, a request that she vehemently refuses. Withdrawal, rationalization, daydreaming—all function to guard her against future exposure to the same frustrating experience, the same repeated failure. We should note here, however, that a traumatic event more often accentuates a previous tendency to withdraw than causes such a tendency to originate. Not every woman who is deserted by a man reacts by withdrawing.

Withdrawal may also be manifested by a man who is afraid that no one will want to hire him. Although he keeps reading newspaper ads and consulting his friends about promising openings, he is always a little too late in applying for a job. His delay is a form of withdrawal. By applying a day or two late he does not expose himself to the possibility of being rejected. In this sense, the effects of withdrawal are similar to those of rationalization. The real problem is not faced and therefore cannot be resolved.

Some people avoid the problems and conflicts of everyday life by *withdrawing into illness.* They may not deliberately make themselves ill, but they do become especially sensitized to physical disturbances that other people would scarcely notice.

What we popularly describe as *narrow-mindedness* is also a form of withdrawal. The narrow-minded person is unwilling to expose himself to ideas contrary to his own. He dismisses as propaganda anything that opposes his own prejudices. He avoids opinions that threaten his own. He withdraws from contacts with people who disagree with him. True, to some extent we are all selective in what we read and listen to. But when this selectivity becomes so pronounced that it blurs our perception of reality, then it is maladjustive.

Apathy and *lack of interest* may also be symptoms of withdrawal. Some people, in order to justify their withdrawing, profess a lack of interest in others; and lack of interest becomes an additional defense mechanism. Withdrawal in its most acute form is seen in schizophrenia (see Chapter 7), a severe mental disorder characterized by pronounced loss of interest in external affairs and by emotional apathy and seclusiveness.

Withdrawal as a defense mechanism should be distinguished from the need to "get away from it all" that all of us have experienced at times. Such a withdrawal can be beneficial. In fact, it is often essential to productive, creative work, because it can give us a chance to look at ourselves and to evaluate our ideas and our problems. Moreover, not everyone *needs* the same amount of contact with others. Some people have interests they can pursue alone. Some get greater satisfaction out of doing things entirely on their own.

But when withdrawal is adopted as a means of dealing with *inadequacies,* then it reflects maladjustive behavior. And when people remove themselves from society altogether and live like hermits, or when they remain in society but refuse to relate to those around them, we can be fairly sure that they are among those about whom George Homans [1] has this to say:

> If there is one truth that modern psychology has established, it is that an *isolated* individual is sick. He is sick in mind: he will exhibit disorders of behavior, emotion, and thought; he may, as psychosomatic medicine teaches, be sick in body besides. Perhaps, it is better to say that he will have an impaired capacity for maintaining his personal equilibrium under the ordinary shocks of life. This does not mean that, for health, he must be a member of any particular group: not every group will be good for him. It does mean that unless he is a fully accepted member of *some* group—a family, a group of friends, a group of fellow workers—he will be in trouble. And perhaps we need not require him to be a fully accepted member of a group at any

[1] George C. Homans, *The Human Group* (New York: Harcourt, Brace, 1950), pp. 313-14. By permission of Harcourt, Brace and World, Inc.

particular time but only to have been a member at *some* time. A person who has always been isolated may be less able to bear continued isolation than a person who has once known something very different.

To escape isolation, a person must be able to become a member of a group, and that is not just a problem of finding the group. The capacity for relating one's self to other men and women is not inborn but a result of experience and training, and that experience and training is itself social. It begins early in the family, where the child learns the basic imperatives of his society.

Repression

Repression is the process by which painful and anxiety-producing traumatic experiences and ideas are "automatically forgotten." It is a form of self-protective blocking in which "forgetting" occurs more by inhibition than by extinction of material. The blocked material, though not available to consciousness (awareness), nevertheless continues to influence behavior, as is seen frequently in cases of amnesia, phobias, compulsions, or obsessions (see Chapter 6).

The process of blocking traumatic experiences and unpleasant memories from awareness defends us from emotional turmoil and anxiety. Behavior associated with strong social taboos is frequently repressed. Thus in our society a large number of our anxieties and repressions are associated with sexual experiences.

As already implied above, repression interferes with adjustment because even after the original incident has been "forgotten" the tension and emotional disturbances associated with it remain. Some unforeseen occurrence—a chance meeting, an accidental discovery of a long-lost letter—may recall the original emotional turmoil and evoke the original emotional response. In some cases of repression *dissociation* may occur. In extreme form, dissociation may lead to the conditions known as amnesia, split-personality, or fugue, which are described in Chapter 6.

Regression

Regression is the process by which a person unconsciously reverts to earlier, less mature forms of behavior. It represents a psychological retreat into the past to escape from present threats and conflicts. Thus the behavior selected generally reflects such characteristics as *infantilism* (behavior associated with infants, such as crying, violent temper outbursts) or *rigidity* (illustrated by someone continuing to tug at a door he had already found locked, without exploring any other possibilities for opening it).

An example of regressive behavior is seen when an older child reverts to infantile behavior after a new baby has arrived in the family. He may begin to crawl or wet himself, even though he has long since learned to walk and use the toilet. Regression may occur at any age level. The following case history is another example.

> The mother of a seventeen-year-old girl complained that the girl's behavior had become increasingly destructive and irrational during the past few months. Her general behavior was very childish, she spoke in simple sentences, giggled a great deal, and had to be fed and cleaned as if she were an infant. Her history showed a highly unstable family background. When she was four years old her parents began to have violent quarrels, and when she was seven they separated. The mother was given custody of the child, a factor that further upset the child because she was greatly attached to her father. She became increasingly sullen and withdrawn, tendencies that were further accentuated by another violent encounter between her parents some years later. After that she refused to go to school, and while her mother was at work she would destroy the clothes her mother made for her and create complete disorder in the house. At one such time she found a photo of herself as a five-year-old. It showed her with a baby bob and, because of poor lighting, without eyebrows. Immediately she cut her hair, shaved off her eyebrows, and began to imitate the expressions and posture of the photographed child. These actions, together with the childish behavior described earlier, gave a clear picture of regression to a time that she remembered as a relatively happy one.[2]

The occurrence of regression in frustrated children was demonstrated experimentally in a study of a group of thirty children.[3] Each child's ability to play constructively was determined by studying him closely for a half-hour period, during which he was free to play

[2] Jules H. Masserman, *Principles of Dynamic Psychiatry* (Philadelphia: Saunders, 1946), p. 64.

[3] R. G. Barker, T. Dembo, and K. Lewin, "Frustration and Regression: An Experiment with Young Children," *University of Iowa Studies in Child Welfare*, XVIII, No. 1 (1941), 1-314.

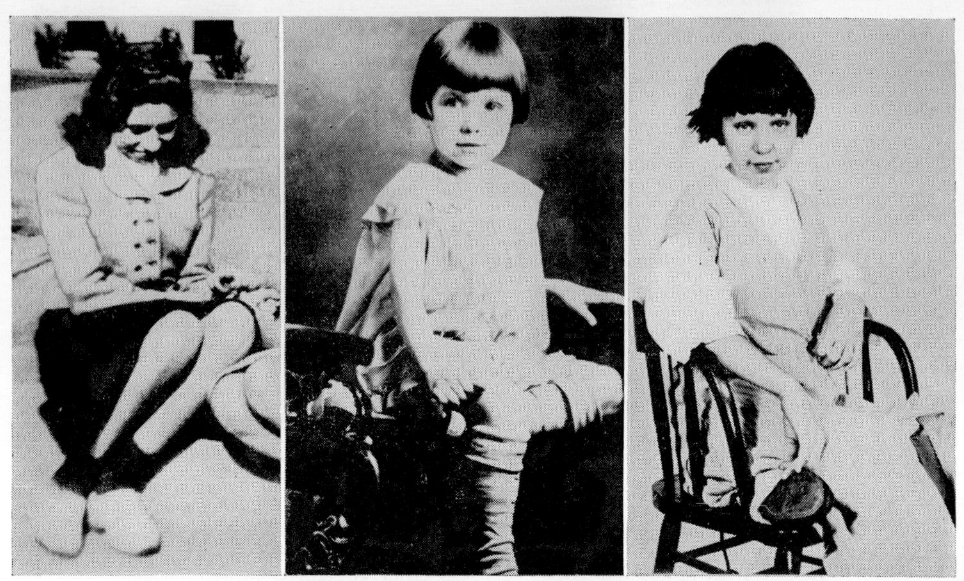

Regression. These three photographs illustrate the case history given in the extract on page 139. Left: before finding baby picture. Center: baby picture. Right: imitating baby picture. (After Romano and Renneker. From Jules H. Masserman, Principles of Dynamic Psychiatry. *Philadelphia: W. B. Saunders Company, 1946.)*

with different toys. Following this, the children were shown some beautiful new toys. But after they had been allowed to inspect the new toys for a few moments they were led back to their old ones, and the new ones were locked away.

Then the children were again observed in the same play situation in which their constructiveness had already been scored. The frustrating experience of being exposed to tempting new toys without being allowed to play with them produced striking examples of regression in their level of constructiveness. The average regression for the group was 14 months. Only five children showed no regressive behavior.

Regressive behavior may occur especially during periods of *separation crisis,* when, for example, a person leaves home for a new and distant place. When people leave one culture for another culture, they often experience what we term *cultural shock.* Both the separation crisis and the cultural shock may lead to feelings of depression, prolonged crying, intense loneliness—the typical symptoms of *home-*

sickness. What we call homesickness is thus a regressive form of adjustment to a new and threatening environment. Such homesickness may also be encountered in young married persons. A new bride or bridegroom may flee from the challenge of the adjustments demanded by the marriage relationship to the former childlike dependency enjoyed at home. As might be expected, homesickness reflects dependency. Consequently it is more likely to occur in people who have been overprotected and overindulged, and therefore denied the opportunity to develop the independence necessary to make separation from home more tolerable and enjoyable.

Nature and Function Summarized

From the foregoing description of the various defense mechanisms, certain general principles concerning their nature and function can be summarized as follows:

1. Defense mechanisms serve to cope with frustrations. They are learned forms of behavior.

2. Defense mechanisms serve to protect self-esteem and to relieve feelings of guilt and anxiety.

3. Whether defense mechanisms are adjustive or maladjustive depends on how much they are used. Occasional daydreaming or withdrawal can be a source of relaxation and strength, but when these tendencies lose their temporary nature and become permanently more satisfying than reality—when the imagined world becomes consistently more desirable than the real world—they are maladjustive.

4. Defense mechanisms also cease to be adjustive:

a. when they obscure the source of our conflicts or the real nature of the problem confronting us;

b. when they lead to cumulative maladaptations, that is, when a person who has failed to obtain a job begins by saying he did not want the job anyhow ("sour grapes" mechanism), goes on to blame others for his failure (scapegoating), and finally starts to daydream about being a successful businessman without actually making any effort to become one;

c. when they prevent a person from making an objective analysis of himself in relation to his problem and blind him to the possibility of alternative courses of action.

For Additional Reading

Ackerman, Nathan W. and Marie Jahoda, *Anti-Semitism and Emotional Disorder*. New York: Harper, 1950.

Barker, R. G., T. Dembo and Kurt Lewin, "Frustration and Regression: An Experiment With Young Children," *University of Iowa Studies in Child Welfare*, XVIII, No. 1 (1941), 1-314.

Berkowitz, Leonard, *Aggression. A Social Psychological Analysis*. New York: McGraw-Hill, 1962.

Cameron, Norman, *The Psychology of Behavior Disorders*. Boston: Houghton Mifflin, 1947.

Horney, Karen, *Our Inner Conflicts*. New York: Norton, 1950.

Jourard, Sidney M., *Personal Adjustment*. New York: Macmillan, 1958. See especially Chapter 10: "Defense of the Self-Structure."

Keister, M. E. and R. Updegraff, "A Study of Children's Reactions to Failure and an Experimental Attempt to Modify Them," in *Readings in Social Psychology*, eds. T. M. Newcomb and E. L. Hartley. New York: Holt, 1947, pp. 291-296.

Lazarus, Richard S., *Personality and Adjustment*. Englewood Cliffs, N. J.: Prentice-Hall, 1963.

Masserman, Jules H., *Principles of Dynamic Psychiatry*. Philadelphia: Saunders, 1946.

May, Rollo, *The Meaning of Anxiety*. New York: Ronald, 1950.

Miller, D. R. and E. G. Swanson, *Inner Defense and Conflict*. New York: Holt, 1960.

Murphy, Gardner, *Personality. A Biosocial Approach to Origins and Structure*. New York: Harper, 1947.

Shaffer, Laurence Frederic and Edward J. Shoben, Jr., *Personality and the Psychology of Adjustment. A Dynamic and Experimental Approach to Mental Hygiene* (2nd ed.). Boston: Houghton Mifflin, 1956.

Smith, Henry Clay, *Personality Adjustment*. New York: McGraw-Hill, 1961. See especially Chapter 11: "Personality Mechanisms."

Snygg, Donald and Arthur W. Combs, *Individual Behavior* (rev. ed.). New York: Harper, 1959. See especially Chapter 9: "The Availability of Perceptions in the Field."

Symonds, P. M., *The Dynamics of Human Adjustment*. New York: Appleton-Century-Crofts, 1946.

CHARACTERISTICS OF NEUROTIC BEHAVIOR

CLASSIFICATION AND DESCRIPTION OF THE NEUROSES

Anxiety Reactions

Phobic Reactions

Obsessive-Compulsive Reactions

Dissociative Reactions

Conversion Reactions

Depressive Reactions

Hypochondriac and Neurasthenic Reactions

CAUSES OF NEUROTIC BEHAVIOR

Heredity

Past Experiences

The Contemporary Situation

FUNCTIONS SERVED BY NEUROTIC BEHAVIOR

The Neuroses

6

If the defense mechanisms—
our "first line of defense"—
cannot sufficiently protect us
when our feelings of security and adequacy
are threatened by frustration,
we may mobilize a "second line of defense"—
the *psychoneuroses*—
known more simply as
the *neuroses*.
We may define the *neuroses* as
disorders reflected in our ways

of thinking, feeling, and behaving, produced by severe emotional tensions that our defense mechanisms could not adequately control.

As with the defense mechanisms, neurotic symptoms represent an attempt to cope with inner conflicts and situational pressures that threaten us. The defense mechanisms—which constitute a less seriously maladjustive means of handling anxiety—may continue to be employed in behavior characterized as neurotic.

Characteristics of Neurotic Behavior

1. Neurotic behavior is more maladjustive than the defense mechanisms, but less maladjustive than the psychoses (discussed in Chapter 7).
2. Neurotic symptoms are unconsciously developed and not consciously selected.
3. Neurotic symptoms are functional in nature; that is, they are not based on organic deficiencies. Neurotic behavior is therefore referred to as *psychogenic,* meaning caused by emotional, not physical, problems.
4. Neurotic behavior is characterized by inappropriateness and rigidity. It is inappropriate, for example, to wash one's hands every 10 minutes whether they need washing or not. This same behavior is rigid as well, in the sense that the neurotic feels *compelled* to go through his ritual of washing his hands regardless of the difficulties he meets in doing so.
5. Neurotic behavior is self-related for ego protection rather than situation-related for problem solving.
6. Neurotic behavior seldom reflects lack of orientation to the environment—the neurotic is in touch with reality.
7. The neurotic recognizes the inappropriateness of what he is compelled to do, even though he does not understand the origin or function of his symptoms.
8. Neurotic behavior is not likely to endanger the person himself or others.
9. Neurotic behavior seldom requires hospitalization.
10. Neurotic behavior generally includes disturbed interaction with others, thus making it difficult for the neurotic to achieve satisfactory interpersonal relationships.

Classification and Description of the Neuroses

In addition to the general characteristics just listed, neurotic behavior falls into more specific patterns of symptoms, on the basis of which we can identify and describe a variety of specific neuroses. Classifications of neuroses differ somewhat with different authorities, but they generally include the following:

1. Anxiety reactions
2. Phobic reactions
3. Obsessive-compulsive reactions
4. Dissociative reactions
5. Conversion reactions
6. Depressive reactions
7. Hypochondriac and neurasthenic reactions

Let us consider briefly the distinguishing characteristics of behavior disturbances found under these classifications.

Anxiety Reactions

Anxiety reactions are characterized by an emotional state of intense and persistent apprehension and fear. They are usually accompanied by one or more of a number of physiological reactions, such as palpitation of the heart, sweating, a sense of pressure in the head, dryness in the mouth, and feelings of dizziness or faintness. A person suffering from an anxiety neurosis may be in a *chronic* state of apprehension, or may be seized with *temporary* attacks of intense fear. He may not know the cause of his anxiety reaction, which can be a kind of "free-floating" fear, not related to any one stimulus. He may, for example, have an intense apprehension of impending danger, illness, or death but be unable to give any details about these apprehensions.

This intense anxiety is spoken of as *neurotic anxiety* and should be distinguished from *normal anxiety*. Normal anxiety is the kind of apprehension and tenseness that all of us may experience in preparing to meet a situation that may be somewhat threatening. We might feel such anxiety before giving a talk; just before appearing on stage; or before we start at a new job or a new school.

Phobic Reactions

When the intense fear of an anxiety reaction becomes focused and displaced upon a definite (but often transitory) object, we speak of a phobia or a *phobic reaction*. Phobias are exaggerated and illogical fears related to specific people, objects, or situations. A person who feels panic when a feather comes out of a pillow, for example, may know this intense fear is irrational but still be unable to control it. All of us are familiar with the more common phobias: *claustrophobia*, the fear of confined spaces; *agoraphobia*, fear of open spaces; *mysophobia*, fear of contamination; *acrophobia*, fear of high places; and so on. People may also develop phobias about blood, germs, animals, and many other things.

Phobic reactions may be divided into simple and complex types. Simple phobic reactions may be directly learned from the behavior of others. A phobic parent, for example, may teach a child to fear insects, the dark, or lightning. Complex phobic reactions may be persistent, maladjustive responses to an originally terrifying object or situation. They are attempts to prevent or avoid strong anxiety by repressing the fear of the actual danger and displacing that fear onto some portion of, or symbolic substitute for, the actual danger. By fleeing the symbolic substitute the neurotic person avoids recognizing the real cause of his anxiety.

For example, the adult who, as a child, was attacked by a bulldog may now be terrified not only of dogs but also of cats, birds, and even fur pieces. This shift of fear reactions from one stimulus object to another is an example of displacement. Here the displacement may be due to simple generalization of the original fear-evoking stimulus.

What a person consciously fears depends on his own psychological needs. Thus a woman's morbid fear of germs may serve to satisfy her need for self-protection by displacing her real (but unacceptable) source of anxiety-suicidal impulses. Simultaneously, her fear of germs helps her to avoid situations in which she might give vent to suicidal impulses. Phobic reactions, therefore, may result from internal as well as external sources of danger. "Danger" in a given situation may be the neurotic's own impulses or desires—unconscious desires or impulses that he has repressed because they are unacceptable to him.

Obsessive-Compulsive Reactions

The central characteristic of the *obsessive-compulsive reaction* is a persistent repetition of an unwanted and often symbolic thought or act. *Obsessions* are characterized by the recurrence of undesired and disquieting thoughts, often making a person feel he is a victim of his own ideas. A man might be haunted, for example, by the fear that he will step in front of an oncoming car. A woman might be obsessed with the idea that she will harm her baby. Some people are obsessed by thoughts about sexual activities, others by fears of "losing" their minds.

Compulsions are acts a person performs without knowing why or without consciously wishing to do so. The compulsive person is aware that what he is doing is situationally unnecessary or undesirable, and yet he cannot resist doing it. Often the victim of a compulsion will give up even trying to find an explanation or justification for his behavior, other than to say, "I simply cannot help myself." One of the most common compulsions is the one, already mentioned, in which a person feels compelled to wash his hands over and over again, even though they may be perfectly clean. Other compulsions are *kleptomania*, which is the compulsion to steal, and *pyromania*, the compulsion to set fires.

Phobias, obsessions, and compulsions may occur alone or in combination. Someone who has a phobia about contamination, for example, may unconsciously fall victim to the hand-washing compulsion. Some phobias may be complicated by obsessions. A man haunted by thoughts of an object or situation he fears may become just as distraught as if he were actually meeting the object or situation face to face.

As with other neurotic behavior, the obsessive-compulsive symptoms are an attempt on the part of the individual to protect himself against stress and anxiety by displacing his fears or guilt feelings.

The hand-washing compulsion, for example, may indicate a person's deep-seated fear of having sinned or been "dirty" and his need, therefore, to atone for his sins through his symbolic cleansing act. By concentrating on the symbol, rather than the pent-up emotions behind it, he avoids having to face disturbing facts. The symbol becomes an outlet for releasing tensions and controlling anxiety.

Dissociative Reactions

In *dissociative reactions* a person's ways of thinking, feeling, and behaving become separated from normal consciousness and function as separate activities. Dissociation is a form of psychological compartmentalization. It is the phenomenon that allows Sunday saint and weekday sinner to function in peace within the same personality. Dissociation may occur in varying degrees, ranging from the mild type experienced by all of us in such acts of absent-mindedness as unconscious doodling while on the telephone, to the severe and complete type encountered in multiple personality disorders. The dissociative reactions are neurotic attempts to escape inner conflict and anxiety by separating from awareness certain unwelcome ideas, feelings, or drives. Probably basic to this dissociation is the phenomenon of repression. The following are examples of dissociative reactions.

AMNESIA *Amnesia* is characterized by the inability to recall past experiences where such recall is to be expected. Its scope may be restricted to an inability to recall certain events related to a particular time, place, or type of experience, or it may extend to a total loss of memory for most of one's past. An example of partial amnesia would be the loss of memory associated with the shock of being involved in an accident that was fatal to a friend. Traumatic episodes associated with conflict or with sexual assault may lead to partial amnesia. An attack of amnesia may persist for a day, a week, a month, a year, or longer.

FUGUE The word *fugue* means *flight* and refers to a prolonged period of amnesia during which the person usually leaves his home and job and begins a new life with a new name and identity. As a rule skills and abilities are not affected by this loss of memory. With recovery, the earlier events are again remembered, but the experiences during the period of a fugue are usually forgotten. Examples of fugues are reported in newspapers occasionally, in stories telling of victims who forget their identities and run away from home and familiar surroundings, "coming to" later in some distant place, dazed, confused, and unable to remember how they got there or who they are.

MULTIPLE PERSONALITY From fugue it is but a step to *multiple personality.* This is a condition in which an individual shows two or more distinct sub-personalities, which make him different persons at different times. The story *Dr. Jekyll and Mr. Hyde* presents a classic literary example, and the story *The Three Faces of Eve* describes a recent actual case of multiple personality.

Ordinarily each of us plays several different roles during the course of a day. We may assume the role of husband, father, employer, philanthropist, or sportsman, acting quite differently in each one. But we recognize ourselves as unified, integrated personalities no matter how diverse these roles may be. In multiple personality, however, the integration or relatedness is missing. The victim is unable to reconcile the traits of one personality and role with the other or others. Frequently the one personality is unable to recall—or can recall only dimly—the acts and thoughts of the other.

In summary, the amnesia victim deals with his conflicts and anxieties by forgetting unpleasant and disturbing events; the fugue victim also deals with his by forgetting his past, but in addition takes flight into a different life; and the multiple-personality victim deals with his emotional problems by a fairly complete dissociation of functions, characteristics, and roles.

Dissociative reactions may be found in emotionally immature people who want to escape from anxiety-producing situations but who see themselves as unable to do so without suffering intense feelings of guilt or fear. A neurotic solution to this problem is dissociation of the experience that the person cannot face and deal with constructively.

Conversion Reactions

In the *conversion reactions,* often classified as conversion *hysteria,* anxiety and emotional conflict are "converted" into physical symptoms of disease or disability. With this unconscious choice of defense, the person may go blind, become paralyzed, or develop a tic or tremor—all with no discernible physical basis. The physical symptoms may appear where no organic pathology ever existed, or they may retain the characteristics of an earlier illness. In the latter case, the patient unconsciously exploits a symptom suggested by the former illness. When a patient does this it is often difficult to distinguish the hysterical conversion reaction, an *unconscious* defense, from deliberate *malingering* which is a *conscious* feigning of sickness or disability.

Conversion reactions fall into three categories: *hysterical sensory disturbances, hysterical paralysis,* and *hysterical motor disturbances.* In hysterical sensory disturbances, the functioning of one or more of the senses is disturbed. The victim may become blind; lose his sense of smell; or show disturbances in the sense of touch, with sensations that the skin is tingling or "crawling." Hysterical paralysis may involve partial or complete loss of the voice, paralysis of one or more limbs, or even paralysis of half the body. Motor disturbances may involve loss of muscular control, as seen in tics, in involuntary nervous twitching of the head or parts of the face, and in muscular tremors.

Like other neurotic symptoms, the conversion reactions lack any organic basis. They develop out of feelings of anxiety and are symbolic of underlying conflict. The symptoms serve to lessen anxiety and so usually meet the immediate needs of the patient, allowing him to make at least a short-range neurotic adjustment.

Depressive Reactions

In *depressive reactions* a person tries to deal with personal anxiety by going into a state of depression, characterized by withdrawal from stimulation, lack of interest, loss of initiative, feelings of hopelessness, and feelings of worthlessness and self-doubt. All of us may have experienced these symptoms in varying degrees. When encountered in their moderate form we generally speak of them as *dejection*. When, however, these symptoms appear in more acute form, we speak of a neurotic depressive reaction (sometimes also called reactive depression). However, this depression must also be distinguished from the more severe psychotic depressions found in involutional melancholia and manic-depressive reactions (discussed in Chapter 7).

Intense feelings of dejection, pessimism, and discouragement, often accompanied by an intense foreboding of danger, are symptoms encountered in neurotic depression. Marked feelings of ambivalence about an experience may also be associated with this depression. We are ambivalent toward a person or experience when contradictory feelings, such as love and hate or acceptance and rejection, "pull" us in psychologically opposite directions. For example, a neurotically depressed soldier whose life was spared in combat while his best friend was killed may be troubled by feelings of ambivalence about his right to enjoy life. He may even occasionally have feelings of guilt about his friend's death and believe himself responsible for it.

The extent of the depression depends on the depressed person's predisposition to feelings of inadequacy, the extent to which he regards the world as unfriendly and hostile, the severity of his traumatic experience, and the degree of ambivalence he has toward the experience. A tendency to be self-blaming and self-punishing and to be narrow and inflexible could also influence the extent to which neurotic depression develops.

Hypochondriac and Neurasthenic Reactions

In *hypochondriac* and *neurasthenic reactions* the individual is excessively preoccupied with how he feels physically. The hypochondriac feels physically unfit. The neurasthenic feels tired.

The complaints of a hypochondriac may run the whole gamut of man's ills—indigestion, stomach-aches, heart or lung trouble, glandular ailments, urinary disturbances, sore muscles. Hypochondriacs spend much of their time in doctors' offices or poring over popular medical books and journals looking for remedies. Many seem to "enjoy" poor health and do not appear discouraged about their symptoms, operations, tribulations, or their expenditures in trying to find relief. Often the hypochondriac becomes the dupe of quacks.

The key symptom of neurasthenia is an exaggerated feeling of fatigue, and neurasthenia is often called the "fatigue neurosis." The neurasthenic complains of exhaustion and a feeling of general weakness. He feels mentally and physically tired, and often complains that he cannot concentrate. Difficulties that appear small to others may upset him greatly. He is very irritable, and this is often accompanied by emotional exhaustion and feelings of depression. Sometimes, in the absence of any organic basis, he may develop physiological symptoms, such as headaches, backaches, numbness in various parts of the body. Often the neurasthenic will show diminished sexual vigor, at times becoming impotent. Neurasthenia is often difficult to diagnose because many of its symptoms may have their origins—though not their causes—in some temporary or chronic physical condition. The physical condition, however, serves here as the "psychological excuse" to develop the other symptoms that are found in the neurasthenic picture.

Case histories of neurasthenics reveal that the symptoms of pronounced fatigue rarely come from strenuous mental or physical activity. Rather, the fatigue seems to be associated with emotional tension which arises from an inability to resolve disturbing emotional difficulties.

The main difference between the neurasthenic and the hypochondriac is that the former complains of bodily fatigue and "all over" discomfort, while the latter tends to focus complaints on a specific organ or function of his body. Instead of being tired all over, he has a heart that does not work right, or a kidney that will not let him function adequately. Both, however, show abnormal concern about their own well-being.

These symptoms, like the neurotic symptoms already discussed, serve important functions in that they help to provide needed protection against the admission of inadequacy or failure. Hypochondriac and neurasthenic symptoms provide a "physical" excuse to the neurotic for not trying things in which he anticipates failure.

Causes of Neurotic Behavior

We pointed out that the difference between normal and neurotic behavior is one of degree, and that the same dynamic processes concerned with the satisfaction of needs that motivate normal behavior can be observed in the behavior of the neurotic person. Remembering that in all behavior not single factors but combinations of factors tend to operate, let us now consider how neurotic behavior is related to such factors as *heredity, past experiences,* and the *contemporary situation.*

Heredity

The influences of heredity on neurotic behavior are difficult to ascertain, as it is almost impossible to differentiate between a person's inherited characteristics and those he acquires early in life. For example, the attempt to link a patient's mental illness with heredity by tracing the incidence of mental disorders in his family usually fails, because, even if the incidence of disorders is high, one cannot tell whether the patient acquired predisposing characteristics through heredity or through close and frequent contact with afflicted members of the family. In general it is more accurate to assume that neurotic behavior as described above is a "learned" way of behaving rather than one influenced by an inherited predisposition.

Past Experiences

Our experiences from earliest childhood on help to shape the way we think, feel, and behave and so influence our behavior toward normality or neuroticism. In addition, certain specific experiences may promote the learning of behavior which is more defensive, maladaptive, or neurotic. Someone who encountered considerable illness as a child, for instance, may in times of stress fall back on illness and physical complaints in an attempt to solve his problems. Or, to cite a different kind of past experience, someone who has been subjected to much training and pressure to be orderly, or clean, or on time, or to adhere strictly and often irrationally to certain rules and regulations, may develop an obsessive and compulsive disposition about such behavior.

The social experiences we had with others in the process of growing up may influence the manner in which we approach our problems. Someone who has been rejected as a child, for example, will want to love and be loved as much as or more than others, but he may be afraid lest he be rejected again. This approach-avoidance conflict, the desire to approach a person, while at the same time fearing to do so, appears to be a fundamental problem encountered by the neurotic.

Another fundamental conflict often observed is that between the needs of the individual and the demands of society that these needs be satisfied in certain prescribed ways and at certain specified times. As the child grows up he develops many needs. These must be satisfied in socially acceptable ways, and often this involves delayed gratification and requires assistance from others. But if help and guidance are not forthcoming, the child's world becomes threatening, hostile, dangerous. Maladjustive ways of dealing with such conflicts may develop early in life, and since such maladjustive methods do reduce tension to a certain extent (although they do not resolve the conflict), they persist and become preferred ways of responding. Even so, the individual may carry on his daily activities fairly well as long as no new disturbances occur.

The Contemporary Situation

A third factor that has a bearing on whether or not someone resorts to neurotic behavior is his present situation. He may function quite adequately unless special stresses or pressures appear—a serious quarrel between husband and wife, a serious financial problem, loss of a job. Then he may develop neurotic symptoms. Cases of war neuroses are also examples of individuals breaking down under increased stresses and pressures.

Whether we develop neurotic symptoms or not depends on several interrelated factors in our present situation. They are (1) the particular experiences or problems confronting us; (2) our sensitivity or responsiveness to these experiences at this particular time; (3) our adaptability, that is, our ability to handle the experiences; and (4) how much support we get from others with whom we are in close and frequent contact. Put another way, whether anyone "breaks" or not depends on *what happens, how he reacts to it, what he can do about it,* and *how he relates to others.* An exploration of these four factors is essential to an understanding of the adjustment of any given individual. One person may react deeply to disturbing experiences and yet not become neurotic because he has adequate ways of handling the situation. Another may break under less trying problems because he lacks the techniques for dealing with them, because he may have limited capacities for controlling his emotional reactions to them, or because he cannot communicate adequately about them with others.

We may summarize this discussion by saying that *environmental changes, acting upon an organism with a certain receptivity, will evoke certain reactions, depending on what facilities (innate or learned) the organism has at its disposal for adjusting to the stimulus.* Cause-and-effect relationships operate in neurotic behavior just as they do in any other behavior, although the causes and motives leading to neurotic symptoms may be difficult to discover or understand. Nevertheless, seeing neurotic behavior in this perspective may make it easier for us to regard it (in ourselves or in others) as behavior that needs to be studied and understood rather than to be condemned or rejected.

Functions Served by Neurotic Behavior

Neurotic behavior patterns are unconscious attempts to deal with conflict situations. It is important to emphasize that the behavior patterns are selected and developed unconsciously. Although the symptoms of conversion reactions, for example, may be similar to characteristics observed in malingering individuals, there is an important difference. The malingerer is aware that he is attempting to get out of a conflict or choice by developing a symptom; the neurotic is not.

What is the primary value of these unconscious neurotic behavior patterns? They are ways of dealing with anxiety and conflict—even if only temporarily successful. We shall more readily understand the tension-reducing function of the neuroses if we consider for a moment the restlessness and anxiety that we all experience when anticipating an important event in our lives. By looking at this normal anxiety, we may facilitate our understanding of the more intense and neurotic anxiety. For instance, if we are expecting a visit from a close friend whom we have not seen for a long time, if we are waiting for an appointment that may lead to our securing a better job, if we have only a few hours left before taking an important examination, we are likely to become increasingly anxious. In order to calm ourselves, we may turn to such activities as reading or taking a walk in an effort to reduce our tension, even though these activities do not directly help us to deal with the situation that creates the tension. The neurotic is unable to find relief through such normal and acceptable channels.

In addition to its general tension-reducing function, neurotic behavior may serve other, more specific purposes. Neurotic complaints may protect a person from taking on problems that are beyond his ability. The neurasthenic or the hypochondriac, for example, shifts responsibility for his failure or inadequacy to some physical defect over which he cannot be expected to have any control. Consequently others cannot blame him for his inadequacy, and he can maintain his self-respect. By extension, the guilt-ridden person who develops a hand-washing compulsion does not actually free himself from his guilt feelings, but the symbolic act of washing his hands does reduce the guilt feelings for a time. Again, someone who is afraid to face his problems does not solve them by developing hysterical blindness, but he does relieve himself temporarily of his responsibility for dealing with them.

Although it reduces tension temporarily, neurotic behavior may at the same time aggravate the underlying causes of the tension. A person who does not get along well with others may alienate them further by compulsive or obsessive behavior. The rigidity that characterizes his responses makes it difficult for him to learn new, more acceptable ways of behaving.

For Additional Reading

Bennett, Ivy, *Delinquent and Neurotic Children*. New York: Basic Books, 1960.

Bettelheim, Bruno, *Truants from Life*. Glencoe, Ill.: Free Press, 1955.

Cattell, R. B. and I. H. Scheier, *The Meaning and Measurement of Neuroticism and Anxiety*. New York: Ronald, 1961.

Cleveland, E. J. and W. D. Longaker, "Neurotic Patterns in the Family," in *Explorations in Social Psychiatry*, eds. Alexander H. Leighton *et al.* New York: Basic Books, 1957, pp. 167-200.

Coleman, James C., *Abnormal Psychology of Modern Life*. Chicago: Scott, Foresman, 1950.

Committee on Nomenclature and Statistics of the American Psychiatric Association, *Diagnostic and Statistical Manual of Mental Disorders*. Washington, D. C.: American Psychiatric Association Mental Hospital Service, 1952.

Dollard, John and Neal E. Miller, *Personality and Psychotherapy—An Analysis in Terms of Learning, Thinking and Culture*. New York: McGraw-Hill, 1950.

Dorcus, Roy M. and G. Wilson Shaffer, *Textbook of Abnormal Psychology* (4th ed.). Baltimore: Williams and Wilkins, 1950.

Fenichel, O., *The Psychoanalytic Theory of Neuroses*. New York: Norton, 1945.

Horney, Karen, *The Neurotic Personality of Our Time*. New York: Norton, 1937.

Hunt, J. McV., ed., *Personality and the Behavior Disorders*. New York: Ronald, 1944.

Kubie, Lawrence S., *Neurotic Distortion of the Creative Process*. Lawrence, Kan.: University of Kansas Press, 1958.

Maslow, A. H., *Motivation and Personality*. New York: Harper, 1954.

May, Rollo, *The Meaning of Anxiety*. New York: Ronald, 1950.

Opler, Marvin K., *Culture, Psychiatry and Human Values. The Methods and Values of Social Psychiatry*. Springfield, Ill.: Thomas, 1956.

Schneidman, Edwin S. and Norman L. Farberow, eds., *Clues to Suicide*. New York: Blakiston, 1957.

Thigpen, C. H. and H. M. Cleckley, *The Three Faces of Eve*. New York: McGraw-Hill, 1957.

The Psychoses

7

If defense mechanisms and neuroses

are our first and second "lines of defense"

against severe emotional tension,

we may consider the *psychoses*

as the final line of defense.

People who are too disturbed

to maintain even the limited adjustment

the neuroses afford

may become *psychotic*.

The differences between

a normal and a neurotic person,

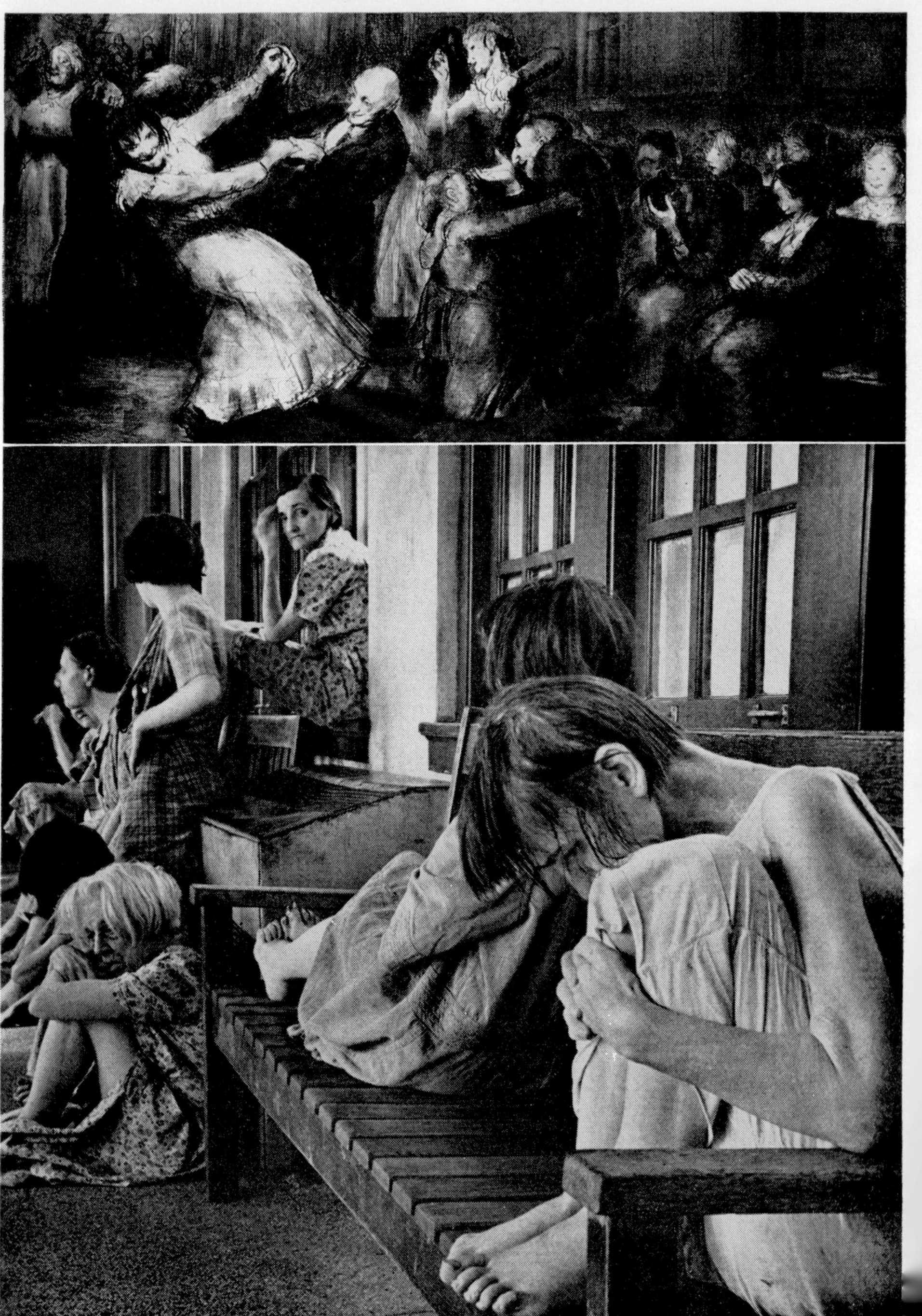

Because the psychotic person has lost contact with reality, hospital or institutional care is generally required. The painting at the top, Dance in a Madhouse *by George Bellows, offers the artist's conception of what a mental institution was like in 1917. Below is a contemporary photograph showing a group of hospitalized psychotic patients. (Top: courtesy of the National Gallery of Art, Washington, D. C. Bottom: New York Public Library.)*

or a neurotic and a psychotic, are mainly differences in *degree* of disturbance.

The psychoses constitute the most severe forms of mental disorders, and each year approximately 150,000 persons so afflicted are admitted to mental institutions in this country. This figure includes only first admissions—not patients who have been released and who are returning. But not all psychotics enter hospitals. Many are cared for at home or in institutions that do not classify them as psychotic.

Since the changes in a person's behavior that indicate the presence of a psychosis may occur gradually—sometimes almost imperceptibly—it is difficult for untrained persons to detect such changes when they first occur. Only when behavioral disturbances become severe do relatives and friends become concerned about them.

One way of looking at the relationship between mental health and the neuroses and psychoses is presented in Figure 1. As this figure indicates, a stable person in an environment of average stress would show behavior characterized as normal or healthy. As the amount of environmental stress increases and the person correspondingly shows more instability, the various neuroses may appear. If environmental stress increases still more, and individual instability increases, then psychotic behavior may emerge. We may thus view our behavior as falling on a continuum, with normal or healthy behavior at one end and psychotic behavior at the other, but with many intermediate conditions in between. The differences, as we have already indicated, are mainly differences in *degree* of disturbance, rather than in *kind*.

We shall summarize here the main characteristics of psychotic behavior, describe and classify the major psychoses, discuss the causes of such behavior, and comment briefly on types of treatment that are used.

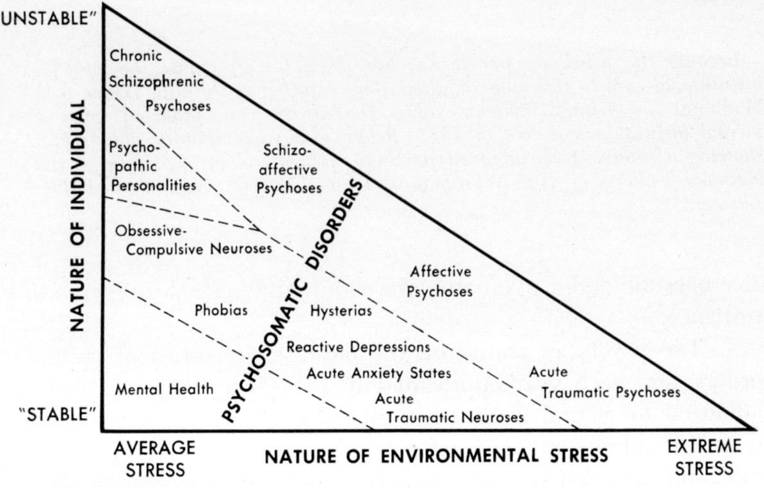

Figure 1. Psychosomatic disorders. (Source: Judd Marmer, M.D., and E. Pumpian-Mindlin, M.D. "Toward an Integrative Conception of Mental Disorder," Journal of Nervous and Mental Disease, *III, 1950, 19-29. By permission of the authors and the* Journal of Nervous and Mental Disease.*)*

Characteristics of Psychotic Behavior

Although each psychosis has its particular symptoms, all have certain characteristics in common. These are as follows:

1. Psychotic behavior is characterized by severe disturbances in thinking, feeling, and behaving, and the patient must generally be hospitalized.
2. Psychotic behavior is characterized by loss of contact with reality. There are severe distortions in what the person perceives or feels and severe disturbances in his social relationships. His breaks with reality often include hallucinations and delusions.
3. In psychotic behavior the *total* personality is involved. That is, the psychosis usually manifests itself in everything the person does.
4. Unlike the neurotic person, the psychotic has no insight into his disturbances and does not realize there is anything wrong with him. This is part of his loss of contact with reality.
5. The psychotic's behavior frequently endangers himself or others. This is one reason for hospitalization.

We may define psychoses, then, as a group of serious behavior disorders that:

1. Involve the entire personality;
2. Are characterized by loss of contact with reality (including loss of relationships with others); and
3. Can render the person dangerous both to himself and others.

Classification and Description of the Psychoses

The psychoses are usually classified as either *functional* or *organic*. Functional psychoses are those behavior disorders for which we can detect no organic basis. They originate in psychological disturbances, that is, they are *psychogenic*. Organic psychoses are caused or accompanied by physiological and neurological disorders affecting the brain.

The Functional Psychoses

The functional psychoses to be discussed in this section are: (1) schizophrenia, (2) paranoia, (3) the manic-depressive psychosis, and (4) involutional melancholia.

SCHIZOPHRENIA Schizophrenia, which often appears in adolescence or early adulthood, is characterized by disturbances in reality relationships, as manifested by disorganized ways of thinking, feeling, and behaving. The name indicates that the schizophrenic person "splits" from the world—not, as is ocasionally believed, that he has a split personality. He lives in his own private world, out of touch with reality and with other people. He usually suffers from delusions, and therefore he may ascribe his difficulties to the malice or interference of other people. He may even believe that his behavior is influenced by magic, by strange powers and forces; and he may claim to hear voices that tell him what to do. Frequently the schizophrenic is indifferent and apathetic, but his mood may change suddenly and inexplicably. He may turn against, even attack, someone he previously trusted and loved. Often his mannerisms are stereotyped or ritualistic, as in the case of the patient who could never sit down without first turning around three times. The schizophrenic may shut himself off from all mental or emotional contact with others, perhaps sitting alone for hours, rigid and motionless, and refusing to talk to anyone.

Schizophrenia has been divided into four subgroups: *simple, hebephrenic, catatonic,* and *paranoid.* In each of these groups, certain characteristics predominate, although sometimes the symptoms of one group may appear in others. A person may also pass from one subgroup to another in the course of an illness.

A person afflicted with simple schizophrenia is withdrawn, unconcerned, apathetic. He is not usually subject to emotional outbursts or to hallucinations and delusions. If he does have hallucinations or

The catatonic schizophrenic assumes odd positions for long periods of time. (New York Public Library.)

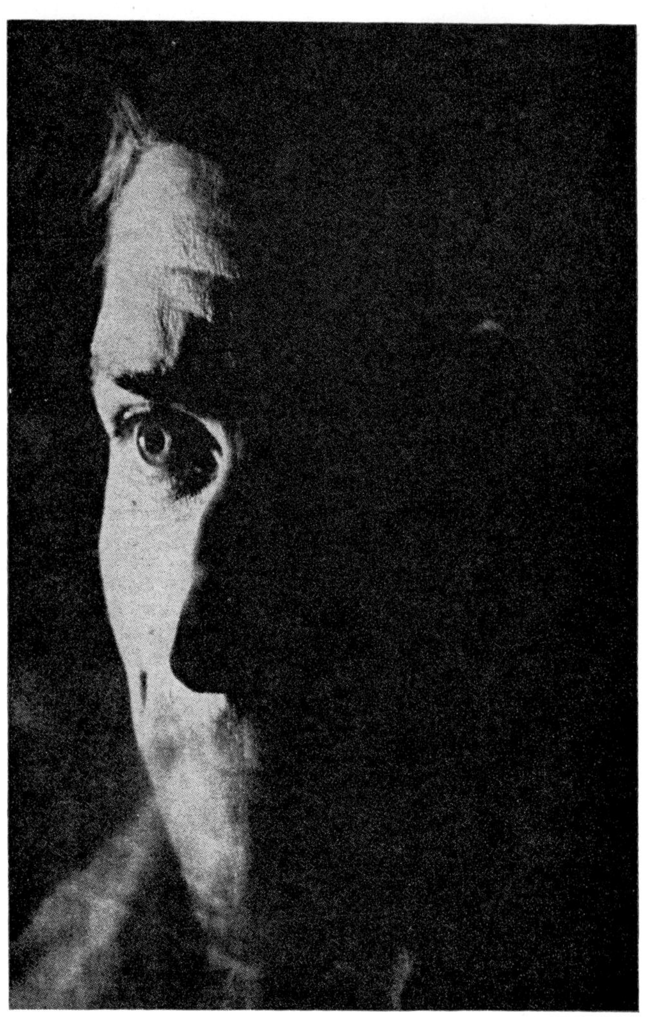

His suspicions that others are plotting against him can make life a nightmare for the paranoiac. (New York Public Library.)

delusions, he is generally very secretive about them, and they can be discovered only by careful investigation.

The hebephrenic schizophrenic appears silly and laughs and giggles without any apparent reason. He may show delusions and hallucinations. His mannerisms may appear purposeless.

In catatonic schizophrenia motor symptoms predominate, although there are also intellectual or emotional disturbances. The patient may be overactive or listless, excitable or taut. He may sit

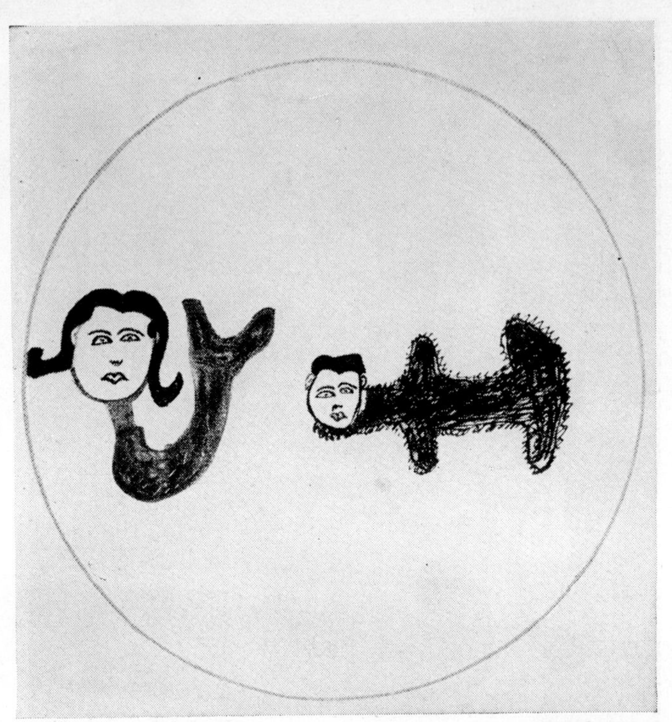

Delusions. A paranoid patient has elaborated on a photograph of sunspots. By giving the spots human features, he can fit them into his private magic system of delusions. (Courtesy of H. Lehmann, M.D., Montreal, Verdun Protestant Hospital, and Ayerst, McKenna and Harrison, Ltd.)

motionless or he may assume odd positions or postures, such as standing on one foot or curling up into a ball. Once he takes a position, he will often resist all efforts to make him change it, being negativistic in this as in other ways. He may refuse to speak to anyone for long periods of time, and he may appear stuporous and withdrawn. But in spite of this apparent indifference, he may be aware of what goes on around him and later recall much of what happened.

The paranoid schizophrenic shows his autistic and unrealistic thinking mainly through persecution complexes, in which he sees himself threatened by all kinds of evils, and through delusions of grandeur, where he may believe himself to be a famous historical, religious, or political figure. The delusions usually change often and they come and go quickly. As the illness progresses, the patient may become increasingly suspicious, resentful, hostile, and at times even aggressive. The patient may be excessively concerned with religious matters and rituals.

PARANOIA Paranoiac disorders, which often develop between the ages of 35 and 55 years, are characterized by suspicions that become more and more numerous and finally develop into whole systems of highly organized delusions. The highly organized, permanent, and systematic nature of the delusions distinguishes paranoia from the paranoiac *tendency* in certain schizophrenics.

Paranoiac delusions are based partly on incorrect interpretations of events and partly on false premises. If the paranoiac's original premise is fairly reasonable, he may be able to argue his case logically, consistently, and convincingly. The paranoiac nature of his claims often becomes apparent only after prolonged contact and conversations with him have revealed the meager evidence on which he bases his conclusions and have shown that he will not even consider alternative explanations.

At times the paranoiac succeeds in convincing others that he is rational and objective, because in general his appearance and actions seem quite normal. His characteristic delusional system appears to be isolated from the rest of his personality pattern, his contact with reality broken at one point only, this gap being filled by the delusional system.

The paranoiac's delusion usually takes the form of a persecution complex. He is convinced that others are out to hurt him or interfere with his life. Being markedly egocentric and suspicious, he builds up a private world in his delusions, a pseudo-world that replaces the real one that others inhabit. For example, he may develop the delusion that others are trying to poison him or to control his thoughts by special waves from another world. Or he may see himself as a religious savior, and this viewpoint may color all his attitudes toward his associates.

Since the paranoiac shows little additional mental deterioration, he often formulates clear and logical plans for warding off the imagined persecutions or affronts of others. Such plans may even involve a decision to kill his "enemy," which indicates the danger in such delusions.

THE MANIC-DEPRESSIVE PSYCHOSIS The manic-depressive psychosis is characterized by marked emotional exaggeration and vacillation rather than by the intellectual distortions just described for schizophrenia and paranoia. In the *manic phase,* we observe great excitement, elation, overactivity, and flight of ideas. The patient is extremely happy; he feels well and is optimistic. He laughs frequently and may try to cheer others. At the same time, however, he is easily distracted; his mind and conversation wander haphazardly. The manic is always on the go—talking to others, organizing parties, arranging furniture, trying to promote big deals (such as selling the Brooklyn Bridge). But his thoughts, feelings, and activities are unstable. If he meets interference or if someone contradicts him he becomes irritable and suspicious. At times, he has wild delusions, thinking of himself as an emissary of God, a great military genius, or a famous political figure. Occasionally he has hallucinations and he may hear voices advise him, flatter him, or inspire him. Usually the manic suffers from rapid heart action and high blood pressure induced by his exertion and activity. He may lose a great deal of weight and, because of his overexcitement, be unable to sleep.

On the basis of increasing intensity of the reaction, three kinds of manic behavior may be distinguished: *hypomania,* characterized by a condition of moderate increase in excitement, activity, and flightiness; *acute mania,* characterized by a more exaggerated increase; and *delirious mania,* characterized by the most extreme form of overactivity and excitement. As the manic condition intensifies, the patient's speech becomes increasingly incoherent, his moods are unstable, his restlessness more extreme. When he suffers from delirious mania he lacks insight. His judgment is impaired and he may lose his sense of shame. His speech may become heavily obscene, and he may expose himself and make open sexual advances to others. He may lose weight rapidly and become physically exhausted.

The *depressive phase* of manic-depressive psychoses is characterized by retardation of ideas and movement (called *psychomotor retardation*), by sadness and despondency, sometimes by stupor or suicidal attempts, and by intense feelings of inadequacy and hopelessness. The patient is indifferent to other people. Nothing cheers him. Thinking requires a tremendous effort, and his speech is slow and hesitant. He resists any sort of activity, moves slowly if at all, and often sits in the same place for long periods of time. His bodily processes slow down perceptibly. Constipation, loss of appetite, and loss of weight may occur. In women menstruation may stop. Where the manic patient appears to have a high opinion of himself, his depressive counterpart is plagued by guilt feelings. He may harbor the delusion that he has committed an unpardonable sin, a delusion nourished by hallucinations, by voices that speak to him accusingly of his crimes and faults.

Four varieties of the depressive phase may be distinguished, depending on the intensity of the symptoms: the mild form, simple retardation, acute depression, and depressive stupor. As the depression increases, the danger of suicide usually increases also. When the patient reaches a state of depressive stupor, he becomes so apathetic that he must be fed. He feels increasingly guilty, bemoans his worthlessness, and condemns himself unceasingly.

In some cases of manic-depressive disorders, only the manic stage is present; in others only the depressive phase; in still others, the mixed or circular types, there is an alternation between the two extremes, frequently with an intervening period of normality (see Figure 2, page 172).

INVOLUTIONAL MELANCHOLIA Another severe affective disturbance is involutional melancholia. This depressional melancholia generally occurs around the time of the menopause or climacteric, which can begin from ages 40 to 55 in women and from 50 to 65 in men. The involutional melancholic manifests an "agitated depression" in which depression combines with restlessness. His restlessness is seen in his inability to work, to finish a task, or to sleep; his depression shows itself in crying spells and in feelings of sadness, guilt, and worthlessness. He may have mild delusions of persecution; become excessively concerned about bodily functions; and—as a result of his sense of uselessness and guilt—may even contemplate suicide.

Although physiological and endocrine changes accompanying change of life may contribute to the onset of involutional melancholia, it is generally believed that the major causes of the disturbance are psychological. If the causes were physiological, everyone undergoing change of life would experience the symptoms of melancholia, which is not what happens at all. What, then, are some of the psychological factors contributing to involutional melancholia? An older person may see himself as slowing down, feel that his life is behind him, that the world is passing him by, and that he is no longer as important to others as he once was. He realizes that former opportunities cannot be recaptured and feels that the future holds less promise. His reactions to these perceptions can bring on the melancholia and agitated depression, which may represent a final, though maladjusted, attempt to do something (as seen in the agitation) although feeling hopeless (as seen in the depression).

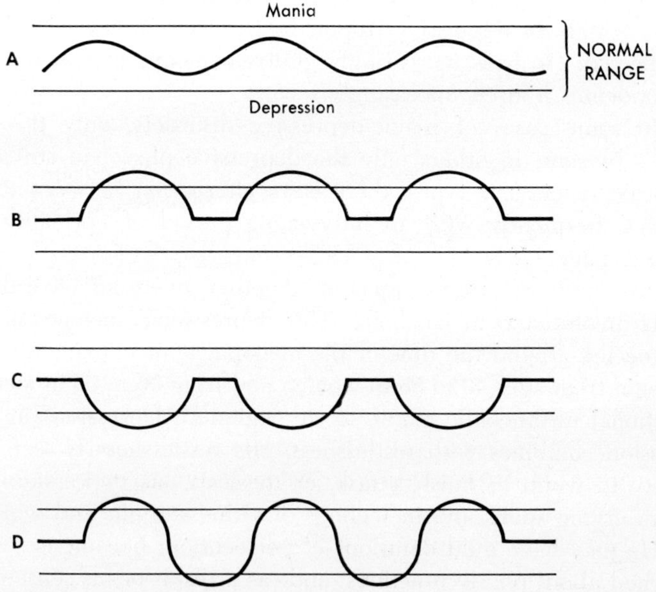

Figure 2. Manic-depressive psychosis. Changes of mood occur in the normal person (A), but in the psychotic the swings in moods go beyond the normal limits. Different sequences are shown in (B)–recurrent mania; in (C)–recurrent depression; and in (D)–circular type.

The Organic Psychoses

Organic psychoses are responsible for about 40 to 50 per cent of all first admissions to mental hospitals in this country, the functional psychoses accounting for the remainder.

These disorders may stem from a wide variety of causes, but damage or injury to the brain or other parts of the central nervous system is always involved. The chief symptoms are:

1. Impairment of orientation;
2. Impairment of such intellectual functions as comprehension, use of information previously acquired, and learning of new materials;
3. Impairment of memory;
4. Impairment of judgment, often including impairment of the ability to behave in accordance with accepted standards of social conduct; inappropriate behavior including lack of interest in personal appearance; neglect of responsibilities; and anti-social behavior;
5. Emotional changes, such as increased general irritability, oversensitivity, suspiciousness, and emotional instability characterized by mood swings without apparent cause.

We shall discuss in this section the four major types of organic psychoses: (1) psychoses associated with infectious diseases, as illustrated by general paresis; (2) psychoses associated with toxins, as illustrated by alcoholic psychoses; (3) psychoses associated with head injuries; and (4) psychoses associated with old age.

PSYCHOSES ASSOCIATED WITH INFECTIOUS DISEASES The most important psychoses associated with brain infection or central nervous system infections from bacteria or viruses are *general paresis, epidemic encephalitis,* and *epidemic cerebrospinal meningitis.* As an example of this kind of psychosis we shall briefly discuss general paresis.

General paresis is a serious behavior disturbance resulting from brain and nerve tissue damage caused by the spirochetes of syphilis. The disease afflicts about 2 per cent of those who contract syphilis. The main symptoms of paresis are: (1) the absence of, or sluggishness in, certain reflexes such as the pupillary reflex; (2) various tremors, particularly trembling hands and tremors of the lips and tongue, and speech distortions; (3) intellectual disturbances including loss of memory, especially for recent events; (4) development of delusions, the patient imagining himself to be Napoleon, Babe Ruth, or President of the United States; (5) mood changes, often leading to severe depression, although these moods sometimes swing from depressive to manic within short periods of time; and (6) an unsteady, shuffling gait known as locomotor ataxia, developed by some patients and indicating that they have lost the ability to obtain sensory feedback from their legs and must drag them along the ground in order to walk. The consequence of all these symptoms is a generalized intellectual and personality deterioration.

PSYCHOSES ASSOCIATED WITH TOXINS Psychotic disturbances may result from a variety of toxic and metabolic effects: from drugs or gases; from the effects of nutritional disturbances, as in the case of pellagra and alcoholism; from endocrine disturbances; and from the chemical effects of various endocrine gland dysfunctions, such as thyroid or adrenal dysfunction. For illustrative purposes we shall briefly describe psychotic behavior associated with alcoholism.

The best known of the alcoholic reactions is an acute reaction called *delirium tremens.* This disturbance is most strikingly characterized by severe tremors of the hands and tongue. The patient is acutely ill and disturbed. He is confused and unable to respond to outside stimuli, and he has vivid and frightening hallucinations, usually of rats, snakes, and other small animals. He often has high fever, a rapid and weak heart beat, a coated tongue, and sometimes convulsive seizures. The delirium typically lasts from three to six days and is usually followed by a deep sleep. The death rate from heart failure or exhaustion is as high as 10 or 15 per cent.

Another frequent after-effect of prolonged alcoholism is *Korsakow's psychosis,* named after the Russian psychiatrist who first described it. Korsakow's psychosis is not an acute reaction, like delirium tremens, but it is a chronic disturbance. Its most characteristic mental symptom is loss of memory for recent events. The patient fills out the missing gaps in his memory by improvising stories, a process called *confabulation.* Other symptoms include a painful inflammation of the nerve trunks, loss of feeling of certain skin areas, and wrist-drop (the patient is unable to raise his hand).

Korsakow's psychosis results from a deficiency in "B" complex vitamins due to the nutritional disturbances accompanying prolonged use of alcohol. In treatment, therefore, the patient usually receives heavy injections of vitamins. But treatment seldom leads to complete cure, and some memory defects and other behavior disturbances usually remain. These defects are considered symptoms of psychological rather than physiological deterioration, however, for post-mortem studies of the brains of people who have died of a Korsakow's psychosis reveal no gross organic lesions.

The symptom picture for the alcoholic psychotic usually includes emotional blunting and loss of intellectual vigor. Often he appears unable to control his reactions. For example, he is moved to tears, laughter, or anger at the slightest provocation. His judgment, memory, and capacity to work show signs of deterioration. In later stages of the disease, further organic complications often appear, such as gastritis, cirrhosis of the liver, heart disease, and nephritis.

PSYCHOSES ASSOCIATED WITH HEAD INJURIES Head injuries, or more precisely, brain injuries, may lead to a number of personality disturbances, the kind of disturbance largely depending on what part of the brain is damaged. Most brain injuries are caused by blows to the head, usually sustained in accidents (notably traffic accidents) and in warfare. In fact, many important discoveries concerning brain damage have resulted from studies of head injuries sustained in battle.

A person who has suffered a brain injury may exhibit a number of symptoms. He may be temporarily dazed, lose consciousness for several days, become nauseous and vomit, or develop severe headaches or dizziness. Quite frequently he becomes delirious on regaining consciousness. Finally he may lose all sense of time and place and suffer from hallucinations. The study of brain injuries points up the interweaving of psychological and physiological factors in human behavior. People sustaining apparently identical damage may develop entirely different symptoms, and psychologists are increasingly inclined to relate a patient's symptoms to the way he acted and behaved before he was injured. The patient who shows a severe depressive psychotic reaction, for example, may already have been despondent before the accident occurred. His history may show an inclination toward despondency over a period of years in his life. Similarly, a patient who becomes morbidly dependent after the acute phase of the psychosis has passed probably lacked self-reliance even before his accident. Research has shown that even the chronic headaches that are sometimes after-effects of brain injuries seem to be more closely related to the personalities of the victims than to the extent and location of the organic damage. Many symptoms of brain injury can probably be interpreted as efforts by the patient to cope with the limitations his injury imposes and with the anxieties and fears related to these limitations.

PSYCHOSES ASSOCIATED WITH OLD AGE The psychoses associated with old age, commonly called *senile psychoses,* are chronic disorders of the aged. They are marked by damage to brain tissue and by serious behavior disturbances involving loss of memory; rigidity of behavior (i.e., stubbornness and insistence on one's own way); extreme irritability and suspiciousness; confusion and incoherence; and at times severe depression accompanied by feelings of hopelessness and extreme guilt. Suspiciousness and irritability may be so severe as to be classified as paranoiac, and mental confusion may extend to delusions and hallucinations. A famous literary figure considered an example of a senile psychosis is Shakespeare's *King Lear.*

Not all elderly people fall victim to senile psychoses. The biological changes associated with aging, as with the organic brain damages resulting from head injuries, may not in themselves be sufficient to explain the changes in the behavior of some older persons. In many, the factors of aging are accessory rather than primary causes of mental disturbances. In senile psychoses, as in involutional melancholia, there appears to be an interplay of organic and psychological factors. Let us look a little more closely at some of the psychological factors associated with aging that may contribute to the appearance of senile psychotic behavior.

1. Fear of dependence and uselessness. As a person ages he begins to fear retirement, unemployment, financial insecurity, loss of mental clarity and manual skills, and the possibility of having to rely on children for support.

2. Fear of illness. Failing health often becomes a problem as people get older. They no longer see or hear as well as they used to; reflexes slow down; strength begins to ebb; and functions such as digestion and circulation grow sluggish.

3. Fear of isolation. Fear of isolation is often related to fear of illness. The specter of invalidism haunts older people, threatening to shut them off further from their already shrinking contacts. And in addition, the deaths of his friends and of his spouse and the loss of

contact with his colleagues on the job all intensify an older person's feeling of isolation and sense of the imminence of personal death.

We have already mentioned some of the symptoms of senile psychoses. The person may be depressed and highly irritable, and he may insist on his own way. In addition his interests may narrow. Books, magazines, and newspapers that formerly interested him now lose their appeal. His conversation becomes increasingly cluttered with recollections, often highly glamorized. "In the good old days when I was young . . ." becomes his standard device for introducing his views and for rejecting changes. Such a person can be difficult to live with, and younger people may find him boring, intolerant, and odd. And if they allow their feelings to show through, the older person may begin to feel that he is not wanted.

As more people live to an advanced age, the problem of senile psychoses becomes increasingly important, not only in terms of treatment but particularly in terms of prevention.

PSYCHOSOCIAL FACTORS IN ORGANIC PSYCHOSES The organic psychoses we have described may be influenced by psychosocial factors. The same psychosis, resulting from brain injuries or other organic damage, for example, can give rise to a wide range of behavioral symptoms. It is almost as if the organic disease is sometimes only a kind of trigger, a trigger that sets off one or another group of symptoms according to the patient's particular psychosocial experiences.

In line with this question of psychosocial influences, we must also note that severe organic lesions of the nervous system do not necessarily lead to serious psychotic disorders. As a matter of fact, when behavior disorders do occur many clinicians now seek to explain them in terms of adjustment difficulties which may have preceded the organic damage. The organic lesion is often viewed as a precipitating factor, rather than the cause of certain psychotic behavior. It is therefore not surprising when, as happens frequently, the apparent removal of the organic trouble does not automatically clear up the behavior disorder.

We can say, therefore, that psychotic behavior, like neurotic behavior, results from the individual's attempts to cope with circumstances.

Causes of Psychotic Behavior

The causes of psychotic behavior are probably as diverse as the forms it assumes. Heredity, constitutional predisposition, faulty parent-child relations, social stresses and social disintegration, psychological frustrations, endocrine dysfunction, and brain infections can all be included among the multitude of antecedent conditions whose interaction may be related to the onset of a psychotic disorder. For our discussion we shall consider these pathogenic (illness-producing) factors under the headings of (1) hereditary, (2) psychosocial, and (3) physiological causes.

Hereditary Factors

It has frequently been observed that mental disease tends to run in families, and for this reason some people believe, and legends have often suggested, that mental illness is hereditary. While some statistical investigations have seemed to substantiate the belief that similar hereditary factors in a family may lead to similar behavior disturbances, it should be pointed out that this statistical evidence is far from clear-cut. The effects of similar environments are difficult to assess. Family members who may seem to have inherited similar mental disorders have inherited not only their parents' *genes* but also their *social environment.*

One way of distinguishing between the influences of heredity and environment is through the study of identical and fraternal twins. In one such study [1] it was found that in 86 per cent of the cases where one *identical* twin showed schizophrenic behavior, the other did likewise. Among *fraternal* twins, however, if one developed schizophrenia only 14 per cent of their twins did likewise. This would seem to suggest that a genetic disposition towards susceptibility may come with similar heredity (as in the case of the identical twins), with less susceptibility as genetic similarity decreases (as in the case of the fraternal twins). With manic-depressive psychoses the correlation was even

[1] F. J. Kallmann, *Heredity in Health and Mental Disorder* (New York: Norton, 1953).

closer. In 96 per cent of the cases the second identical twin showed the same disturbance. Among fraternal twins the figure was 26 per cent.

Psychological research seems to indicate that newborn infants have certain consistent reaction tendencies; and some psychologists believe that these reaction tendencies (for example, to be generally responsive to stimulation versus being nonresponsive) are influenced by hereditary factors. But no conclusive evidence linking psychoses to these reaction tendencies has yet been advanced.

The belief that hereditary factors influence our behavior is also present in what may be termed the *constitutional* view, which relates organic or bodily predisposition and build to personality and behavior characteristics. The most thorough attempt to study the relationship between body build and personality was made by W. H. Sheldon [2] at Harvard University. Sheldon believed that every body or physique could be described in terms of three factors: (1) *endomorphy*, the fatty and visceral component, (2) *mesomorphy*, the muscular and bony component and (3) *ectomorphy*, the tall, thin, delicate component. In Sheldon's research, each of these three components tended to be associated with certain personality characteristics. Endomorphy tends to be associated with extraverted, comfort-loving, relaxed personalities; mesomorphy with characteristics of assertiveness, desire for action, and aggressiveness; and ectomorphy with intellectual interests, introversion, need for solitude, and minimal need for others.

Other investigators have failed to define similar relationships, but it may be well to remind ourselves that our general physical appearance can influence how others react to us. Compare the differences in men's reactions to pretty or homely girls, or the reactions of women to short and fat or tall, handsome, and well-built men. Such reactions by others may, over a period of years from early infancy on, influence the way we think and feel about ourselves and behave towards others.

Psychosocial Factors

Let us consider briefly how such factors as a person's relationship to his parents and others, the neighborhood in which he lived, and the cultural forces to which he was ex-

[2] W. H. Sheldon and S. S. Stevens, *The Varieties of Temperament* (New York: Harper, 1942).

posed might contribute to the development of a serious behavior disorder. One study[3] examining the relationships between social environment and mental disturbances found that the *incidence* of psychoses was greatest among people living in the central business districts, next highest in the adjacent rooming-house areas, and lowest in suburban residential areas. The *type* of psychoses was found to vary with social conditions. The incidence of paranoiac schizophrenia, for example, occurred most often in first-generation immigrant neighborhoods. This study points to the possible influence of such factors as poverty, stress-producing cultural experiences and cultural conflict, and social disorganization on the number and kinds of psychoses occurring. In general, these findings have been supported by other studies.

Another study[4] found that the number of mental disturbances, the kinds of disorders, and the frequency and nature of treatment, were related to social status. For example, the rates of incidence of the psychoses varied inversely with class, with the highest incidence rates in the lowest classes. For the neuroses, however, the opposite relationship was found, with the lowest rates in the lowest classes, and the highest rates in the highest classes. The findings also suggest that *types* of neuroses may be related to social class. Obsessive-compulsive reactions were found more often in the upper classes while conversion reactions prevailed in the lower classes.

It would appear, then, that severe and prolonged conflicts between an individual and his social environment—as seen in disturbed relationships with his parents, his neighborhood, and his cultural norms—are instrumental in preparing the grounds for later psychotic reactions.

Physiological Factors

Infectious diseases, brain tumors, head injuries, toxins, and other organic injuries or dysfunctions can lead to psychoses. The behavior disturbances that sometimes accompany old age, such as senility and defects resulting from hardening of the arteries, are also classified as psychoses resulting from physiological

[3] Robert E. O. Faris and H. Warren Durham, *Mental Disorders in Urban Areas* (Chicago: University of Chicago Press, 1939).

[4] August E. Hollingshead and Frederick C. Redlich, *Social Class and Mental Illness: A Community Study* (New York: Wiley, 1958).

causes. The role of physiological factors in certain other types of psychoses is not clear, but renewed interest in investigating them has arisen out of biochemical studies showing that certain chemicals, such as lysergic acid, have induced temporary disorganization of thought processes, inducing delusions and hallucinations similar to those experienced by schizophrenics.

The Treatment of Psychoses

In the chapter on *psychotherapy* we take up in detail various methods for treating both neurotic and psychotic behavior disturbances. Here we merely mention some of the main forms treatment of psychoses can take, noting that the different forms can be employed both separately and in combination.

1. *Hospitalization.* Care in a hospital or sanitarium may give a patient a way to escape severe environmental stresses, provide simplification of his psychological and emotional interactions, and offer him custodial care, which includes careful attention to his physical wants. Prognosis for recovery with custodial care varies with the nature of the disturbance, but many patients recover or improve as a result of hospital care.

2. *Shock methods.* Psychotic patients have been treated with a variety of shock methods, the most common of which are insulin shock, metrazol shock, and electric shock. These methods appear to help some patients, but seem of little value to others. Exactly how shock methods effect improvement is not yet known.

3. *Psychosurgery.* Psychosurgery is a procedure in which nerve fibers connecting the frontal lobes of the brain are severed from the thalamus, resulting in a decrease of anxiety and tension for the patient but also resulting in loss in understanding, in ability to plan and initiate activities, and in judgment.

4. *Chemotherapy.* In recent years a great many drugs have appeared that influence the behavior of disturbed persons. The most widely known of these are the tranquilizing drugs. Chemotherapy is presently an area of considerable research interest.

5. *Psychotherapy.* Psychotherapy makes use of psychological techniques in treating behavior disorders. How psychotherapy operates and the various forms it can take are discussed in Chapter 15, but it should be mentioned in passing that psychotherapy is used much more frequently with neurotic than with psychotic patients. This is so partly because psychotics are much more difficult to deal with and partly because there are so few psychotherapists in the hospitals caring for psychotics.

Currently, increased emphasis is being given to *prevention* of mental illness, a better understanding of cause-and-effect relationships as they operate in our psychological development, and the establishment of more psychological counseling centers and clinics. This has gradually helped to lower the number of admissions to mental hospitals. At the same time, with the help of the treatment techniques just mentioned, the number of those discharged is increasing. In fact, about as many people are now being discharged from mental hospitals as are being admitted.

For Additional Reading

Appleby, Lawrence, Jordan M. Scher, and John Cummings, eds., *Chronic Schizophrenia.* Glencoe, Ill.: Free Press, 1960.

Arieti, Silvano, ed., *The American Handbook of Psychiatry.* New York: Basic Books, 1959.

Clausen, John A. and Marian Radke Yarrow, eds., "The Impact of Mental Illness on the Family," *The Journal of Social Issues,* XI, No. 4 (1955).

Culpin, M., *Mental Abnormalities, Facts and Theories.* New York: Longmans, Green, 1950.

Dorcus, R. M. and G. W. Shaffer, *Abnormal Psychology* (4th ed.). Baltimore: Williams and Wilkins, 1950.

Dunham, H. Warren, *Sociological Theory and Mental Disorder.* Detroit: Wayne State University Press, 1959.

Eaton, J. W. and R. J. Weil, *Culture and Mental Disorder.* Glencoe, Ill.: Free Press, 1955.

Fischer, S., *Principles of General Psychopathology.* New York: Philosophical Library, 1950.

Fitzgerald, O. W., *Personality and Psychosis*. Baltimore: Williams and Wilkins, 1951.

Freeman, Howard E. and Ozzie G. Simmons, *The Mental Patient Comes Home*. New York: Wiley, 1963.

Goldhamer, H. and A. Marshall, *Psychosis and Civilization*. Glencoe, Ill.: Free Press, 1953.

Gurin, Gerald, Joseph Veroff, and Sheila Feld, *Americans View Their Mental Health* (Monograph Series No. 4 of the Joint Commission on Mental Illness and Health). New York: Basic Books, 1960.

Hall, Calvin S. and Gardner Lindzey, *Theories of Personality*. New York: Wiley, 1957. See especially Chapter 9: "Sheldon's Constitutional Psychology," pp. 336-377.

Hollingshead, August B. and Frederick C. Redlich, *Social Class and Mental Illness. A Community Study*. New York: Wiley, 1958.

Herrold, Kenneth and Dorothy Lee, eds., "Sociocultural Approaches to Mental Care," *The Journal of Social Issues*, VIII, No. 4 (1952).

Hughes, Charles, Marc-Adelard Tremblay, Robert N. Rapoport, and Alexander H. Leighton, *People of Cove and Woodlot. Communities from the Viewpoint of Psychiatry* (Vol. 2 of The Stirling County Study of Psychiatric Disorder and Sociocultural Environment). New York: Basic Books, 1960.

Jaco, E. Gartley, *The Social Epidemiology of Mental Disorder: A Psychiatric Survey of Texas*. New York: Russell Sage, 1960.

Kallman, F. J., *Heredity in Health and Mental Disorder*. New York: Norton, 1953.

Kaplan, Bert and Thomas F. A. Plaut, *Personality in a Communal Society: An Analysis of the Mental Health of the Hutterites*. Lawrence, Kan.: University of Kansas Press, 1956.

Landis, C. and M. M. Bolles, *Textbook of Abnormal Psychology*. New York: Macmillan, 1950.

Leighton, Alexander H., *An Introduction to Social Psychiatry*. Springfield, Ill.: Thomas, 1960.

———, ed., *Explorations in Social Psychiatry*. New York: Basic Books, 1957.

———, *My Name Is Legion. Foundations for a Theory of Man in Relation to Culture* (Vol. 1 of The Stirling County Study of Psychiatric Disorder and Sociocultural Environment). New York: Basic Books, 1959.

Maslow, A. H. and B. Mittleman, *Principles of Abnormal Psychology*. New York: Harper, 1951.

Myers, Jerome K. and Bertram H. Roberts, *Family and Class Dynamics in Mental Illness*. New York: Wiley, 1959.

Noyes, A. P., *Modern Clinical Psychiatry* (4th ed.). Philadelphia: Saunders, 1953.

Ojeman, Ralph H., ed., *Recent Contributions of Biological and Psychosocial Investigations to Preventive Psychiatry*. Iowa City: State University of Iowa, 1959.

O'Kelly, L. I., *Introduction to Psychopathology*. Englewood Cliffs, N. J.: Prentice-Hall, 1949.

Opler, Marvin K., ed., *Culture and Mental Health: Cross-Cultural Studies*. New York: Macmillan, 1959.

Passamanick, Benjamin, ed., *Epidemiology of Mental Disorder*. Washington, D. C.: American Association for the Advancement of Science, 1959.

Perry, J. W., *Self in Psychotic Process*. Berkeley: University of California Press, 1953.

Plunkett, Richard J. and John E. Gordon, *Epidemiology and Mental Illness*. New York: Basic Books, 1960.

Pollak, Otto, *Social Science and Psychotherapy for Children*. New York: Russell Sage, 1952.

Rose, Arnold M., *Mental Health and Mental Disorder. A Sociological Approach*. New York: Norton, 1955.

Scher, Sam C. and Howard R. Davis, eds., *The Out-Patient Treatment of Schizophrenia: A Symposium*. New York: Grune and Stratton, 1960.

Schilder, P., *Introduction to a Psychoanalytic Psychiatry*. New York: International University Press, 1951.

Schneider, Kurt, *Clinical Psychopathology*. New York: Grune and Stratton, 1959.

Seward, Georgene, *Psychotherapy and Culture Conflict*. New York: Ronald, 1956.

Shaffer, G. W. and R. S. Lazarus, *Fundamental Concepts in Clinical Psychology*. New York: McGraw-Hill, 1952.

Social Aspects of Mental Health. *International Social Science Journal*, XI, No. 1 (1959).

Srole, Leo *et al.*, *Mental Health in the Metropolis: The Midtown Manhattan Study*. New York: McGraw-Hill, 1962.

Strecker, E., *A Basic Psychiatry*. New York: Random House, 1952.

Sullivan, H. S., *Interpersonal Theory of Psychiatry*. New York: Norton, 1953.

Taylor, W., *Dynamic and Abnormal Psychology*. New York: American Book, 1954.

Ulett, George A. and D. Wells Goodrich, *A Synopsis of Contemporary Psychiatry* (2nd ed.). St. Louis: Mosby, 1960.

Weinstein, Edwin A., *Cultural Aspects of Delusion. A Psychiatric Study of the Virgin Islands*. New York: Free Press of Glencoe, 1962.

PART THREE

Areas of Adjustment

A. Family Structure and Function

THE STRUCTURAL ORGANIZATION OF THE FAMILY

THE FUNCTIONS OF THE FAMILY

Reproduction

Protection and Care of Children

Socialization of Children

Education of Children

Conferment of Status

Assumption of Economic Obligations

Recreation

Satisfaction of Psychological Needs

B. The Dynamics of Family Interaction

THE HUSBAND-WIFE RELATIONSHIP

Marital Expectations

Factors in Marital Success

THE PARENT-CHILD RELATIONSHIP

Negative and Positive Patterns of Interaction

Special Problems

ADJUSTING TO FAMILY CRISES

How Crises Disrupt Family Life

How Families Deal with Crises

Techniques for Reducing Tension

DIVORCE

Family Adjustment

A. Family Structure and Function

The *family* is the oldest social institution
known to man.
Although its specific structure has differed
in different times and places,
it has been, in most cultures,
the basic unit of social order. In our culture
the large family unit that included
grandparents, parents, children—

and possibly an aunt, uncle, or cousin, all together under one roof, has almost disappeared; and the small family unit, consisting, as a minimum, of husband and wife or parent and child has taken its place.

As we shall see in this chapter, family roles have undergone modification during the transition from large to small family units. In addition, some functions once performed by the family have been taken over, in varying degrees, by groups outside the home; and families have begun learning to pay more attention to certain other functions that affect the personal adjustments of their individual members.

To facilitate discussion we have organized this chapter into two sections. The discussion of family structure and function will be followed by a consideration of the dynamics of family interaction.

The Structural Organization of the Family

Family structures differ according to location of authority. In the *patriarchal* family, the father is the ultimate authority; his word is almost law to his wife and children. In a *matriarchal* family, the mother or grandmother controls, although the father may retain his position of chief provider. In the *adult-centered* family, all major decisions are made jointly by husband and wife, and many tasks, such as the training of children, are jointly shared. In the *democratic* family, decisions and responsibilities are shared by all members. Figure 1 illustrates diagrammatically the decision-making process in these four types of family structure.

One or another of these structural types may be characteristic of a culture. All four are found in American society, but rarely in pure form. Each formal structure is subject to many variations, and it should be remembered that although structure may indicate the status relationships within a family it does not necessarily indicate the actual location of authority. The father may be the nominal family head, but the actual reins of control may be held by the mother or one of the children. Such factors as intelligence, health, and temperament affect the interaction among family members and contribute to the variation.

American family structure has changed considerably since the beginning of the twentieth century. The father has relinquished some of his authority to the wife and even in some instances to the children. Although the father continues to be the chief provider in most families, decisions are now often jointly made. In one study of urban communities only 25 to 30 per cent of those interviewed said their fathers made the major decisions in the family when they were children. Almost 50 per cent said their mothers made major decisions and another 20 per cent said the mother and father played equal roles. About half indicated that the children also had a voice in family affairs.[1]

[1] Scott Greer and Ella Kube, *Urban Worlds* (Los Angeles: Laboratory in Urban Culture, Occidental College, 1955).

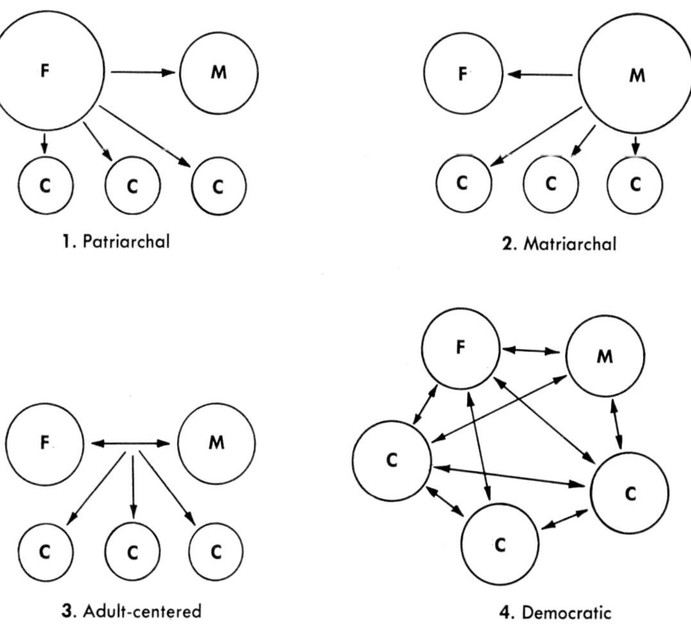

Figure 1. Decision-making in four types of family. The status of each member of the family differs and is perceived as being different by other members of the family. The arrows indicate the direction of influence.

Although one structural type may be predominant in a culture, subcultural variations may occur. Students of the family have traced the development of well-established, class-typed family patterns revealing distinctive differences, for example, in child-training. Even within a homogeneous cultural group no two families are exactly alike, because cultural norms alone do not determine such factors as intelligence, health, and temperament.

The Functions of the Family

Family functions, like family structures, vary from time to time and place to place. In some cultures, for example, most of the functions concerned with satisfying a person's needs are performed in the family. In others only certain of these functions are carried out by the family, the remainder being delegated to other groups. In our own culture we can discern eight main areas where the culture expects the family to assume varying degrees of responsibility. These are: (1) reproduction, (2) protection and care of children, (3) socialization of children, (4) education of children, (5) conferment of status, (6) assumption of economic obligations, (7) recreation, and (8) satisfaction of psychological needs.[2]

To what extent does the contemporary American family accept responsibility for these functions? Let us consider each of them.

Reproduction

Approximately 96 per cent of the children in this country are born to married couples, substantiating the family's acceptance of its reproductive function. But even this reproductive function has been modified by our culture. Such terms as *family-planning* and *child-spacing* have become familiar to us as various *birth-control* methods have been recognized and generally accepted. Today, many families not only decide how many children they are going to have, but also when they will be born. To date, however, this sort of planning predominates in the upper and middle classes.

[2] Robert F. Winch, "The Modern Family," in *Family, Marriage and Parenthood,* eds. Becker and Hill (New York: Holt, 1952), p. 779.

Protection and Care of Children

In our culture parents are held responsible for the protection and care of their children, and most children do grow up within the family home. Only 2 per cent of the children in this country are brought up in foster homes or institutions. A survey of variations in family patterns has indicated that care of children is almost universally a function of the family, although how this function is fulfilled may vary.[3] In recent years attention has been called to some groups where protection and care of children is not a family function, notably in the Israeli kibbutz.[4] Under this system, an infant is placed in a nursery when the mother returns from the hospital after the birth of her baby. It remains there in the care of nurses so that the mother is freed for other duties. B. F. Skinner, in his book *Walden Two*, presents a fictionalized version of how such an arrangement might be carried out in an American utopia.[5]

Although the American family continues to assume major responsibility for the care of children, various social agencies are prepared to offer assistance if the parents become physically or financially handicapped. Since 1912, the U. S. Children's Bureau has been concerned with all aspects of child life and has made available to parents brochures, pamphlets, and booklets containing valuable advice on child care. The World Health Organization is attempting to do the same thing on an international scale. During the last quarter century there has been considerable legislation in the United States regarding child welfare. Parents no longer have the absolute authority over their children that once was permitted. Juvenile authorities endeavor to make certain that the rights of children are upheld.

Groups and individuals outside the family have been concerned with the protection and care of children in other ages and cultures as well as in our own. The medicine man, the midwife, or the priest has been called upon in many societies to help avert dangers confronting

[3] Clyde Kluckhohn, "Variations in the Human Family," in *A Modern Introduction to the Family*, eds. Norman W. Bell and Ezra F. Vogel (Glencoe, Ill.: Free Press, 1960), pp. 45-51.

[4] Melford E. Spiro, *Kibbutz: Venture in Utopia* (Cambridge, Mass.: Harvard University Press, 1956).

[5] B. F. Skinner, *Walden Two* (New York: Macmillan, 1948).

the child. But extensive planning, in which local community, county, state, and nation join hands, is fairly recent.

Socialization of Children

In most cultures the family is the fundamental institution for transmitting the basic cultural values and mores. But because the standards to be transmitted vary and because different methods are employed, the process and content of socialization vary from family to family and from culture to culture. For example, among the Zuñi Indians of the southwestern United States, personal crises, such as birth, death, marriage, and divorce, are minimized; and the child is trained for individual submission. By contrast, the Mundugamor child of New Guinea grows up in an atmosphere of violence and is expected to be aggressive and combative.

Students of family life in our own country have noted marked differences between the processes of socialization of middle-class and working-class children. In one important investigation in this field, nearly 400 suburban mothers of children in public kindergartens were interviewed.[6] The subjects came from middle- and working-class environments. Information was sought that would answer three questions: (1) What are the customary practices of child-rearing in this suburban group and how much do practices differ within it? (2) What effects do different types of child-rearing practices have on the personalities of young children? (3) What kinds of mothers engage in what kinds of child-rearing practices? It was found that the middle-class mothers tended to be more permissive toward their children and to use less physical punishment and ridicule than did the working-class mothers. Concerning the children's education, more than two-thirds of the middle-class mothers expected their children to go to college, as compared to less than one-fourth of the working-class mothers.

Other researchers have also found interesting contrasts. Working-class families, for example, tend to encourage children to assume adult responsibilities at an earlier age than do middle-class families, who shield and protect their children as long as possible. Again, working-class training stresses utilitarian control over the environment rather

[6] Robert R. Sears, Eleanor E. Maccoby, and Harry Levin, *Patterns of Child Rearing* (Evanston, Ill. and White Plains, N. Y.: Row, Peterson, 1957).

than the expression of ideas, whereas middle-class training stresses the expression of ideas as a large factor in success.

The methods a culture accepts for socializing children change over a period of time. Most of us are aware how the methods recommended in the United States for the care and training of children have changed during the last five decades. As conceptions of the child's basic nature changed, ideas about how the child should be reared were modified accordingly. In the beginning the child was assumed to possess dangerous impulses and an essentially sinful nature, against which the parents were advised to wage a constant battle. But gradually this conception disappeared and the baby came to be regarded as almost completely pure and harmless. Children have benefited as a result. They are no longer treated like demons.

Many methods are used in the process of socialization: some direct, some indirect. A child may be instructed in culturally approved habits by his parents or he may learn them indirectly by the more subtle method of being praised when he obeys and punished when he rebels. Reward and punishment may take various forms. Some of the methods used reinforce one another; others are contradictory and leave the child uncertain and anxious.

As with child care and protection, the function of socialization is not left to the family alone. Schools, churches, and other social organizations play an important role. In fact, everyone a child associates with for any length of time will affect his socialization.

Education of Children

The extensive system of public and private education in this country furnishes ample evidence that the education of children is not confined to the family. Of course, socialization is an educative process, but fairly little of what we call "formal" education takes place in the family. Few parents are competent to teach all of the many specialized skills that make up our school curricula. Perhaps the most important thing parents can do to assist in the education of their children is to impart to them a receptive and sympathetic attitude. Parents who talk about "all the rubbish children are taught in school these days" are not likely to instill in their children a desire to take advantage of educational opportunities. The family is

A child whose family has emphasized the pleasures to be derived from books and other educational opportunities is more likely to approach school eagerly and confidently than is the child who has heard his parents or grandparents ridiculing various aspects of formal education. (A Lehner-Kube photograph.)

of course expected to arrange for each child to receive the type of formal education appropriate to his interests and abilities.

Religious education was formerly an important family function, but it has been shifted to Sunday Schools, the parochial schools, and other denominational institutions.

Conferment of Status

Not only has everyone a certain status within his family, as we mentioned in discussing family structure, but through the family a certain rank and position in his society. His family status is related to the functions he serves within the family. His social status is related to his family's position and reputation in the community. He can have high status in a low-status family, or vice versa.

The kind of neighborhood a person lives in, the church he attends, the groups to which he belongs are usually family determined—and all help confer a certain social status on him. By the time he reaches adolescence, the matter of "position" in society becomes significant, and if he finds that his family's status is lower than that of people with whom he would like to associate, and that, as a result, some of his hopes have little chance of fulfillment, severe conflict may result. It is important to keep in mind that the family does not exist as a closed system, in isolation from other families. It must be viewed, instead, in the context of interaction with the broader society.

Even after an individual moves away from his home community, the behavior, manners, and speech habits he has acquired within the family circle may still identify him as belonging to a specific socio-economic level and continue to determine his social status.

Assumption of Economic Obligations

Whether it produces the goods it requires or buys them from others, the modern family is expected to meet its own minimum economic needs. Today, however, the urban family is not a self-sufficient economic unit. Many of the goods and services it needs must be acquired from sources outside the home. It is no longer economically advantageous for members of such a family to stay together and to work together, as families may still do in relatively isolated rural communities. The usual pattern in the urban family is for the husband to be the provider, although an increasing number of women now also earn wages.

Here, too, outside organizations can, if necessary, help a family fulfill its functions. If the provider is temporarily unable to support the family adequately, governmental relief agencies or charitable organizations can provide assistance.

Recreation

Many families spend their leisure time together and join in such recreational activities as swimming, back-yard barbecues, do-it-yourself projects, games, watching television, or making excursions to resorts. The pattern of recreational activity changes with different stages of family life. Family projects are frequent while the children are pre-adolescents, but by the time children enter high school, their interest in family projects has often dwindled. After they grow up and marry, however, they may discover new interests in common with their parents, leading once again to the planning of joint activities.

In our culture, where so much commercial entertainment is available and where personal mobility (through widespread ownership of cars) is so high, many recreational activities take place away from

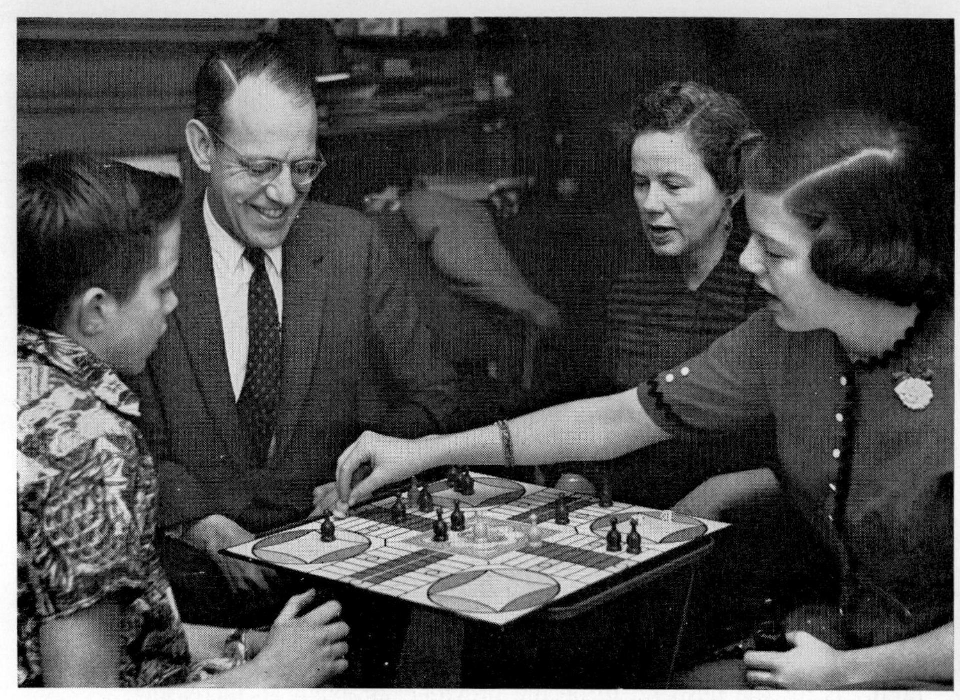

Sharing recreational activities during leisure hours is an important family function. (From Monkmeyer, by Nancy Hays.)

home. The elaborate plans and preparations that once played an important part in family recreation projects are no longer necessary. Now family members need only decide what they would like (and can afford) to do. Where members formerly would have stayed together to cooperate in the only recreation available, they now find they cannot always agree on a choice from among so many possibilities and are more likely to go separate ways.

Satisfaction of Psychological Needs

As agencies outside the home have assumed increasingly more of the traditional family functions, family members, particularly parents, have learned to recognize psychological needs that arise within the family circle and to spend more time satisfying them. Satisfaction of psychological needs has always been one of the family's most important functions. Adults as well as children need affection and love, acceptance and recognition, all the factors that contribute to emotional security. If its members possess sufficient psychological insight and sensitivity, no group is better qualified than the family to help satisfy psychological needs. The close associations family members have enjoyed, the confidences they have shared, the familiarity with one another's personality characteristics that has developed—all these can help one member to know what relief measures another needs. The intimate understanding that parents feel for their children, for example, often leads them to apply intuitively the appropriate psychological remedies.

We have already seen that it is almost inevitable for a person living in these times to feel threatened and bewildered. Almost daily he encounters disparities between real and ideal culture patterns and finds himself in situations in which the old ways of behaving no longer apply. In order to alleviate the tensions such situations engender, he turns to the intimate family circle for reassurance, for love, and for a sense of belonging.

Many serious emotional crises as well as many criminal incidents could be prevented if parents were better informed on the most effective methods for handling emotional needs—their own as well as those of their children. But the fact that so many people today display serious emotional disturbances indicates that their families were frequently unable to cope with their needs.

B. The Dynamics of Family Interaction

In order that we may better understand how family relationships affect personal adjustment and the satisfaction of psychological needs, we turn now to a consideration of the dynamics of family interaction. Although a family reflects the mores, values, and behavior patterns of its culture, no two families are exactly alike. Each family pattern derives from the interaction of the distinctive personalities of its members. Families are constantly changing. New members are born into them, grow up, and leave to establish careers and families of their own. Older members pass away. All these changes affect, to some degree, the adjustment of the other members.

In this section we shall consider in detail the husband-wife relationship, the parent-child relationship, and adjustment to family crises.

The Husband-Wife Relationship

When people marry they enter into a new relationship, yet they bring to it the same behavior patterns, needs, and attitudes that characterized their former relationships. We shall consider here two aspects of the husband-wife relationship: (1) marital expectations and (2) factors in marital success.

Marital Expectations

The interactive adjustment that occurs between husband and wife is determined in the beginning by the hopes and expectations that each partner brings to the marriage. How does the girl regard her future husband? How does the boy expect his future wife to behave? In other words, what *roles* does each expect the other to play?

Young people who have not learned to view marital roles realistically, who have not prepared themselves for marital responsibilities, are almost certain to be disappointed by the hard facts they will eventually encounter. Yet engaged couples frequently tend to idealize each other, to cast each other in roles that do not fit.

During the courtship period, for example, a young man whose apartment is always topsy-turvy and who forgets to take his laundry out until he has nothing left to wear may appear at his girl friend's house looking neat and dapper in his one clean shirt and his one good suit. He takes her dancing when he would really rather play poker with the boys from the office. He likes the way she looks and the way she dresses. He imagines her playing the role of the perfect wife he has seen on a television serial written by a writer who may have been divorced several times. He pictures her cooking his meals, washing his clothes, mending his socks, taking care of his children, keeping the house clean, and still looking like the girl in the shampoo advertisements. He decides to marry her.

The girl, on her part, has spent her monthly allowance at the beauty parlor and has memorized the weekly news magazine so she'll appear up to date on current events. Pretending to be sophisticated, she orders a martini at the restaurant because she doesn't know any other drinks. She tells the boy she does most of the cooking at home, when actually her mother can hardly persuade her to set the table. All the while she is cherishing an expectation that the man she marries will look and act like a combination of several different movie stars.

Both boy and girl are playing roles that do not fit, while at the same time casting the potential mate in a role that does not fit. Extreme as this situation may sound, it indicates the way many young people approach marriage. It exemplifies the sort of behavior to be avoided. These are the marriages that do not last, that swell the divorce statistics. Fortunately, most couples establish their marriages on a firmer foundation, taking into consideration such matters as financial security, standard of living, companionship, and the opportunity to share in the making of decisions.

If a marriage is to last, the partners must be able to see each other realistically. Furthermore, they need to agree beforehand on the kind of life they wish to achieve together and the methods they will employ in achieving it. Such a mutual understanding does not guarantee that each partner will always be able to anticipate what the other will do; nor does agreement about a way of life guarantee that all expectations will be fulfilled. But these things do serve to establish confidence between the partners that they will be able to work out any problems, and that, therefore, they will be able to build a mutually satisfying relationship.

During the last two generations people's conceptions of marital roles have altered significantly, and this change is responsible for many conflicting expectations. When a woman unquestioningly assumed the *wife-and-mother* role, her expectations about how her role should be filled matched those of her husband fairly well. But today's woman has more roles to choose from. She can still be a wife and mother, of

If a boy and girl contemplating marriage allow themselves time for realistic planning they may avoid many of the disappointments that disturb impulsively married couples. (From Monkmeyer, by Max Tharpe.)

course, but if she prefers she can assume a *companion* role, or a *partner* role.

Each role has its characteristic obligations and privileges. The wife and mother earns the respect and gratitude of her husband and children by devoting her life to child-rearing and homemaking, subordinating her interests to those of her family. The companion enjoys a more romantic relationship, one which permits her to share more activities with her husband and which offers leisure time to pursue social and educational opportunities. In return she is expected to retain her beauty and charm, to remain intellectually alert, and to assist her husband in acquiring advantageous social contacts. In the third role, the partner role, the wife shares equal authority with her husband. Economically independent, she is expected to contribute to the family income. She must be willing to dispense with special privileges, such as appeals to chivalry.

These three roles may overlap, of course. It has been noted that women tend to stress the privileges of the roles in their marital expectations, while men tend to stress the obligations.

Factors in Marital Success

Since people retain the same personalities after marriage, the effect of their personality traits, habits, and attitudes plays an important part in the success or failure of their marriages. A woman who has always been domineering is not likely to become suddenly submissive after she marries, and her husband may rebel at finding himself "henpecked." The man who has always been inept at his job will probably not be transformed into a model employee by marriage, able to earn all the luxuries his wife might like to acquire. But although people's past experiences do affect their marriages, they *can* learn new ways of behaving and assume new roles. New responsibilities may bring out previously undeveloped character potentialities.

As the marriage relationship develops, cooperation and enjoyment may increase, or friction and crises may occur. Previously unrecognized personal differences may be handled in a way that will help enrich the marriage relationship, or they may become sources of irritation and conflict. Disagreements, even about such matters as money, religion, morality, friends, in-laws, or raising children, need not lead to conflict. The attitude with which both partners approach these disagreements is decisive. If one or both of them takes an "I-know-I-am-right" attitude the chances of reaching a satisfactory solution are slim. But if each makes an honest effort to understand the other's point of view and is willing to compromise on minor points, the differences can probably be ironed out.

Data from studies investigating factors which influence marital success are summarized in Table 1. The factors are grouped into the following five areas: (1) personality characteristics, (2) cultural backgrounds, (3) social participation, (4) response patterns, and (5) sex factors. Each area is identified as *favorable, unfavorable,* or *unrelated to marital success.*

Table 1 **Basic Background Factors in Marital Success**

Favorable	Unfavorable	Unrelated
Personality Characteristics		
Permissive and considerate attitudes (both)	Lacks self-confidence (husband)	Extraversion-introversion
Cooperative attitudes (both)	Man daydreams and woman does not	Friendliness or offishness
Compatibility of temperament	Man feels inferior and woman does not	
Combinations where neither is neurotic	Woman makes friends easily and man does not	
Combinations where both are intellectually superior	Self-sufficiency in facing troubles alone (both)	
	Proneness to argue points (wife)	
	Unhappy temperament (both)	
	Variability in moods (both)	
	Feelings easily hurt (both)	
Cultural and Family Background		
Similarity of cultural backgrounds	Dissimilarity in cultural and family backgrounds	Number of siblings
Similarity of educational level	Wife's cultural background higher than husband's	Birth order in family
Father of high occupational level (both)	Residence in the city during childhood	Differences in educational achievements of parents
Firm but not harsh home training (both)		Modernist or fundamentalist religious beliefs
Happiness of parents' marriage (both)		Economic circumstances at marriage
Happiness of childhood (both)		
Conservative home backgrounds		
Sociability Factors		
Frequency of attendance at church and Sunday school	Unconventionality with respect to religion, sexual ethics, drinking	Number of persons with whom one has "kept company"
Number of friends (both sexes)	Religious inactivity	
Residence in single-family dwellings		
Social conservatism		

Favorable	*Unfavorable*	*Unrelated*
Response Patterns		
Love based on companionship	Romantic infatuation as basis of love	Amount of "petting" before marriage
Length of acquaintance before marriage	Disapproval of marriage by parents (especially husband's)	Fear of pregnancy
Similarity between parent of opposite sex and affianced (both)	Conflict with father (both)	
Strong attachment to father (both)		
Sex Factors		
Sex information received from parents first (both)	Premarital intercourse by either or both (low but negative relationship to subsequent marital adjustment)	Sex techniques used
Frank and encouraging attitudes of parents toward child's curiosity about sex (important for husband)	Fear of sex (wife)	Frequency and duration of intercourse
Similarity in sex desires	Prudishness and excessive modesty (wife)	Degree of pain experienced by wife at first intercourse
Orgasm capacity in wife	Husband-wife differences in strength of sex drive	Methods of contraception used
Amount of pleasure wife experienced at first intercourse		

Source: Willard Waller and Reuben Hill, *The Family, A Dynamic Interpretation*, rev. ed. (New York: Dryden, 1951). Revised copyright, Holt, Rinehart and Winston, Inc. By permission.

By way of amplifying this table let us summarize some of the major findings of one of the pioneers in the field, psychologist Lewis M. Terman. His study was based on a sample of 792 married couples, who filled out a personality schedule of 233 items dealing with interests, attitudes, likes and dislikes, habitual response patterns, and opinions about what constitutes the ideal marriage.

By noting the individual items that differentiated people with high and low happiness scores, Terman derived descriptive composite personality pictures of the happily and unhappily married. These composites are not exact likenesses of anyone but represent the patterns characteristic of the happier or less happy groups. The personality pictures for happily married men and women, which follow, will serve as illustrations.

> Happily married women, as a group, are characterized by kindly attitudes toward others and by the expectation of kindly attitudes in return. They do not easily take offense and are not unduly concerned about the impressions they make on others. They do not look upon social relationships as rivalry situations. They are cooperative, do not object to subordinate roles, and are not annoyed by advice from others. Missionary and ministering attitudes are frequently evidenced in their responses. They enjoy activities that bring educational or pleasurable opportunities to others and like to do things for the dependent or underprivileged. They are methodical and painstaking in their work, attentive to detail, and careful in regard to money. In religion, morals, and politics they tend to be conservative and conventional. Their expressed attitudes imply a quiet self-assurance and a decidedly optimistic outlook on life.
>
> Happily married men show evidence of an even and stable emotional tone. Their most characteristic reaction to others is that of cooperation. This is reflected in their attitudes toward business superiors, with whom they work well; in their attitude toward women, which reflects equalitarian ideals; and in their benevolent attitudes toward inferiors and underprivileged. In a gathering of people they tend to be unselfconscious and somewhat extroverted. As compared with unhappy husbands, they show superior initiative, a greater tendency to take responsibility, and greater willingness to give close attention to detail in their daily work. They like methodical procedures and methodical people. In money matters they are saving and cautious. Conservative attitudes are strongly characteristic of them. They usually have a favorable attitude toward religion and strongly uphold the sex mores and other social conventions.[7]

The *background* factors which Terman found most predictive of marital happiness were:

1. Superior happiness of parents
2. Childhood happiness
3. Lack of conflict with mother
4. Home discipline that was firm, but not harsh
5. Strong attachment to mother

[7] Lewis M. Terman, *Psychological Factors in Marital Happiness* (New York: McGraw-Hill, 1938), pp. 145-146; 155.

ceptable to himself; if he feels rejected, he learns to see himself as lacking in the qualities that would make him acceptable.

The relationship established between the child and his parents is significant also for the child's *social* development. If his parents have treated him with respect, he will probably approach others with confidence. If his parents have nagged him and found fault with him, he may treat outsiders as though he expects them to nag and criticize him, too. If his parents have overprotected him, he is likely to lack initiative and to depend too much on others.

Parents may relate to their children in a number of ways. Some of these patterns of interaction encourage satisfactory adjustment. Let us call these *positive* patterns. Others may be expected to cause adjustment difficulties. We can call these *negative* patterns. No parent, of course, can always be expected to choose the positive method of dealing with a problem, the one that a psychologist might recommend. Even the psychologist himself would not be able to predict the exact result of handling a single incident one way rather than another. Mistakes are bound to occur. Moreover, parents suffer emotional ups and downs that affect their handling of a particular incident at a particular time; and so sometimes they will employ positive patterns and sometimes they will not. What one parent does may sometimes neutralize or overbalance what the other does.

But if in the over-all handling of the child the positive patterns outweigh the negative patterns, the child will have a reasonable chance to achieve satisfactory adjustment. Let us consider some of these patterns, the negative first and then the positive.

Negative Patterns of Interaction

The negative patterns we shall discuss are: (1) rejection, (2) overprotection, (3) overindulgence, (4) authoritarianism, (5) ambivalence, and (6) monopolization.

REJECTION Parents who are indifferent or hostile to a child, who abandon, isolate, or seclude him, who lock him up in a room or punish him at the slightest provocation, are rejecting him. Sometimes parents threaten to send the child away, or to deny him something he wants. But perhaps the most disturbing form of rejection a child can experience is to be humiliated by his parents in front of others. We are all familiar with the mother and father who constantly hold up visiting children as examples for their own to follow, or who criticize their child to friends and relatives while the child is within hearing distance.

Parents rarely admit they are rejecting a child. They are always ready with explanations for their actions, often including the remark, "It's for the child's own good." And sometimes, to be sure, there are valid reasons for sending the child to visit his grandparents or for leaving him with the neighbor next door. Isolated or occasional instances of such behavior do not mean rejection. But when such behavior occurs repeatedly, and especially when it is done for the convenience of the parents alone and not for the pleasure of the child,

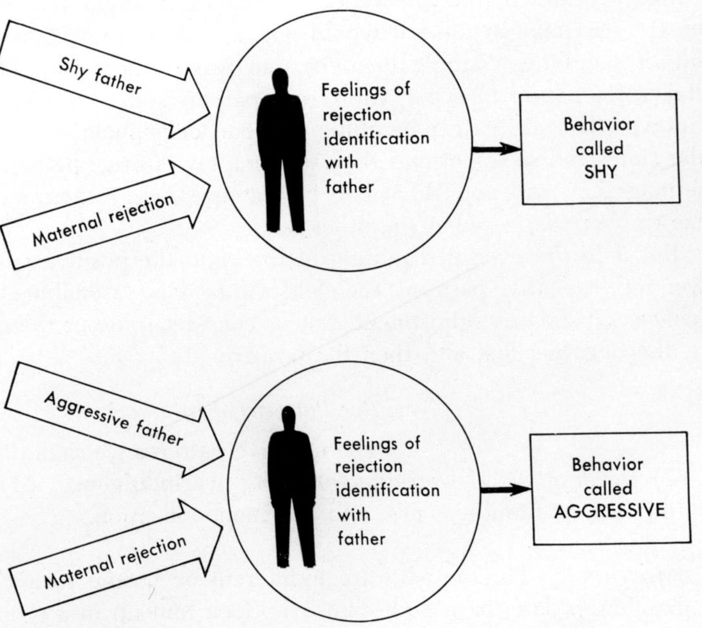

Figure 2. The experience of maternal rejection may lead to different forms of behavior, depending on other influences in the life-space of the child.

then the child is almost certain to feel that his parents do not love him or want him.

The rejected child may react in many ways. One of the more common is to resort to attention-getting behavior in an unconscious effort to win his parents' affection. Usually this attempt defeats itself, because in seeking attention the child merely succeeds in annoying his parents still more. Sometimes a rejected child will become hostile and rebellious and this hostility creates new adjustment problems. Evidence also indicates that rejection may result in physiological, mental, and social retardation. Warm parental relationships are indispensable if a child is to achieve satisfactory adjustment.

OVERPROTECTION At the opposite extreme from rejection is overprotection, which is usually an expression of anxiety on the part of parents. The child may have become the misplaced target for an anxiety that is in no way related to him. Perhaps another child in the family has died and the parents are fearful that something may happen to the one who remains. Perhaps the father's job often takes him away from home; and the mother, worrying that the child may be injured or hurt in the father's absence, will not let the youngster out of her sight. Or perhaps the father has died; and the mother, seeing her child as "all that she has left," is unwilling to share him with others and thus deprives him of outside contacts. In her fear that she may lose the child, she watches over him, helps him dress far beyond the time when he needs such help, accompanies him to school when other children are going by themselves. Sometimes parents overprotect a child *because* they are rejecting him. They may feel so guilty about not wanting the child that they overprotect him in an effort to make amends. Such insincerity confuses the child and contributes to his feelings of inadequacy.

As a result of all this, the child is denied the opportunity to learn for himself. When he starts to school he often finds he is unable to compete on an equal footing with other children. Having become overly dependent, he fails in situations that require initiative and independence. Such failures may discourage him. To avoid further frustrations he may withdraw into the home, and a vicious circle is established. Or, instead of withdrawing, he may become overly aggressive.

OVERINDULGENCE Closely related to overprotection is overindulgence. The overindulged child frequently becomes the tyrant of the family. All his wishes are granted if at all possible. Although he appears to control the family, he is actually dependent on his parents. He is likely to develop an exaggerated self-regard and an unwillingness to share with others, and, accustomed to having his wishes satisfied, he does not develop much tolerance for frustration.

As with overprotection, overindulgence may be a symptom of rejection. Parents may become overindulgent when they feel guilty about not wanting the child, and so proceed to bring him gifts and cater to his whims in an effort to assuage their guilt.

AUTHORITARIANISM In contrast to overindulgence, authoritarianism characterizes parents who enforce excessive discipline, who demand strict obedience and quickly punish any deviation from prescribed behavior. Frequently the parents set standards the child cannot possibly meet. And like the overprotected and overindulged child, the sternly disciplined youngster may become highly dependent on his parents, since all his decisions are made for him. Or he, too, may grow

Left: when a door will not open and a mother does not come, it is easy for a child to feel unwanted and unloved. Feelings of rejection can develop if such experiences are frequent or prolonged. (A Lehner-Kube photograph.) Right: the parent who wishes to reprimand a child and yet—at the same time—does not wish to upset him is experiencing ambivalence. (From Monkmeyer.)

defiant and aggressive as the overprotected and overindulged child does.

AMBIVALENCE A mixture of positive and negative feelings, which psychologists call ambivalence, characterizes all close personal relationships. Consequently there are times when even the most loving parent has mixed feelings about his child, perhaps because he is fatigued or upset. It is important for parents to realize that such mixed feelings are normal and understandable. Otherwise they may feel guilty when they discover themselves growing hostile and angry. Then, feeling guilty, they may resort to overprotection and overindulgence in an effort to make amends. Ambivalent feelings express themselves in inconsistent behavior, and the child, unable to predict his parents' reactions to specific situations, becomes anxious and uncertain.

Parents cannot avoid occasionally feeling hostile toward their children, but it is important for them to learn how to control their anger. If they realize that their children are sure to provoke them, that such provocation is natural and normal, they will cease to be troubled and embarrassed when they sometimes see their young charges as reckless demons. Nor will they need to excuse their doubts and mixed feelings. If, however, their feelings of hostility are constant and excessive, they should seek professional help.

MONOPOLIZATION Some parents try to be everything to their children, try to usurp roles that properly belong to other people in the child's social world. The father who wants to be a constant playmate to his son may make it difficult for the boy to get along with others his own age, either by keeping him isolated from them or by causing the boy to have unrealistic expectations—to expect, for example, that his peers will provide the same sort of constant encouragement or unselfish cooperation that he is accustomed to getting from his parents. Such children may become overly attached to one or more of their parents and resist making friends with their peers.

Positive Patterns of Interaction

The positive patterns we shall discuss are: (1) unqualified love, (2) sensitivity, (3) permissiveness, and (4) reasonable techniques of control.

UNQUALIFIED LOVE If a child is to achieve emotional security and satisfactory adjustment it is essential that he be accepted *as he is.* He must receive unqualified love—love that is not dependent on how he behaves, love that is not withheld when he is "bad" or awarded only if he is "good."

Some parents are so eager to bring their children up properly that they set impossible standards for them and then feel justified in correcting them for falling short of these standards. Actually these parents succeed only in making their children feel inadequate and therefore unloved and unwanted. Rather than giving their children the benefits of unqualified love they are in fact causing them to feel just as rejected as the child who is actually unwanted.

In contrast, children who are encouraged to do the best they can, but who receive generous praise and affection in spite of the mistakes they inevitably make, do, as a rule, feel sure that their parents love them. Such children can usually develop a self-confidence that permits them to adjust more easily to the anxiety-producing situations accompanying the growing-up process. To give this unqualified love the parent must possess tolerance, security, understanding, and kindness.

SENSITIVITY Parents who are sensitive to their children are quick to detect their emotional needs. They can sense, for example, when a child needs sympathy, approval, or reassurance. Such parents are aware that when problems arise there is, for each individual child, a considerate way to handle them and an appropriate time in which to do it. They can tell when the child's mood is receptive to suggestions and when suggestions would only irritate or upset him.

Sensitivity enables parents to guide their children tactfully, with a minimum of emotional upsets. Children of sensitive parents know in turn that their rights will be respected, their needs considered, and their intentions understood. In other words they know they have nothing to fear from their parents. Parental sensitivity, then, reduces a child's fear and anxiety, leaving him free to develop satisfactory adjustment patterns.

PERMISSIVENESS In a permissive home atmosphere, the child can develop his potentialities and learn the necessary motor and social skills without feeling undue pressure. The demands on him are kept in line with his abilities and his level of development, so that he will not become discouraged by failing to achieve what is beyond his capacities.

A parent need not feel, however, that in order to be permissive he must always let the child have his own way. What he should do is to set reasonable limits that guide the child without frustrating or discouraging him. Children need to learn that certain restrictions must be accepted, not only to protect themselves from injury and to help them develop intellectually and socially, but also to guarantee the rights and safety of others. It is important that they develop dependability and a sense of responsibility toward others.

REASONABLE TECHNIQUES OF CONTROL The child learns what is expected of him through certain techniques of control exerted by his parents, techniques usually involving praise or punishment. Ordinarily, parents reward the child for behavior they wish to encourage and punish him for behavior they wish to eliminate. But family standards differ both in the form in which praise and punishment are expressed and in the extent to which they are used. Some parents, for example, are highly autocratic, demanding obedience and punishing frequently for disobedience. These parents seldom help their children to understand the standards set for them. In other families positive sanctions far outweigh negative ones in helping children to learn accepted ways of behaving.

Punishment is almost certain to arouse hostility or resentment. It is a risky practice, one which does much damage. Frequent punishment, therefore, may irreparably damage the parent-child relationship. Punishment has few benefits. Furthermore, as a training device it is apt to be ineffective. The child doesn't learn *what* to do but only what *not* to do. The wise parent will keep punishment at a minimum and try instead to direct the child's drives into constructive channels, showing him ways of behaving that satisfy his needs without being destructive.

Both praise and punishment are external controls. As a child develops, these external controls are gradually supplemented or replaced by internal controls growing out of the child's acceptance of

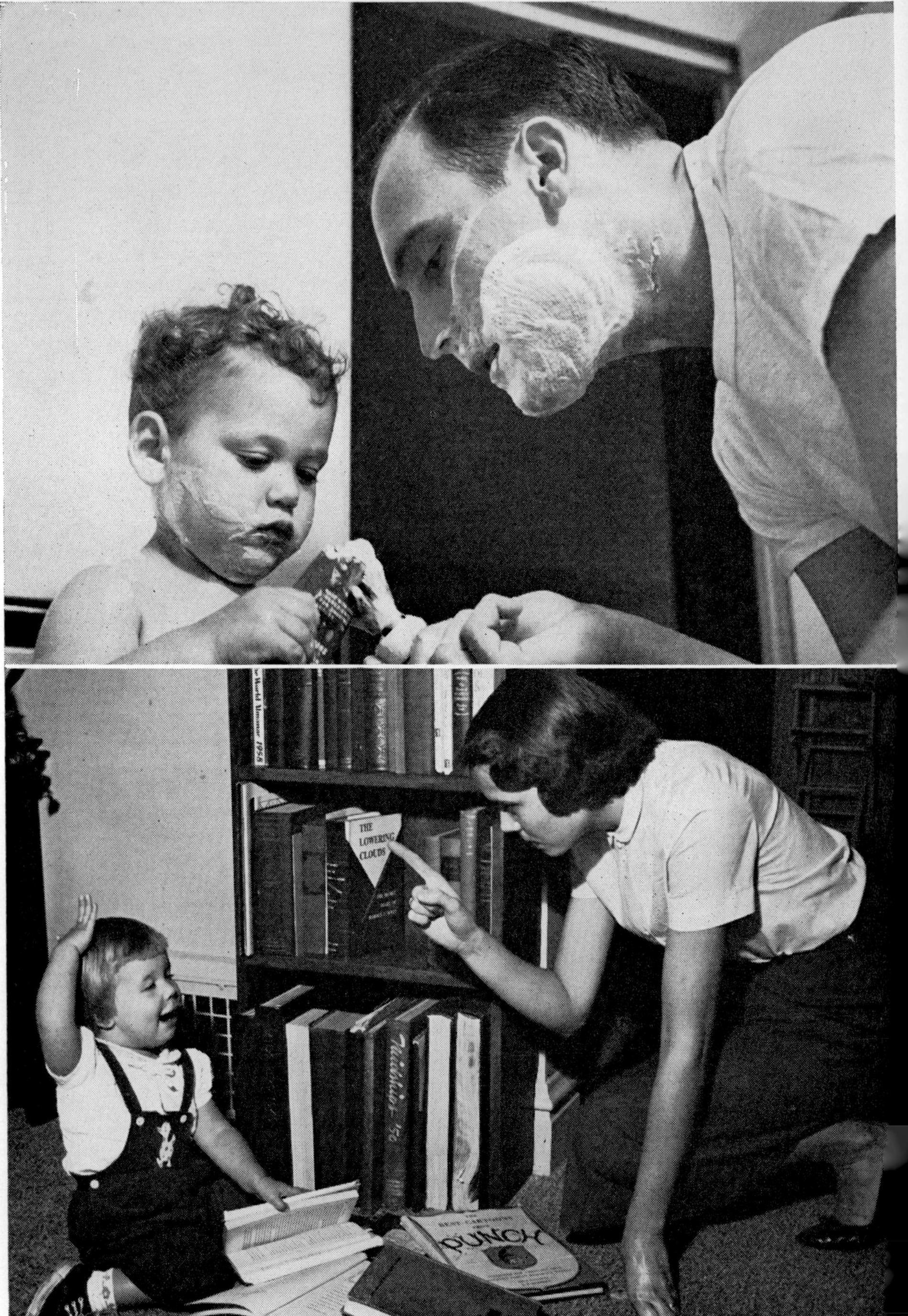
THE
LOWERING
CLOUDS
PUNCH

The sensitive, permissive parent gives his child a chance to satisfy his curiosity about the world—in a reasonably controlled environment. (From Monkmeyer, by Rae Russel, and Al Bloom.)

his parents' standards of conduct. Having accepted these standards, he is able to follow them even when his parents are absent. Often a child will rehearse these standards in his play. If he deviates from them he may feel ashamed or guilty. He is developing a *conscience.*

We can conclude this discussion of negative and positive patterns of interaction by repeating a point we made at the beginning: that it is inevitable for parents to make frequent mistakes. But if they can manage to strike a balance between extremes of overprotection and rejection, between excessive exercise of authority and utter lack of guidance, between too much and too little attention, between pushing their children into adult roles too fast and retarding them too long at a certain level of development, they will be giving their children a reasonable chance to develop satisfactory adjustment patterns.

Special Problems

Because they occur so frequently in our culture, we shall mention briefly two special problems that may disrupt the smooth functioning of the family. One problem is that of *sibling rivalry.* The other is that posed by *working mothers.*

SIBLING RIVALRY Even for the well-adjusted child the arrival of a new baby creates some tension and anxiety, and these tensions can become quite serious if the older child feels insecure and rejected. Sometimes parents devote all their attention to a new arrival, reinforcing the older child's sense of insecurity and rejection. If this happens, the older child may begin to look on his new brother or sister as a rival for his parents' affection. This is especially true of the overprotected and overindulged child. The older child's anxiety and insecurity often prompt him to try to call more and more attention to himself. Frequently he regresses temporarily to behavior patterns typical of a much younger child. He may, for example, cry a great

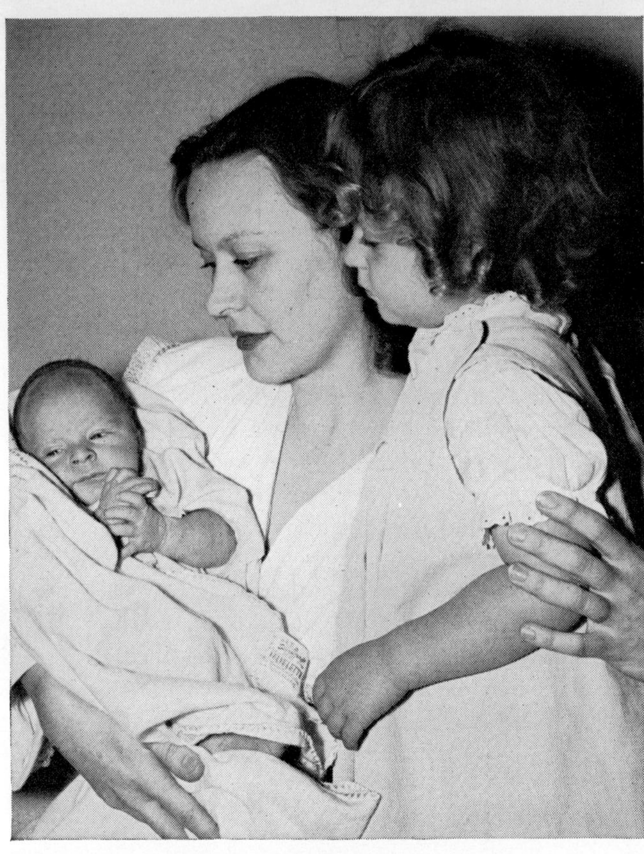

This mother is helping a child to welcome a new arrival. Older children need to be reassured that their parents will continue to love them even after a new baby joins the family. (A Lehner-Kube photograph.)

deal, crawl on the floor, start wetting himself again, or demand to be fed like the new baby.

An older child can be prepared for the arrival of a new baby and helped to feel the new arrival belongs as much to him as to the parents. He can be encouraged to welcome the new baby as a playmate, not to see him as a feared and hated competitor.

WORKING MOTHERS Most mothers who work do so because their families need additional income, but many others prefer jobs to housework. In a recent survey [8] of 2,500 high-school seniors, 96 per cent of the girls were found to want to be homemakers, but half of these wanted to combine their homemaking with a career.

The conflict that frequently occurs between a woman's desire for a career and her function as a homemaker can have several harm-

[8] Ralph H. Turner, unpublished research.

ful consequences. If she chooses a career her children may receive inadequate care. But if she gives up her desire for a career she may tend to resent her children and to some extent reject them. Or she may go the opposite extreme and emotionally smother them.

But none of these consequences is inevitable. Provided a mother can make adequate arrangements for the care of her children, much depends on the kind of work she does and why she does it. If economic necessity compels her to take a job she does not enjoy, then the physical and emotional strain may leave her so fatigued that she cannot relate satisfactorily to her children even when she is with them. But if she enjoys her work, she may also be free to enjoy and care for her children when she has the opportunity.

Adjusting to Family Crises

A *crisis* is a critical or decisive moment, a turning point in a course of events. Some crises erupt only after a long build-up of related tension-producing situations. Other crises occur suddenly and require rapid and efficient action. Frequently one crisis may occur as the result of an attempt to adjust to another crisis or series of crises. Any crisis can, if poorly handled, lead to further crises.

Let us begin our discussion by observing some of the disruptive effects certain types of crises can produce.

How Crises Disrupt Family Life

SUDDEN INJURY When a member of the family is injured—in an automobile accident, for example—immediate action is required on the part of at least one other family member. Someone has to make sure that the injured person receives proper medical attention. Other details such as filing insurance claims or consulting with law-enforcement authorities must be attended to, and these require the postponement or abandonment of previous appointments and plans. If these duties fall to the father, his business may have to be temporarily neglected. If they fall to the mother, the household routine will be interrupted, and some of the children's needs may not be fulfilled.

PROLONGED ILLNESS Prolonged illness or the long convalescence that can follow an injury may require a family to make drastic adjustments. Even if the family can bear the financial burden, some members usually have to take on additional duties until the disabled member recovers. No matter how well-loved the invalid may be, the strain and tension that result from his constant need for attention, added to the concern for his welfare, can produce a severe emotional crisis in the family.

UNEMPLOYMENT Unemployment may compel a family to retrench on many fronts—to move to a poorer neighborhood, to see less of old friends, to send children to a different school. The father, as we have seen, is traditionally regarded as the provider, and his failure to maintain his family, regardless of the reasons, may reduce his status both within the family and in the larger community. Such loss of status may in turn damage his self-concept. If the period of unemployment is prolonged indefinitely, the resulting psychological disturbances, both to him and to other members of the family, may lead to serious consequences.

MILITARY CONSCRIPTION When homes are broken up by military conscription serious problems arise for members of the family. If the husband and wife are not to be separated for an indefinite period, the family must often break its ties in its home community and move to another town—even at times to another country. If the wife decides to stay at home with the children while the husband is away, the family faces another unnatural situation. A number of tension-producing problems can arise in either situation, and in many cases the individuals involved do not know how to cope with them. The result, again, may be a severe emotional crisis.

Crises such as these can arise in any family. How disruptive they will be depends on the severity of the situation, on the resources and resourcefulness of the family members, and on their interpretations of and attitudes toward the situation.

How Families Deal with Crises

Whether a crisis arises from factors outside the family (a layoff from a job) or from unsatisfactory patterns of interaction within the family itself (the efforts of one member to dominate the others), the solutions attempted will depend on the personalities of the family members and on already established patterns of family interaction. For example, when Mr. Jones lost his job, nobody in the family blamed him. A conference was held and everyone pitched in to help out. Mrs. Jones found a part-time job. The older children took care of the younger ones. Everyone made some sacrifices. As a result, Mr. Jones' self-confidence remained high and his self-respect remained intact.

But when Mr. Green lost his job, a different set of reactions appeared. Almost immediately he and Mrs. Green began quarreling, and she repeatedly called him a failure, sometimes in front of the children. His ego and confidence shattered, Mr. Green began drinking, and eventually the family was broken up by divorce.

Some family crises, such as illness, unemployment, and conscription, require only temporary readjustments (although temporary readjustments may at times have more far-reaching effects than the members anticipate). Other crises may bring permanent or irrevocable repercussions and require long periods of reorientation by family members.

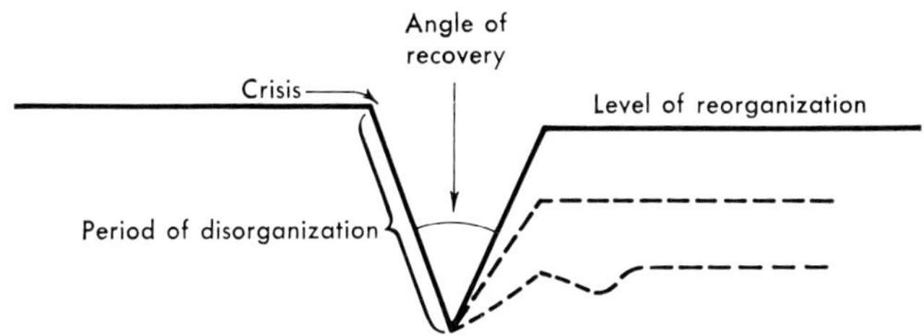

Figure 3. Profile of adjustment to crisis: crisis–disorganization–recovery –reorganization. (Adapted from Willard Waller and Reuben Hill, The Family: A Dynamic Interpretation, *rev. ed. New York: Dryden, 1951, p. 465. Reproduced by special permission of the Dryden Press, Inc.)*

Although families respond to crises in different ways, all usually pass through a series of recognizable, though overlapping, stages in dealing with them. First comes *disorganization,* then *recovery,* and finally *readjustment.* During the stage of disorganization a family might know, for example, that the father was soon to be conscripted or the mother hospitalized for an operation. On the other hand, the crisis might strike suddenly, as in the case of an injury caused by an accident. When the crisis can be anticipated in advance, some family members may prepare for it. Others, by contrast, may become hysterical and fail to make any preparations at all. In either case, when the crisis does finally arrive some members may be numbed, confused, or severely depressed. At the height of the impact a process of recovery sets in. This may involve long weeks of trial-and-error learning, during which the family gradually becomes familiar with the new situation. It is during this process of familiarization that readjustment procedures begin to be set in motion.

Any one of these stages can be met and handled in a variety of ways. One family, for example, may become quickly demoralized by a crisis while another may rise to the occasion efficiently and effectively. The period of recovery in one family may be short, in another agonizingly long. The level of readjustment finally attained may constitute an exact reconstruction of the conditions before the crisis, or it may be one in which the family is handicapped by severe financial burdens or the responsibility of caring for a permanently disabled member. A severe financial setback may never be recouped. A bitter quarrel may leave lasting scars.

Techniques for Reducing Tension

Families may try to solve their own problems; they may turn to friends and relatives for help; or they may seek the advice of a professional therapist. No matter which procedure they follow, certain techniques and attitudes can help them to achieve satisfactory adjustment and avert further crises. Essential to all of them is a realistic, *problem-solving* attitude.

First, it is essential that family members *keep their channels of communication open.* A good many family members, when they become angry or upset, react by refusing to talk to each other. They go off into corners, lock themselves in their rooms, or find other means of enforcing an angry silence. But if the members of a family will not talk to each other, there is little hope for any sort of progress toward adjustment or solution of their problems. An unsolved problem stands like a silent barrier between members as long as one or the other refuses to talk about it. A problem cannot be solved by refusing to discuss it.

A second technique is to foster *objectivity*. This includes attempting to understand the problem not only from our own point of view but also from the point of view of other members of the family. It also means attempting to understand the sources and the nature of the problem and to discover ways of solving it, rather than merely trying to find someone on whom to put the blame. Objectivity is encouraged when attention is directed away from the self and how to protect one's own "rights" or "honor" and concentrated on the problem itself and how it is to be solved. A fault-finding attitude inhibits an objective approach.

Finally, many problems can be eased and more readily solved if they are approached with a *sense of humor*. A sense of humor often helps a person to see his problems in a new perspective and reduces disruptive emotions. Often, however, humor may be possible only after objectivity has been attained.

Divorce

A crisis, as we have seen, may often represent an attempt to adjust to one or more other crises. This is the case with divorce, which represents such a severe family crisis that we shall discuss it separately.

In 1867, when the Census Bureau published divorce statistics for the first time, there were 0.3 divorces per 1,000 population. Eighty years later, in 1946, divorces hit a record high, 4.3 per 1,000 population. After that the rate decreased somewhat, to 2.2 per 1,000 population in 1957,[9] but even this rate represented an increase of over seven times from 1867.

Along with these changes, and closely associated with them, has come a more permissive attitude. Divorced persons are no longer burdened with an intense social stigma. We often hear it said that divorce is made too easy. But the fact that the divorce rate is increasing does not necessarily mean that marriages are any less happy

[9] U. S. divorce rate per 1,000 population for selected years. National Office of Vital Statistics, *Special Reports*, L, No. 7 (1959), 181.

now than 50 or 100 years ago. In the past many couples suffered through unhappy marriages because of convictions that divorce was immoral or because they feared the disgrace that divorce might bring to them. But we should note also in this connection that many couples, faced with no other way out, often resolved to try to make the best of their situations and often succeeded in converting unhappy unions into happy ones.

But although social changes help to explain the over-all increase in divorce rates, they do not help us understand why one marriage ends in divorce while another does not. In general terms, many divorces result from the fact that the emotional needs of one or both partners in the marriage are not met—and since marriage today is expected to serve primarily the psychological needs, where this does not occur, divorce often follows.

Often a marriage will not end in divorce if the partners to the union believe that other considerations may be more important than their own immediate personal happiness. There may be children, and parents may hesitate to take a step they believe will bring grief and sadness to the youngsters. Again, a wife who might otherwise seek divorce may refrain from doing so because she dreads the responsibility of raising the children by herself.

There are many other considerations a divorce-seeking couple should keep in mind, considerations that may temper the first flush of relief that goes with anticipated freedom. Daily living habits will have to be reorganized as the divorced couple takes up separate residences. It may become apparent only then that although both parties are now less anxious and tense they also miss the many pleasant things they used to do together. And maintaining separate households increases economic burdens. If the children stay with the mother the husband is usually required to help support both households. If he is unable to meet these obligations, the mother may have to take a job.

This last-mentioned readjustment is one of the more serious that the divorced woman has to make, especially if there are small children and if she has been given custody of them. It means that she has to make arrangements to have the children cared for while she is at work. She may also have difficulty finding a job, especially if she has never worked outside the home before and has no special job training.

The couple's social life will also be affected. Undoubtedly both have had many mutual friends, and now one or the other may find himself excluded from functions or gatherings they used to attend together. If the couple formerly spent much time with people the husband came to know in his work, the wife may be "left out" after the divorce to avoid embarrassment or awkwardness to all concerned. Or the two may have been very friendly with relatives who now are likely to take sides in the divorce issue and who may ostracize the partner they consider guilty. Sometimes couples separate with little resentment or antagonism and remain friends after the divorce. Under those circumstances, their friends may not hesitate to invite them together. More often, however, such joint invitations will be avoided, and one of the divorced partners will have to seek new friends.

In addition to having to reorganize their daily habits and their financial and social relationships, the divorced couple will face psychological repercussions often not anticipated at the begininng of the separation. Sometimes only one of the mates wants the divorce. For the other the separation may mean rejection, sorrow, and feelings of failure. Even if both members want the divorce, their failure to attain the happiness they expected from marriage may cause severe disillusionment and depression. The severity of these adjustment problems will vary according to the divorced couple's individual needs and resources, both psychological and economic. The social support they receive from others will also affect their adjustment. But even if adjustment problems are severe, they may at times be preferable to the unrelieved tensions of an unhappy marriage.

Many people feel that any advantages that may accrue from a divorce will be small compensation to the couple if the separation affects their children adversely. Although more divorces occur among childless families than among families with children, the proportion of the latter is quite high. It is pertinent, then, to inquire into the effects of divorce on children.

How much the children suffer depends largely on the nature of the husband-wife and parent-child relationships. If the parents are resentful and vindictive toward one another, they may deeply disturb a child. If he has previously identified himself with both of them, he will be torn by his double loyalties. This conflict often is accentuated when custody is assigned to both parents, who may then compete for the child's affection. The child, in turn, may exploit this relationship for his own purposes. A child may also be disturbed by the fact that he is now different from many other children because either his father or his mother no longer lives at home with him. But whatever unfortunate effects a divorce may have on a child, they are probably no worse than the consequences of his being exposed daily to the spectacle of an unhappy marriage. In some cases the child may actually welcome the divorce for putting an end to the bickering, quarreling, and hostility of his parents.

For many, divorce is by no means the end of marital experience. It has been estimated that over 90 per cent of the women who have obtained a divorce by the age of 30 will eventually remarry.[10] Both cultural pressures and individual needs influence the desire to reestablish a full household. Informal adult groups are frequently composed of couples, and the unmarried person, whether single or divorced, does not fit in. Usually he is asked to bring a friend of the opposite sex. If he can not, his friends may try to find one for him.

The divorced mother is frequently urged or advised to marry again because of the strong feeling that children need two parents in the home. She herself may find the daily responsibility of maintaining a household for herself and her children too great a burden to handle alone. Factors such as these, added to the need for adult affection and for sexual experience, lead many divorcees to seek new marital partners.

[10] William Goode, *After Divorce* (Glencoe, Ill.: Free Press, 1956).

For Additional Reading

Ackerman, Nathan W., *The Psychodynamics of Family Life: Diagnosis and Treatment of Family Life*. New York: Basic Books, 1958.

———, Frances L. Beatman, and Sanford N. Sherman, eds. *Exploring the Base for Family Therapy*. New York: Family Service Association of America, 1961.

Bakke, E. W., "The Cycle of Adjustment to Unemployment," in *A Modern Introduction to the Family*, eds. Norman W. Bell and Ezra F. Vogel. Glencoe, Ill.: Free Press, 1960.

Bandura, Albert and Richard H. Walters, *Adolescent Aggression: A Study of the Influence of Child-Training Practices and Family Interrelationships*. New York: Ronald, 1959.

Bell, Norman W. and Ezra F. Vogel, eds., *A Modern Introduction to the Family*. Glencoe, Ill.: Free Press, 1960.

Bettelheim, Bruno, *Dialogues with Mothers*. New York: Free Press of Glencoe, 1962.

Blitsten, Dorothy, *The Family*. New York: Random House, 1962.

Blood, Robert O., Jr., *Anticipating Your Marriage*. Glencoe, Ill.: Free Press, 1956.

——— and Donald M. Wolfe, *Husbands and Wives: The Dynamics of Married Living*. Glencoe, Ill.: Free Press, 1960.

Bowlby, John, *Maternal Care and Mental Health*. New York: Columbia University Press, 1951.

Bronfenbrenner, U., "The Changing American Child—A Speculative Analysis," *Journal of Social Issues*, XVII, No. 1 (1961), 7-18.

Christensen, Harold T., *Marriage Analysis: Foundations for Successful Family Life*. New York: Ronald, 1958.

Clausen, John A. and Marian Radke Yarrow, eds., "The Impact of Mental Illness on the Family," *Journal of Social Issues*, XI, No. 4 (1955).

Despert, J. Louise, *Children of Divorce*. New York: Doubleday, 1962.

Duvall, Evelyn M., *Family Development* (2nd ed.). Philadelphia: Lippincott, 1962.

Erikson, Erik E., *Childhood and Society*. New York: Norton, 1950.

Fishbein, Morris and Ruby Jo Reeves Kennedy, eds., *Modern Marriage and Family Living*. New York: Oxford University Press, 1957.

Folson, Joseph K., "Value Analysis and the Resolution of Marital Conflict," *Merrill-Palmer Quarterly*, VI (January 1960), 105-113.

Glidewell, John C., ed., *Parental Attitudes and Child Behavior*. Springfield, Ill.: Thomas, 1961.

Goode, William, *After Divorce*. Glencoe, Ill.: Free Press, 1956.

Havighurst, Robert J. and A. Davis, "A Comparison of the Chicago and Harvard Studies of Social Class Differences in Child Rearing," *American Sociological Review*, XX (1955), 438-442.

Hess, Robert D. and Gerald Handel, *Family Worlds. A Psychosocial Approach to Family Life*. Chicago: University of Chicago Press, 1959.

Hill, Reuben, *Families under Stress*. New York: Harper, 1949.

Jacobsen, Paul H., *American Marriage and Divorce*. New York: Rinehart, 1959.

Jones, Eve, *Raising Your Child in a Fatherless Home*. New York: Free Press of Glencoe, 1962.

Kephart, William M., *The Family, Society, and the Individual*. Boston: Houghton Mifflin, 1961.

Kluckhohn, Florence R., "Family Diagnosis: Variations in the Basic Values of Family Systems." *Social Casework*, XXXIV (Feb.-Mar. 1958), 63-72.

Koos, Earl Lomon, *Families in Trouble*. Morningside Heights, N. Y.: King's Crown, 1946.

Landis, Paul H., *Making the Most of Marriage* (2nd ed.). New York: Appleton-Century-Crofts, 1960.

Lee, Alfred McClung and Elizabeth Lee, *Marriage and the Family*. New York: Barnes and Noble, 1961.

LeMasters, E. E., *Modern Courtship and Marriage*. New York: Macmillan, 1957.

Levy, John and Ruth Monroe, *The Happy Family*. New York: Knopf, 1947.

Miller, D. R. and E. G. Swanson, *The Changing American Child*. New York: Wiley, 1958.

Mudd, Emily Hartshorne and Aron Krich, eds., *Man and Wife: A Sourcebook of Family Attitudes, Sexual Behavior, and Marriage Counseling*. New York: Norton, 1957.

Murphy, Gardner, "New Knowledge about Family Dynamics," *Pastoral Psychology*, XI (September 1960), 39-47.

Parsons, Talcott and R. F. Bales, *Family, Socialization and Interaction Process*. Glencoe, Ill.: Free Press, 1955.

Queen, Stuart A., Robert W. Habenstein, and John B. Adams, *The Family in Various Cultures* (2nd ed.). Philadelphia: Lippincott, 1961.

Sears, Robert R., Eleanor E. Maccoby, and Harry Levin, *Patterns of Child Rearing*. Evanston, Ill.: Row, Peterson, 1957.

Spiro, Melford E., *Children of the Kibbutz*. Cambridge, Mass.: Harvard University Press, 1958.

Sussman, Marvin B., ed., *Sourcebook in Marriage and the Family* (2nd ed.). Boston: Houghton Mifflin, 1963.

Symonds, Percival M., *The Dynamics of Parent-Child Relationships.* New York: Teachers College, Columbia University, 1949.

Terman, Lewis M., *Psychological Factors in Marital Happiness.* New York: McGraw-Hill, 1938.

Waller, Willard and Reuben Hill, *The Family. A Dynamic Interpretation* (rev. ed.). New York: Dryden, 1951.

White, Robert W., *Lives in Progress. A Study of the Natural Growth of Personality.* New York: Dryden, 1952.

Whiting, Beatrice B., *Six Cultures. Studies in Child Rearing.* New York: Wiley, 1963.

Winch, Robert F., *Mate-Selection: A Study of Complementary Needs.* New York: Harper, 1958.

———, Robert McGinnis, and Herbert Barringer, *Selected Studies in Marriage and the Family* (rev. ed.). New York: Holt, Rinehart and Winston, 1962.

Zimmerman, Carle C. and Lucius F. Cervantes, *Sucessful American Families.* New York: Pageant, 1960.

SCHOOL AS A NEW EXPERIENCE

THE HOME-SCHOOL RELATIONSHIP

THE TEACHER-CHILD RELATIONSHIP

THE PEER-GROUP RELATIONSHIP

THE DYNAMICS OF LEARNING

Areas of Learning

Factors Responsible for Learning

Aids to More Effective Learning

SCHOOL AS A LIFE SITUATION

School Adjustment

9

The *school* stands second

only to the home

in influence exerted on our lives.

At home

our parents are primarily responsible

for what we learn.

After we enter school

the teacher takes over.

Her aim is to help us to benefit from

the accumulated experience and knowledge

of those who have lived before us.

Our teachers are a link between ourselves and our social and cultural heritage.

More than 40 million children are enrolled in school each year in the United States. More than a million teachers help them to learn. We Americans have always placed great faith in education, and our extensive school system testifies to this faith. The system ranges all the way from nursery school through post-graduate doctoral facilities. And in recent years the adult education movement, stressing the need for continuous learning beyond formal schooling, has provided many new opportunities for people to learn, explore, and discover.

But we begin to learn long before we start to school, and what we learn at home during the first five years of our lives determines, to a large extent, our reactions to subsequent learning situations. At birth we are endowed with a certain learning potential. The manner in which this potential is fostered and developed by our parents, teachers, and friends exerts a direct influence on the kind of adults we become. Such learning involves not only the acquisition of factual information but also the development of attitudes and the selection of goals.

School as a New Experience

When children start to school they encounter many new experiences. They look forward to this new world with pleasure if their parents and others close to them have encouraged such expectations. It is hoped that children will view school as an exciting place, one in which to make new discoveries and find new friends, one where interesting adults—the teachers—are waiting to guide them. It is hoped that children will have developed enough self-confidence to cope adequately with the many facets of this new world.

Even when these conditions are met, children are likely to feel some anxiety on their first day of school. But this anxiety will be greatly increased if their parents have failed to prepare them. If parents have emphasized only negative aspects of the school situation—that the things to be learned are dull and useless, that the teacher will punish them if they don't behave, that their classmates will ridicule them for

Our educational system ranges from nursery school through adult-education extension courses. Classes may be held out of doors, in a regular classroom, in a graduate-school seminar, or in any other place where teacher and students can gather. The curriculum encompasses every subject known to man. (Top left, courtesy Pacific Oaks College; top right, from Monkmeyer, by Al Bloom; bottom, New York University.)

their idiosyncrasies—their enthusiasm and self-confidence will be undermined; and school, instead of being eagerly anticipated, may become a threatening situation.

Parents are not the only ones who help to color a child's school expectations. Older playmates, brothers and sisters, even casual visitors, may reinforce or counteract parental influences. A playmate who talks about his happy relationship with his teacher, or a brother who voices a dislike for his teacher, will affect the child's attitude toward school. Although his parents' views will continue to affect a child's attitudes and behavior all the way through school, the actual situation encountered will revise them somewhat. And through the child the school might in turn modify the parents' views.

After a child starts to school, he begins to look to his teacher, as well as to his parents, for affection, acceptance, and guidance. A good teacher, therefore, recognizes two main areas of responsibility toward the child. She must first help him to acquire knowledge by creating an atmosphere in which he feels free to learn. But she must also be sensitive to his emotional needs and do whatever she can to gratify these needs in order to assure him of her acceptance and support. At school a child usually finds himself competing for attention against many more children than at home; and the teacher must try to see to it that no children feel slighted as a result of this competition for her attention.

School sets in motion the process that enables a child eventually to become independent, a process which the mother and father may facilitate by gradually reducing parental discipline in favor of self-discipline. Often parents find this difficult to do. Many make the mistake of attempting to assert authority in areas where authority is no longer needed.

The child entering school, then, is confronted with many new experiences, experiences which may be gratifying and stimulating or which may lead to frustration and anxiety. Just how he will adjust to these experiences depends on a number of things. One study, for example, points out that a school child's mental health depends on how effectively he establishes appropriate relationships with his teachers and with the other students and on how readily he acquires knowledge and skills.[1] In understanding a child's adjustment to school the *total* situation must be taken into account.

[1] F. H. Sanford, "Proposal for a Study of Mental Health in Education," *First Annual Report,* Joint Commission on Mental Illness and Health, Appendix H, 1956.

The Home-School Relationship

The parent-child relationship, and the emotional reactions it arouses, influences the child's behavior in school. If, for example, a child has been overprotected—encouraged to depend on his mother for support and guidance—he will have developed few resources of his own for dealing with unfamiliar situations. Unable to cope with the new problems of school, he may begin to feel inadequate and inferior to his classmates. Eventually he may withdraw and, by isolating himself from new situations and problems, deprive himself further of opportunities to learn to handle them. A disturbing cycle of failure and insecurity may result.

By contrast, a child who has been rejected at home may react in several ways, each of which will have a different effect on his school relationships. Without realizing it he may become aggressive, unconsciously demanding at school the attention he is denied at home. But since aggressiveness is more likely to arouse antagonism than affection, he may soon find his schoolmates and teachers rejecting him just as his parents do. Another possibility is that a child rejected at home may regard himself as inferior, just as the overprotected child does. He may become afraid to mingle with the other children or to speak up in class. For this reason his needs may be overlooked. Thus, whatever his reaction—aggression or timidity—the child who needs love most may be least likely to receive it.

A number of other preschool experiences can affect a child's school adjustment. He will be influenced by his parents' comments about their own school experiences and by their remarks about what he himself can expect. He will be affected, perhaps too much, by remarks made by other children. The feelings implicit in the remarks of others may often be more significant than the remarks themselves. If, for example, a mother declares, "I'll be glad when you start to school; maybe then I'll have some peace around here," she may give her child the impression that school is a place for unwanted children and that attendance at school is some sort of a punishment. Or if she says, "You won't be able to do *that* in school—just wait until the teacher sees you," she may suggest to her child that teachers are tyrants who will bully him. Another mother might complain about how inconvenient it is to have to drive the child to school, or how expensive it is to buy books and clothes, or what a nuisance it is to have to get up so early. As a result her child may feel uncomfortable about all the trouble he is causing her.

Damage can also be done by painting too bright a picture. A mother may be so eager to instill in the child a favorable attitude toward school that she overdoes the job and arouses unrealistic hopes and expectations. When these expectations fail to materialize, the child may become disappointed and resentful.

Sometimes a mother's comments to the teacher on the first day of school create a problem or erect a barrier between the teacher and child. An oversolicitous mother may tell the teacher that her child is "very sensitive" and must therefore be treated carefully, at the same time implying by her tone of voice that she would not trust the child with the teacher if the law did not require it. Such intimations might arouse in some teachers feelings of irritation and hostility toward the mother that later will be displaced onto the child. The mother has inadvertently created an unfavorable climate for her child.

It is safe to say, then, that school problems are often basically home problems. A child who is disturbed at home brings his problem to school, where it becomes a school problem in the sense that teachers and school authorities must deal with it. The most effective way to correct it, of course, is to straighten out the source of the difficulty at home. All too frequently, however, parents are unwilling to accept responsibility. The following case illustrates how parents refused to accept responsibility for such a problem.

Victor was a ten-year-old boy, rather heavy for his age, who had difficulty getting along with other children. He would insult them, bump into them, push them, or trip them "by accident" whenever he had the opportunity. In the classroom he was restless, talked a great deal, and disturbed the teacher and the other students. In general, he made a nuisance of himself. Whenever the teacher attempted to admonish Victor, he would blame someone else. "He made me do it," he would say. Or "It's her fault." He also accused the teacher of picking on him.

The teacher tried to alert the parents to the necessity of discovering the causes for Victor's behavior and correcting them. But they took the attitude that it was the school's problem, not theirs. Finally, when the boy had to be sent home because he had struck a girl, the father telephoned the principal, accusing the teacher of mistreating his son and declaring he had advised the boy he need no longer obey her.

Victor was eventually transferred to another school, but his undesirable behavior continued.

We might point out that the father's comments reflected not only his own attitudes, but also those of his son. Both believed that the school was in the wrong, that the teachers and principal had it in for Victor, and that others were to blame for what he did. When Victor's case was finally brought to the attention of a therapist, he found that the boy came from an unhappy home. His father and mother quarreled violently and often beat him. He was not close to either parent, which probably contributed to the difficulty he had in making friends in school. Before such a boy could be helped, his parents would need to be made to see: (1) that their own attitudes and feelings were responsible for their child's adjustment difficulties and (2) that they would have to correct their home environment before their son could benefit from his school experiences.

Parents who are very anxious to have their children do well in school often create more problems than they solve. In the following case a father who wanted to help his young daughter to read better actually prevented her from learning to read at all.

When seen by the psychologist, Lynn, age 10, a bright-eyed, beautiful girl who was very popular with her schoolmates, had not yet learned to read. She was excellent in arithmetic and other school work; but her reading level was barely that of a second-grader, and she had not yet learned to associate the written letter with spoken sounds.

A diagnosis of Lynn's reading problem and a history of its origin disclosed that her father had attempted to teach her to read before she started to school. He had bought a copy of an elementary reader and would sit down with Lynn to give her a lesson. Invariably the lesson ended with the father becoming violently angry and upset because Lynn did not learn to read as rapidly as he thought she should. By the time she actually started to school, Lynn had grown so emotionally disturbed about reading that she could not accept the guidance of her teachers and keep up with her classmates. In Lynn's case, as in Victor's, a home problem became a school problem.

The solution to Lynn's problem involved reducing her emotional reactions about reading, special remedial procedures, and instructions to her father to refrain from further efforts to teach her.

Parents, children, and teachers might all benefit from a counseling clinic designed to prepare them for a child's entrance into school. Such counseling—by helping parents (1) to understand how their attitudes affect their children's approaches to school, and (2) to realize that problems upsetting children in school are often brought from home—might lead to an improved home situation that would make both parents and children happier and minimize the number of home-school problems. The result would be an easier job of teaching for the teacher and an easier job of learning for the child.

The Teacher-Child Relationship

As we have seen, the teacher plays an important role in a child's intellectual and emotional development. As a parent-substitute she faces many of the same responsibilities parents face, multiplied by the number of children in her charge. The child looks to his teacher, as to his parents, for satisfaction of his needs. He seeks help in understanding the world and guidance to help him feel secure in his part of that world. A skillful teacher can create a wholesome atmosphere, in which each child is permitted to develop his potentialities as fully as possible.

Because it has become recognized that personality is so important in teaching, the number of degrees a candidate for a teaching post has earned can no longer be the sole measure of her qualifications. Today's teacher must be a scholar, psychologist, counselor, and guide all rolled into one. In order to understand children she must be able to understand herself. She must have an appreciation of her own needs,

A skillful teacher makes every effort to understand and encourage each child. (Hank Kranzler.)

of how she reacts when these needs are frustrated, of the kinds of defenses she uses, and of the possible influences her unresolved problems may have on her pupils. The well-adjusted teacher can help her pupils to adjust. The maladjusted teacher will probably create new problems for them, or intensify already existing ones. The emotionally healthy teacher who has an appreciation of the psychological principles governing behavior will regard each child as unique, an individual whose personal characteristics must be considered in relation to the total learning situation. Such a teacher will be able to help the shy child to grow in confidence, the emotionally starved child to feel loved and accepted, and the aggressive child to sublimate or overcome his feelings of hostility.

The kind of leadership a teacher furnishes exerts a significant influence on the effectiveness of the learning situation. Some teachers prefer to teach in an *authoritarian* atmosphere, setting themselves up as the final authority, demanding unquestioning obedience, and being quick to punish if they are disobeyed. The authoritarian teacher is essentially self-orientated; she believes that in order to control her class she must appear infallible. She displays little understanding or tolerance when children misbehave or go counter to her wishes. Her restrictive attitude suppresses the spontaneity and creativity of her children and creates an atmosphere of emotional tension, insecurity, and hostility.

In contrast, the *democratic* teacher emphasizes the personal value of each student as part of the total social group. Instead of setting herself up as one who knows it all, who tells others what to do and when and how to do it, the democratic teacher assumes the role of a resourceful leader, ready to help her students in any way she can. She encourages each pupil to participate in the group, thereby stimulating spontaneity and creativity, rather than discouraging them. Her methods of discipline inspire desirable behavior while still protecting the feelings of each pupil. The democratic teacher does not feel that her prestige is threatened if she cannot answer a question. And she recognizes that students will make mistakes and that they will profit from them. She is careful never to ridicule a student who is slow to learn, recognizing that each of her charges is an individual, and adjusting her materials and methods to meet the problems created by individual differences.

The Peer-Group Relationship

No matter how democratic the home or school may be, a child usually occupies a subordinate position, since in all critical situations adults make the decisions. And no matter how sensitive to his needs these adults may be, they have the advantage in age, maturity, and experience.

But in the peer group the child enjoys equal status. Being liked by his schoolmates, being included in their play, being able to do the things they do—all such experiences provide emotional support for his acceptance of the total school situation. Whether he is accepted or rejected by his peers may often determine whether he likes or dislikes school.

The behavior of his peers provides the child with standards against which to evaluate his own attitudes and behavior. Often he may accept what he is taught in class only after he has talked it over with his friends. Rules about fair play, honesty, and responsibility, which parents and teachers may have tried to explain, often become meaningful only after they have been applied in peer relationships.[2]

The Dynamics of Learning

Since we go to school essentially *to learn,* we shall consider, in this section (1) the *areas* of learning and (2) the interrelated, contributory factors that influence *what* we learn, *how* we learn, and *how much* we learn.

[2] For a detailed discussion of the functions of the peer group in the school see Robert J. Havighurst and Bernice L. Neugarten, *Society and Education* (Boston: Allyn and Bacon, 1957). See especially Chapter 5: "The Peer Group."

His relationships with his peers in school enable the child to evaluate his own attitudes and abilities. (Courtesy Pacific Oaks College.)

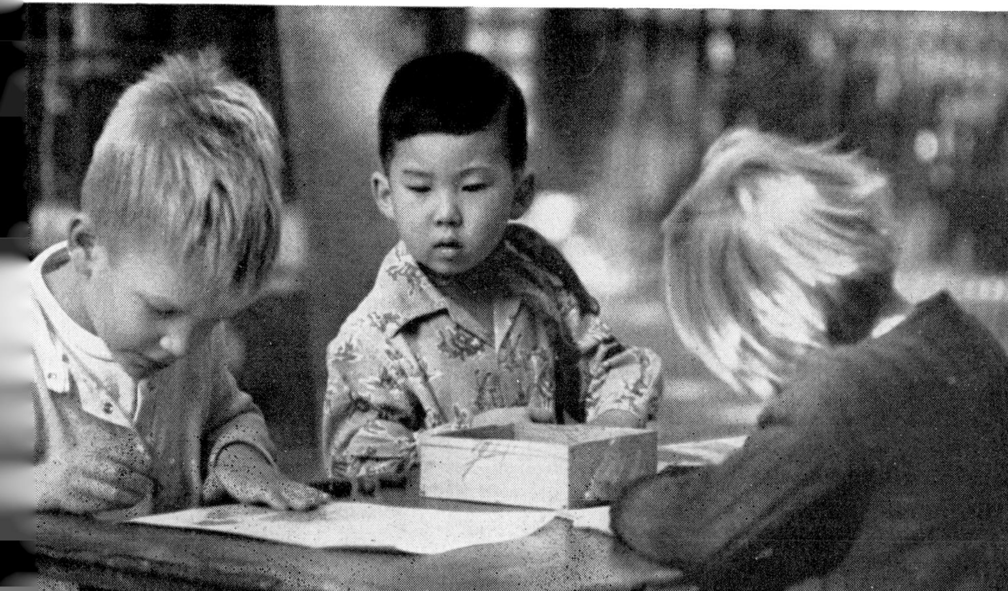

Areas of Learning

We may distinguish four areas of learning. Although each is distinct from the others, they may be closely interrelated in the learning process. A single learning situation may be limited to one of them or it may encompass a combination of several of them. These areas are:

1. Motor learning—acquiring muscular skills and techniques.
2. Social learning—acquiring skills for getting along with others, with our peers as well as with those in authority.
3. Emotional learning—developing and training our feelings and attitudes.
4. Intellectual learning—acquiring factual information and discovering how it is used in solving problems.

Factors Responsible for Learning

The factors principally responsible for what, how, and how much we learn—all of them subject to individual variation—are: (1) opportunity, (2) learning potential, (3) motivation, (4) discipline, (5) level of aspiration, (6) language skills, (7) competition, and (8) cooperation. All are interrelated in our learning process. Let us briefly consider each of them.

OPPORTUNITY Adequate opportunity is essential to learning. Without it no one could initiate a purposeful learning process. School provides such an opportunity, but how a student utilizes it will be determined by the other factors that contribute to the learning process.

It must be pointed out, however, that although school provides an opportunity for learning, schools do not offer *equal* opportunities to all children. The educational system acts as a selecting agency. Not all those who enter first grade will enter high school; not all who begin high school will graduate; and not all who graduate will go to college. The number remaining in school gets progressively smaller.

The four areas of learning: upper left, motor learning; upper right, social learning; lower left, emotional learning; lower right, intellectual learning. (Standard Oil Co. of N.J.; Detroit Public Schools; from Monkmeyer, by Sybil Shelton; Hank Kranzler.)

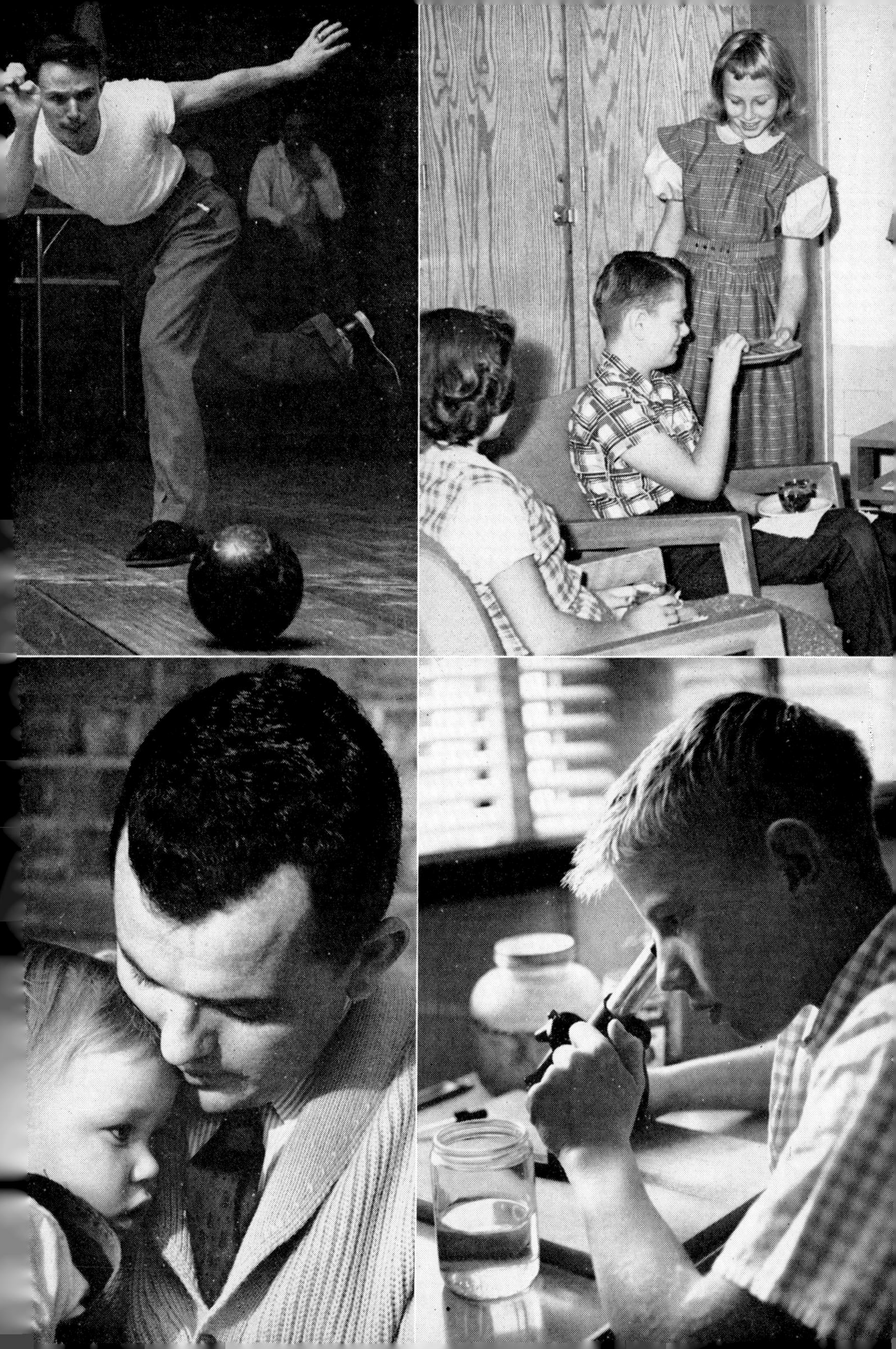

What are the bases for this selection? One is the ability and performance of the student. Numerous studies have shown that to a considerable extent the schools select the ablest for continued education. But these studies have also shown that young people from the upper-class and upper middle-class socio-economic levels are more likely to go on to college, while the able young people of working-class status frequently discontinue their education at the end of high school.

In part, availability of financial resources, or lack of resources, explains this difference. In part, it is due to parental expectations and pressures. Upper-class and middle-class parents are more likely to urge their children to go to college than are working-class parents. Class bias of teachers is another factor.

The motivation of the student is affected by these influences. All of them combine to create a state of unequal opportunity. The schools, being a part of the culture, reflect and are faced with the culture's problems. The struggle over segregation and integration in the schools highlights one of these problems: creating equal educational opportunities for all.

LEARNING POTENTIAL An individual's *learning potential* determines the level of intelligence he is capable of attaining. Results obtained from intelligence tests indicate that learning potential varies greatly from individual to individual. It varies not only according to the *amount* or *intellectual level* of the material, but also according to the *kind* of material a given individual can assimilate. One student may, for example, possess the ability to learn mathematics quickly and easily. He may progress rapidly toward an understanding of extremely advanced mathematical principles. But he may never learn to spell. Another may be able to grasp complicated philosophical theories, but geometry may make little sense to him. Still another may not be able to learn either to spell or to add and subtract. These examples may sound extreme, but they do serve to indicate the kinds of variation that can occur.

The fact that learning potential is not the *only* determiner of what we actually do learn is due partly to *motivation* and partly to the complexity of contributory factors that either facilitate or hinder our *opportunities* to learn. Learning potential, then, is modified by motivation and by opportunity. We do not learn as much as we can learn if we do not wish to learn it or if we have no chance to learn it. All of us are restricted by these modifying factors. Few of us ever really learn as much as we are capable of learning.

Much of our educational emphasis today involves discovering and measuring differences in learning potential so that children may be guided accordingly.

MOTIVATION We have already mentioned motivation as an influential factor in the learning process. By *motivation* we mean here simply the *urge to learn.* Generally when we are urged to learn something it is because, for one reason or another, we *need* to learn it. In a sense the entire learning process has its basis in this dynamic interaction between our needs and their satisfaction. We learn what we need to learn in order to satisfy other physiological and psychological needs.

A child's urge to explore his environment is an important factor in his learning. This urge to explore, often called curiosity, leads to the acquisition of new skills, new information, and new attitudes. The child, like the adult, wishes to understand what goes on around him. He is always asking how, what, why, and where. These questions constitute the basis of his quest for knowledge. Similarly, many an adult pursuing answers to such questions has acquired a new motive to learn.

Someone highly motivated to learn will create his own opportunities if necessary. We have all heard of self-taught men whose determination to learn and to advance themselves in the world motivated them to walk miles to the nearest library, to go without food in order to buy books, or to take any job they could find in order to pay for their education. By contrast, we also know of indifferent students who are not sufficiently motivated to take advantage of excellent educational opportunities.

Motives to learn must usually compete with motives that attract us to activities that interfere with learning.

> There are parents and teachers to be pleased, one's contemporaries to be dealt with, one's sense of mastery to be developed. At the same time, interests are developing, the world opens up. Schoolwork is only

> a part of the quickened life of the growing child. To different children it means different things. To some it is the road to parental approbation; to others it is an intrusion on the social world of contemporaries, and is to be handled by the minimum effort that will "get by." The culture of the school may be anti-intellectual or quite the opposite. And within this complex picture there is the subtle attraction of the subjects in school that a child finds interesting.[3]

This awakening and developing of interest is one of the main functions of education and is one of the most desirable and stable motives for learning.

DISCIPLINE When we speak about motivation and its effect on learning, we must also consider the closely related factor of *discipline,* particularly as it pertains to techniques of *reward* and *punishment.* We are motivated *toward* something we wish to attain or *away from* something we wish to avoid—toward rewards and away from punishment. Reward and punishment are the two principal techniques for controlling behavior. They are also the two basic approaches to discipline, by which we mean the control methods used in school to encourage students to do certain things and to discourage them from doing others. Former methods of discipline stressed painful punishment or the threat of it to control children's behavior. Such a negative system of discipline may insure obedience, but the child conforms simply to avoid pain. Under a constant rain of warnings and intimidations he may grow hostile and antagonistic toward the teacher and school situation and develop feelings of inferiority.

Current disciplinary methods emphasize principles of good mental health and are more concerned with guiding, rewarding, and suggesting than with dictating, criticizing, and punishing. Modern discipline is *positive* discipline in that it emphasizes the accomplishments of the child and minimizes his failures and shortcomings, thus making him feel more adequate and secure and safeguarding his ego needs. Positive discipline insures not only that a child will behave as desired, but also that he will be encouraged to develop wholesome

[3] Jerome S. Bruner, *The Process of Education* (Cambridge, Mass.: Harvard University Press, 1960), pp. 72-73. Reprinted by permission of the President and Fellows of Harvard College from Jerome Seymour Bruner, *The Process of Education,* 1960.

attitudes and feelings toward himself and the educational process. It enables him to establish effective, long-range *self-control.*

We might note here that all children, regardless of the kind of discipline they are exposed to, will inevitably encounter a certain amount of criticism and social or group disapproval. But such experiences need not leave a child depressed, insecure, or frustrated if he has learned to regard them as normal accompaniments to living and has developed enough self-confidence to cope with temporary setbacks calmly and rationally. Developing the self-confidence that will enable him to endure such experiences without losing faith in himself is an essential part of his education.

LEVEL OF ASPIRATION We see, then, that much of our behavior is directed toward achieving success (rewards) and avoiding failure (punishment). Such expectations regarding future performance we call *level of aspiration.* When we are called upon to perform a task, we generally have a fairly good idea, based on past performances, about whether or not we can do it; and we try to avoid situations in which we expect to fail while seeking out those in which we can expect to succeed. The quality of our performance in each undertaking will influence our future estimates of our abilities.

The term, *level of aspiration,* refers to the goals we set for ourselves and the plans we make for attaining them. The term, *level of achievement,* refers to the goals we attain. In school, for example, the level of aspiration often refers to the kind of grades we hope and work for. Sometimes there is considerable difference between levels of aspiration and levels of achievement.

Our level of aspiration should be determined bv our abilities, by the opportunities we have to use these abilities, and by our willingness to surmount difficulties. Very often we ignore one or more of these factors. For example, a boy with an IQ of 90 who wants to become a doctor does not have a realistic level of aspiration. Evidence indicates that an IQ of approximately 120 is the minimum required for success in medicine. Likewise, the 120-pound freshman who has his heart set on making the first-string football team must learn that determination and enthusiasm, important though they may be, cannot compensate adequately for lack of brawn. The student, however, who makes good grades in all his subjects and who is particularly adept at mathematics, sets a realistic level of aspiration in deciding to study engineering.

Good teachers can help students appraise their abilities realistically, select attainable goals, and plan how to reach those goals. Many high schools have set up guidance services to assist in this sort of planning. Helping a student toward a realistic appraisal means not only preventing him from setting his achievement sights too high but also from setting them too low. Someone with high ability may often set a low standard of achievement because he feels inadequate and insecure, perhaps as a result of negative discipline practiced by his parents or teachers. His parents may have set unrealistically high standards for him in an area in which he could not excel and then criticized and punished him when he fell short. For example, they may have wanted him to excel in a sport for which he had no particular skill. Or they may have insisted that he study law and join his father's law firm when actually he wanted to be an architect. The same mistake is made by the mother who expects her six-month-old daughter to acquire proper toilet habits or her three-year-old son to display the social skills and manners of an adult.

Students subjected to experiences of this sort may set low goals for themselves solely to insure success. But since their goals are too easy to attain they become lazy. They *need not* work so they *do not* work. Consequently they do not learn *how* to work.

We should set goals we can reach, but only by putting forth our best efforts. If the goal is set far in the future, various sub-goals should be interspersed along the way. The student striving to become an engineer, for example, will be encouraged as he completes individual course requirements, since their completion indicates he is progressing toward his goal.

Since level of aspiration is so influential in determining how much people will learn, schools have a responsibility to help students set realistic goals and plan for their attainment. Aspirations must not be out of proportion to abilities. The goals set must be feasible.

LANGUAGE SKILLS Human society itself is derived from the ability of men to communicate with one another through speech and writing. Language not only facilitates communication between people but also, in its written form, provides the means by which man preserves knowledge and skills and passes them on to his contemporaries and his descendants. Language enables him to select, identify, and manipulate aspects of a situation; generalize about it; express attitudes toward it; relate it to other situations in the past and future; direct his own actions and the actions of others with respect to it; and evoke in others similar attitudes and tendencies.

The acquisition of *language skill,* then, is an essential factor in learning. To develop a good vocabulary—by informing ourselves of the exact meanings of words and then using them correctly—is to acquire not only the key to greater understanding but also the badge that distinguishes an educated man. It is important also to recognize these two additional features peculiar to the use of language: (1) To be fully effective, a word must *symbolize* the *same thing* or the *same idea* for all who use it; but (2) at the same time, words do *not* always mean the same thing to different people. Even between two members of the same family slight differences in interpretation may occur, because everyone sees the connotations of words in the light of his own experiences. A skilled user of language never loses sight of these two features and takes them into account when making his own interpretations. Many arguments, by the way, might be avoided if the participants took the trouble to define their terms carefully. Difference of opinion is often a matter of confused wording.

One of the school's chief responsibilities is to help the student to acquire skill and facility in the use of language, to become aware of subtle variations in the meanings of words, to establish finer distinctions between ideas and closer relationships between a topic and the symbols that describe it. With each new field that he explores the student acquires a new vocabulary that enables him to describe, relate, and explain accurately the subject matter of that field. Language provides us with a valuable tool, upon which all other learning depends.

COMPETITION *Competition*—that is, activity in which two or more people strive to outrace each other to the same objective, or to reach the objective more efficiently, or to prevent others from reaching it at all—is familiar to us from early childhood and influences much of what we learn. The competitive aspects of our lives are reinforced by many influences. Even before starting to school, brothers and sisters are often pitted against one another, encouraged by their parents to outdo one another in tests of strength or skill. In school, competition continues. Pupils are constantly contending for the highest grades, for awards and prizes, or for increased prestige. Athletic contests reinforce this alarming emphasis. In college, competition for grades is a source of marked anxiety to many; and it can become so intense that some students strive not so much to learn as to get good grades, even if they have to cheat to get them.

The following four consequences of excessive competition among secondary-school students have been pointed out: (1) Slow learners despair and grow discouraged as they begin to fall behind their classmates. (2) Average students are under constant stress to keep up their work. (3) The brightest students develop exaggerated feelings of superiority. (4) Students within a given progress bracket develop attitudes of "aggressive non-cooperation" toward others in their group in an effort to maintain their relative positions in their bracket.[4]

[4] J. J. Fuller and J. N. Baker, "Competition vs. Cooperation in the Classroom," *Secondary Education,* VIII (1939), 134-137.

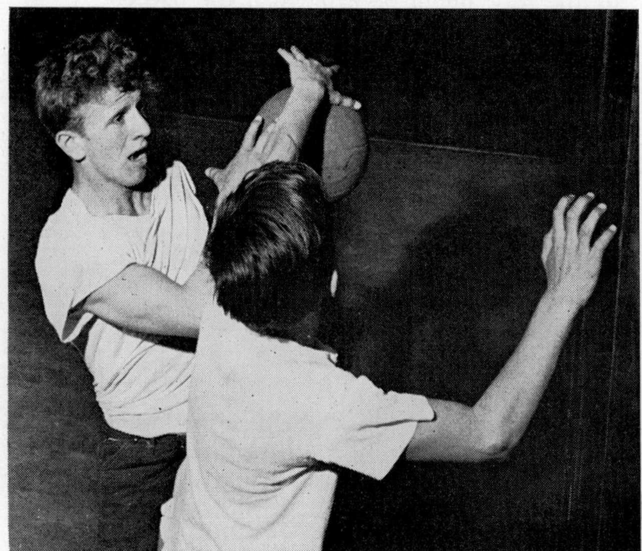

Too much emphasis on competition as a learning technique can produce undesirable consequences. Carefully prepared regulations are as essential to competitive learning as they are to competitive games. (Standard Oil Co. of N.J.)

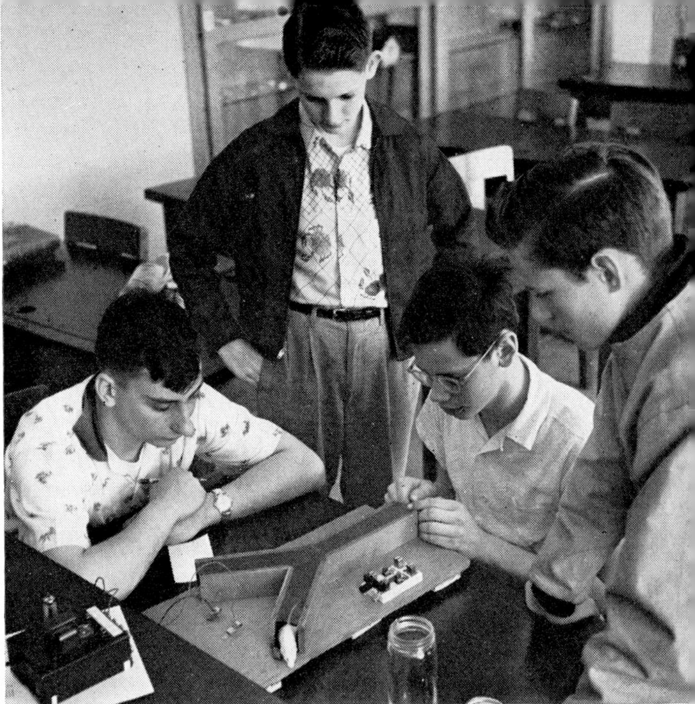

Cooperation leads to understanding of and identification with the group in the interest of achieving a common goal. But it is also essential to develop the ability to study and develop alone. (From Monkmeyer, by Nancy Hays.)

Those who encourage competition are usually urging individuals with different learning potentials and different physiological and psychological qualifications to try to achieve the same goals. It would seem therefore that the value of competition in the learning process is questionable. Unless the students who compete are grouped according to interest, ability, and learning potential and then permitted to compete only against others in their own group—and only on certain otherwise relaxed occasions—it would seem that organized competition should be kept to a minimum. Under the circumstances listed above, however, competition may stimulate motivation without harmful consequences.

COOPERATION In contrast to competition, cooperation encourages students to work together toward a common goal—to pool their efforts, so to speak. This means that each is permitted to contribute to the group effort according to his own abilities. Rather than being asked to do something he *cannot do very well,* he is urged to do more of what *he is able to do best.* When pupils are placed in situations that encourage them to cooperate, they manifest the following behavior characteristics: (1) They work together in setting the goal and in planning ways of achieving it. (2) They contribute whatever efforts are needed to attain the goal. (3) They share alike in the responsibilities for success or failure in the pursuit of the task at hand. (4) They become more goal-centered and less self-centered.[5] Thus, in the cooperative situation we see a tendency toward mutual aid and understanding and identification with the group effort, as against the fear, hostility, and anger so frequently found in intensively competitive situations.

The so-called *progressive education* movement stresses this principle of cooperation in the classroom while at the same time recognizing that the student must also be encouraged to work *alone*. Of course, a child must at times strive to develop new skills—must try, that is, to do things that are hard for him in order that they may eventually become easier. But children should be permitted to learn these new skills in a relaxed atmosphere, one that permits them to proceed at their own speed and that takes into consideration their individual motivations.

Aids to More Effective Learning

The student's main job is to learn, but all too often he does not know how. Inability to learn well prevents him from benefiting as much as he might from his school experiences. He will be more effective in school if he modifies his approach to learning in the light of the following factors: (1) definite goals, (2) perspective, (3) distributed effort, (4) active study approach, (5) problem orientation, and (6) application. We shall discuss each of these factors briefly.

DEFINITE GOALS We have seen that we must be motivated if we are to learn. We must, that is, have goals whose achievement requires learning. In order to understand why we are in school, why we are studying a certain course or reading a certain book, we need to understand how these present activities relate to more distant goals. This assumes, of course, that we have a goal or goals. All of us know students who enrolled in a university simply because they did not know

[5] Fuller and Baker, *Secondary Education,* VIII.

what else to do or because their parents talked them into it. They are not interested in their work and consequently do not bother to learn very much. The student who enrolls in order to work toward a specific goal will work harder and learn more, even though he may have to sacrifice comforts and pleasures to do so.

If the subject matter we study is to contribute to the attainment of our goals, we must be able to define those goals. And we should frequently remind ourselves of them. A goal that we cannot hope to reach immediately may slip out of sight; and as we lose sight of it, we may lose interest in it. Sub-goals, as previously stated, help prevent this loss of motivation.

PERSPECTIVE We see a course of studies in correct perspective if we see it as part of a total goal-oriented program and not as an end in itself. Without a sense of perspective we shall find it difficult to separate the significant from the insignificant. It is always wise to view a problem or a subject in its entirety before trying to break it down into its component parts. If we approach a new book, for example, by reading through the table of contents, we immediately get an over-all view of the subject matter presented and a clear idea of how the chapters are related. By getting the total picture into focus we facilitate our understanding of each individual chapter.

DISTRIBUTED EFFORT Research indicates that we learn better and retain longer if we distribute our learning efforts over a number of short periods instead of trying to master an entire assignment all at once. Even if we have little time for study, we can intersperse our intense periods of concentration with occasional five-minute breaks. Sometimes it helps just to walk around the room, or to glance at a magazine article or write a letter. When we return to the material we are studying we discover that our ability to concentrate has been increased by this brief freshener. Where possible it is even more desirable to put the work down long enough for a quick swim, a game of tennis, or a visit with a friend.

The benefits to be derived from distributed effort seem to apply equally to motor learning, such as learning to play golf, and to intellectual learning, such as memorizing chemical formulas.

The best kind of spacing depends, of course, on individual motivation and available time, and each student must work out his own method. It is helpful if a definite schedule can be arranged. Establishing a schedule relieves us of the necessity of making daily decisions about when to work and when to play, and permits us to enjoy our recreational periods without worrying about when the work will get done. Similarly, if we know that we have set a definite time for recreation, we shall be less likely to resent our work as being a constant hindrance to play. We will not be constantly distracted from our work by reminders of other things we would rather be doing.

ACTIVE STUDY APPROACH Learning is more efficient if we approach it actively. An active study approach may mean something as simple as assuming a "work position"—for example, sitting at a desk while reading rather than lying in bed. It may also mean taking notes, perhaps briefly summarizing the material as we read it, or jotting down ideas and questions it suggests. One way we can make the material "really stick" is to rephrase it in our own words. Another active approach may involve voluntarily competing with ourselves or with others—others whose past achievements indicate that their interests and learning potential closely resemble our own—in seeing how much work we can do and how well we can do it. Such competition may motivate us to get the job done rather than to procrastinate. Satisfactory distribution of effort also contributes to an active study approach.

PROBLEM ORIENTATION When we are trying to learn, it is important to be problem-oriented rather than self-oriented. By this we mean that in trying to solve or to understand a problem we must focus our attention on the problem itself and not on our own feelings as they relate to it. Most of us can no doubt remember occasions when a mathematical problem just would not come out right, or when a foreign language passage just would not make sense. The chances are that after struggling for a while and becoming frustrated we began to think of the problem as unsolvable or the passage as untranslatable. And we probably also accused the teacher of making unrealistic demands. In other words, we had ceased to view the problem as a problem and were now seeing it as a form of torture inflicted on us by a tyrant.

Such a situation is most likely to occur when we do not really want to study in the first place. In such a mood, we are more likely to attack the assignment as an enemy than to approach it as simply something to learn or to solve with a reasonable amount of effort. We are emotionally upset, we feel sorry for ourselves, and we cannot see a problem as merely a problem. Before we can solve it, therefore, we must deal with the emotional disorders it arouses. Once these are eliminated, a swift solution may present itself.

In other words, we should apply to the learning situation the same problem-solving attitude that is essential in any area of adjustment. In cases where emotional reactions consistently interfere with the learning process, professional therapy may be advisable.

APPLICATION By application we mean putting to use the information and the skills we are acquiring. In school one of the simplest ways to do this is to help a younger brother or sister—or a fellow student who is falling behind—with homework.

Usually when we apply knowledge we are not aware that we are doing so. For example when someone asks you how to spell a word and you are able to tell him, you probably do not realize that you are applying knowledge. Yet even in so simple an act, you experience the feeling of pride that accompanies the application of your knowledge.

Student discussions are an application of knowledge. School projects, club activities, formal debates, and part-time jobs are other examples. One sort of knowledge that can be regularly applied is our information regarding personal adjustment.

Once we become aware of the value of application, we will search for opportunities. And the more opportunities we find, or create, the more we will be motivated to continue learning. The challenge of searching for knowledge that can be applied is a continuous stimulant to learning. The harder it was to acquire your knowledge the more stimulating applying it will be. And the more often you apply it and the more intensely you become aware of applying it, the more eagerly you will anticipate new opportunities. The pleasure you get from the experience will encourage you to learn still more in order to experience the pleasure more often.

School as a Life Situation

We often hear the remark that school is a preparation for life. In the sense that in school we prepare for our life's work, this is true. But it is not true in the sense that school is a preparation and nothing more. School *is* life. It is a situation in which we find, though perhaps in somewhat milder form, almost all the problems we encounter in later life. In school, therefore, *we learn to live by living.*

The way we handle our problems in school can serve as a measure of our ability to handle those we shall meet later on. How well do we learn what we need to learn? How well do we adjust to school discipline, to authority, and to other aspects of an organized social activity? How do we get along with other people—with those in our own class, with younger students, with older students, with those whose interests and backgrounds are similar to ours, with those whose interests and backgrounds are different? What kind of close attachments do we form? Can we comfortably give and receive affection? The answers we give to these questions while we are still in school will indicate what our adult attitudes and behavior patterns will be.

By providing us with problems like those we must face later on, school gives us more than just intellectual training. True, it is important to master the subject matter of our courses, but it is equally important to learn to consider and to respect other people. We live by our feelings as well as by our intellects. How we feel toward other people often determines how we interact with them—with peers, elders, and prospective employers. And if our manner of interacting displeases everyone who might employ us, we may never be given an opportunity to use the information and skills we have acquired. In this respect it is interesting to note that about 90 per cent of those who lose their jobs do so not because they cannot do the work, but because they cannot get along with others.

School, then, is not merely a place in which to acquire "book-learning." It is also a place in which to acquire "life-learning." It is a place in which to learn to understand and evaluate, to like and get along with all kinds of people. It is an opportunity to expand our world.

For Additional Reading

Barzun, J., *The House of Intellect.* New York: Harper, 1959.

Bruner, Jerome S., *The Process of Education.* Cambridge, Mass.: Harvard University Press, 1961.

Bühler, C., Faith Smitter, and Sybil Richardson, *Childhood Problems and the Teacher.* New York: Holt, 1952.

Charters, W. W., Jr. and N. L. Gage, *Readings in the Social Psychology of Education.* Boston: Allyn and Bacon, 1963.

Coleman, James S., *The Adolescent Society. The Social Life of the Teenager and Its Impact on Education.* Glencoe, Ill.: Free Press, 1961.

Dinkmeyer, Don, *Motivating Children to Learn: The Encouragement Approach.* Englewood Cliffs, N. J.: Prentice-Hall, 1963.

Farnsworth, D. L., *Mental Health in College and University.* Cambridge, Mass.: Harvard University Press, 1957.

Fisher, Margaret B. and Jeanne L. Noble, *College Education as Personal Development.* Englewood Cliffs, N. J.: Prentice-Hall, 1960.

Getzels, Jacob W. and Philip W. Jackson, *Creativity and Intelligence. Explorations with Gifted Children.* New York: Wiley, 1962.

Glidewell, John C., ed., "Mental Health in the Classroom," *Journal of Social Issues,* XV, No. 1 (1959).

Harris, Irving D., *Emotional Blocks to Learning.* Glencoe, Ill.: Free Press, 1961.

Harris, S. E., ed., *Higher Education in the United States: the Economic Problems.* Cambridge, Mass.: Harvard University Press, 1960.

Havighurst, Robert J. and Bernice L. Neugarten, *Society and Education.* Boston: Allyn and Bacon, 1957.

Hayakawa, S. I., "Meaning, Symbols and Levels of Abstraction," in *Readings in Social Psychology,* eds. T. M. Newcomb and E. L. Hartley. New York: Holt, 1947.

Hilgard, E. R., *Theories of Learning* (rev. ed.). New York: Appleton-Century-Crofts, 1956.

Hughes, Everett C., *Students' Culture and Perspectives: Lectures on Medical and General Education.* Lawrence, Kan.: University of Kansas Law School, 1961.

Jacob, P. E., *Changing Values in College.* New York: Harper, 1957.

Jones, H. E., "The Environment and Mental Development," in *Manual of Child Psychology* (2nd ed.), ed. L. Carmichael. New York: Wiley, 1954, pp. 631-696.

Lewin, K. *et al.*, "Level of Aspiration," in *Personality and the Behavior Disorders* (Vol. 1), ed. J. McV. Hunt. New York: Ronald, 1944, pp. 333-378.

Mayer, Martin, *The Schools.* New York: Harper, 1961.

McCarthy, D., "Language Development in Children," in *Manual of Child Psychology* (2nd ed.), ed. L. Carmichael. New York: Wiley, 1954, pp. 492-630.

McClelland, D. C., J. W. Atkinson, and E. L. Lowell, *The Achievement Motive.* New York: Appleton-Century-Crofts, 1953.

——, A. L. Baldwin, U. Bronfenbrenner, and F. L. Strodtbeck, *Talent and Society.* Princeton, N. J.: Van Nostrand, 1958.

McConnell, T. R., ed., *Selection and Educational Differentiation.* Berkeley: Field Service Center and Center for the Study of Higher Education, University of California, 1959.

Mead, G. H., "Language and the Development of the Self," *Readings in Social Psychology,* eds. T. M. Newcomb and E. L. Hartley. New York: Henry Holt, 1947.

Neill, A. S., *Summerhill: A Radical Approach to Child Rearing.* New York: Hart, 1960.

Riesman, D., *Constraint and Variety in American Education.* New York: Doubleday, 1958.

Rokeach, Milton, *The Open and Closed Mind.* New York: Basic Books, 1960.

Ryans, David G., *Characteristics of Teachers: Their Description, Comparison, and Appraisal.* Washington, D. C.: American Council on Education, 1960.

Sanford, F. H., "Proposal for a Study of Mental Health in Education," *First Annual Report.* Joint Commission on Mental Illness and Health. Appendix H, 1956.

Sanford, Nevitt, ed., *The American College. A Psychological and Social Interpretation of Higher Education.* New York: Wiley, 1961.

Sanford, Nevitt, "Personality Development During the College Years," *Journal of Social Issues,* XII, No. 4 (1956).

Sarason, Seymor B. *et al., Anxiety in Elementary School Children.* New York: Wiley, 1960.

Smith, Henry P., *Psychology in Teaching.* Englewood Cliffs: Prentice-Hall, 1962.

Thelen, Herbert A., *Education and the Human Quest.* New York: Harper, 1960.

Warner, W. L., R. J. Havighurst and M. B. Loeb. *Who Shall Be Educated?* New York: Harper, 1944.

Wedge, B. M., ed., *Psychosocial Problems of College Men.* New Haven: Yale University Press, 1958.

Witty, P., ed., *The Gifted Child.* Boston: Heath, 1951.

THE TRANSITION FROM SCHOOL TO WORK

FACTORS AFFECTING JOB SELECTION

Socio-Economic Considerations

Interests

Abilities

Job Requirements and the Labor Market

WORKING WOMEN

FACTORS AFFECTING JOB SATISFACTION

Fears Arising on the Job

Personal Approach to the Job

Conditions on the Job

JOB SATISFACTION AND PERSONAL ADJUSTMENT

Job Adjustment

10

For most of us
the end of school means the beginning
of full-time employment.
The *job* we choose must earn us a living.
We hope it will also afford
pleasant, stimulating experiences.
The kind of job we hold,
or whether or not we hold a job,
exerts considerable influence on our lives.
Most men,
and a large number of women,

are gainfully employed; and the work they do determines where they will be and what they will do throughout a significant portion of their lifetime.

Thus, in addition to providing a livelihood, a job performs a number of other functions. To begin with, our occupational status largely determines our *social identity*. Frequently one of the first questions we ask about another person is: "What does he do?" or "Where does he work?" The friendships we establish, the prestige we acquire, the roles we play in the community are related to the socio-economic position in which our job has placed us. Even in the job situation itself our particular assignment influences the kind of associations we engage in with other members of the working staff.

Our job is also important to our self-concept, which is determined by our social identity as well as by the characteristics we value in ourselves. If we see ourselves as competent to handle the technical and social skills our job requires, and if others confirm this competence, we feel confident and self-assured—fairly well satisfied with our self-concept. But if we feel inadequate to cope with the demands of our job, or if others question our competence, we may become discouraged and our self-concept may be damaged.

Our job, then, performs various complex functions and serves many different needs—needs for belongingness, for self-esteem and self-respect, and for self-expression, as well as the need for food and shelter. We must, therefore, weigh these factors carefully in choosing both a career and a specific job in that career. If possible, it may help to try several different jobs in order to find the one that best satisfies our needs.

The Transition from School to Work

The period of transition from school to full-time employment is a time when we give up for good many roles and values we acquired as children that are out of place in adult life. In our society this transition from childhood and adolescence to maturity is often accompanied by anxiety and insecurity. Usually, during their last year of school, young people regard apprehensively the imminent necessity to assume adult roles and to establish their own places in the world.

At whatever point we enter full-time employment—after high school, after college, or after completing graduate work—the change from school to work means new tasks and new responsibilities. First, we are now expected to become self-supporting. Second, we compete with others for jobs that must be regarded not merely as means of temporary support but rather as determiners of our future. Third, even though mediocre work may have somehow brought us to graduation, we now must learn to do our jobs to the best of our abilities, for an employer may not settle for mediocre work. Fourth, in school we associated with a large group of peers with whom we could share similar problems, and we could look for help and guidance from our teachers as well. At work, however, we may hesitate to discuss our problems and may need to solve them without much assistance or sympathy from others. Finally, we must learn new technical and social skills.

Personal needs or desires figure strongly in the transition from school to work and often lead to decisions having life-long consequences. For example, a high school graduate who wishes to get married right away may decide against going to college. He may even refuse to take a job that requires a long apprenticeship, in spite of the fact that it offers good possibilities for advancement. Another young person may pass up similar opportunities because of severe financial need or because of the desire to escape parental domination. Such conflicting needs must often be resolved when we are considering a job. It is important to avoid impulsive decisions.

Factors Affecting Job Selection

"What kind of work do I like to do?" "What kind of work am I able to do well?" Before taking any job we should ask ourselves these two questions.

We do not, as a rule, suddenly decide on a particular job without giving the matter some advance thought. As children, many of us want to be firemen, policemen, nurses. During adolescence, we change our minds and decide to become pilots, actresses, or professional athletes. Finally, as adults, we may settle on something entirely different. These changes reflect our growing awareness of ourselves and the world around us.

The choices we make as children, from about six to eleven, are called *fantasy choices.*[1] We choose activities that appear pleasurable and attractive, ignoring other aspects of the occupations of which these activities are a part. The choices of adolescence are *tentative choices,* in which we begin to ask ourselves not only, "Do I like it?," but also, "Am I able to do it?" By this time we have had a chance to gain a more realistic picture of what certain occupations demand. We have been exposed—by our families, our schools, and our friends—if not to specific

[1] For a discussion of the developmental stages in occupational choice, see Eli Ginzberg, Sol W. Ginsburg, Sidney Axelrad, and John L. Herma, *Occupational Choice, An Approach to a General Theory* (New York: Columbia University Press, 1951).

As children we make fantasy choices. A girl may dream of becoming a ballerina; a boy may dream of becoming a fireman. (From Monkmeyer, by Lew Merrim, and Leo Dewys.)

jobs, at least to certain attitudes toward work, certain value judgments about different kinds of work. We have had a chance to discover some of our own interests and to explore our abilities. Many of us have held part-time jobs during the school year and have worked full-time during the summer vacations. In this way we have discovered our preferences and learned what others expect of us. Such experiences help us determine what we can or cannot do well, what sort of social relationships certain kinds of jobs provide, and what sort of satisfactions and frustrations each type of job has to offer. Consequently by the time it becomes necessary to take a job or prepare for a career, we can at least eliminate those we are certain would not suit us, even though we may not have definitely decided on a lifetime career.

By adulthood, then, many of us can make *realistic choices.* That is, we can consider a job in relation to other preferences and demands. We may, for example, have to weigh our desire to stay in our home town, where jobs are scarce, against better opportunities in another part of the country. Or we may have to choose between a job that will fulfill a lifelong ambition to travel and one that will fulfill our wish to become independent of family support as soon as possible. The job we finally do choose is likely to represent a compromise between our needs and wishes and our opportunities.

This last period of realistic choice has been subdivided into three stages: *exploration, crystallization,* and *specification.*[2] During the exploration stage the young person acquires background experience and information by exploring different subjects in school or college, by talking with teachers and advisors, or by trying his hand at different jobs. During the crystallization stage he assesses the different possibilities open to him and commits himself to a certain occupational field. In the specification stage he reviews the alternatives within his chosen field and selects a career objective. If, for example, he has decided to become a psychologist, he specifies the particular branch of psychology he will pursue—whether it be clinical, industrial, or social psychology, vocational counseling, child guidance, or some other field of specialization.

Five characteristic work periods have been distinguished in the

[2] Ginzberg *et al., Occupational Choice.*

normal lifetime.[3] They are: (1) the *preparatory* work period, during which the child is socialized to the work patterns of American society and during which the school and the home provide early work experiences; (2) the *initial* work period, during which the young worker is able to earn his first wages and to begin learning about the adult work world; (3) the *trial* work period, described as the early years of struggle to obtain a secure, satisfying, well-paying job; (4) the *stable* work period, during which the individual becomes established in his life's work and puts down roots in his community; and (5), the *retired* work period, during which the withdrawal from active work marks the end of his career.

Having taken a general look at the process of vocational choice, let us now consider four sets of factors influencing this choice. They are: (1) socio-economic considerations, (2) interests, (3) abilities, and (4) factors having to do with job requirements and the labor market.

Socio-economic Considerations

Family background influences occupational choice in many ways. The socio-economic position of the family strongly influences the jobs children choose or set their sights on. In his book, *Elmtown's Youth,* August Hollingshead [4] reports that the vocational goals of the high school students queried reflected, on the whole, the social class of their parents. Figure 1 depicts the relationship between class and vocational desires. There is a striking decrease in the choice of professional and business careers as we go from the upper-middle to the lower-lower class. Only 7 per cent of the latter choose such careers, as compared to 77 per cent of the former. What happens is that the young person is exposed not to all of society but only to a certain segment of it. Within that segment, he hears only about certain kinds of occupations—those typical of his class—and comes to accept almost as a matter of course that some day he too will be working at one of them.

It is also interesting to note that as we descend the social scale in

[3] Delbert C. Miller and Wm. H. Form, *Industrial Sociology: An Introduction to the Sociology of Work Relations* (New York: Harper, 1951). See especially Part 4: "The Social Adjustment of the Worker," pp. 517-786.

[4] August B. Hollingshead, *Elmtown's Youth. The Impact of Social Classes on Adolescents* (New York: Wiley, 1949), pp. 284-287.

Figure 1, we find more children undecided about their careers. Only 3 per cent in Class II have not made up their minds, but 41 per cent in Class V are undecided.

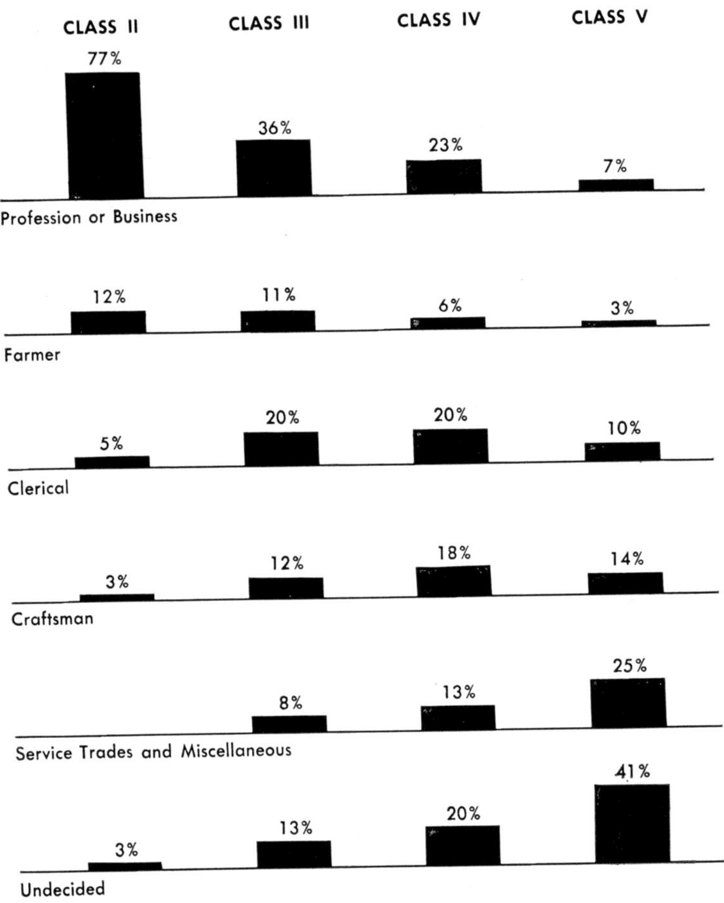

Figure 1. Vocational choices of Elmtown high school students from the upper-middle, lower-middle, upper-lower, and lower-lower classes (classes II, III, IV, and V respectively). (Reprinted with permission from A. B. Hollingshead, Elmtown's Youth. *New York: Wiley, 1949, p. 286.)*

It would be misleading, however, to point out only the occupational *stability* from one generation to the next. Considerable occupational *mobility*, downward as well as upward, is also evident. Sons do hold jobs that differ from those of their fathers. Comparing the occupations of fathers with those held by their sons, one study [5] found that although the largest percentage of sons held the same occupational status as the fathers, many did not. For example, 45 per cent of the sons of white collar workers also held white collar jobs. But 55 percent were distributed through other occupational categories, as shown in Figure 2.

We need to account, then, not only for occupational *stability* but also for occupational *mobility*. Changes in the economy affect changes in the distribution of occupations. The parents' way of life, and particularly their hopes and expectations for their children, may influence them to encourage the children to improve or alter their socio-economic positions. Children, on their part, may rebel against the "rut" they believe their parents to be in. The influence of peer groups and of others outside the family circle may be important. Native abilities and interests and the way in which they are encouraged or frustrated may be decisive. Probably most of these factors play some part in determining the kind of job we choose and how well we succeed in it.

Family, class, and other social pressures do not, as a rule, *compel* the young person to choose his profession on the basis of his position in society. If he seems to restrict his choice to certain occupations, it is usually because he has accepted the values and norms to which he was exposed as a growing child. Since these values and norms have become part of his own way of thinking, they naturally influence his vocational choice.

Many young people set their aspirations beyond what they can hope to achieve, while others do not aim as high as they should. This gap between aspiration and possible achievement will be discussed more fully later in the chapter, when we consider the factors that make for work satisfaction. It is enough to say here that in this gap lies one of the chief causes of occupational frustration and discontent.

Some parents encourage their children to make their own deci-

[5] Richard Centers, "Occupational Mobility of Urban Occupational Strata," *American Sociological Review,* XIII (1948), 197-203.

sions concerning a career. Others try to dictate what jobs their children should take, regardless of aptitudes or preferences. A doctor, for example, may try to persuade his son to follow in his footsteps, even though the boy may have no interest in medicine. A mother may try to persuade her boy to become a lawyer because of the social prestige associated with such a career. It is possible, of course, for children to be happy in careers chosen by their parents if a satisfactory parent-child relationship has been established and if the children possess the interests and skills required by the career. But frequently the desires of the parents do not coincide with the interests of the children.

Although all kinds of jobs are essential to the functioning of our economy, they vary in prestige value. When we ask people to

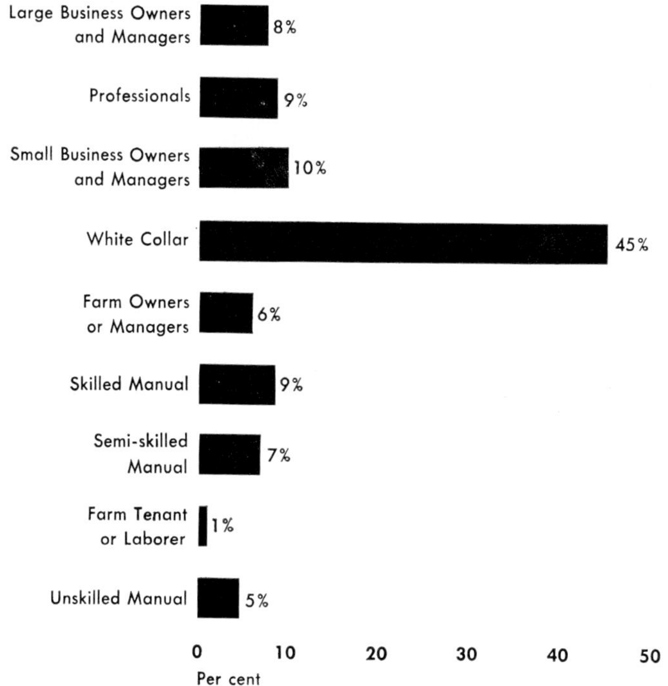

Figure 2. Jobs held by sons of white-collar workers. (Based on data from Richard Centers, "Occupational Mobility of Urban Occupational Strata," American Sociological Review, *XIII, 1948, 198.)*

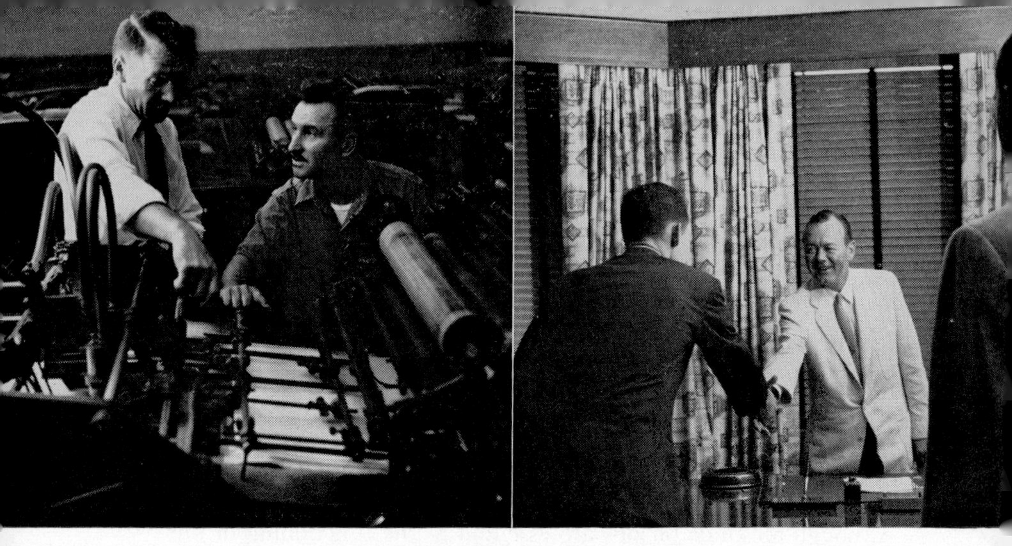

Although all kinds of jobs are essential to the functioning of our economy, they vary in prestige value; and this is a significant factor in job selection. (Left: Standard Oil Co. of N.J. Right: Cities Service Company, by J. Alex Langley.)

rank occupations according to status, we find that they assign the highest rank to the professions and to business executive positions; intermediate rank to the skilled trades, technical occupations, and occupations in the distribution field; and the lowest rank to semi-skilled and unskilled occupations.[6] On the whole, the same ranks are assigned to these occupations by all people, regardless of their own positions in the occupational hierarchy. However, a few studies have shown that different jobs are regarded from a different perspective, depending upon individual viewpoint. One, for example, showed that manual workers tended to evaluate their own jobs higher than clerical positions, whereas clerical workers reversed this rating.

A hierarchy of occupations is a part of the American tradition. Related to it is the culturally induced conviction that a man should better himself, that progress up the occupational ladder is a mark of success. But Donald Paterson, in discussing the conservation of human talents, attributes the choice of high-prestige occupations to what he calls false values permeating our society. He says:

> If we really believed in the essential dignity of labor, no matter how menial, and that the welfare of our society is really dependent

[6] Maether E. Deeg and D. G. Paterson, "Changes in Social Status of Occupations," *Occupations*, XXV (1947), 265-268.

upon the contributions of workers in every occupational group, the prestige hierarchy would disappear and each occupation would be ranked as equal to every other occupation. Since this is not so, the vocational counselor is confronted by tremendous resistance to wise occupational choices by innumerable youngsters and adults who seek jobs with high prestige rather than jobs for which they are best fitted.[7]

Interests

Our interests are dynamic factors in vocational choice because they direct our attention toward certain activities and occupations. If an interest is strong enough, it can motivate us to study, to seek training, and to overcome social and financial handicaps. If we are enthusiastic about the opportunities and challenges a job offers, we will be much more willing to tolerate hardships and delays than if we are only mildly interested in it.

Interest in an occupation can derive from a number of sources. It may arise because the work is of intrinsic value to us. For example, if we like to help people we may choose social work; if we are interested in the creative possibilities of children and young people we may decide to teach; or if we are curious about plants, we may select a career in biochemistry or experimental agriculture. In these instances our interest lies in the nature of the work itself. But interest may also arise from such considerations as money, prestige, and status. And it is possible of course that a job will satisfy both interests.

Parents may stimulate their children's interests by talking about their own jobs or by indicating in a number of ways the glamour, prestige, and other rewards that attach to certain occupations. And if a young person shows an ability for one of these positions, his interest will increase that much more. Interest may also be a consequence of work well done. If someone receives approval and praise for doing something well, and if his emotional needs are satisfied by what he does, he is likely to concentrate on these activities. Subsequently he may learn to enjoy his work because of the satisfaction he derives from it, without regard to praise or approval. His interest becomes self-sustained, independent of support from others.

Interests may also grow out of school and work experiences. For

[7] Donald G. Paterson, "The Conservation of Human Talent," *The American Psychologist*, XII, No. 3 (March 1957), 134-144.

many young people college years are a period for exploring interests and activities. For those who do not go to college the early years of work serve the same function. During this exploratory period young people are introduced to new activities and a wider range of job possibilities from which to discover new interests. They may meet teachers, scientists, doctors—people who enjoy their work so much they leave a lasting impression. Or they may meet people who care so little about their jobs that they discourage any interest.

Abilities

Although interests channel our vocational aspirations in certain directions, they do not entirely determine them. Interest in a job is important, but a person must also display the

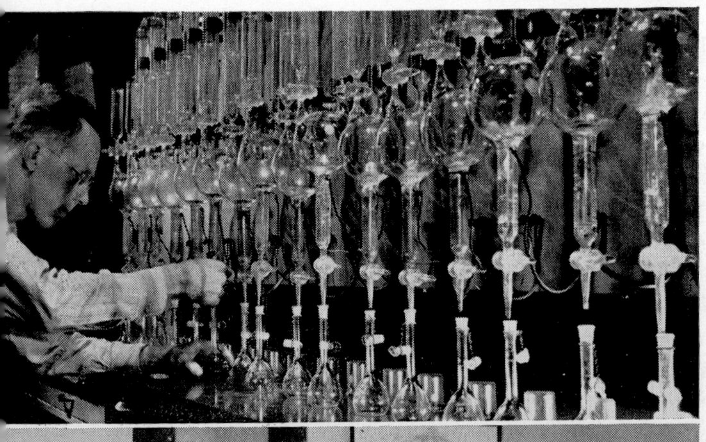

Different jobs require different aptitudes and different levels of intelligence. Some emphasize manipulative skills. Others emphasize social skills. (Top: Standard Oil Co. of N.J. Bottom: E. I. du Pont de Nemours & Company.)

necessary ability. We may, for example, be interested in painting or engineering but lack artistic talent or mathematical ability. In that case our interest may lead us down a blind alley as far as career choice is concerned. It is important, therefore, to consider thoroughly our abilities in relation to our interests.

Different occupations require different levels of intelligence. Many require, in addition, special abilities and aptitudes, and many tests have been developed to assess them. Some jobs demand a great deal of mathematical ability or good perception of spatial relations. Others require special motor skills, perhaps quick muscular reactions, good coordination, or fine manual dexterity. In still others resistance to fatigue, good eyesight, or ability to endure extremes of temperature are essential. And social skills—the ability to meet people easily and to work well with them over long periods of time—are of paramount importance in many occupations. Before we choose an occupation demanding any of these skills or aptitudes, we should determine whether or not we can meet the requirements.

The fact that we can do something well, however, does not mean that we are sufficiently interested in it to choose it for an occupation. Some abilities do not lead to satisfactory vocational choices. It may also be that our abilities would be useful in vocations we do not know about. Aptitude tests can help us discover our abilities, and vocational guidance counselors can advise us on job possibilities.

Job Requirements and the Labor Market

What we bring to a job must be considered in relation to what the job expects of us and what jobs are available. It is necessary, therefore, not only to assess our interests and abilities, but also to learn something about the labor market, both locally and nationally. We must determine, insofar as possible, what qualifications are essential to success in any occupation we may be exploring as a possibility.

If we find that ability is the chief requirement for a job we are considering, and if we are confident that we possess that ability, then we may choose the occupation if we are sincerely interested in it, no matter how difficult the work or the working conditions may seem. But if we believe that ability is of minor importance and that such factors as

Table 1 **Attitudes of Occupational Strata: Why People Succeed**

	N	*Ability*	*Ability plus other factor*	*Luck*	*Pull*	*Better oppor-tuni-ties*	*Combi-nation of luck, pull, and oppor-tunities*	*Don't know*	*For abilities differences are significant between:*
National	1,092	45.1%	14.4%	6.1%	7.5%	20.3%	2.8%	3.8%	
Urban									
A. All business, professional and white collar	426	52.1	19.2	2.6	6.2	16.4	2.1	1.4	A + B
B. All manual workers	413	35.8	12.2	9.4	11.9	21.0	4.1	5.6	B + A
1. Large business	54	62.3	20.8	0.0	0.0	16.9	0.0	0.0	1 + 5, 6, 7
2. Professional	73	46.6	31.5	2.7	5.5	11.0	2.7	0.0	2 + 7
3. Small business	129	51.9	20.2	3.1	6.2	14.7	1.6	2.3	3 + 6, 7
4. White collar	171	51.5	12.9	2.9	8.2	19.9	2.9	1.7	4 + 6, 7
5. Skilled manual	162	41.9	14.8	6.8	10.5	19.1	2.5	4.4	5 + 1, 7
6. Semi-skilled manual	174	34.5	10.9	8.6	11.5	23.6	5.7	5.2	6 + 1, 3, 4
7. Unskilled manual	77	25.9	9.1	16.9	15.6	19.5	3.9	9.1	7 + 1, 2, 3, 4, 5
Rural									
C. Farm owners and managers	153	56.2	9.2	5.9	3.3	21.6	1.3	2.5	C + D
D. Farm tenants and laborers	69	31.9	8.7	11.6	2.9	36.2	1.4	7.3	D + C

Source: Richard Centers, "Attitude and Belief in Relation to Occupational Stratification," *Journal of Social Psychology*, XXVII (1938), 169. By permission of The Journal Press.

influence and connections determine success, we may choose the job only if we believe we can cultivate the right acquaintances and make the necessary contacts.

A survey [8] of a representative cross-section of the adult, white, male population disclosed some interesting differences in attitudes toward qualifications for success. The subjects were asked: "Do you think that most people are successful because of ability, luck, pull, or the better opportunities they have had?" The responses included 45 per cent who rated ability alone as the determiner of success; and 14 per cent who chose ability plus luck, pull, or opportunity. Pronounced differences, however, were found in the attitudes expressed by people in different occupational levels. In Table 1, reading from the lower to the upper occupational levels, we see a steadily increasing number who believe in ability or ability plus some other factor as the determining element in success. At the same time, fewer and fewer designate luck, pull, or better opportunities. We are not concerned here with whether these beliefs actually do indicate the factors responsible for success. Rather we are interested in the fact that such beliefs affect job aspirations.

Over the last few decades, there have been decided shifts in the kinds of work people do. In 1930, 23 per cent of the labor force was employed in agriculture, as compared to only 9 per cent today. On the other hand, opportunities have expanded greatly in the manufacturing, distributive, and service fields. A breakdown of the occupations in the United States in 1962 is shown in Table 2, page 278.

Experts in population analysis project continued changes of considerable proportions for the future. Such changes are graphically represented in Figure 3, which indicates for the decade 1960-1970 a 40 per cent increase in professional and technical workers and considerable increases among proprietors, managers, and clerical, sales, skilled, and service workers. It is important to note that job opportunities will increase fastest in occupations requiring the most education and training.

Within each of the occupational categories listed there is a high degree of specialization. This is one of the outstanding characteristics

[8] Richard Centers, "Attitude and Belief in Relation to Occupational Stratification," *Journal of Social Psychology*, XXVII (1938), 159-185.

of our economic life. The Federal Security Agency lists about 600 occupational fields and approximately 40,000 separate jobs in its *Dictionary of Occupational Titles.* Although many of these jobs call for similar interests and abilities, the picture is still highly diverse and offers the individual much freedom of choice.

We should note that the problem of vocational choice exists only in a free society, where the individual is free to choose an occupation. In a free society the son need not follow in his father's footsteps, and the laborer who is dissatisfied with his job is free to change it. Of course this does not mean that changes will not involve some hardship, or that a worker's obligations to his family will not prevent him from making such a change. But it does indicate the absence, in general, of societal prohibitions of such change.

In the final analysis, however, freedom of vocational choice is meaningful only if it is possible for everyone to choose the job he wishes and for which he is qualified. A glance at the employment advertisements in many newspapers will reveal that not all jobs are equally available to all qualified people. Job discrimination, whether because of age, sex, race, or religion, may lead to tensions, conflict,

Table 2 ***Major Occupation Groups of Employed Persons, by Sex, June, 1962 (Thousands of Persons 14 years old and over)***

Occupation Group	*Total*	*Male*	*Female*
Professional, technical and kindred workers	10.9%	10.8%	11.2%
Farmers and farm managers	3.9	5.5	.7
Managers, officials and proprietors, excluding farm	10.7	13.6	4.8
Clerical and kindred workers	14.7	6.8	30.4
Sales workers	6.3	5.8	7.3
Craftsmen, foremen and kindred workers	12.8	18.9	.8
Operatives and kindred workers	17.4	18.8	14.7
Private household workers	3.3	.1	9.5
Service workers, except private household	9.5	6.6	15.1
Farm laborers and foremen	4.7	4.4	5.1
Laborers, excluding farm and mine	5.8	8.6	.3
Total employed in the civilian labor force	*69,539*	*46,311*	*23,228*

Source: *Employment and Earnings,* IX, No. 1 (July 1962), 6.

and frustration. Furthermore, discrimination represents a loss to society. This is due to the fact that a person who knows that certain potential employers are likely to discriminate against him may, in order to avoid unpleasantness, take a job beneath his abilities. Society will be the loser, because that person will not be producing at his full potential.

Since restrictive practices vary with different parts of the country, it is important for a job-seeker to study regional labor markets. Fair employment practices laws in some states increase the likelihood that job-seekers there will be able to enter occupations closed to them in other states.

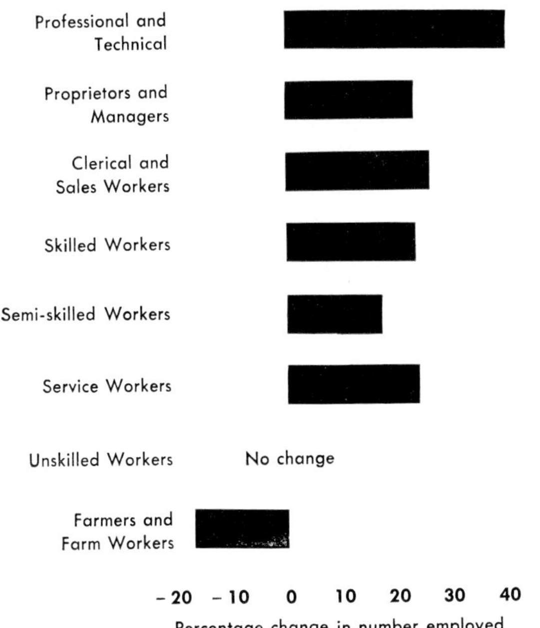

Figure 3. Occupational opportunities, 1960-1970. Job opportunities will increase most rapidly in occupations requiring the most education and training. (Adapted from Ewan Clague, "Demographic Trends and Their Significance," in The Changing American Population, *ed. Hoke S. Simpson. New York: Institute of Life Insurance, 1962, p. 19)*

Regional considerations are important in other respects. In one area there may be a labor shortage; in another, the market may be glutted. The home town may not need another lawyer or engineer, but there may be many good opportunities elsewhere.

If we have narrowed our choice to a given occupational field but still are undecided about a specific job, we can turn to a number of sources for information. Many public libraries have books and pamphlets listing and describing hundreds of occupations. High schools and colleges often have teachers qualified and willing to act as vocational counselors, and many educational institutions maintain vocational guidance bureaus. We can often get valuable tips from friends or relatives working at the jobs we are interested in.

But whatever our sources, there are several questions we need to have answered if we want to get as complete a picture of an occu-

What kinds of duties are involved in the job we are considering? Would we be expected, for example, to instruct others, as in the first photograph, or to function as part of a team, as in the second photograph? It is important to answer such questions to our own satisfaction before accepting a job. (Top: Cities Service Co., by J. Alex Langley. Bottom: Pacific Oaks College.)

pation as possible. It is easy to be misled by the label a job carries and the prestige it affords. We need to make a thorough analysis of each occupation we are considering. The following outline may serve as a guide.

1. *Duties.* What kinds of activities are involved? Are these activities connected primarily with people, ideas, or things? Does the job involve indoor or outdoor work? Will traveling be required? Are the tasks highly repetitive or does the job offer variety?

2. *Working conditions.* What are the physical conditions at the place of work? Are there safety hazards? What are the hours of work? Do the hours fall into a set schedule or are they flexible? What are the provisions for vacation and recreation? How long does it take to travel to work?

3. *Payment.* What is the salary? Can raises be expected? Are there employee fringe benefits?

4. *Opportuntties for advancement.* Is promotion possible? What is the basis for advancement? How often is advancement possible? Are there exceptional opportunities for advancement?

5. *Education and training required.* How much general education is necessary? Is trade school training required? Is there a long period of professional preparation? How much will training cost? If training takes place on the job, is the employee paid while he is learning? Is previous work experience necessary?

6. *Personal qualifications.* What special aptitudes and abilities are required? Are there any special physical requirements?

7. *Social relationships on the job.* What is the status of the person holding this job in relation to others of the staff? Does he have to assume a great deal of responsibility for his own work and the work of others or does he mostly carry out orders and assignments. Does the job call for teamwork or for solitary effort? Are there organizations, such as unions or business and professional groups, to which he can or must belong?

8. *Special advantages.* Is the job an important one in the community? Is there scope for initiative and special talents?

It is very likely that not all answers to these questions will be satisfactory. Perhaps the job pays less at the start than we had hoped for. But opportunities for advancement may compensate for this disadvantage. Perhaps we like most of the working conditions but find that we must spend a long time traveling to and from the job, or perhaps must even change our place of residence. We have to weigh the different criteria set down in the outline and evaluate the advantages against the disadvantages.

Working Women

Certain distinctive aspects that differentiate the situation of the working woman from that of the working man require her to deal with adjustment problems that he does not encounter. We shall discuss them briefly in this section.

From 1890 to 1962 the proportion of women in the labor force has almost doubled, going from 17 to 33 per cent. When we speak of working women, we refer to women who are gainfully employed in work other than running their own homes and raising their children. During World War II the number of working women increased greatly, and although it decreased again after the war, it continued at a higher than prewar level.

The war gave special impetus to the employment of women by creating a demand and by supplying the necessary social sanctions. But other long-term trends must also be considered. Perhaps the most significant of these is the shift in family functions. Many things women formerly made in the home are now prepared elsewhere, and labor-saving devices have been introduced into the household. Also, families are smaller. Accordingly, household duties of wives and mothers have decreased, allowing time for activities outside the home.

The employment of women is related to certain significant stages in their lives. There is a peak of employment among women aged eighteen or nineteen. After that the proportion decreases until around the age of thirty. Then it begins to rise again and there is another peak

Working women fulfill a variety of functions in our society. Top: nurse, secretary. Bottom: librarian, laboratory technician. (From Monkmeyer; by Max Tharpe, Lew Merrim, Nancy Hays, Al Bloom.)

around age fifty. These fluctuations reflect stages in the family cycle marked by the following events: completion of school, marriage, birth of last child, entrance of last child in school, marriage of last child, and death of husband.

Family status affects the likelihood of being in the labor force for both men and women. As shown in Figure 4, single men are less

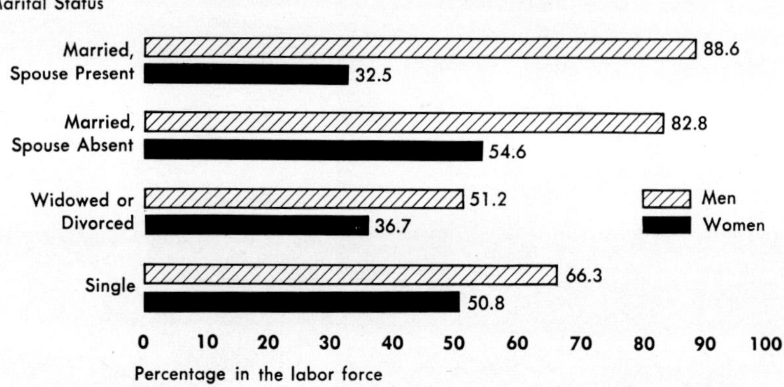

Figure 4. Employment status by marital status and sex, June 1962 (includes only civilian and noninstitutional population). (Source: Bureau of Labor Statistics, U. S. Department of Labor, Employment and Earnings, *IX, No. 1, July, 1962, 4.)*

likely to be working than married men, almost all of whom are in the labor force until they reach retirement age. For women, the stages of the family cycle affect much more strongly the likelihood of their employment. Thus, married women whose husbands are living with the family are less likely to be in the labor force than are single women. Women who have been or are married but who have never had children are more likely to be employed than are mothers. Among the mothers, those with older children are more likely to be employed than those with young children.

Attitudes toward women's working underscore and probably reinforce the distribution of women in the labor force. In a cross-cultural study[9] most of those interviewed expressed the following opinions concerning women's work: unmarried women *must* work; married women without children *may* work; married women with small children *must not* work.

Why do married women work? Why do they take on this function of wage earner in addition to that of wife and mother? The reasons are many and by no means the same for all women. Some women work principally because of economic necessity. Their husbands may be temporarily or permanently disabled, or there may be other emergency expenses to meet. Where there is no such economically compelling need, the wife's earnings may still help the family to maintain or improve its standard of living. Some women work because household duties bore them or do not occupy enough of their time. Some work because of a strong desire for adult associates. Others work because they want to make use of their education and training, or because they found earlier work experiences highly satisfying. This last would be especially true of women in professional and semi-professional work.

How does the employment of housewives and mothers affect their marriages? Does the wage-earner role conflict with the wife-and-mother role? Can the housewife be competent and satisfied in both roles? A good many articles on this question have appeared in popular magazines—phrased in terms of "career woman" versus "mother"—but the few research projects that have considered the problem have presented contradictory findings. Thus one study reports no difference in the marital adjustment of employed and unemployed wives,[10] and another finds evidence that employed women have smaller families and a higher divorce rate.[11] A more recent investigation shows more marital conflict among couples where the mother is employed and indicates that divorce and separation are more likely to occur among such couples.[12] In all cases there are indications of role conflict.

[9] "Images of Women in Society," *International Social Science Journal*, XIV, No. 1 (1962), 18.

[10] Harvey J. Locke and Muriel Mackensprang, "Marital Adjustment of the Employed Wife," *American Journal of Sociology*, LIV (May 1949), 536-539.

[11] Ernest Havemann and Patricia Salter West, *They Went to College* (New York: Harcourt, Brace, 1952).

[12] F. Ivan Nye, "Employment Status of Mothers and Marital Conflict, Permanence, and Happiness," *Social Problems*, VI (Winter 1958-59), 260-267.

Even if the working mother is employed full time, the major responsibility for running the household and caring for the children usually still falls on her. The demands on her may be too great and the resulting worry and fatigue may adversely affect her family life. The situation may be aggravated if relatives and friends reproach her for her dual role. Their criticisms may, of course, be due to deficiencies in her performance as wife and mother. But it may also be that their attitudes toward working women are such that, no matter what her performance, they will disapprove. If they believe that "a woman's place is in the home," her assumption of any other role will be unacceptable to them.

An important factor, of course, is the husband's attitude toward his wife's employment—whether he supports it or resents it. By support we mean that he shows more than a mere tolerance of her dual role, that he willingly shares in her achievements as well as in her setbacks and problems, that he is willing to work out practical adjustments in homemaking routines and leisure activities in order to ease his wife's responsibilities, and that he is proud of her achievements and feels no need to be on the defensive about her dual role. Such wholehearted support is possible only when the husband does not feel threatened by his wife's career. Whether or not he feels threatened will in turn largely depend on the views he holds concerning the proper role of women in marriage, and on the support he receives for these views from others in his environment.

Changing role expectations are partly reflected in the opening up of new occupational fields for women. The traditional functions of women—care of the sick, bringing up children, making and caring for clothes, preparing and serving food—characterize many of the paid occupations which employ the largest number of women. But millions of women are employed in jobs which have no such connection with the home. Though the largest number of women work in clerical positions (see Table 2, page 278), a growing though still small number work in such traditionally male professions as medicine, law, and engineering. Today we are even considering the possibility of space careers for women.

So far we have considered the possible role conflict of the wife and mother who is working. What about women who give up their jobs when they get married and start raising a family? Do they experience any conflict about shifting from a job to motherhood?

A group of mothers, the majority of whom had worked at some time during their lives, were asked if their work experiences had in any sense "spoiled" them for assuming their later roles as wives and mothers. Of those who had worked at some time, 48 per cent stated that they were delighted to have become pregnant. By contrast, only 29 per cent of those who had never worked expressed this delight.[13]

This group of mothers was also asked how they felt about giving up their work. Their answers are shown in Table 3.

Table 3 ***Responses Given by Mothers Concerning Their Feelings About Giving Up Their Work***

Response	*Percentage*
Much sacrifice. Enjoyed work, felt it was important, didn't want to give it up to have children	6
Some sacrifice. Mixed feelings. Glad to have family, but enjoyed some things about work.	13
No sacrifice. Indifferent, didn't particularly enjoy working, didn't mind giving it up.	33
The opposite of sacrifice; glad to give up work, more than ready to start having family.	28
Never worked.	7
Not ascertained (including: gave up work for reason other than marriage).	13

Source: Robert R. Sears, Eleanor E. Maccoby, and Harry Levin, *Patterns of Child Rearing* (Evanston, Ill.: Row, Peterson, 1957), p. 46. Reprinted by permission of Harper and Row, Publishers, Inc.

According to the authors of this study, these responses

> . . . appear to suggest that a woman's enjoyment of a job outside the home does not necessarily interfere with her acceptance of the maternal role when the time comes for the advent of children. In fact, if a woman shows a certain amount of interest and involvement in her work, whatever it is, the prognosis is better for her interest in (and enjoyment of) motherhood than if she is indifferent to her work. One cannot but wonder whether enjoyment of outside work and mother-

[13] Robert R. Sears, Eleanor E. Maccoby, and Harry Levin, *Patterns of Child Rearing* (Evanston, Illinois: Row, Peterson, 1957), p. 45.

hood are not both reflections of an underlying "style" of dealing with whatever life situation the individual woman finds herself in.[14]

These and other questions revealed that almost all the women in this study felt that motherhood was their primary job and expressed little or no conflict between the demands of a career and the demands of child-rearing.

Today almost every young woman expects to hold a job when her schooling is completed—at least until she marries, probably continuing into the early part of her marriage, and possibly again later on. But at the same time, marriage will probably continue to be the primary concern of most women. Nevertheless, since women not only enter the labor force after school but may re-enter it again later in their married life, it is probable that the number of young women seeking job-training will continue to increase.

Having considered the problems women face in reconciling their roles as workers and as wives and mothers, let us look now at the kind of problems they encounter in the working world itself. A group of Los Angeles businesswomen listed their problems, as follows:

Items listed as most important
- How to achieve recognition of abilities
- How to communicate decisions or directions without causing resentment
- How to improve personal relationships with associates
- How to accept responsibilities

Items listed as second in importance
- How to overcome prejudices that limit advancement, i.e.,
- How to be recognized as an individual rather than as a woman
- How to achieve compensation equal to that of men for the same job
- How to achieve equal opportunity for advancement
- How to contain resentment caused by obvious discrimination in job opportunities and salary because of sex
- How to educate men to accept women as equals
- How to improve ability to communicate effectively with job superiors
- How to utilize special feminine characteristics to promote rather than to defeat business goals

[14] Sears, *et al.*, *Patterns of Child Rearing*, p. 46.

Items listed as third in importance
- How to motivate self to sustain efficient job performance and derive job satisfaction
- How to retain identity as a woman in a man's world

We can see from this list that women share with men the problems in the first group plus the problem of communication listed in the second group and that of motivation listed in the third. But they have a separate group of problems based entirely on the attitudes of men toward working women. These they share with all minorities who experience the effects of discrimination.

It is interesting to note in passing that none of the problems that are listed here related to the fact that some of the women were married.

Factors Affecting Job Satisfaction

Many different factors contribute to our job satisfaction. Some of them, such as wages, working hours, employee benefits, and relationships with employers and co-workers, relate directly to the job. Others are more closely related to the kind of people we are—dependent or domineering, perfectionist or willing to get by with as little effort as possible, ambitious or indifferent. Still other factors derive from our group relationships outside the job, that is, from the satisfactions we get from our families, our standing in the community, or from participating in work-connected groups such as unions, business organizations, or professional associations.

Business and industry have become increasingly concerned with individual work satisfaction and with work-group morale. A high labor turnover—too many dissatisfied workers leaving the job—is expensive, especially where prolonged training is required to fill the vacancies. A number of employers have initiated or cooperated in studies of employee satisfaction and morale. Such studies have shown repeatedly that although pay, hours of work, and physical working conditions are important to job satisfaction, other factors, such as recognition for good work, a fair hearing for grievances, and congenial co-workers are at least equally important. We might call these psychological or social factors.

As part of an extensive survey on how Americans view their mental health, a group of employed men were questioned as to the things they liked and did not like about their jobs.[15] The replies were grouped into *ego* satisfactions and dissatisfactions and *extrinsic* satisfactions and dissatisfactions. Ego satisfactions related to the work itself —how interesting and varied it was; the skills it required; the opportunities it offered for the exercise of responsibility, independence, and competence; and the extent to which it gratified interpersonal and friendship needs. Extrinsic satisfactions were those concerned with money, job security, and working conditions. The findings, reported by occupational categories, are presented in Table 4. All of those interviewed indicated that ego satisfactions were more important to them than extrinsic satisfactions, but significant differences were evident among different occupational groups. Eighty per cent of the professionals and technicians reported ego satisfactions exclusively. By contrast, only 29 per cent of unskilled workers did so. Apparently those in higher status jobs *get* more ego satisfaction in their work; but they also *seek* it more, and as a result, experience more frustration when they fail to achieve it.

Fears Arising on the Job

We cannot be satisfied in a job if we are perpetually afraid that something is going to go wrong. Since they affect job satisfaction, let us consider some fears we face on the job. Different work situations may give rise to different fears, but almost any occupation can produce the following: (1) fear of failing, (2) fear of not getting along, (3) fear of not being able to learn, (4) fear of displacement, and (5) fear of new responsibilities.

[15] Gerald Gurin, Joseph Veroff, and Sheila Feld, *Americans View Their Mental Health,* Joint Commission on Mental Illness and Health Monograph Series No. 4 (New York: Basic Books, 1960).

FEAR OF FAILING A frequent fear among workers is that of not being able to do the job satisfactorily. This fear may be unrelated to a worker's capabilities. Even when he possesses the necessary ability to do the job well, he may still fear that he may fail. Such fear, whether realistic or not, inevitably reduces job satisfaction.

FEAR OF NOT GETTING ALONG While fear of failure is usually tied most closely to the question of ability to perform, the fear of not getting along has to do with social relationships. The fear may focus on not getting along with one's boss or supervisor and thus relate to a fear of authority; or it may focus on not getting along with one's peers or one's subordinates—the latter in the case of a person who has supervisory responsibilities. How well a worker can get along with other workers, is of course, an important factor in his job satisfaction and performance.

FEAR OF NOT BEING ABLE TO LEARN The fear of not being able to learn new skills, or to learn them fast enough, is related to fear of failing. When new job demands arise, particularly in technological areas where changes occur very rapidly—electronics or space-age

Table 4 ***Relationship Between Occupational Status and Sources of Job Satisfaction among Employed Men***

Source of ob Satisfaction	*Profes-sionals, tech-nicians*	*Managers, pro-prietors*	*Clerical workers*	*Sales workers*	*Skilled workers*	*Semi-skilled workers*	*Unskilled workers*	*Farmers*
ntion only ego satisfactions	80%	68%	39%	60%	54%	40%	29%	58%
ntion both ego nd extrinsic atisfactions	16	20	35	29	28	31	26	17
ntion only ex-rinsic satis-actions	2	9	24	7	14	24	29	17
ntion no reasons or liking job	...	...	2	2	2	3	8	1
t ascertained	2	3	...	2	2	2	8	7
otal	100%	100%	100%	100%	100%	100%	100%	100%
umber of men	(119)	(127)	(46)	(55)	(202)	(152)	(84)	(77)

Source: Gerald Gurin *et al.*, *Americans View Their Mental Health*, p. 159. By permission of Basic Books, Inc.

aviation, for example—the worker must not only be able to do a good job today but also remain up to date in his knowledge and skills, so that he will be able to do a good job tomorrow.

FEAR OF DISPLACEMENT Fear of displacement may be brought on as younger workers push to replace older ones, by age, or by the possibility of replacement by automation. Today machines are displacing men in many kinds of work. So many have been displaced that national retraining programs have been inaugurated to help them find other work.

FEAR OF NEW RESPONSIBILITIES Many people stand in the way of their own advancement because they fear accepting new responsibilities. Responsibilities may be seen as threatening because they require the utilization of new technical or social skills. It is well known that many technically competent people are not able to function at their highest levels of ability because of their reluctance to assume responsibilities.

There is no simple answer to the problem of handling these fears. Individual resourcefulness, company and union assistance, and education programs are all being utilized in the search for solutions.

Personal Approach to the Job

The attitudes with which we approach our jobs influence the satisfaction we get from them. Consequently we can contribute toward our own job satisfaction. The following approaches may be helpful: (1) realistic self-appraisal, (2) tolerance for delayed gratification, and (3) willingness to compromise.

REALISTIC SELF-APPRAISAL We must be able to take a close look at our weaknesses and strengths, appraising our goals in the light of what we can realistically expect to accomplish and evaluating what others expect of us in terms of our own resources. If, for example, we choose a demanding job because of its prestige appeal without considering whether we have either the ability to handle the work or the kind of temperament required to stand the strain, we may soon become frustrated and discouraged.

TOLERANCE FOR DELAYED GRATIFICATION In a job, as in most other endeavors, it is often necessary to endure hardships and wait for rewards, which may come only after long periods of concentrated effort. It is important not to become disgruntled because rewards do not appear as soon or as frequently as we would like. The rewards at the top of the ladder cannot be grasped the moment one starts to climb. If a person wants to become an actor, for example, he must be willing to begin at the bottom—to spend many months, or even years, doing "bit" parts and "stand-in" roles—before he can hope to see his name in lights.

WILLINGNESS TO COMPROMISE It is unlikely that any one job will satisfy all needs and wishes. If a person insists on holding out for what he believes to be the "ideal job" he may never get a job at all, or he may find himself drifting from job to job in a futile search.

Psychologically, success or failure, satisfaction or dissatisfaction in our work is determined by our level of aspiration. If the gap in either direction between our level of achievement and our level of aspiration remains too wide for too long, we may grow dissatisfied. If, on the other hand, we succeed in reaching one goal, we may raise our ambitions a little and strive with greater persistence and confidence toward further goals.

Conditions on the Job

Among the conditions that contribute to job morale are: (1) job specifications, (2) adequate communication, (3) authority relationships, (4) rewards and punishments, and (5) organizational image. Let us consider them briefly.

JOB SPECIFICATIONS We must clearly understand what our work and that of our co-workers entails, and our co-workers must know exactly what our responsibilities are as well as their own. Such understanding is necessary to prevent employees from exploiting one another by "passing the buck" and to avoid duplication of work. Duplication, for example, is not only wasteful but also discouraging, especially for employees who are interested in their work and try to do their best.

Usually we are hired for a job because we have qualifications that enable us to assume certain responsibilities and perform certain tasks. If, after we have started working, other duties outside of our field of interest or ability are thrust upon us, tensions are likely to develop that could have been avoided if the job specifications had been clearer. However, if job specifications are too rigidly defined, individual initiative may be stifled.

ADEQUATE COMMUNICATION Morale is improved if communication is a two-way affair, not merely a matter of transmitting instructions and orders from management to worker, but a channel that is open in the other direction as well. The extent to which our suggestions are recognized or our grievances considered will be an important factor in our job satisfaction.

AUTHORITY RELATIONSHIPS All work situations involve hierarchical relationships. Different jobs carry different responsibilities and different authority and prestige. Some people can carry authority gracefully—are tactful, considerate, and yet firm when necessary. Others, however, are stern, inflexible, and demanding, and their requests are met with resentment or perhaps even ignored. That the quality of immediate supervision is a decisive factor in morale on the job has been demonstrated in a number of studies. In one,[16] about 8,000 employees in non-supervisory positions in a large utility company were asked to fill out a questionnaire dealing with work satisfaction and morale. On the basis of the answers, 40 groups with high morale and 40 groups with low morale were selected and compared in their responses to this question: In what way does your immediate boss supervise you? Table 5 shows the relationship between supervision and morale. Notice that the outstanding response differences between the two groups occur in the extent to which the supervisor is interested in the welfare of the employees and in the greater flow of communication between supervisor and employees.

[16] D. Katz, "Morale and Motivation in Industry," in *Current Trends in Industrial Psychology* (Pittsburgh: University of Pittsburgh Press, 1949).

Table 5 ***Functions Ascribed to Supervisor in High and Low Morale Groups***

The statement that the supervisor	*was made in the high morale groups by*	*was made in the low morale groups by*	*Difference*
Arranges the work and makes work assignments	67%	69%	– 2%
Enforces the rules	54	54	0
Keeps the men supplied with materials and tools	36	41	– 5
Makes recommendations for promotions, transfers, and pay increases	61	22	39
Keeps the men informed on what is happening in the company	47	11	36
Keeps the men posted on how well they are doing	47	12	35
Hears complaints and grievances	65	32	33

Source: D. Katz, "Morale and Motivation in Industry," in *Current Trends in Industrial Psychology* (Pittsburgh: University of Pittsburgh Press, 1949), p. 167. By permission of the University of Pittsburgh Press.

SYSTEM OF REWARDS AND PUNISHMENTS The employee who knows his work will be appreciated is more likely to put forth his best efforts than one who fears it will be ignored or taken for granted. Even when we know we have done a good job, it adds to our satisfaction to find that others are also pleased with it. But if we have made a mistake we prefer to be corrected in private in a friendly, helpful manner rather than be reprimanded publicly. To be criticized in front of friends and colleagues is embarrassing and humiliating and may damage our self-concept.

We need to feel that rewards are distributed fairly. To be singled out for a lone award may profit us economically, but if our co-workers suspect favoritism they will view us with hostility. Arbitrary assignments of rewards tend to demoralize a work group.

ORGANIZATIONAL IMAGE Organizational image refers to what we think about the company that employs us and how we feel toward the people we work with. Do we get along well with our colleagues, or do petty jealousies and personal likes and dislikes impair the efficiency of the group? Are we proud to be identified with the firm we work for, or would we rather not mention our place of business?

Job Satisfaction and Personal Adjustment

Job satisfaction or dissatisfaction can affect our adjustment in other areas. The extent to which this is true depends upon the importance we attach to our jobs—that is, to the meaning the job holds for us. If the job we hold is our central life interest and therefore extremely meaningful to us as a means of self-expression and self-actualization, it will have a more far-reaching effect on our adjustment than would a job that was nothing more than a convenient means of earning a livelihood.

Since much of a man's life is spent on the job, it has frequently been assumed that his work must always represent a central life interest, that job adjustment must represent a crucial indicator of general life adjustment, and that if a man's job did not provide a high degree of satisfaction, his whole life would be disrupted and his adjustment in all other areas jeopardized.[17] But such an effect would occur only if the job were really of central importance, and recent research has indicated that nearly three out of every four workers do not regard their jobs as a central life interest.[18] When the job does not constitute a central life interest, it provides less ego gratification, to be sure. But it also causes less ego frustration.

It is also possible to trace a reverse process in which work adjustment is affected by general adjustment. People who seek therapy for what appear to be vocational difficulties often find that the source of their problems lies not in their work but in some other area. For example, the emotionally disturbed person, the person who lacks confidence in himself, who feels insecure in his relationships with others, may encounter a good many problems on the job for which the job itself cannot be held responsible.

[17] Gerald Gurin *et al.*, *Americans View Their Mental Health.* See especially Chapter 6, "The Job," pp. 143-174.

[18] Robert Dubin, "Industrial Workers' Worlds," *Social Problems,* III, No. 3 (January 1956), 131-142.

For Additional Reading

Bakke, E. Wight, *Bonds of Organization: An Appraisal of Corporate Human Relations*. New York: Harper, 1950.

Bendix, Reinhard and Seymour M. Lipset, eds., *Class, Status, and Power: A Reader in Social Stratification*. Glencoe, Ill.: Free Press, 1953.

Blum, Milton L., *Industrial Psychology and Its Social Foundations* (rev. ed.). New York: Harper, 1956.

Centers, Richard, *The Psychology of Social Classes*. Princeton, N. J.: Princeton University Press, 1949.

Dubin, Robert, *The World of Work: Industrial Society and Human Relations*. Englewood Cliffs, N. J.: Prentice-Hall, 1958.

Durand, John D., "Married Women in the Labor Force," *American Journal of Sociology*, LII (November 1946), 217-224.

French, John R. P., Robert L. Kahn, and Floyd C. Mann, eds., "Work, Health and Satisfaction," *The Journal of Social Issues*, XVIII, No. 3 (July 1962).

Friedan, Betty, *The Feminine Mystique*. New York: W. W. Norton, 1963.

Friedman, Eugene A. and Robert J. Havighurst, *The Meaning of Work and Retirement*. Chicago: University of Chicago Press, 1954.

Friedmann, Georges, *The Anatomy of Work*. New York: Free Press of Glencoe, 1961.

Ginzberg, Eli, Sol W. Ginsburg, Sidney Axelrad, and John L. Herma, *Occupational Choice. An Approach to a General Theory*. New York: Columbia University Press, 1951.

Gross, Edward, *Work and Society*. New York: Thomas Y. Crowell, 1958.

Hartley, Ruth E., "Children's Concepts of Male and Female Roles," *Merrill-Palmer Quarterly*, VI (January 1960), 83-91.

Havemann, Ernest and Patricia Salter West, *They Went To College*. New York: Harcourt, Brace, 1952.

Herzberg, Frederick, Bernard Mausner, and Barbara Bloch Snyderman, *The Motivation to Work* (2nd ed.). New York: Wiley, 1959.

Hoffman, Lois Wladis and Frederick Hoffman, "Social Change and Motivations for Having Larger Families: Some Theoretical Considerations," *Merrill-Palmer Quarterly*, VI (July 1960), 235-244.

Hollingshead, August B., *Elmtown's Youth. The Impact of Social Classes on Adolescents*. New York: Wiley, 1949.

Hughes, Everett C., "Work and Self," in *Social Psychology at the Crossroads,* eds. J. H. Rohrer and M. Sherif. New York: Harper, 1951.

"Images of Women in Society," *International Social Science Journal,* XIV, No. 1 (1962).

Jacques, Elliott, *The Changing Culture of a Factory*. London: Tavistock, 1951.

Jahoda, Marie and Joan Havel, "Psychological Problems of Women in Different Social Roles," *Educational Record,* XXXVI, (1955), 325-335.

Kahn, Robert L. and Nancy C. Morse, "The Relation of Productivity to Morale," *Journal of Social Issues,* VII, No. 3 (1951), 8-17.

Komarovsky, Mirra, *Women in the Modern World*. Boston: Little, Brown, 1953.

Lipset, Seymour M. and Reinhard Bendix, *Social Mobility in Industrial Society*. Berkeley and Los Angeles: University of California Press, 1959.

Lundberg, Ferdinand and Marynia F. Farnham, *Modern Woman, the Lost Sex*. New York: Harper, 1947.

Maier, Norman R. F. and John J. Hayes, *Creative Management*. New York: Wiley, 1962.

McGregor, Douglas, *The Human Side of Enterprise*. New York: McGraw-Hill, 1960.

Mead, Margaret, *Male and Female*. New York: Morrow, 1949.

Miller, Delbert C. and William H. Form, *Industrial Sociology*. New York: Harper, 1951.

Morse, Nancy C., *Satisfactions in the White-Collar Job*. Ann Arbor: University of Michigan Press, 1953.

———, and Robert S. Weiss, "The Function and Meaning of Work and the Job," *American Sociological Review,* XX (April 1955), 191-198.

National Manpower Council. *Womanpower*. New York: Columbia University Press, 1957.

Nosow, Sigmund and William H. Form, eds., *Man, Work, and Society*. New York: Basic Books, 1962.

Nye, F. Ivan, *Family Relationships and Delinquent Behavior*. New York: Wiley, 1958. See especially Chapter 6: "Employed Mothers and Delinquent Behavior," pp. 53-59.

———, and Lois Wladis Hoffman, *The Employed Mother in America*. Chicago: Rand McNally, 1963.

Paterson, Donald G. "The Conservation of Human Talent," *American Psychologist,* XII (March 1957), 134-144.

Pitt, Gavin A. and R. W. Smith, *The Twenty-Minute Lifetime: A Guide to Career Planning.* Englewood Cliffs, N. J.: Prentice-Hall, 1959.

Reiss, Albert J., Jr., *et al., Occupations and Social Status.* New York: Free Press of Glencoe, 1961.

Roe, Anne, *The Psychology of Occupations.* New York: Wiley, 1956.

Rosenberg, Morris, *Occupations and Values.* Glencoe, Ill.: Free Press, 1958.

Sears, Robert R., Eleanor E. Maccoby, and Harry Levin, *Patterns of Child Rearing.* Evanston, Ill.: Row, Peterson, 1957.

Smith, Leonard P., *Career Planning.* New York: Harper, 1959.

Spiro, Melford E., *Children of the Kibbutz.* Cambridge, Mass.: Harvard University Press, 1958.

Super, Donald E., *The Psychology of Careers.* New York: Harper, 1957.

——— and J. Crites, *Appraising Vocational Fitness* (rev. ed.). New York: Harper, 1962.

Sutermeister, Robert A., *People and Productivity.* New York: McGraw-Hill, 1963.

"The American Female," special supplement in *Harper's Magazine,* CCXXV (October 1962), 117-180.

Thompson, Clara, "Cultural Pressures in the Psychology of Women," in *A Study of Interpersonal Relations,* ed. P. Mullahy. New York: Hermitage, 1949, pp. 130-146.

Tiffin, Joseph and Ernest J. McCormick, *Industrial Psychology* (4th ed.). Englewood Cliffs, N. J.: Prentice-Hall, 1958.

United States Department of Labor, *Spotlight on Women in the United States,* 1956-57, Washington, D.C.: Government Printing Office.

Whyte, William Foote, *Men at Work.* Homewood, Ill.: Dorsey and Irwin, 1961.

———, *Money and Motivation.* New York: Harper, 1955.

"Working Women," special issue of *Marriage and Family Living,* XXIII (November 1961).

Zweig, Ferdynand, *The Worker in an Affluent Society.* New York: Free Press of Glencoe, 1962.

THE AVAILABILITY OF LEISURE

THE FUNCTIONS OF LEISURE

THE CHARACTERISTICS OF LEISURE

THE ACTIVITIES OF LEISURE

FACTORS INFLUENCING CHOICE OF LEISURE ACTIVITIES

Personal Factors

Social Factors

LEISURE AS A PROBLEM

Interests—Too Few or Too Many

The Effect of Work Experiences

Lack of Experience with Leisure

The Fear of Leisure

THE CREATIVE USE OF LEISURE

Adjustment to Leisure

11

When we think of *leisure*

we think of time to spend loafing,

time when no demands are being made on us,

time to devote

to any activities we choose.

Obviously, then,

our so-called *free* time

is not always *leisure* time.

For even when we escape from the demands

of our regular daily activities—

jobs, housework, classes—

other pressures and obligations frequently interfere to prevent us from doing what we would really like to do.

Before we turn to the question of adjusting to leisure, then, we might consider the availability of leisure in relationship to the various demands that are made on our supposedly unoccupied time.

The Availability of Leisure

If out of a 24-hour day we spend seven hours sleeping and one to three eating, we still have fourteen left. If eight of these are spent at work, we still should have six hours left on week days; while on week-ends, theoretically, we should have fourteen hours a day to devote to our own pursuits. This comes to a total of 58 hours, considerably longer than the average work week.

Figure 1 illustrates the average amount of time spent away from the job by today's workers as compared to the averages for every previous decade since 1850. We can see from this chart that there has been a steady shortening of the work week and a corresponding increase in the amount of time left over.

A portion of this time must be spent covering the increasing distances between the home and the office or factory. But even the remainder may not necessarily be considered as leisure time. To understand why, let us consider the following facts.

First, many people whose work weeks have been reduced to 35 hours have taken on second jobs in order to improve their financial positions. At the end of 1959, three million people in this country, or about five per cent of those employed in 35-hour-a-week jobs, were also filling secondary jobs. Second, even those who hold only one job have other obligations that take up their time after working hours. Sometimes these obligations may be connected with their jobs. They may be required to attend union or company meetings. They may need to entertain clients or business associates. They may have enrolled in trade, business, or professional courses in order to become more proficient at their work. Certain other obligations center around family affairs. There may be children to chauffeur; PTA meetings to attend; sick relatives to visit and run erands for; extra chores to do around the house; food, clothing, and other necessities to shop for. When we must devote our so-called free time to these tasks, it is not, strictly speaking, leisure time. Finally, a good many people need more than the seven hours' sleep suggested at the beginning of the section.

Even the leisure time that statistics show to be available is not equally available to everyone. The increase in free time resulting from the shortened work week is by no means equally distributed throughout all socio-economic strata of our population. It has been greatest among plant workers and office clerks, much less, if at all, among professional and top management groups.

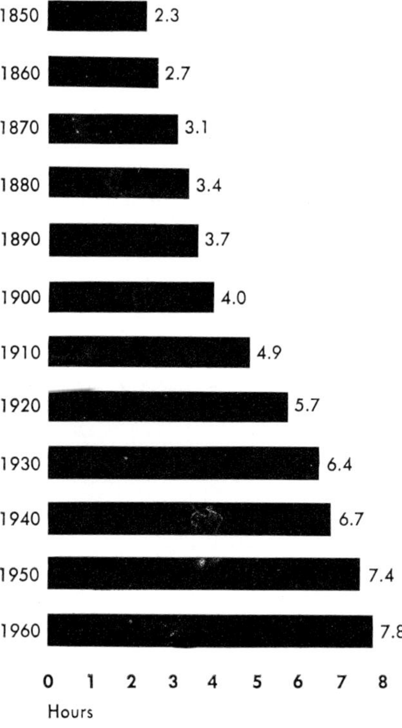

Figure 1. Hours free after work, eating, and necessities—1850-1960. Projected on a six-day work week. Includes seven hours sleep, one hour eating, two hours miscellaneous. (Source: Max Kaplan, Leisure in America: A Social Inquiry. *New York: Wiley, 1960, p. 38. By permission of John Wiley and Sons, Inc.)*

Regardless of these various factors, most of us do have some leisure time, although the amount varies from person to person. The more limited our leisure, the greater our need to make good use of what is available. Keeping this in mind, let us consider the functions we might like our leisure time to fulfill.

The Functions of Leisure

Diverse as leisure activities may be, we can distinguish three major functions they perform for the individual. The first is that of *rest and refreshment.* Having worked all day, we may not want to do anything but loaf. Tired, both physically and psychologically, from our job and from meeting our other obligations, we rest to relieve fatigue, to refresh ourselves, and to restore our energy.

The second function is *entertainment or amusement.* Leisure activities may compensate for the dullness and monotony of our work, or they may help to take our minds away from the pressures and responsibilities of a highly demanding job.

The third function is *enrichment.* Leisure offers us the oppor-

The functions of leisure: rest and refreshment might be achieved by relaxing in a hammock, entertainment or amusement by singing songs with friends, enrichment by visiting a museum. (Center: from Monkmeyer, by Lew Merrim. Others: Lehner-Kube photographs.)

tunity to develop interests, and aspects of our personalities, which otherwise might never find expression. In a leisure situation we can explore an object or a person more fully and objectively than when driven by an urgent need or a demanding goal. In the latter situation our attention would be narrowed, and only those aspects that might be instrumental in meeting the need or reaching the goal would be perceived and attended to. In our leisure time we can pause to think, to explore, to orient ourselves more fully in the world we live in. The exploration may take many forms. We may pursue and cultivate physical and intellectual interests, we may participate in community affairs, we may find creative expression for interests that would otherwise be neglected. This enriching function often leads writers on leisure to see it as essential to the development of a great civilization.

The Characteristics of Leisure

What are the characteristics that turn *free* time into *leisure* time?

As we have already indicated, leisure time must be time in which we feel *free from demanding pressures and obligations.* Furthermore,

leisure time must be time in which we can *freely choose what we want to do.*

In this respect, we might point out why the function of leisure is disturbed when the activities we engage in may not be freely chosen. We have said that leisure must rest and refresh us. It cannot do so when we are in a state of tension. Inability to exercise freedom of choice is likely to create this tension. We become tense, for example, if we must spend our leisure time alone when we long for company. We become tense in company if we would like to be alone. Similarly, we may get tired of swimming or of dancing long before our friends do, but we are denied our freedom of choice because we must wait until they too are ready to go home. We may get tired of playing bridge, but if we stop playing it disrupts the game. Whenever we go along with an activity because we feel that we *should* or *must,* the time spent is not experienced as leisure because the activity is not freely chosen. It is felt as an infringement on our free time, and this infringement is likely to create or increase tension in us. The psychological significance of leisure lies in its *tension-relaxing capacity.* Leisure is something to be enjoyed, something to help diminish tension and anxiety.

Finally, to qualify as leisure, free time must be *welcome.* The value of leisure is lost when free time is forced upon us, as it would be in periods of unemployment or after compulsory retirement. Usually such enforced idleness is regarded as a deprivation and in such an atmosphere leisure pursuits cannot flourish. Such time is not experienced, psychologically, as leisure. Even when the basic needs for food and shelter are adequately met, as they may be in retirement, a new concept of the meaning of time and a new way of relating to people must be developed if leisure is to be meaningful.

The Activities of Leisure

What do people do with their leisure time? A number of studies have attempted to answer this question, but their answers are many and often contradictory. To evaluate the answers we must recognize that they depend on a number of things. They depend first on the *kinds of people* interviewed—young, middle-aged, or old; men or women; rich or poor; the highly educated or those with little education; people on farms or in cities. The answers will also depend on the

Creative hobbies, sports, and parties are popular leisure-time activities. (Top right: Cities Service Company, by Anthony Linck. Others: from Monkmeyer, by Al Bloom, and Lew Merrim.)

time of the year we conduct the study. In July we are apt to get different answers from those we obtained in December. Again, the answers will vary according to *the way we collect our information*. Do we ask people what they did yesterday, or do we ask them what they did last month? Or did we ask them to keep a daily record for a month? Finally, how we proceed in a particular study depends on the *purpose* of our inquiry. A local agency concerned with leisure activities for young people in a small town will use methods different from those of a federal agency planning a budget for leisure facilities for older men and women.

These, then, are some of the considerations we have to keep in mind in evaluating leisure-time studies. Now let us look at a specific study,[1] conducted with a national sample of the population, which will give us a broad picture of the kinds of leisure activities people engage in. The findings are presented in Table 1.

As we see, by far the largest percentage of those interviewed named watching television as one of their leisure activities. Spectator activities outside the home, however, ranked very low. Only 4 per cent attended sports events, only 3 per cent went to movies in a regular theater, only 1 per cent to a play, concert, or opera.

The leisure activities listed here might be differentiated according to whether they are *spectator* or *participant activities*, *solitary* or *social* activities, and whether they are engaged in *at home* or *away from home*. Sometimes people tend to make value-judgments against one such category and in favor of another. For example, someone who prefers participant activities might decry the extent to which people choose to watch television or engage in other spectator activities. But such censure often fails to take into account the wide variations in the *quality* of spectator activities and the *psychological meaning* of such activities for the individual. Watching television, for example, can mean watching such diverse offerings as symphony concerts, puppet shows, legitimate plays, comic acts, discussion panels, musical reviews, news commentaries, Westerns, travelogues, and gangster, detective or doctor serials. Psychologically it can mean a stultifying

[1] *The Public Appraises Movies*, Vol. II, A survey for Motion Picture Association of America, Inc. (Princeton, N. J.: Opinion Research Corporation, December 1957).

addiction or an opportunity to expand our world. It can offer escape or enrichment.

A good many activities could be listed in more than one category. Thus baseball can be either a spectator or a participant activity, depending on whether we are playing or watching others play. Furthermore, it can qualify as either a profession or as a leisure sport. As the latter, through Little League or neighborhood competitions, it provides an enjoyable leisure-time activity for children and parents alike. As the former it offers outstanding athletes an opportunity to earn enviable incomes.

If we observed a large number of people enjoying their favorite

Table 1 ***Percentage of Population Engaging in Various Leisure Activities "Yesterday"***

Rank	*Activity*	*Percentage of all respondents*
1	Watching television	57
2	Visiting with friends or relatives	38
3	Working around yard and in garden	33
4	Reading magazines	27
5	Reading books	18
6	Going pleasure driving	17
7	Listening to records	14
8	Going to meetings or other organizational activities	11
9	Special hobbies (woodworking, knitting, etc.)	10
10	Going out to dinner	8
11	Participating in sports	8
12	Playing cards, checkers, etc.	7
13	None of those listed	7
14	Spending time at drugstore, etc.	6
15	Singing or playing a musical instrument	5
16	Going to see sports events	4
17	Going to movies in a regular theater	3
18	Going to drive-in movies	2
19	Going to dances	2
20	Going to a play, concert, or opera	1
21	Going to lectures or adult school	1

Source: *The Public Appraises Movies*, Vol. II. (Percentages in above table add up to more than 100 because many people gave more than one answer.) By permission of the Opinion Research Corporation and the Motion Picture Association of America, Inc.

leisure activities it would soon become apparent that almost any activity can qualify as a leisure activity. One man's work is another man's pleasure. Gardening, sewing, cooking, woodwork, to list but a few examples, can serve as either hobbies or as areas of employment. It is not the content of an activity that marks it as a source of leisure-time enjoyment, but rather the attitude and orientation with which we approach it. Another distinguishing factor is that a job organizes and regulates our time in line with specific demands to meet and tasks to accomplish, whereas if we undertake a similar activity as a leisure pursuit we are free to shape it and explore it as we wish. Furthermore, if the activity does not come up to our expectations we can give it up.

Factors Influencing Choice of Leisure Activities

We have emphasized that leisure is time perceived as free from urgent demands and pressures, time in which we may choose what we want to do. But leisure is also anchored to and influenced by our total life experience. As with other aspects of behavior, our leisure behavior is influenced by personal factors—our needs, interests, and abilities—and by social factors—our positions and roles in various groups, the standards we adhere to, and the opportunities available to us.

Personal Factors

In Chapter 3 we discussed the physiological and psychological *needs* that motivate our behavior. With the exception of the need for rest, it is primarily the psychological needs that we seek to satisfy through our leisure behavior. Our choice of leisure activities is particularly directed toward the satisfaction of needs left unsatisfied by our other areas of activity. The need for belongingness and love, for example, may lead us to spend our leisure time with friends or to participate in group activities. The informal social gatherings we attend during our leisure time enable us to get to know people better because, in the relaxed atmosphere these gatherings afford, we are under no obligation to accomplish anything and so can observe people from various angles. Other needs lead us to other activities. The needs for esteem or for competency, for example, may lead us to spend our leisure time reading or learning skills which will enable us to demonstrate our mastery. The need for self-actualization may lead us to spend our leisure in creative pursuits.

Personal *interests* give direction to our needs. They influence our selection of methods to satisfy our needs. Needs as such may be rather amorphous. Even though we may feel a need for esteem or for self-actualization, we cannot satisfy it unless we have some idea of the area in which we wish to develop our competency or creativity. Such needs can lead in a variety of directions. A need for competency, for example, may stimulate an interest in learning about a foreign country or about native wild flowers; in learning to play a musical instrument or to raise chickens in the backyard.

In addition to interests, we must also have the *ability* to pursue those interests. If we are interested in learning to play the piano, for example, but lack musical ability, the interest is not likely to contribute to the development of an enjoyable leisure activity. Probably it will gradually disappear. Interests may lead us to try various activities, but they can flourish and be sustained only if we have the ability to follow through.

Social Factors

It frequently happens that all the members of a family spend a large proportion of their time away from home. Most husbands and many wives go to work. Children go to school. But in the evenings and on weekends family members are free to enjoy a certain amount of leisure time together, and each member can exert an influence on the activities of the others.

Parents influence their children's leisure behavior in many ways—by their own attitudes toward leisure, by the leisure activities they themselves choose, by their permissive or restrictive attitude toward choice of activities, and by the resources which they make available and the diversity of interests they encourage or help their children develop.

Young parents frequently engage in child-centered leisure activities. (From Monkmeyer, by Roy Pinney.)

Children, in turn, influence the leisure behavior of their parents. Leisure activity is shaped to a considerable extent by the particular stage of the *family cycle* in which the individual finds himself. Parental leisure time, and particularly that of the mother, is frequently channeled into child-centered activities, such as participating in school projects or helping with such organizations as the Boy or Girl Scouts. Quite a few leisure activities are planned to accommodate both adults and children. Visits to the zoo, picnics in the park, barbecues in the backyard, trips to the beach can be enjoyed by both parents and children. When parents wish to spend part of their leisure away from the children—go to a concert or a movie, for example—they must first make sure that the children will be cared for by a competent sitter. And they must add the expense of the sitter to the cost of the outing. Only older couples whose children have left home can indulge in impromptu leisure-time activities.

Single people and childless couples base their choices of leisure activities on a different set of factors. Few of their activities are likely to be child-centered, and more of their time can be devoted to their own interests.

The individual's style of life is in many ways significantly affected by his *socio-economic* status, and this status may also be reflected in his use of leisure time. A number of studies have examined this relationship, and usually they have found that leisure behavior differs according to the socio-economic level.

One such study [2] grouped leisure activities into spectator-type activities, commercial-type activities, and craftsmanlike activities and asked members of five occupational groups how they spent most of their leisure. As indicated in Table 2, pronounced differences in participation in these types of activities were noted according to occupations, which are ranged on the table from the highest to the lowest economic level.

[2] Alfred C. Clarke, "The Use of Leisure Time and Its Relation to Levels of Occupational Prestige," *American Journal of Sociology,* XXI (June 1956), 301-307.

Table 2 ***How Five Occupational Groups Spend Most of Their Leisure (Percentage in each group)***

	Occupational Group				
Activity	(*highest*) I	II	III	IV	(*lowest*) V
Spectator	25.7%	22.9%	41.3%	36.1%	23.9%
Non-spectator	74.3	77.1	58.7	63.9	76.1
Number responding	(120)	(96)	(126)	(98)	(96)
Commercial	3.8	4.2	7.7	7.9	10.1
Non-commercial	96.2	95.8	92.3	92.1	89.9
Number responding	(124)	(98)	(130)	(104)	(99)
Craftsmanlike	19.9	21.4	21.9	23.2	30.3
Other types	81.1	78.6	78.1	76.8	69.7
Number responding	(124)	(98)	(130)	(104)	(99)

Among the activities included in the *spectator* category were watching television, attending motion pictures, lectures, plays and musical events, attending sports events, such as football, baseball, basketball, boxing, wrestling, and auto races.

Commercial activities included bowling, attending theatrical plays, motion pictures, playing pool or billiards, spending time in a café or tavern, attending a night club, dancing, attending sports events. If the activity generally involved the payment of a fee, it was classified as commercial.

Craftsmanlike activities included model building, sculpturing, painting, various forms of woodworking.

Based on data from Alfred C. Clarke, "The Use of Leisure Time and Its Relation to Levels of Occupational Prestige," *American Journal of Sociology,* XXI (June 1956), 305-306. By permission of the American Journal of Sociology and the University of Chicago Press.

The percentage of people devoting most of their leisure to commercial and craftsmanlike activities increases steadily from highest to lowest occupational level. Percentages of those spending most of their leisure in spectator-type activities also differ markedly with occupational level, but the pattern of differences is not the same as the pattern for commercial and craftsmanlike activities. Here a considerably higher percentage is found in the middle occupational group than in the highest or lowest group.

These differences in leisure activities among occupational groups reflect different standards of leisure behavior and different needs which the individual seeks to satisfy in his leisure time. The author of the study speculates, for example, that interest in craftsmanlike activities in the lowest occupational group develops because the man who spends his working hours on a job where he produces only a small part of a finished product, or who is engaged in more or less intangible personal relationships, derives great satisfaction from creating a complete, tangible product.

The groups they belong to outside their jobs influence people's use of leisure. Boys and girls are expected to play different games and often are very emphatic about what is boys' play and what is girls' play. Such *sex differences* continue to influence the leisure-time activities of adults. There are, to be sure, many activities which both men and women take part in, and which they enjoy together, but there are also others which are considered to be almost exclusively male or female activities. Knitting, for example, would be considered quite an unorthodox leisure pursuit for a man, but women are free to knit almost wherever and whenever they please.

Different *age groups,* as well, may spend their leisure time in different ways. A young person tends to choose strenuous games or adventurous pursuits more often than does an older person.

Finally, *cultural backgrounds* also influence leisure activities. Different nationality groups celebrate different special holidays, for example, and devote them to different kinds of activities. And certain religious groups adhere to standards which forbid some kinds of activities—such as dancing or playing cards—that other people are free to enjoy.

Leisure as a Problem

Free time that could be leisure time becomes a problem when we see it as empty time that we do not know how to fill in a meaningful, enjoyable way. When this happens we may become bored or discontented as we watch others who seem to be enjoying their leisure. We may become anxious, feeling that we are missing out on something. We begin to worry about not having enough fun, or to doubt that we are capable of having as much fun as we should. Such doubts and anxieties may drive us into hectic activities that keep us always on the go, as though by staying compulsively busy we could escape our uncertainties about ourselves. And though we may seem to succeed for a time, we actually find little real enjoyment. Such use of free time fails to serve the functions of leisure, because neither the boredom nor the mad rush is relaxing or enjoyable, and because our activities are not freely chosen.

Why does this happen? We shall consider a number of factors that contribute to making free time a sterile experience.

Interests–Too Few or Too Many

Some people have never developed any interests to pursue in their leisure time. Their lives are narrowly circumscribed. They may function adequately in situations in which external obligations and demands regulate their behavior, for instance, in their jobs. But when these external props are missing, time hangs heavy on their hands. They seem to lack the inner resources to overcome boredom. Even when some interest may faintly stir, they may lack the necessary skills for cultivating it; and the interest may not be strong enough to motivate them to learn these skills. Nor do they perceive free time as an opportunity to explore and develop interests.

Others have too many interests. A diversity of interests is an asset if we know how to choose among them. But if we are driven to pursue all of them we will find neither enough time nor enough energy to explore any one fully. We will find it impossible to spend our time in a leisurely manner, and we will end up exhausted rather than relaxed.

The Effect of Work Experiences

Our leisure is separate from our work and other experiences but not isolated from them. Some kinds of work may have such a pervasive negative effect on people that they destroy the potential benefits of free time. If our work is profoundly unsatisfactory, we may be unable to enjoy our free time because we are too fatigued, not so much physically as emotionally. We may find it very hard to shake off the depression which often accompanies such fatigue, and this depression can undermine our ability to enjoy our free time.

On the other hand, some people may be so highly involved in their work and so ambitious to advance themselves that they cannot use their free time for leisure. Instead, they are driven to utilize it as a means of furthering their occupational and social ambitions. They plan dinner parties, join clubs, attend professional meetings, read books—all potential leisure activities. But instead of enjoying these experiences they transform them into non-refreshing, non-amusing, non-enriching steps toward the achievement of a particular goal.

Lack of Experience with Leisure

Extensive leisure time often finds people unprepared to cope with it. If, for example, they have been spending all of their free time studying for a job, they may not have developed the interests or skills that will enable them to transform newly acquired free time into leisure time. The same problem often arises with people who are newly retired. One author [3] reports remarks of union leaders to the effect that the frequent breakdowns among men forced to retire may be due to their lack of any experience in handling extensive free time.

Retired or not, if we are inexperienced in handling leisure we may tend to perceive it as an obligation and thereby suffer the tensions discussed earlier. Since leisure time is available to us we may feel that we are obligated to enjoy it, and that the only way to do so is to

[3] David Riesman, "Leisure and Work in Post-Industrial Society," in *Mass Leisure,* eds. Eric Larrabee and Rolf Meyersohn (Glencoe, Ill.: Free Press, 1958), 363-385.

follow the examples of others who seem to be enjoying it. If, therefore, our acquaintances seem to enjoy playing golf on Sundays, we may feel obliged to play golf too, whether we like it or not. We may even try to convince ourselves that we do like it.

The problem is that we have no concept of what leisure is supposed to be, no models to follow except the examples set by our friends or our acquaintances. Therefore, we follow these examples even though they may not suit us.

On the other hand, we may lose our desire to try anything at all and just become bored, depressed, and withdrawn.

The Fear of Leisure

Leisure would be less of a problem, and many of us would have more leisure time, were it not for the fact that we are a little afraid of leisure. The cultural heritage handed down to us by the hard-working settlers of our country has given us the feeling that it is somehow immoral to be idle and that we have no right to enjoy ourselves for more than short periods at a time. We are somewhat appalled when we visit other countries and discover their more leisurely mode of existence. We have been brought up on such expressions as, "The Devil finds work for idle hands." We have heard people derided as "lazy, good-for-nothing loafers." As children we may have seen our parents hurrying back and forth—doing their own jobs and then, in their free time, devoting their energies to community projects, home-improvement projects, and church or school projects—and this may have given us the impression that we must always make ourselves useful too. We are afraid to loaf, we are afraid to relax, we are afraid to enjoy ourselves—unless we can justify the few hours or the few days we "allow ourselves" by working overtime before and after.

The Creative Use of Leisure

When we speak of the creative use of leisure time we are not referring to any particular kind of leisure activity or accomplishment. We are referring, rather, to the *emergence of something new,* to a *growth experience,* in our lives. For one person this may be new understanding of a friend; for another the discovery of a new book; for another an insight into a puzzling problem, coming to him as he relaxes in the backyard; and for still another the joy of taking a friend to a favorite spot in the mountains.

Leisure cannot always be creative. At times we are too weary and need to rest and sleep; at other times we need to be diverted from pressures and worries that intrude on our free time. But leisure appears to be most satisfying when used creatively in the sense we have indicated here.

Leisure time provides us with an *opportunity* for exploring and developing new interests and new skills and for increasing our understanding of ourselves and of others. It can give us many satisfactions, perhaps the best of which are those that make us sensitive to further new experiences. To pass up this opportunity repeatedly would be to miss out on enriching our lives.

For Additional Reading

Anderson, Nels, *Work and Leisure.* New York: Free Press of Glencoe, 1962.

Brightbill, Charles K., *Man and Leisure, a Philosophy of Recreation.* Englewood Cliffs, N. J.: Prentice-Hall, 1961.

Clarke, Alfred C., "The Use of Leisure Time and its Relation to Levels of Occupational Prestige," *American Journal of Sociology,* XXI (June 1956), 301-307.

De Grazia, Sebastian, *Of Time, Work, and Leisure.* New York: Twentieth Century Fund, 1962.

Denney, Reuel, "American Youth Today," *Daedalus* (Winter 1962), pp. 124-144.

Dewhurst, J. F. *et al., America's Needs and Resources.* New York: Twentieth Century Fund, 1955.

Donahue, Wilma *et al.*, eds., *Free Time: Challenge to Later Maturity.* Ann Arbor: University of Michigan Press, 1958.

Editors of Fortune, *The Changing American Market.* Time Inc., 1955.

Ennis, Philip H., "Leisure in the Suburb: Research Prolegomenon," in *The Suburban Community,* ed. William M. Dobriner. New York: Putnam, 1958, pp. 248-270.

Galbraith, John Kenneth, *The Affluent Society*. Boston: Houghton Mifflin, 1959. See especially Chapter 24: "Labor, Leisure and the New Class."

Graham, Saxon, "Social Correlates of Adult Leisure-Time Behavior," in *Community Structure and Analysis*, ed. Martin B. Sussman. New York: Thomas Y. Crowell, 1959.

Greenberg, Clement, "Work and Leisure under Industrialism." *Commentary*, XVI (July 1953), 54-62.

Havighurst, Robert J. and Kenneth Feigenbaum, "Leisure and Life-Style." *American Journal of Sociology*, LXIV (1959), 309-404.

Himmelweit, Hilde, *Television and the Child*. Oxford: Oxford University Press, 1958.

Kaplan, Max, *Leisure in America: A Social Inquiry*. New York: Wiley, 1960.

Larrabee, Eric and Rolf Meyersohn, eds., *Mass Leisure*. Glencoe, Ill.: Free Press, 1958.

Lundberg, G. A., M. Komarovsky, and M. A. McInery, *Leisure: A Suburban Study*. New York: Columbia University Press, 1934.

Neumeyer, Martin H. and Esther S. Neumeyer, *Leisure and Recreation* (3rd ed.). New York: Ronald, 1958.

Pieper, Josef, *Leisure the Basis of Culture*. New York: Pantheon, 1952.

Plant, James S., *Personality and the Cultural Pattern*. New York: The Commonwealth Fund, 1937. See especially Chapter 12: "Recreation."

Riesman, David, *Individualism Reconsidered*. Glencoe, Ill.: Free Press, 1954. See especially Chapter 13: "Some Considerations on Changes in Leisure Attitudes."

Rosenberg, Bernard and David Manning White, eds., *Mass Culture: The Popular Arts in America*. Glencoe, Ill.: Free Press, 1957.

"Sociological Aspects of Leisure," *International Social Science Journal*, XII, No. 4 (1960), 509-602.

"The Uses of Leisure," *American Journal of Sociology*, LXII (May 1957).

Veblen, T., *The Theory of the Leisure Class*. New York: The Modern Library, 1899.

White, Clyde R., "Social Class Differences in the Uses of Leisure," *American Journal of Sociology*, LXI (September 1955), 145-150.

Wolfenstein, Martha, "The Emergence of Fun Morality," *Journal of Social Issues*, VII (1951), 15-25.

ATTITUDES TOWARD SEX

Psychological Factors

Physiological Factors

ATTITUDES TOWARD LOVE

Psychological Factors

Physiological Factors

FACTORS IN MATE SELECTION

Impersonal Factors

Interpersonal Relationships

Personal Needs and Characteristics

PSYCHOSEXUAL RELATIONSHIPS IN MARRIAGE

WHY SOME PEOPLE DO NOT MARRY

Psychosexual Adjustment

12

In the United States,
matters of *sex* and *sexual adjustment*
are discussed more freely today
than they were fifty,
or even twenty, years ago,
but they are still surrounded
by a good deal of secrecy
and misinformation.
Young people cannot always find
books to enlighten them
or adults willing to explain.

Many parents and teachers still hesitate to discuss objectively one of the most important aspects of our lives.

In the pages that follow, therefore, we shall attempt to provide concise factual information on the subject and we shall consider some of the distorted ideas many of us still hold about it.

Psychological and physiological factors are jointly responsible for the attitudes we develop toward sex and love; and these attitudes in turn determine the quality of our psychosexual adjustment. Since our culture considers the sex relationship as ideally a love relationship, we tend at times to think of one as inseparable from the other. Therefore, our attitudes toward sex are reflected in our love relationships, and our attitudes toward love are reflected in our sex relationships. Here, insofar as possible, we shall consider our attitudes toward sex and toward love separately and discuss the psychological and physiological factors affecting the development of each.

Attitudes Toward Sex

We Americans are amazingly inconsistent in our approach to sex. On one hand we glorify it. Wherever we turn, at whatever hour of the day or night, sex rushes in upon us from the pages of our magazines and newspapers, from paperback book covers, from billboards, from television and radio. We heap adulation on shapely starlets and make lavish productions of our beauty contests. Sex has come to be an essential ingredient in many of our novels.

Yet, on the other hand, most of us seldom discuss sex unless we are exchanging jokes or gossiping about it. Many people still maintain puritanical attitudes and attempt to discourage those who advocate frank discussions and the circulation of accurate information. As a result, many have been denied access to the knowledge they need if they are to establish the satisfactory sexual relationship with a legally recognized mate that forms the basis of our entire sociocultural system. With so much at stake, adequate circulation of information is essential. Enforced ignorance leads only to error, and then to dissatisfaction and disillusion. Personal and marital problems frequently revolve around matters of sex. We cannot reduce the incidence of these problems by ignoring their sexual aspects.

Psychological Factors

Our use of the term *psycho*sexual indicates the importance of psychological attitudes in sexual adjustment. Where do these psychological attitudes come from? Parents' responses to their children's early sex curiosity probably play a major role in determining them. Thus, parents may exert significant influence over their children's eventual marital happiness. The process by which a child derives his own attitudes toward sex from the attitudes of his parents can begin while he is still very young. It develops not only as a result of what they say but also—and perhaps primarily, from *how* they say it—that is, from the emotional overtones that accompany their answers or instructions. In a sense, there is no parent who does *not* give sex education. Even one who is embarrassed and refuses to answer a child's question is contributing to his education by conveying the impression that discussions of sex—and, therefore, sex itself—are embarrassing and taboo. Furthermore, the child is likely to pick up the withheld information in some less desirable way.

In addition to learning about sex functions, the growing child and adolescent learn sex roles. Differential training for boys and girls begins in early childhood. They are given different kinds of toys and encouraged to engage in different activities. The mother and father serve as examples of typical male and female behavior. When boys and girls begin to date in their teens, they gain further insight into their respective sex roles.

We see then that sexual expression is socially conditioned and patterned, just as are our other physiological drives. Man's ability to reason, to judge, and to recognize certain standardized forms of social behavior has greatly modified his sexual activity. Previous experiences in interpersonal relationships influence choices of sexual partners. If, for example, a person has categorized love and sex into two opposing compartments labeled "good" and "bad," he may avoid sexual relations with anyone he loves and respects. Their different attitudes toward sexual matters may lead one person to frequent and promiscuous intercourse and another to abstinence from intercourse altogether.

Differential training in sex roles begins early in life. The little girl is pretending to sew—regarded as primarily a feminine activity. The little boy is learning to fish—regarded as primarily a masculine activity. (Lehner-Kube photos.)

We must, then, take into account psychological and social factors, as well as physiological factors, when considering sexual behavior.

Physiological Factors

How a person reacts to the physiological changes of puberty is largely determined by his earlier development. The course of development that leads to mature sexual adjustment in our culture may be divided into three periods. The first of these is the *infancy* period. During infancy, most children show an interest in their sexual organs and frequently may be observed touching and examining them. Before long they become curious about siblings, both brothers and sisters. These early interests and actions, however, have no sexual meaning or significance as they do in the adult. Sexual significance is acquired through learning the social meaning of such behavior. An understanding mother, who does not become upset over her child's natural curiosity about his sex organs, will help the child to develop a healthy attitude toward sex. But a mother who punishes her child for playing with his sex organs, or who refuses to answer his questions, may cause him to regard sex as something "unspeakable and untouchable."

Infancy gives way to the *latency* period, a neutral period that supposedly contributes little to later sexual development. At this time the child's curiosity about sex seems to diminish. It has been pointed out, however, that not all cultures have such a neutral period. Its occurrence in our own culture, therefore, may spring primarily from the sex-repressive nature of the culture itself.

During the third, the *puberty* period, the child becomes increasingly interested in sexual activity. Physiologically he has matured, but psychologically and socially he has not. He is learning the new ways of behavior required by new roles. He is in a transition period during which he must cast off his childhood dependency and learn to become an independent adult. He must assume new responsibilities and certain of his culture's mores and values.

It is at this time that the adolescent begins to have dates and to learn about "boys" or "girls." Before long he finds himself involved in the conflict surrounding the question of premarital sexual relations. How much petting is permissible and how far it should be carried is a frequently perplexing problem for adolescents and young adults. Their physiological capacity to engage in sexual relations must be weighed against the sociocultural mores. Wide cultural variations exist in the handling of premarital sexual behavior. Some cultures place relatively few restrictions on sexual activity outside of marriage. Our own culture forbids it; but there is often a considerable discrepancy between mores and practices, and each individual must evaluate the moral issue for himself. Many different decisions are possible. Some people reject the moral prohibitions without suffering psychological disturbances. Others reject the prohibitions but feel guilty and ashamed. Still others accept the cultural mores and observe the prohibitions. The prohibitions, incidentally, are likely to be especially strong if they are supported by religious ethics that consider extra-marital sexual activity sinful.

The frequency of premarital intercourse is influenced by individual training as well as the general mores. There are subcultural variations, for instance, among people of different educational backgrounds. The Kinsey report [1] shows that by the age of 21 only 49 per cent of those with some college education have had premarital intercourse, as compared to 77 per cent of those who did not go beyond high school and 84 per cent of those who did not go beyond grammar school. This would indicate that the mores forbidding premarital intercourse operate more effectively among those who have had more education. This trend, however, seems to be reversed where other sexual outlets are concerned. Masturbation and petting to a climax increase as the education level rises.

BIOLOGICAL FUNCTIONING At the end of puberty, around the ages of twelve or thirteen in girls and fifteen to seventeen in boys, the sex organs attain full maturity. At this time boys and girls become

[1] G. M. Gilbert, "Sex on the Campus," *About the Kinsey Report. Observations by 11 Experts on Sexual Behavior in the Human Male*, eds. D. P. Geddes and E. Curie (New York: New Amercian Library, 1948), pp. 70-74.

physiologically—but not necessarily psychologically—ready to mate.

The male sex glands, the testes, are composed of two types of cells, one producing sperm cells, or spermatozoa; the other acting upon all other cells of the body and producing such secondary male sex characteristics as beard and general hairiness, deep voice, broad shoulders and so forth.

The spermatozoa are extremely small, approximately one five-hundredth of an inch in length on the average. In a normal ejaculation, from 200,000,000 to 400,000,000 may be released. The spermatozoa are carried in the semen, which is a fluid ejaculated by the male during the orgasm or sexual climax. The penis is the male organ of copulation, through which the semen and spermatozoa are brought near the opening of the uterus in the female. To transmit them the penis must become rigidly erect in order to enter the female genital tract. Erection occurs during periods of sexual excitement, when the blood supply to the genital organs of both male and female is greatly increased and the vessels and erectile tissue become engorged. The skin surface around the end of the penis contains many sensory nerve endings, thus making the whole genital area very sensitive.

The female sex glands are the ovaries, located in the pelvis on either side of and immediately adjacent to the womb (also called the uterus). The ovaries serve a double function for the female as do the testes for the male; i.e., they produce the ova or egg cells and cause the appearance of secondary female sex characteristics, such as breasts, broader hips, and a rounder, softer figure.

After puberty, the egg cells mature and, under normal conditions, are discharged from the ovaries at the rate of one ovum for each menstrual cycle, i.e., approximately every 24 to 28 days. This process is called ovulation and generally occurs about the middle of the menstrual month, which is about twelve to fifteen days after the beginning of the last menstrual period. The discharged ovum is carried along the Fallopian tubes, where fertilization ordinarily takes place. The fertilized egg then passes into the uterus, which provides space for its growth during the period of gestation. During the development of the egg in the ovary, changes take place within the uterus and especially in the uterine lining, preparing it to receive the fertilized egg. If the egg is not fertilized, a large part of the uterine lining is sloughed away about every 24 to 28 days. The bleeding that follows constitutes the menstrual flow.

The uterus opens through the cervix into the vagina. The cervix is a canal-like opening through which the spermatozoa enter and through which the menstrual flow leaves the uterus. The vagina, which is a membranous tube or vestibule, is the female organ of copulation. Surrounding the external opening of the vagina is a membranous fold called the hymen. The hymen is almost always ruptured during the first sexual intercourse, but may be broken before then in other ways.

The external genital organs of the female are the vulva, which consists of the major and minor lips, and the clitoris. Under sexual excitement the clitoris, analogous to the penis in the male, becomes firm and erect. The clitoris is richly supplied with nerve endings and is, therefore, highly sensitive; it is the chief, though not the only, source of erotic sensation in women.

Although physical contact probably is the most potent stimulus to sexual excitement, it may arise from many other sources which, through a process of association and conditioning, have become sex-connected symbols. Once aroused, sexual excitement is kept going chiefly by the autonomic nervous system, resulting in a pleasurable sensation of excitement that builds up until an *orgasm*, or climax, is

Love has many meanings: "a feeling of being wanted;" "a desire to take care of another;" "a desire to be together forever." (From Monkmeyer, by Sybil Shelton, Lew Merrim, Eva Luoma.)

reached. In the male, the orgasm is crowned by the ejaculation of semen; in the woman, by a similar climactic response but without ejaculation. The orgasm is followed by a sudden release of tension accompanied by a desire for relaxation and rest.

Attitudes Toward Love

Thousands of people get married each year. If they were asked, "Why did you get married?" the most frequent reply would be, "Because we were in love." If they were then asked, "What does 'love' mean to you?" their answers would include such ideas as: "a feeling of being wanted," "a feeling of being needed," "a feeling of caring more for someone else than I do for myself," "a feeling of intense sexual attraction," "a feeling of tenderness and empathy," "a feeling of companionship," "a desire to be together forever," "a desire to take care of someone," "a desire to make someone happy."

The word *love,* then, even when used only in the context of love between a husband and a wife, encompasses many different attitudes. The scope of its meanings increases even further when we speak of

"mother" love; "father" love; "brotherly" love; the love of friends or self; of God, country, or life; or of wine, women, and song. The complexities inherent in the idea of love are further highlighted when we consider it in such contexts as "being" in love, "falling" in love, "making" love, "knowing" love, "losing" love, or "buying" love.

Can we unscramble these attitudes and come up with—if not a specific definition—at least a general description that encompasses all of them? We might begin by considering the origin of the word. One view holds that it comes from the Sanskrit word *lubhyati*, meaning "he desires." Another attributes its origin to the German word *lieben* (to love) which was originally spelled *leiben* (meaning *body*), thus *bodying*, the sexual contact of bodies. Webster defines love as a "feeling of strong personal attachment induced by sympathetic understanding, or by ties of kinship; ardent affection."

Next, if we break down these attitudes into their components we find that:

(1) One person thinks of love as a highly subjective *sensation* of varying degrees of intensity.

(2) Another person thinks of love as a process of focusing upon or relating to a *love object*.

(3) Still another person thinks of love as a specialized type of *behavior*.

If we then put these components back together we can include them all by saying that people think of *love* as *a sensation stimulated by a love object that produces a special kind of behavior toward that love object*.

What do people think this loving behavior is? By the same process of reducing many attitudes to a few general ideas we might distinguish four elements found in all loving behavior.

Loving behavior, is: [2]

1. Behavior in which one person *cares* for another. This might include physical care, as is evident in a mother's love for her child, or as might be evident in a person's love (care) for animals, plants, other persons. "Love is the active concern for the life and the growth of that which we love."
2. Behavior manifesting *responsibility* toward another; not in the

[2] Erich Fromm, *The Art of Loving* (New York: Harper, 1956).

sense of duty, but more in the sense of a voluntary commitment to respond to his needs.

3. Behavior showing *respect* for another in the sense of accepting him *as he is,* not as we might like him to be to serve our needs. It implies absence of domination or exploitation as well as appreciation of individuality.
4. Behavior which seeks *knowing* the other person to the fullest possible extent. This implies a desire to sense his feelings, and a willingness to understand rather than judge him.

Psychological Factors

We have already seen in other chapters how the extent to which our psychological needs are satisfied affects our attitudes toward other people and our methods of interacting with them. We have spoken often of the human being's needs to give and to receive affection and of the effects that can result when these needs are not satisfied. We have seen that the individual who receives little love will resort to various types of behavior in an effort to obtain the love he has been denied and that, in many instances, this behavior only produces the opposite effect.

People have different attitudes toward love and different capacities to give and to receive love because they have undergone different love experiences and love training. Attitudes toward love and capacities to behave lovingly are *learned.* Those of us who never learned as children to act lovingly or to accept loving behavior must try to learn as adults. A consideration of the four elements characteristic of loving behavior—care, responsibility, respect, and knowledge—can enable us to assess how much of our behavior toward others, and theirs toward us, is loving behavior. It can also help us to assess how much we manifest *self-love,* by caring for ourselves, feeling responsible for our own welfare, respecting ourselves, and knowing (or understanding) ourselves. Love of self forms the basis for love of others and exerts an important influence on our attitude toward love. If, for example, we reject, hate, or disregard ourselves, we are likely to develop similar attitudes toward others. Many people need to replace unhealthy "unselfishness" with healthy "selfishness." They must learn to love and to consider *themselves* so that they will be willing and able to love and to consider *others.* The saying "Love thy neighbor as thyself" can serve a useful purpose only if we do love ourselves.

Physiological Factors

We have noted several times that it is often difficult to separate physiological factors from the psychological effects accompanying them, and once again this should be kept in mind as we consider physiological factors affecting our attitudes toward love.

In each of the three periods of psychosexual development, a child fixes on characteristic love objects. In psychoanalytic terms, the three periods are labeled *narcissistic* (infancy), *homosexual* (latency), and *heterosexual* (puberty). During the narcissistic period, the infant and small child finds pleasure primarily in his own body; he is his own primary love object. He shows no preferences for either sex. He does not identify and choose acording to sex. As he grows older and enters the latency period, the "gang," or homosexual, stage emerges. (As used here, the word homosexual has no connotations of sex satisfaction. Rather, it refers to the child's choosing those of his own sex as associates and playmates.) Groups and clubs of the same sex are formed and the opposite sex is avoided.

As the child approaches puberty, as the secondary sex characteristics appear, and as he begins to feel the influence of various social and psychological factors, he begins to show an interest in the opposite sex. At first, however, his interest is generalized. A boy, for example, is interested in girls but not in any one particular girl. The same is true of the girl's interest in boys. The tendency to go together in groups and to shift attention to first one person and then another is characteristic of this stage. But as the adolescent grows older, this generalized interest in the opposite sex narrows more and more until it is finally concentrated on a single person.

The choices people make depend to a considerable extent on their previous experiences. If at an earlier date a young person suffered some embarrassment or shame or some traumatic experience with someone of the opposite sex, he or she may be very cautious in approaching others or may seek out only those people with whom he or she can be sure of feeling comfortable and at ease. Thus, the interpersonal relationships established at each level of development exert significant influence on psychosexual growth.

It is possible, of course, for sexual relations to take place without love, affection, or respect between the partners. It is also possible for a man and woman to love each other and yet fail to achieve sexual satisfaction. A love relationship is characterized by the enjoyment of an ongoing interaction between two people, while a sexual relationship is characterized by a periodic rise and release of tension. Sexual pleasure is most satisfying when it results from and is accompanied by love and desire for the partner. Where satisfaction is sought without regard for the partner, the sexual relationship becomes an exploitative one, in which the partner is merely a tool. If, on the other hand, the desire to give and the ability to receive are mutually shared, sexual pleasure is greatly increased. Successful integration of both the love and the sexual relationships enriches the total marital experience.

Factors in Mate Selection

The cult of "romantic love" has long flourished in America. From childhood on most of us cherish the sentimental notion that fate has decreed for each of us a perfect mate. Our culture encourages us to idealize the love object that we are some day "destined to meet." We relish examples of "love at first sight" and often claim that "as long as two people love each other, nothing else matters." This romantic love concept is the stock in trade of motion pictures, popular fiction, radio and television serials, and commercial advertising; and when we consider the feelings of inferiority and insecurity that characterize adolescence, we can understand why young people so eagerly accept a concept that promises so much, and why they tend to attribute to their potential mates characteristics they do not possess. Young people who accept the romantic illusion tend to think of love and marriage in terms of impossible perfection. They expect marriage to be a sort of effortless ecstasy, where "love conquers all." Such idealized projections frequently crumble under the harsh realities of everyday married life.

When young people start dating they have a great deal to learn about one another as well as about the culturally acceptable ways of behaving. We have already noted that when heterosexual contacts are first initiated they are directed toward members of the opposite sex in general. Furthermore, when boys and girls reach this stage in their development they are shy and somewhat insecure. Some try to cover up their embarrassment by showing off. Others may be so uncomfortable that they try to avoid members of the opposite sex.

When dating becomes serious and a boy and girl begin to consider marriage, they have entered the courtship stage. Each has made a specific, tentative choice, and the expectations aroused during this courtship period play a significant role in marital satisfaction. Such expectations must be understood not only in sociocultural terms but also in terms of the needs and the personality of each individual.

Let us now turn our attention to a consideration of the factors that direct us toward the specific choice that leads to marriage. These can be grouped into three categories: (1) impersonal factors, (2) interpersonal relationships, and (3) personal needs and characteristics.

Impersonal Factors

Environmental and social conditions that determine, for example, *how many* potential mates we are likely to encounter, are significant factors in mate selection. Certain cities and states are known to have more unmarried men than women, others to have more unmarried women than men. In general, urban centers have a slight excess of women, rural areas an excess of men. If this sex ratio is markedly unbalanced, some people will be unable to find mates.

Table 1 ***Rural and Urban Sex Ratios in the United States, 1960 (Males per 100 females)***

Area	*Sex ratio*
Rural	104.3
Urban	94.1
National ratio	97.1

Source: Bureau of the Census, Department of Commerce, Washington, D. C., 1961.

Residential proximity plays an important role in mate selection in spite of the great geographical mobility in our culture. When we speak of residential proximity, however, we mean not only *physical* proximity but also—and perhaps more significantly—*social* proximity. People living in the same neighborhood, for example, are likely to have a similar economic and social status, be members of the same neighborhood clubs or organizations, attend the same churches, and belong to the same ethnic groups. Since people most frequently marry within their own socio-economic class, and since people living in the same neighborhood generally share the same class level, we may expect residential proximity to figure prominently in marital choice.

A person with many social contacts has, of course, a wider choice than one who is more isolated and confined. Many people find their marriage partners among school or church acquaintances. Others marry people they meet through business contacts. But though business contacts do lead to a good many marriages, we should remember that in certain jobs, the chances of meeting eligible people are slim. In library work, social work, or teaching, for example, a woman has few chances of finding a man.

Other places that figure in the selection of mates are homes of friends and relatives, recreational facilities, resorts, and clubs.

Finally, *cultural restrictions* influence choices. If these restrictions are accepted by the individual they will limit his choice. Restrictions on racial intermarriage constitute one example, those on religious intermarriage another. "Marrying below one's class" constitutes a more ambiguous situation. It implies being subject to possible social disapproval. However, the very fact of ambiguity may discourage a person from choosing someone outside his own socio-economic level.

Many studies of the impersonal factors in mate selection have documented the fact that there is considerable homogamy in this country; i.e., most marriages take place between couples of the same class, religion, ethnic group, and educational level. All of these factors combine to define "the field of eligibles" [3] from which the individual can then choose according to his personal experiences and needs.

Interpersonal Relationships

The interpersonal relationships an individual has experienced in his associations both at home and away from home influence mate selection. For example, the emotional in-

[3] Robert F. Winch, *Mate Selection* (New York: Harper, 1958).

tensity of a son's or daughter's attachment to one or another parent is a significant factor, whether the emotion is love, hate, or ambivalence. Thus, if a man was over-protected by his mother, he may seek a wife who will deal with him in the same way; that is, he may seek a mother substitute. Or the opposite may occur. A woman whose father was strict and domineering may look for the antithesis of her father, someone who is gentle, kind, and even-tempered.

Similarly, marital choice is affected by the satisfaction people get from relationships outside the family. A person who is always embarrassed and awkward with members of the opposite sex may feel reluctant to seek a mate at all. Whether or not such a person marries may depend on whether or not he or she is singled out by a potential mate who is able to reassure him and increase his self-confidence. A person who meets other people easily, however, who looks forward to making new friends and who feels at ease in company, will be less

Young people who cannot relate comfortably to others may find mate selection difficult—as, for example, the girl in the left photograph, whose date is losing interest in her. In the right photograph we see young people who apparently enjoy making new friends and who will probably have a wide circle of acquaintances from whom they can select potential mates. (From Monkmeyer, by Sybil Shelton, and Lew Merrim.)

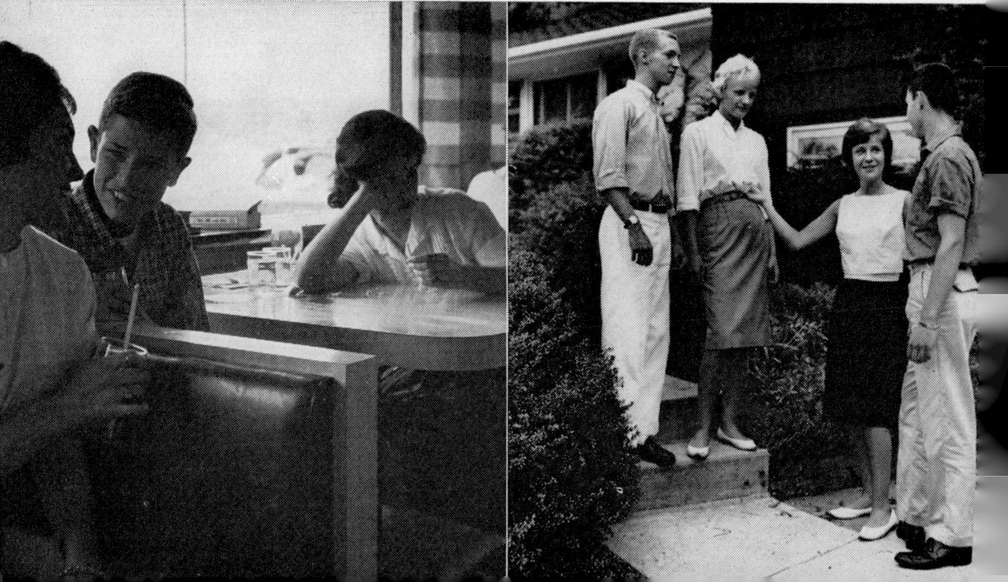

restricted in his choice and will probably base his selection of a mate on a different set of standards.

From these various relationships with others, both within the family and without, people usually form images of the desirable spouse, images reflecting their personal needs and social experiences. The images, however, are not necessarily constant. In childhood, for example, the ideal mate image may closely resemble the parent of the opposite sex, as reflected in the little boy's remark to his mother, "I want to marry you when I get big." This parent image is later modified by images of other relatives and of motion-picture stars, athletic heroes, and the like. For some imaginative adolescents the ideal mate image may be strong enough to provide physical as well as personality and social characteristics. Such ideal mate images may operate as more or less conscious factors in mate selection. The actual choice might correspond rather closely to the ideal, but in most instances the individual probably compromises or comes to realize that other factors are more important.

The following case study illustrates how a daughter's devotion to a monopolizing father affected her choice of a mate and at the same time interfered with her ability to adjust to marriage.

From the time she was a very little girl, Dorothy's father, a successful corporation lawyer, arranged to spend almost all his time with her and introduced her to a great many intellectual activities. He taught her to read, took her to concerts, to museums, even to political meetings. Her mother always remained at home, and Dorothy regarded her as a dull, uninteresting person who wasted her life in useless activities. She regarded her father as her ideal. She considered him handsome, intelligent, cultured, well-informed, and urbane. At a very early age she decided to become a lawyer, like him.

Dorothy continued this pattern of going out socially with her father through most of high school. Although she occasionally went to parties with the other boys and girls, she never dated any single boy until her senior year. Then she became strongly attached to a boy and they began going steady. After a few months they became engaged and Dorothy told her father. He was extremely angry, saying she was too young to know her own mind. But Dorothy did not alter her decision to marry the boy.

A few weeks later, however, when her fiancé placed the engagement ring on her finger, Dorothy became greatly disturbed emotionally and suffered an inexplicable feeling of guilt which she shrugged off as "just nerves." Her father still opposed the engagement and violently objected when, a few months later, she told him of her marriage plans. Her mother, however, was more amenable and decided that Dorothy knew what was best for her own happiness. With the mother's permission, it was decided that Dorothy would be married in a simple civil ceremony.

During the ceremony, as Dorothy looked at the judge, she experienced a feeling very much like the one she had felt when the engagment ring was put on her finger. She was nervous, emotionally upset, and somehow felt extremely guilty. Again she attributed the feeling to "nerves." After the ceremony the couple immediately left for a honeymoon. The wedding night, however, was a very unhappy experience for Dorothy. Although she loved her husband very much and desired physical contact with him, attempts at sexual intercourse aroused only the now familiar feelings of guilt and emotional turmoil.

After several repetitions of this experience, Dorothy sought psychological help. During the course of psychotherapy she began to realize the great depth of her attachment to her father. She also was able to recognize that her husband bore a striking resemblance to her father—a resemblance that her friends had previously pointed out but that she had been unable to see. She also recognized new significance in the fact that her husband's first name was the same as that of her father. She came to understand the feelings of guilt she had experienced. The engagement ring, she saw, had been a symbol of an impending marriage which would separate her from her father. She saw also that the judge had reminded her of her father. She realized that one of the reasons she had been originally attracted to her husband was his resemblance to her father, and she understood that her feeling of guilt in connection with sexual intercourse was due, in part at least, to her unconscious identification of one with the other. Gradually Dorothy was able to accept the fact that her husband was not her father and that she loved him for many qualities uniquely his own. Her relationship with her husband improved considerably and she gradually approached a happier, more normal marital adjustment.

Various studies have shown that parent-child relationships are among the most important factors influencing marital adjustment. The kind of psychological climate in which people grow up influences not only their choices of mates but also their ability to adjust to marriage. Furthermore, since the family is the main socializing agent in our culture, attitudes and values can be better understood when seen against the family background. Although there is a definite tendency for the children of happy marriages to have happy marriages themselves, the fact that parents were unhappily married does not necessarily indicate that their children's marriages will fail. However, a happier marriage will result if each partner is aware of the other's family background. Each can then better understand the other's personality, values, and goals.

Personal Needs and Characteristics

The fact that we feel at ease with some people and uncomfortable with others indicates that some people meet our conscious and unconscious needs and that others do not. One of the most important needs operating in mate selection is one we have already considered in previous chapters—the need for acceptance and recognition. People want their marital partners to accept them as they are, to love them in spite of their faults, and to make them feel important by encouraging them, praising them, and needing them. Most of all, they want to share with their mates a mutual need and respect.

But selecting a mate who appears to satisfy our needs does not insure satisfactory adjustment. A domineering man, for example, may choose a wife he can dominate. An insecure woman may select a husband who protects her and makes all her decisions for her. Such relationships serve only to reinforce maladjustive tendencies. Furthermore, as we saw when we discussed family adjustment, people sometimes hide their true identities until after they are married. A business woman, for example, may think she is marrying a man who will let her stay home and raise a family, only to discover after she is married that her husband expects to live on her salary.

By contrast a marriage between two people who respect each other's differences, who have taken time to get to know each other, who recognize each other's strong points and are not disturbed by each other's weaknesses, and who share a number of interests, have a strong basis for assuming that they can mutually satisfy each other's needs.

Our personal needs influence our selection of goals, as we have already seen; and our goals give direction to our lives. In selecting a mate, therefore, it is important that the goals of one prospective spouse be compatible with those of the other. If the ambitions of husband and wife lead in opposite directions, neither is likely to sympathize with or support the other. If the wife, for example, wants to be secure financially, but the husband is not particularly interested in making money, tensions may soon appear. Basic differences over politics or religion may also become sources of conflict—particularly where the rearing of children is concerned.

Thus, when a man and a woman are considering marriage, it is important for them to discuss the kind of family life they would like to have, where they would like to live, whether they would like to have children or not, how they would like to spend their leisure time, and so forth. Each needs to be aware of the other's expectations in as many areas as possible. People frequently tend to assume that, once the marriage ceremony has taken place, either (a) their areas of disagreement will be automatically eliminated, or (b) their mates will voluntarily relinquish their disparate opinions, or (c) the differences that remain will not significantly affect their marital relationships. It is far more likely, however, that these differences will take root, to sprout later on in a number of unsuspected directions. It is important to realize that when a difference of opinion prevents one or the other partner from achieving something important to him, the resulting resentment and hostility may turn a minor difference into a major disagreement.

Personal characteristics, if they are easily recognizable, may figure strongly in the conscious choice of a mate. We may choose someone whose habitual behavior pattern is pleasing to us. But one important personal characteristic that is frequently overlooked is level of emotional maturity. Emotional development often lags far behind physical and intellectual development; and it is a trying experience to live with an adult who is emotionally a child, no matter how mature he or she may be physically or intellectually. Many such marriages end in divorce or separation.

There are a number of clues to emotional immaturity. One is excessive dependence on others. An overly dependent person may have been strictly disciplined as a child and never permitted to develop the self-confidence essential to emotional maturity. The person who must always have his own way is also emotionally immature. He may have been excessively indulged or extremely frustrated as a child. Another sign of emotional immaturity, and a great source of marital tension, is moodiness. A man married to a moody wife never knows when she will be cheerful and when she will be gloomy. Her emotional states may seem unrelated either to events or to his own behavior. Incidents that almost anyone else would take in stride may depress her or elate her excessively; and it is difficult to anticipate which reaction will materialize. Such behavior in one spouse can cause the other to become uncertain, tense, and irritable. The emotionally immature person also frequently resorts to defense mechanisms. He may rationalize or withdraw or daydream in order to escape facing his problems.

In selecting a mate it is helpful to be aware of these signs of emotional immaturity.

Psychosexual Relationships in Marriage

Clinical case material shows that sexual disharmony frequently accompanies marital discord, and for this reason many people assume it is a *cause* of marital difficulties. But many writers in this field believe that sexual maladjustment is more often a *symptom* of marital unhappiness than a cause. And in cases where it is a cause, it is rarely the only one. As John Levy and Ruth Munroe express the relationship in their book, *The Happy Family:* [4]

> Now the appearance of snowstorms is regularly preceded by the dropping of leaves from the trees. Nevertheless we do not consider

[4] J. Levy and R. Munroe, *The Happy Family* (New York: Knopf, 1947), p. 109. Reprinted by permission of Alfred A. Knopf, Inc.

> the fall of leaves responsible for snow. We know very well that the coming of winter produces both these effects. Just so it may be that some fundamental struggle between husband and wife brings about sexual disharmony and the other evidences of discord which make them consider their marriage a failure. Actually the relationship between sexual incompatibility and the failure of marriage is very intricate. I believe that close study of the problem will show us that it is both cause and effect, and also perhaps just an accompaniment, an expression of general lack of harmony.

Once sexual maladjustment arises it may aggravate other conflicts that are already throwing the marital relationship off balance. What were minor irritations may, after sexual maladjustment develops, become major sources of conflict. We discussed some of these other sources of irritation in Chapter 8.

Table 2 ***Length of Time Required to Adjust in Sex Relations and Happiness in Marriage***

Length of time required	*Very happy*	*Happy*	*Average*
Satisfactory from the beginning	53%	36%	11%
1-12 months	61	30	9
1-20 years	43	38	19
Never satisfactory	11	36	53

Source: Judson T. Landis and Mary G. Landis, *Building a Successful Marriage*, 4th ed. (Englewood Cliffs, N. J.: Prentice-Hall, 1963), p. 308. (This study included 409 couples.)

Here we shall focus on psychosexual factors that are significant to the marital relationship.

As in other areas of adjustment, sexual adjustment is a continuing process and a learning experience. Some couples may achieve a satisfactory sexual relationship from the beginning of their marriages. Others may never achieve it and still consider their marriages happy ones. In general, however, satisfactory sexual relations are more frequently characteristic of very happy marriages than of less happy ones (see Table 2).

Either spouse may be sexually dissatisfied for a number of reasons. To begin with, it is possible that the sex drive is stronger in one partner and that he or she may desire sexual intercourse more frequently than the other. One study [5] used the ratio between actual and preferred frequency of intercourse as one of the basic sexual adjustment factors, and on the basis of these ratios classified subjects into five categories: (a) marked, and (b) moderate, hunger, when the frequency of preferred intercourse was greater than that of actual intercourse; (c) optimum satisfaction, where the frequencies were the same; and (d) moderate, and (e) marked, satiety, where frequency of actual intercourse exceeded frequency of preferred intercourse. It was found that slightly more than half of the husbands and wives obtained optimum satisfaction; and this group, in general, had the highest happiness scores. The greater the degree of unsatisfied hunger or of satiation the lower the general trend of happiness. It was found also that the happiness of a spouse depended not only on the spouse's own sexual satisfaction, but also on the sexual satisfaction of his partner. For example, even if the husband enjoys approximately the intercourse frequency that he prefers, he as well as his wife will have a moderately low happiness score if his wife suffers marked sex hunger. We should keep in mind, however, that the scores compared are means, and that within each group there is considerable variation.

We might say, then, that in a happy marriage the sexual satisfaction of one partner depends on the satisfaction of the other. Fulfilling the desire of one is a condition of satisfaction for the other. The husband and wife play complementary, not conflicting, roles.

In his summary of the relative importance of sexual and psychological compatibility, Terman stated:

> Our data do not confirm the view so often heard that the key to happiness in marriage is nearly always to be found in sexual compatibility. They indicate, instead, that the influence of the sexual factors is at most no greater than that of the combined personality and background factors, and that it is probably less. The problem is complicated by the fact that the testimony of husband and wife regarding their sexual compatibility is influenced by their psychological compatibility. Couples who are psychologically well mated are likely to show a surprising tolerance for the things that are not satisfactory in their sexual

[5] Lewis M. Terman, *Psychological Factors in Marital Happiness* (New York and London: McGraw-Hill, 1938), pp. 201, 202, 204. By permission of McGraw-Hill Book Company, Inc.

> relationships. The psychologically ill-mated show no such tolerance but instead are prone to exaggeration in their reports on sexual maladjustment. The two sexual factors of genuine importance are wife's orgasm adequacy and relative strength of sex drive in the two spouses.[6]

Frequency of intercourse as such—whether once or twice a month or more than ten times—showed only a very slight correlation with marital happiness. A rather high frequency of intercourse was found in unhappy marriages, which may imply that sex is the only type of communication still satisfying to the husband and wife, or that sex is used as a possible means to revive the waning affection between the partners.

Another factor in sexual adjustment involves the orgasm. Frequently the man arrives at the point of orgasm more quickly than the woman. Unless he restrains himself, she will not find the emotional release the orgasm affords. Yet Terman found that wife's orgasm adequacy was the most important of the sex factors. In the population sample he studied, 67 per cent of the wives said that they experienced orgasm usually or always, and 33 per cent replied that they experienced it rarely or never. The mean happiness score of wives increases as the frequency of adequate orgasm experience increases; the same is true of the happiness scores of the husbands of these wives.

Again these are averages; the range of scores in each group shows a high happiness score for some of the wives who never or rarely experience orgasm and a low happiness score for some who always or usually do.

Women who have strong sex drives can have just as much difficulty reaching an orgasm as women in whom the sex drive is weak. Both conditions are included under the term *frigidity*. The causes for frigidity are not well known. Clinical evidence indicates that many factors are involved. It may stem from biological factors, although endocrine therapy has not generally been successful in effecting cures. Or it may be related to the woman's attitudes toward sex, especially if she learned as a child to regard everything related to the sex act with revulsion. Frigidity may also result from a traumatic experience —an attempted rape, for example.

[6] Terman, *Psychological Factors in Marital Happiness*, p. 376. By permission of McGraw-Hill Book Company, Inc.

Because of the multiplicity of factors, no one method of treatment can be advocated as being the answer in all cases. Help for some of these women may be obtained from psychotherapy or from instruction in sex techniques. Even those women who are not helped may be able to make a happy adjustment with their husbands by reducing the high value they or their husbands may have placed on sex and by emphasizing other values in their marriages.

The counterpart to frigidity in women is impotence in men. Impotence may manifest itself in failure to produce an erection, in premature ejaculation, or simply in a very low sexual interest and drive. Clinical evidence indicates that impotence generally is a psychological problem. Often it is a temporary condition, caused by general tension and fatigue. Where it is more lasting it may spring from disturbed emotional relationships with the wife or from the husband's own personality problems.

It is apparent from a survey of the work in this field that problems of sexual adjustment affect millions of couples. A better understanding of the factors that influence sexual relationships is needed.

Why Some People Do Not Marry

We may consider the question of why people do not marry within the same frame of reference we used in discussing mate selection. A person may not marry because he has no opportunity to meet possible partners. In certain lines of work, as we have already indicated, men and women are relatively isolated from one another, and in some parts of the country the sex ratio is decidedly unfavorable for one or the other sex. And members of socially prominent families who are strongly status-conscious may be very restricted in their choice of mates.

Again, the relationship a person has had with his parents may make the choice of a mate very difficult for him. He may have developed an excessive identification with one or the other of his parents. A man may be very close to his mother, for example—psychologically he may not have been weaned—and in looking for a mate he unconsciously looks for someone to take his mother's place. It is not likely he will find such a mate. Someone else may have been overindulged as a child, and because he is accustomed to having his wishes catered to he may find it difficult to accept the initiative and responsibility that go with marriage.

Closely related to the fear of accepting responsibility is the fear of losing one's freedom or independence. One of the many common expressions implying that getting married is tantamount to losing one's freedom is the description of marriage as "being tied down with a ball and chain."

Many people do not marry because they set their goals too high. Their ideas of what they want in a mate are quite removed from reality. They are searching for a fantasy, an ideal that no one could possibly fit. Often this delusion can be traced to parental influence. A mother may be overambitious for her son and daughter and may instill in them the belief that they are much too good for anyone else. In order to avoid quarreling with their mother, the children may give in to her and wait for the "ideal" mate—who, of course, cannot materialize.

Frequently the idealized picture of the mate is a defense. A person who has been disappointed in love may now set his goal so high that his chances of becoming involved again, and perhaps of again meeting failure and disappointment, are reduced. He is afraid of being hurt again and the idealization functions as a protective armor.

Certain other cultural values and pressures may prevent young people from marrying. First, and this is especially characteristic of the middle class, is the demand that young people make a "good" marriage. Parents usually prefer that their children marry into economically and socially favorable positions, and they tend to fight against the possibility of a child's marrying "beneath his class."

Secondly, a great deal of pressure is exerted against the idea of marrying too young. Although adolescents may be sexually mature, few have the means to support a family. Therefore, early attachments may be broken up, and these breakups may be very disturbing for the individuals involved.

Often pressures that reflect cultural mores are supplemented by other pressures, reflecting the strong personality needs of the parents. The father, for instance, who prevents his son from marrying the girl he wants to marry may justify his action on the ground that he acted for the boy's own good. Actually, however, the father probably has identified himself strongly with his son and hopes to attain through the boy's success and achievements a little of the glory and adulation he himself was denied, perhaps because he married early and had to support a family. The father regards the marriage as a threat to his hopes. The son, on the other hand, is beset by a conflict of loyalties that may well disturb his relationships both with his father and with the girl he loves.

If a marriage is postponed or a love affair broken off, the individuals concerned may build up defenses against future emotional attachments as a safeguard against being hurt again. On the other hand, it is quite possible for individuals to grow rather than to decline in their capacity to love.

For Additional Reading

Baruch, Dorothy Walter, *New Ways in Sex Education: A Guide for Parents and Teachers*. New York: McGraw-Hill, 1959.

Benda, Clemens E., *The Image of Love*. Glencoe, Ill.: Free Press, 1961.

Bowman, Henry A., *Marriage for Moderns* (4th ed.). New York: McGraw-Hill, 1960.

Burgess, Ernest W. and Paul Wallin, *Engagement and Marriage*. Chicago: Lippincott, 1953.

Christensen, Harold T., *Marriage Analysis*. New York: Ronald, 1958.

——— and George R. Carpenter, "Value-Behavior Discrepancies Regarding Premarital Coitus in Three Western Cultures," *American Sociological Review*, XXVII (February 1962), 66-74.

Coleman, James S., *The Adolescent Society*. New York: Free Press of Glencoe, 1961.

Duvall, Evelyn M. and Reuben Hill, *When You Marry* (rev. ed.). Boston: Heath, 1953.

Ehrmann, Winston, *Premarital Dating Behavior*. New York: Holt, 1959.

Ellis, Albert, *The Art and Science of Love*. New York: Lyle Stuart, 1960.

Fromm, Erich, *The Art of Loving*. New York: Harper, 1956.

Geddes, Donald Porter and Enid Curie, eds., *About the Kinsey Report. Observations by 11 Experts on Sexual Behavior in the Human Male*. New York: The New American Library, 1948.

Goode, William J., "The Theoretical Importance of Love," *American Sociological Review*, XXIV (February 1959), 38-47.

Harlow, Harry F., "The Nature of Love," *American Psychologist*, XIII (December 1958), 673-685.

Himmelhoch, Jerome and Sylvia Fleis Fava, eds., *Sexual Behavior in American Society*. New York: Norton, 1955.

Kardiner, Abram, *Sex and Morality*. Indianapolis: Bobbs-Merrill, 1954.

Kephart, William M., *The Family, Society, and the Individual*. Boston: Houghton Mifflin, 1961. See especially Part 4: "Premarital Behavior Patterns," pp. 265-387.

Kinsey, Alfred C., Wardell B. Pomeroy, and Clyde E. Martin, *Sexual Behavior in the Human Male*. Philadelphia: Saunders, 1948.

———, *et al.*, *Sexual Behavior in the Human Female*. Philadelphia: Saunders, 1953.

Koos, Earl Lomon, *Marriage* (rev. ed.). New York: Holt, 1957.

Landis, Judson T. and Mary G. Landis, *Building a Successful Marriage* (4th ed.). Englewood Cliffs, N. J.: Prentice-Hall, 1963.

Landis, Paul H., *Making the Most of Marriage* (2nd ed.). New York: Appleton-Century-Crofts, 1960.

Lantz, Herman R. and Eloise C. Snyder, *Marriage. An Examination of Man-Woman Relationship*. New York and London: Wiley, 1962.

LeMasters, E. E., *Modern Courtship and Marriage*. New York: Macmillan, 1957.

Levy, John and Ruth Munroe, *The Happy Family*. New York: Knopf, 1947.

Locke, Harvey J., *Predicting Adjustment in Marriage*. New York: Holt, 1951.

MacIver, Robert M., *Dilemmas of Youth: In America Today*. New York: Harper, 1961.

Mayer, John E., *Jewish-Gentile Courtships*. New York: Free Press of Glencoe, 1961.

Mead, Margaret, *Male and Female. A Study of the Sexes in a Changing World*. New York: Morrow, 1949.

Merrill, Francis E., *Courtship and Marriage*. New York: Holt, 1959.

Montagu, Ashley, ed., *The Meaning of Love*. New York: Julian, 1953.

Peterson, James A., *Education for Marriage*. New York: Scribner's, 1959.

Reiss, Ira L., *Premarital Sexual Standards in America*. Glencoe, Ill.: Free Press, 1960.

Riesman, David, "Permissiveness and Sex Roles," *Marriage and Family Living*, XXI (August 1959), 211-217.

Schachtel, Ernest G., *Metamorphosis*. New York: Basic Books, 1959.

Seward, Georgene H., *Sex and the Social Order*. New York and London: McGraw-Hill, 1946.

Smith, Ernest A., *American Youth Culture*. New York: Free Press of Glencoe, 1962.

Terman, Lewis M., *Psychological Factors in Marital Happiness*. New York and London: McGraw-Hill, 1938.

Vincent, Clark E., *Unmarried Mothers*. New York: Free Press of Glencoe, 1961.

Waller, Willard and Reuben Hill, *The Family*. New York: Dryden, 1951.

Watts, Alan W., *Nature, Man and Woman*. New York: Pantheon, 1958.

Winch, Robert F., *Mate Selection*. New York: Harper, 1958.

"Youth: Change and Challenge," *Daedalus* (Winter 1962).

Old Age Adjustment

13

Through the folklores

and mythologies of many cultures

run themes of a search

for the fountain of youth.

In our culture

we seem almost to have found it.

Recent statistics indicate

that *one out of every nine Americans*

is sixty-five or over,

and many still lead active lives.

The dramatic extension of life expectancy

in this century has stimulated both scientific research into the *problems our old people face* and social planning built around the facts this research reveals.

The nature of the aging process and the conditions of our culture create certain problems characteristic of the old age group. But still there is no typical old person, and many of the aged may escape most of these problems. The process of aging affects different people in different ways, and culturally engendered frustrations and gratifications vary according to the culture. Each aging person will experience and interpret these frustrations and gratifications according to his own personality, the richness or drabness of his childhood and adult life, and his attitude toward old age. Thus the prevalence of certain characteristic old age adjustment problems should not lead us to believe that all old people face the same kind of problems or respond to these problems in the same way. The following two examples illustrate some of the many different ways elderly people adjust or fail to adjust to their circumstances.

There is no typical old person, but the image of old age as a period of uselessness (left) has faded before the image of old age as a time of new opportunities, as exemplified by Grandma Moses (right). (From Monkmeyer, by Carola Gregor, and Fritz Henle.)

Mrs. E. has just passed her eighty-fifth birthday. She is a handsome woman in good health, although she says she does not have the energy she had ten years ago. She needs a long night's sleep, and therefore rarely goes out in the evening. But she never complains. She has lived a full life, has traveled a great deal, and always has been very active in community affairs. When she was seventy-five she settled in a small town near San Francisco. She likes the relative quiet there but goes to San Francisco several times a year for special events. She says she prefers to live by herself because she likes to have things her own way at home and is too old to adjust her style of living to someone else's. But she has many friends who visit her or with whom she keeps up a lively correspondence. She is still active in community affairs—still is aroused by social injustices, and calls on people, writes letters, and works on committees to help remedy what she considers wrong. She reads a great deal and is well informed on national and international politics. Alert and active, she has little time for complaints and boredom.

Mr. B. is approaching eighty. Like Mrs. E. he is in fairly good financial circumstances, and he lives with his wife and daughter in a comfortable apartment. About ten years ago he retired from a successful import-export business in Brazil and came back to the United States. Since then he has gradually deteriorated. He never had any strong interests outside his business, and when he retired from it he had no resources to fall back on, no interests to keep him going. When he left his business, he also left his acquaintances and friends; and he did not have the zest to make new ones when he returned to this country. Physically Mr. B. is still in fairly good health, but otherwise he has deteriorated to where he is content to do nothing but sit in a chair all day long, often nodding off to sleep, even when there is company. If he goes out he soon becomes restless and wants to go home again. His memory for recent events is almost completely gone, and when he talks at all he fills his conversation with recollections of his childhood days spent on a large farm in Kentucky. His life seems empty, devoid of all interests and meaning.

These two examples indicate why we must establish—while we are still young—interests and behavior patterns that will keep us happy, alert, and productive when we are old. Old age is a condition that all of us will have to face—barring early death. Medical advances (especially the rapid strides made in preventive medicine and the control of infectious diseases), improved sanitation, and a general rise in the standard of living have greatly lengthened our lives. Scientists report that they hope to extend man's average life span to 100 years by the early part of the twenty-first century. The majority of us, therefore, can look forward to enjoying old age as a period of freedom from routine and from time schedules, freedom to be selective about commitments, activities, and friends.

Any man or woman who cultivates his natural gifts to the utmost may, on reaching old age, gain from his immediate circle recognition of the contribution he has made to the world in which he has lived.[1]

Changes that Occur During the Aging Process

As the human being ages, certain physiological, psychological, and intellectual changes occur, but the extent and severity of these changes varies with each individual. Not everyone ages at the same rate. Some people may begin to have trouble with their eyesight or hearing at a relatively early age; others may remain keen-eyed and keen-eared until their seventies or eighties, or even later. We all know people who seem old at forty and others who still seem alert and young at seventy. Furthermore, the different senses do not deteriorate at the same rate. A person may begin to have trouble hearing at age sixty and may be quite deaf by the time he is sixty-five, but his eyesight may remain quite good. Keeping this variability in mind we can, nevertheless, note certain general trends in the aging process.[2]

Changes in Physiological Functions

As people age, vision and hearing steadily decline. Changes in vision include loss of ability to match colors, to distinguish between subtle shadings, and to focus on close

[1] Ethel Sabin Smith, *The Dynamics of Aging* (New York: W. W. Norton & Company, Inc., 1956).

[2] For a comprehensive survey of the problems of aging, see the following volumes: R. J. Havighurst and Ruth Albrecht, *Older People* (New York: Longmans, Green, 1953); James E. Birren, ed., *Handbook of Aging and the Individual* (Chicago: University of Chicago Press, 1959); Clark Tibbetts, ed., *Handbook of Social Gerontology* (Chicago: University of Chicago Press, 1959).

or distant objects. Also, the field of vision narrows. These changes spring primarily from changes in the physical characteristics of the eye. Other sight defects result from changes in the central nervous system. Of hearing defects, the most common is an inability to catch high-pitched sounds. This ailment occurs so frequently that it is regarded as a normal result of aging.

It is important to note than an older person often finds it more difficult to adjust to impaired hearing than to defective vision. In a study [3] of older people in Prairie City, a small Midwestern town, it was found that 38 per cent reported some degree of visual disability that could not be corrected satisfactorily, and 47 per cent mentioned hearing problems. However, very few of these old people *complained* about poor vision. Apparently most of them had made a satisfactory adjustment to it. They found it much more difficult, however, to adjust to impaired hearing, which is more of a social handicap than poor vision because those unable to hear cannot follow a conversation. Nor can they understand sales people or follow stage, screen, radio, or television dialogue. Some actually feel that others avoid them or make fun of their hearing defect. They find it difficult to accept the social isolation that often accompanies defective hearing.

Very little information is available concerning the relationship between the other sensory functions and advancing age. Although anatomists have found that taste buds and olfactory nerves atrophy with age, they have not actually been able to link these facts to loss of taste and smell in older people. Nor have researchers been able to prove that the aged are less sensitive to pain than younger people, although some studies have sought to establish this correlation.

Motor abilities decline with advancing years much as do hearing and vision. Decline in reaction time, speed of muscular movement, and muscular coordination begins in the second or third decade of life, but the rate of decline increases toward the end of life. Again, however, there is a wide range of differences among older people and much overlapping among age groups. Reproductive functions decrease with advancing age in both men and women. The cessation of menstrual flow is a clear sign of the end of reproductive capacity in women.

Although the demands made on the physiological functioning

[3] R. J. Havighurst and Ruth Albrecht, *op. cit.*

of the body are often no greater than those that occur at other age levels, older people have less reserve capacity to meet them. They have a reduced ability to grow new tissue, for example, which means that they recover less quickly from accidents. Bones take longer to knit, and abrasions are slower to heal. The ravages of cancer and other degenerative diseases are harder to throw off, and there is less resistance to some infections. In the minds of many people chronic disease is associated with old age. Actually chronic illness may set in at any age, but its incidence increases progressively with age, as shown in Figure 1.

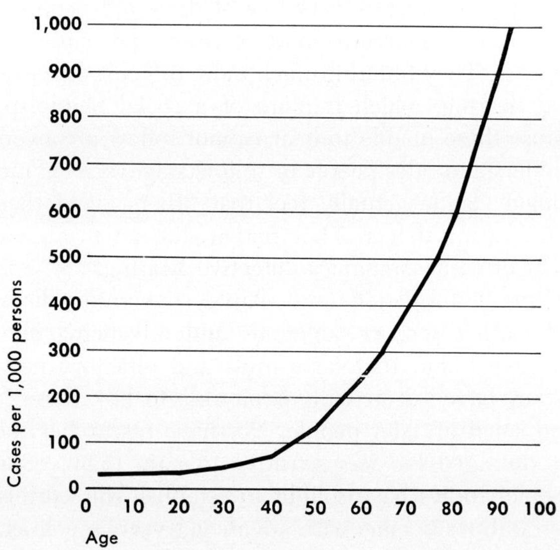

Figure 1. Incidence of chronic diseases and major impairments at ten-year age intervals. The curve shows that the rate of occurrence of chronic diseases increases slowly to 35 people per 1,000 at age twenty-five. In the next 20 years it increases to about 100 per 1,000. After that the rate is accelerated. (Source: Hagerstown, Md., survey, 1923 and 1943. After Ciocco and Lawrence, 1952.)

Much of the disability in the old-age group arises from disorders that are common in persons twenty years younger. At this earlier age these afflictions are not as yet disabling, but they become progressively so with advancing age. It is during this early period that preventive medicine can be most effective.

Changes in Intellectual Functions

Intellectual capacity, as measured by our standard intelligence tests, also changes as we grow older. Studies by a number of investigators have shown that rapid gains in intelligence are made during adolescence, reaching a peak around the age of twenty. Then a continuous, gradual decline sets in. Intelligence test results, however, are composite scores, derived by testing a number of different abilities and averaging the results. We can understand the nature of the changes better by studying the scores for particular abilities. Such studies reveal that older people do poorly on test items that call for speed of performance and relatively new adjustments. The ability to recall digits, work mathematical problems, and reproduce block designs also declines with age. Older people do well, however, on tests dealing with information, comprehension, and vocabulary. In these the accumulated knowledge that comes with age is a definite asset.

Ability to learn usually declines with age. Studies have shown that the extent of this decline depends in part on the kind of material to be learned. It is most pronounced where the new material conflicts with something the subject has previously learned—where, for example, learning a new habit means breaking an old one.

But although it is generally true that mental ability declines with aging, the conclusion needs qualification. First of all we must note that there is great variability within each age group and considerable overlapping among age groups. Second, most of our intelligence tests, especially speed tests, have been standardized on the basis of young people's responses. They may not be entirely valid for older people. Third, motivation is an important factor in all testing, and we cannot assume that younger and older people are equally motivated. On the whole, younger people tend to be more responsive to testing situations and older people more resistant.

Finally, it is difficult to avoid selective sampling. Young people are readily available for testing in our public schools and it is easy to get a fairly representative sample of the total population of any age group in the school years. But we do not find older people in such large ready-made groups, except perhaps in some old age homes, and these are a selective sample. Thus, in evaluating test scores we always have to ask whether the group studied may be taken as representative.

On the whole, abilities that depend essentially on physical or physiological factors show an earlier decline than those that are primarily mental. When we inquire into the subjective awareness of aging, we find that older people mention physical symptoms more often than mental ones. Those who are more highly educated, however, are more likely to mention mental symptoms.

In measuring intelligence, investigators have gone to great lengths to keep the influence of learning at a minimum. But, as we have seen, those test items in which cumulative experience is most important—information, comprehension, and vocabulary—show least decline with age. It is possible, therefore, that although a person's intellectual capacity may decline with age, the decline may be compensated for by his having perfected many special talents through long practice and by his having accumulated wide knowledge and experience. Thus an older person may be creative and productive.

The relationship between age and actual productivity, rather than intelligence, is discussed by Harvey Lehman in his book *Age and Achievement.* Noting the ages at which outstanding figures most frequently made (or first published) their finest creative contributions in science, mathematics, philosophy, literature, music, and painting, Lehman found that superior production was most likely to occur between thirty and forty. For music, for example, the maximum rates of creative productivity occur as follows: [4]

Instrumental selections	25-29 years
Vocal solos	30-34
Symphonies	30-34
Chamber music	35-39
Orchestral music	35-39
Grand opera	35-39
Cantatas	40-44
Light opera and musical comedy	40-44

[4] Harvey C. Lehman. *Age and Achievement* (Princeton, N. J.: Princeton University Press, 1953), p. 325. By permission of Princeton University Press.

But although the highest average output of superior production is in the thirties, the total range for best production extends over several decades. Many notable creative works are produced in late maturity, and, as Lehman points out, any stereotyped conception of later maturity as an unproductive period is quite false. Some of the great philosophers, for example, were still writing and having their works published after they had turned ninety. Individual variations exist at each age level and careful study of the individual is always essential.

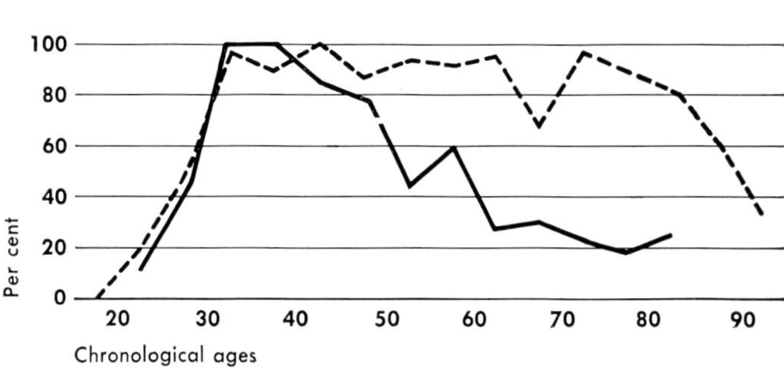

Figure 2. Quantity vs. quality of philosophical output. Solid line indicates age at which the one best treatise (as determined by consensus) of 182 deceased philosophers was written. Broken line indicates ages at which these 182 men published 1,593 books, an average of 8.75 books per man. (Source: Harvey C. Lehman, Age and Achievement. *Published for the American Philosophical Society by Princeton University Press, Princeton, N. J., 1953, p. 47. By permission of Princeton University Press.)*

Although Lehman is concerned with phenomena rather than causes, he does discuss briefly the possible causes for the early maximum rates in creativity. He lists 16 factors as contributing to the decline of these rates. They include decline in physical vigor and sensory capacity; illness and glandular changes; and psychological and social factors such as unhappy marriages, sexual maladjustment, bereavement, preoccupation with practical concerns, less favorable conditions for concentrated work, contentment with early recognition, apathy because of nonrecognition and destructive criticism, increasing inflexibility, decrease in motivation leading to weaker intellectual interest and curiosity, a less stimulating social and cultural environment, psychoses, and the cumulative effects of various kinds of dissipation.

A person's attitude toward aging will depend in part on what he still wants to do—on the goals he has set for himself. Someone with ambitious plans may fear the onset of old age much more than someone who has no particular plans for the future. All behavior and adjustment must always be viewed within a total context, including physiological and psychological changes, environmental influences and pressures, and the way individuals interpret and respond to these factors.

Changes in Personality and Self-Concept

The process of aging also affects emotional life and personality characteristics. The increasing social isolation and uncertainty that mark the lives of many older people lead to emotional instability and anxiety. As his mental dexterity begins to fade, the older person becomes more and more fixed in his attitudes and interests. He loses his time perspective, becomes preoccupied with his day-by-day existence and with the past, and has little hope for the future. Add to these the realization that hearing, sight, and reflexes are declining, and that status and recognition have been lost through retirement, and it is easy to see why old age often presents a difficult adjustment problem.

When despair and depression become too great, neurotic behavior patterns may develop.[5] One of the most common of these is an intense preoccupation with bodily functions (hypochondria). Lack of motivation and decreased energy may combine to produce periods of chronic fatigue usually accompanied by increased irritability. Sometimes fear of reduced sexual potency may lead an older person into excessive eroticism and sexually deviant behavior. Futility may express itself in neurotic depression characterized by self-centeredness and self-disparagement. All these symptoms represent attempts on the part of an older person to find some solutions to the problems con-

[5] For a detailed discussion of neuroses, see N. Cameron, "Neuroses of Later Maturity," in *Mental Disorders in Later Life*, ed. O. J. Kaplan (Stanford, Calif.: Stanford University Press, 1956), pp. 201-243.

fronting him, and they occur when the burdens of adjustment prove too much for him.

It is the psychological functions, more than the intellectual or physiological, that are primarily affected by the factors discussed in the sections that follow.

Sources of Adjustment Difficulties

In addition to having to adjust to the physiological and psychological changes just described, old people must also adjust to certain culturally inspired social and economic trends that complicate their problems. Our concern with these problems is growing because more and more people in our culture are living to advanced ages (see Figure 3)

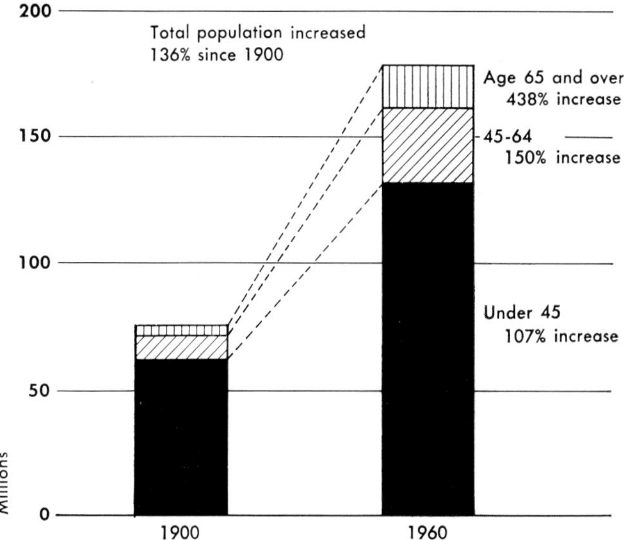

Figure 3. Our population is aging: percentages of population in different age groups. (Source: Federal Security Agency, Fact Book on Aging, *1952. Also, Bureau of the Census, U. S. Department of Commerce,* United States Census of Population, 1960. *Washington, D. C.: Government Printing Office, 1961.)*

and because the physical process of aging when combined with the frustrations our culture imposes may burden many of them to the point of breakdown.

The most dramatic expression of the danger of breakdowns among older people is found in the facts that people sixty or more years old make up approximately one-third of all first admissions to American mental hospitals and that suicide occurs more frequently in the old-age group than in any other. An analysis of admissions to mental hospitals by states and by socio-economic status shows that the rate of admission is highest in lower-class dwelling areas and in areas where the largest numbers of old people reside, namely the Middle Atlantic and New England states and the Pacific Coast areas to which many older people have migrated.[6]

Figure 4 gives the rates of first admissions by age for various mental disorders. As can be seen, schizophrenia and manic-depressive psychoses occur in young adulthood; involutional, syphilitic and alcoholic psychoses occur mainly in the middle years; senile disturbances are most frequent during the older years of 65 and up.

Concerning the senile disturbances, the term *senility* refers generally to progressive physical deterioration, terminating for some persons in marked behavior changes called *senile psychoses.* The term used for the normal changes occuring with age is *senescence.* It refers to aging as a process of change, occuring in such areas as mental, psychomotor, personality, or social functioning. These changes in a particular person are related to such factors as job requirements, roles fulfilled, social expectations, and general cultural demands.

We must keep in mind, however, that the problems of old age are not the same in all cultures. Different cultures regard old age and the aging process in different ways, and even within a culture we find wide differences in attitudes and beliefs about the aged. In our own culture, certain social and economic conditions have aggravated the problems of older people. These conditions are: (1) emphasis on youth, (2) retirement and financial hardships, (3) difficult living arrangements, and (4) feelings of social isolation and uselessness.

[6] H. Warren Dunham, "Sociological Aspects of Mental Disorder in Later Life," in *Mental Disorders in Later Life,* ed. Oscar J. Kaplan (Stanford, Calif.: Stanford University Press, 1956), pp. 157-177

Emphasis on Youth

Our approach to the aged is influenced by the high value our culture places on youth. We see youth as a gay, exciting, dynamic period of life. The young person is full of energy, ready to accept all challenges, bold, confident, courageous, pioneering. The world is wide open for him. We call our young people our most

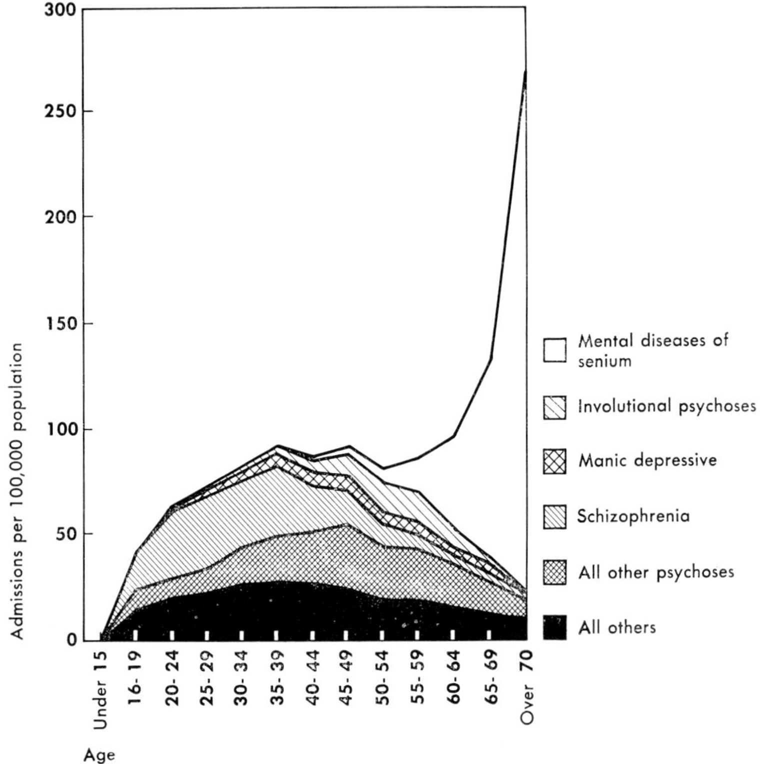

Figure 4. Rates of first admissions for mental disorders, by age. (Source: M. Kramer, "Facts Needed to Assess Public Health and Social Problems in the Widespread Use of Tranquilizing Drugs." Public Health Service, U. S. Department of Health, Education, and Welfare, Publication 486. Washington, D. C.: Government Printing Office, 1956.)

prized possessions, the hope of the future—implying in the same breath that aging is sad and painful, that old people or those beyond middle age are useless and burdensome. If older people accept this evaluation of youth and old age, it is bound to damage their self-esteem.

This attitude is very different from that found in the Japanese culture, for instance, which stresses the advantages of old age. In some Japanese villages men and women hold parties when they reach the age of sixty-one, a privileged age that entitles those who reach it to special respect and privileges in recognition of their wisdom.[7]

Wyndham Lewis has remarked that Americans (and Europeans) try to escape responsibility by refusing to grow up. He felt that dressing in youthful clothes, affecting childish enthusiasms, indulging in the unexacting amusements of childhood were symptoms of a pathological immaturity in our civilization.[8]

Retirement and Financial Hardships

In 1960, as Figure 3 shows, there were in the United States 16.6 million people 65 years of age or more—one out of every nine persons, as compared to one out of every 25 in 1900. While the proportion of those 65 and over has been increasing, however, the percentage of older people who are gainfully employed has radically decreased—from 68 per cent in 1890 to 43 per cent in 1960.

Why do men retire? A number of recent studies have dealt with this question, and almost all of them report that conditions of health and declining physical capacity are given as the main reasons for retirement. The findings from one such study show that approximately three-fourths of the older men no longer in the labor force gave health, age or other personal reasons as the decisive factors in their voluntary retirements. About one-fourth stated that their retirements were involuntary, due to compulsory retirement systems, layoffs, and so on.[9]

Generally, retirement means that income will be reduced and that business and social contacts will shrink. Although many older

[7] John F. Embree, *Suye Mura: A Japanese Village* (Chicago: University of Chicago Press, 1949), p. 214.

[8] Cited in Ethel Sabin Smith, *op. cit.*, pp. 153-154.

[9] P. O. Steiner and R. Dorfman, *The Economic Status of the Aged* (Berkeley: University of California Press, 1957).

persons are covered by pension plans, the income from such plans is ordinarily much lower than the income from wages and salaries. Where the younger man can look forward to advancement and pay increases in his job, the older one must accept the fact that his days of opportunity are over. At best he will be allowed to keep his present job and continue at the same level, but it is more likely that he will have to take another position, one that will mean lowering his standard of living.

We have already seen that many of the child's and adolescent's problems arise as his contacts expand and as he is compelled to adjust to the demands of meeting new people and new and strange situations. Quite the opposite is true for the older person. At retirement his world begins to shrink. He must face the fact that close business associations will be broken, that the stimulation and challenge of his job will be gone.

Compulsory retirement at the age of sixty-five is a controversial matter. Some of the arguments favoring such retirement are:

1. Sixty-five is the age of eligibility for federal government retirement benefits.
2. There is evidence of an increase in incidence of acute and chronic illnesses in people sixty-five and over.
3. Retirement of the aged makes room for young people entering the labor force.
4. Compulsory retirement at sixty-five simplifies administration of retirement programs and enables a company to avoid criticism for discrimination and favoritism.[10]

Opponents of compulsory retirement argue that physiological age is a better criterion than chronological age since the latter does not take into account individual differences in the aging process. They also maintain that the administrative advantages have been greatly exaggerated and that the voluntary retirement programs prevailing in many companies have proved workable. They find voluntary retirement entirely compatible with federal assistance programs. They claim that the objective should be an expanding economy with jobs for all—young and old alike.

[10] Council of State Governments Study, reported by David L. Bowen in an Associated Press News feature, April 16, 1956.

Although attitudes toward retirement vary among different socio-economic groups, it is often true, at least of the industrial worker, that retirement is not voluntary. Business and industry place a premium on the young worker, and although most employers seem willing to retain older workers who have been with them a long time, they do not usually hire older employees.

Since retirement is so often not a matter of choice, but on the contrary is often resisted, it is not surprising that many older people arrive at retirement age quite unprepared to accept the fact that they are no longer needed, that their busy and productive days are over. They want to continue working, and their unwillingness or inability to accept their new situations often intensifies the difficulties they face in adjusting to retirement.

Many experts recommend a system of gradual retirement. A tapering-off process fitted to the individual's interests and abilities would permit him to relinquish his responsibilities gradually, and so gradually accustom himself to less and less work and more and more free time.

Enforced retirement often imposes financial burdens on older people, yet financial security is essential to both physical and psychological welfare. In times of rising costs of living they may find it extremely difficult to support themselves. Aggravating this difficulty is the fact that our society has no clearly established norms concerning the obligation of children to support aged and needy parents. Even if children accept such a responsibility, they may do so unwillingly and in the process make the parent feel unwanted. One study of children's attitudes toward giving an aged parent a home reported that many more accepted than rejected the obligation when the situation presented no special difficulties. But the number of those willing to accept the responsibility decreased rapidly as the hardships or inconveniences connected with such care became more severe.[11] Children do allow the nature of their relationship with their parents to influence their decisions; and this has an important bearing on the psychological security of the parents, since they cannot be sure their children will be willing to care for them later on in life.

[11] Robert M. Dinkel, "Attitudes of Children toward Supporting Aged Parents," *American Sociological Review,* IX (1944), 370-379.

Difficult Living Arrangements

In 1959 a *Life* magazine survey[12] reported that three million American families had aged parents living in their homes. This accounts for approximately 75 per cent of the older people. Of the remainder, some live in homes of their own without relatives; others room or board with non-relatives or live in hotels and institutions.

Many of those who live with their families are loved and resented at the same time. Frequently the younger members of the family accuse the older ones of being meddlesome, of interfering too much, talking too much, finding fault too much. They say that the older people refuse to appreciate the things being done for them. The older ones, on their part, feel that no one appreciates them or remembers all they have done for the family, that no one cares what happens to them, that no one shows them any consideration. Strain and emotional tension are inevitable under such circumstances. Only a lifelong preparation in congenial human relations can keep the tensions under control.

We have become a nation of city dwellers, and living space is at a premium. In a crowded house or apartment an older person is given little opportunity to feel useful. Often he simply feels in the way. For those who still live in rural areas conditions are somewhat better. On a farm older people can still do work related to what they have done most of their lives. They can still contribute to the household in a meaningful way.

Since the early 1950's there has been a noticeable increase in the number of housing projects planned especially for older people. Some of these have been sponsored by communities, some by private investors, and some by the older people themselves. But although housing especially designed for older people can take into account some of their special needs, separating them into special living quarters may also aggravate some of their adjustment problems. For when their contacts are restricted primarily to other older people they feel isolated from the wider community. This difficulty increases when whole communities are planned for the aged, and in recent years the policy of

[12] *Life*, July 13, 1959.

separate communities has been questioned. Current ideas advocate that new communities be developed in such a way as to provide a wide age distribution, that ways be found to accommodate the full family cycle.[13]

Feelings of Social Isolation and Uselessness

Both retirement and living arrangements can contribute to the sense of social isolation and uselessness that many older people experience. Ordinarily adults function in a variety of social roles—as members of work groups or of various civic, religious, or fraternal organizations; as spouses; as parents; as friends. But from the age of about fifty on they may find themselves deprived of many of these roles. Children grow up, marry and move away. Many older people, especially women, lose their mates. Others lose contact with work associates and friends.

Some older people are prepared to accept this deprivation, to adjust easily, and to assume new roles. But others never overcome their loneliness and, falling prey to feelings of self-pity, become demanding and perhaps offensive, alienating the few associates they have left and thereby increasing their isolation. Commenting on this problem, Ethel Smith writes:

> The feeling of being useless, of being unwanted, of being pushed aside, can slow digestion, block elimination, disturb sleep; in short, can make one genuinely ill . . . [often] we say we are emotionally depressed because we are physically ill; whereas the opposite is often truer, that we are physically ill because we are depressed. Once the symptoms are established, the victim is launched on a vicious circle of self-perpetuating mental and physical misery. . . .
>
> When the aged accept as valid society's low estimate of their social worth, they commonly become extremely critical, not of themselves, but of the younger generation; for the cynicism with which the aged too often view the young is the natural projection of their own low self-esteem. To think meanly of one's self through long empty days is an intolerable pain, and the only way to ease that pain is to transfer the burden of inadequacy to someone else. It is the universal human way of shrugging our shoulders in an effort not to care.

[13] Lewis Mumford, "For Older People—Not Segregation but Integration," *Architectural Record*, CXIX (1956), 191-194.

> That more aged persons do not regress mentally to infancy when the body . . . so nearly reproduces the helplessness of the very young, is due primarily to a vigorous self-esteem.[14]

While feelings of isolation and loneliness are frequently experienced by older people, they are by no means experienced by all of them. Recent studies have pointed out that urban living is not always as disruptive of family ties as has often been assumed and that patterns of mutual family assistance persist. Table 1 shows the findings of one such study, which indicate considerable agreement between the expectations retired parents hold concerning their children's behavior and the actual behavior of the children.

Table 1 ***Congruity of Family Assistance Norms with Reported Behavior***

Norms		*Behavior*	
Percentage who say children *should:*		Percentage who say children *do:*	
Visit their parents frequently	84%	Children see them often	76%
After leaving home, keep in close contact	94	Since leaving home, *all* children have kept in close contact	86
Even when children have families of their own, they should keep in close contact	93	*All* children who have families have kept in close contact	86
Take care of their parents when they are ill	60	Help when someone is ill	80
If parents need financial assistance, children should be expected to help	49	Give advice on business or money matters	37
		Give financial help	28
Help their parents	42	*All* children offered financial help	57
Live close by	15	*All* children live close enough so that parents can see them whenever they want to.	50

Source: Gordon F. Streib, "Family Patterns in Retirement," *Journal of Social Issues*, XIV, No. 2 (1958), 55. By permission of *Journal of Social Issues*.

Older people's disappointment in their relationships with their children and their feelings of rejection and loneliness may result not

[14] Ethel Sabin Smith, *op. cit.*, pp. 53-54. By permission of W. W. Norton & Co., Inc.

only from their children's actual behavior but also from the fact that their parents' expectations and demands are too high.

Viewing Old Age Constructively

The saying that an ounce of prevention is worth a pound of cure is recognizably true in old age adjustment. It has been suggested that schools and colleges might offer courses to help students to understand the problems of the aged, in order to learn not only how to prepare for their own old age but also how to cope with the problems of their parents or other aged relatives.

Young people can anticipate old age and make plans for it. It is helpful to remember that even an elderly person must be able to satisfy, at least in part, certain fundamental needs. To be sure, some needs assume less importance with advancing age, but the needs for some degree of affection, recognition, status and self-esteem never disappear completely. If an older person is unprepared for the changes

Many older people have enriched their lives by pursuing old hobbies or learning new skills. (From Monkmeyer, both by Sybil Shelton.)

old age brings, he is confronted with the dilemma of finding new ways to satisfy these needs at a time when his ability to adapt to new experiences and situations has sharply declined. The more interests and skills he has developed in his earlier years, the more resources he will have in old age.

The problems facing older people originate partly in social conditions and attitudes, partly in the physiological and psychological changes accompanying the aging process, and partly in their own personalities—in their outlook on life, their attitudes toward old age. Any approach to satisfactory adjustment must consider all these factors, and often the services of a trained counselor are required to discover unsuspected causes of maladjustment and to suggest solutions that may set an elderly person on the road to healthy, happy living. But many times problems are neither physiological nor psychological in origin. One of the biggest worries of older people concerns money to meet basic needs. Revised hiring and retiring policies in business and industry, adequate pension plans, economical housing arrangements, and provisions for medical care can do much to alleviate this worry.

Fortuately industry is coming to recognize the value of older workers in jobs where quality of work is more important than speed or where judgment and experience count heavily. In recent years, as an indication of the value of age and experience, arrangements were made through the John Hay Whitney Foundation for a small group of retired professors—each an expert in his field—to teach each year at small colleges that could not otherwise afford them. Colleges, professors, and students alike benefited from the experiment. In some cases increased student interest in the subjects these experts taught led to the establishment of new departments. Many of the professors were asked to remain or were invited to lecture at other colleges.

In a few communities job-counseling services for older people have been set up with satisfactory results. The elderly worker will never be in as great demand as the young worker, but interested communities and groups can do much to persuade employers to take advantage of the skills, talents, and productive capacities of older people.

Programs concerned with medical care for older people must give attention both to providing facilities for the sick, especially for the chronically ill, and to preventive geriatrics.[15] We have seen already that many of the disorders of the aged have their genesis in early years. Early detection and treatment can do much to keep these disorders from becoming seriously disabling. Programs for both prevention and care are based on the beliefs that illness and disorders in old age are neither inevitable nor incurable, that the health of older people can be improved, and that rehabilitation is possible. Health programs are valuable both because of the medical help they afford and because they imply a changed attitude toward the elderly. This in turn affects the concept the aged have of themselves.

Increased attention is also being given to living arrangements for the aged, both institutional and private. Many older people will continue to live in their own homes, but for many others some form of group living is necessary or desirable. Recent studies indicate that homes for the aged should not be isolated from the rest of the community. On the contrary, they should be located in urban or suburban areas, where the older people can have access to the larger community and can maintain their contacts with the family and friends.

An example of the kind of housing being constructed for older people is a project recently developed in Cleveland, a fourteen-story apartment building in which rents average $30 a month. On the first floor is located a Golden Age Club, where old people can work in hobby shops and participate in other activities geared to their interests. A special feature is that four of the twelve apartments on each floor are occupied by couples with children under five years of age. These families are moved into another housing development when the children grow older.

Much thought is being given to recreational facilities for the aged, as is evidenced by the many Senior Citizen Centers making their appearance. These centers help older people to extend their circles of acquaintances and to find congenial associates, and at the same time

[15] Gerontology is the scientific study of the phenomena of old age. Geriatrics deals more specifically with the clinical problems of the aged.

A grandchild, a shared newspaper or book, a sociable game—these can provide many pleasurable hours. (A Lehner-Kube photograph; from Monkmeyer, by Nancy Hays; from Cities Service Company, by Russell Lee.)

they provide facilities for a number of activities. A typical example is the Senior Citizens program organized in 1958 by the Junior League of Los Angeles and operated as a community service in an area where living conditions are substandard. More than 100 older men and women—residents of the area and their friends—meet one morning a week in a building the League maintains as a youth center during the remainder of the week. Refreshments, crafts, games, library facilities, and television are available. The program also includes special events such as travelogues, educational lectures, movies, fashion shows, and musical performances. Seasonal celebrations are also held. For the use of these facilities the senior citizens pay a $1 yearly membership fee. More and more communities and civic organizations are establishing similar recreational, educational, and social clubs and centers for the aged.

Not all older people need such community support. Many have interests that make their lives stimulating and productive. Some may enjoy visiting with their children and grandchildren. Others may have many friends. Still others may throw themselves wholeheartedly into church or civic affairs. Older people react in many different ways to the problems confronting them. Many, recognizing their limited physical capacity, turn to less strenuous pursuits and enjoy a more leisurely way of life. Some find retirement an ideal time to do things they always wanted to do but never could find time for. And some, insufficiently motivated to seek out new interests or to indulge old dreams, spend their time reminiscing about the "good old days."

One researcher, David Riesman, has grouped older people's ways of adjusting to their problems into three types of reaction. He calls these reactions the *autonomous,* the *adjusted,* and the *anomic* and he describes them as follows:

> Some bear within themselves psychological sources of self-renewal; aging brings them accretion of wisdom, with no loss of spontaneity and ability to enjoy life, and they are relatively independent of the strictures and penalties imposed on the aged by the culture. Others, possibly the majority, have no such resources within them but are the beneficiaries of a cultural preservative (derived from work, power, position, and so on) which sustains them, although only so long as the

cultural conditions remain stable and protective. A third group, protected neither from within nor from without, simply decays.[16]

In the first, quite small, group—the *autonomous*—Riesman includes such people as Bertrand Russell, Toscanini, and Freud. Their lives were not necessarily well-rounded or balanced; they did not necessarily get along well with others. But their lively interests and creative abilities made old age a rich and satisfying period of life for them. Instead of accepting the cultural definition of old age as a period when a person should slow down and take it easy, they continued to be active and productive in spite of advancing years.

In the *adjusted* group Riesman includes those persons who are kept going primarily by their position and prestige. As long as they can continue to work, the adjusted are able to appear youthful. They are able to carry out the continuous, familiar tasks their environment thrusts upon them, but they are immune to new experiences or new ideas. They are well preserved, but their outward youthfulness actually may mask a stunted psychological growth and inner sterility.

In the *anomic* group are those people who begin to deteriorate when they lose their physiological vitality and when their cultural environment does not provide them with any support. They are, Riesman suggests, the prematurely weary and resigned, and perhaps they were never young. Whatever their backgrounds, they cannot mobilize sufficient inner resources to halt deterioration.

It is not likely that a rich old age is going to materialize out of an empty, sterile past. Nor is constant activity proof that a person is growing up and maturing. A busy life may prevent him from ever developing his own resources. Then, if circumstances change and his activities are suddenly curtailed, he may be appalled by the fact that he has so much time on his hands. The level of adjustment maintained by an older person is to a large extent an outgrowth of the kind of person he was when he reached later maturity. Preparation for old age should not be postponed until old age has already set in.

[16] David Riesman, "Some Clinical and Cultural Aspects of Aging," *American Journal of Sociology*, XLIX (January 1954), 379-383. By permission of the *American Journal of Sociology* and the University of Chicago Press.

It should be kept in mind during the entire period of growing and maturing.

But if we can maintain a favorable self-image, if we can continue to enjoy ourselves, if we can modify our desires and ambitions and cultivate mature methods of achieving our aims, if we can recognize and adjust to reality, if we can gracefully relinquish what must be relinquished, and if we can recognize that the role of the older person is just as valuable as that of the younger person, it should not be difficult for us to achieve a satisfactory old age adjustment.

For Additional Reading

Anderson, John E., ed., *Psychological Aspects of Aging.* Washington, D. C., American Psychological Association, 1956.

Barron, Milton L., *The Aging American: An Introduction to Social Gerontology and Geriatrics.* New York: Thomas Crowell, 1961.

Birren, James E., ed., *Handbook of Aging and the Individual.* Chicago: University of Chicago Press, 1959.

Burgess, E. W., ed., *Aging in Western Societies.* Chicago: University of Chicago Press, 1960.

Cumming, Elaine and William E. Henry, *Growing Old: The Process of Disengagement.* New York: Basic Books, 1961.

Derber, M., ed., *The Aged and Society.* Champaign, Ill.: Industrial Relations Research Association, 1950.

Donahue, W. and C. Tibbitts, eds., *Aging in Today's Society.* Englewood Cliffs, N. J.: Prentice-Hall, 1960.

Federal Security Agency, *Fact Book on Aging.* Washington, D. C.: Government Printing Office, 1952.

Gilbert, Jeanne G., *Understanding Old Age.* New York: Ronald, 1952.

Havighurst, Robert J. and Ruth Albrecht, *Older People.* New York: Longmans, Green, 1953.

———, "Successful Aging," *Gerontologist,* I (1961), 8-13.

Kaplan, Oscar J., ed., *Mental Disorders in Later Life* (2nd ed.). Stanford, Calif.: Stanford University Press, 1956.

Kleemeier, Robert W., *Aging and Leisure: A Research Perspective into the Meaningful Use of Time.* New York: Oxford University Press, 1961.

Lehman, Harvey C., *Age and Achievement.* Princeton, N. J.: Princeton University Press, 1953.

Masserman, Jules H. and J. L. Moreno, eds., *Progress in Psychotherapy,* Vol. 2. New York: Grune and Stratton, 1957. See especially Part III: "Special Problems: Stresses and Techniques in Later Life."

New York Academy of Science, *The Social and Biological Challenge of Our Aging Population.* New York: Columbia University Press, 1950.

Pennington, L. A. and I. A. Berg, eds., *Introduction to Clinical Psychology.* New York: Ronald, 1948.

Pinner, Frank A., Paul Jacobs, and Philip Selznick, *Old Age and Political Behavior.* Berkeley, Calif.: University of California Press, 1959.

Pollak, O., *Social Adjustment in Old Age. A Research Planning Report.* New York: Social Science Research Council, Bulletin 59 (1948).

Pressey, S. L. and R. G. Kuhlen, *Psychological Development through the Life Span.* New York: Harper, 1957.

Reichard, Suzanne, Florine Livson and Paul G. Peterson, *Aging and Personality.* New York: Wiley, 1962.

Shock, Nathan W., *Trends in Gerontology* (2nd ed.). Stanford, Calif.: Stanford University Press, 1957.

Simmons, Leo W., *The Role of the Aged in Primitive Society.* New Haven: Yale University Press, 1945.

Smith, T. Lynn, ed., *Living in the Later Years.* Gainesville: University of Florida Press, 1952.

Streib, Gordon F. and Wayne E. Thompson, eds., "Adjustment in Retirement," *Journal of Social Issues,* XIV, No. 2 (1958).

Tibbitts, Clark, ed., *Handbook of Social Gerontology: Societal Aspects of Aging.* Chicago: University of Chicago Press, 1960.

Tuckman, Jacob and Irving Lorge, *Retirement and the Industrial Worker: Prospect and Reality.* New York: Teachers College, Columbia University, 1953.

Weelwright, Joseph B., "Some Comments on the Aging Process," *Psychiatry,* XXII (1959), 407-411.

Welford, A. T., *Ageing and Human Skill.* New York: Oxford University Press, 1958.

PART FOUR

Achieving Adjustment

THE SIGNIFICANCE OF INDIVIDUAL DIFFERENCES

Relevant and Irrelevant Differences

Differences in Others

Differences in Ourselves

THE SOURCES OF INDIVIDUAL DIFFERENCES

Hereditary Influences

Environmental Influences

MEASURING INDIVIDUAL DIFFERENCES

Major Developments in Measurement

Standardized Measuring Techniques

The Importance of Measuring Individual Differences

Understanding Individual Differences

14

No two individuals are exactly alike.

Each differs in some respect

from everyone else.

However undistinguished his appearance,

however conformist or unoriginal

his ideas,

each person is still identifiably unique.

The manner in which

his abilities and characteristics

have been organized and shaped

by his past experiences,

and the manner in which he directs his behavior toward what he expects from life, combine to differentiate him from others.

We have already seen a number of examples of individual differences. We have seen how different people can react in a variety of ways to the same frustrating experience. We have seen how some elderly people regard retirement as a gateway to futility, while others find in it an opportunity to pursue interests previously denied to them by lack of time. We have seen that teachers must be alert to differences in ability and motivation among their students. Now, in considering the matter of individual differences, we might keep two things in mind: that a difference is not a difference unless it makes a difference, and that the significance of a difference depends on its relevance in a given situation.

The Significance of Individual Differences

Relevant and Irrelevant Differences

When we observe the countless ways in which people may differ, we should remember that not all differences are equally important. Adjustment involves the ability to evaluate which are significant and which are not. When it comes to choosing between two applicants for a job, for example, the fact that one has blue eyes and the other brown is irrelevant. But the training and skill of the applicants *are* relevant factors.

Differences that seem important in the early phases of a relationship may lose their significance later on. A classic example of this is to be found in Melville's great novel, *Moby Dick*. When Ishmael first catches sight of Queequeg, who is to be his roommate for the night, he is appalled by the man's hideous and utterly foreign appearance—so much so that he considers slipping out through the window. But in a very short time, Queequeg's extraordinary consideration and kindness win Ishmael over, and the two become staunch friends.

Physical handicaps are often irrelevant. In recent years employers have learned that physically handicapped people can fill certain jobs very well. Yet in other situations—in athletic contests, for example—

a person with one arm, one leg, or poor eyesight could hardly compete successfully against a perfect physical specimen.

Let us consider this question of relevant differences from another point of view. Suppose we are given a dozen figures of various shapes and sizes, some shaded, some plain. If we are asked to sort the figures according to their *shapes*, whether they are plain or shaded will be irrelevant. If we are asked to group them according to whether they are *shaded* or not, the differences in shape will be irrelevant. So it is with individuals and their differences. They must be evaluated in relation to a purpose.

Sometimes characteristics that are actually quite irrelevant assume importance because of the symbolic meaning attached to them. The "boy with green hair" is not significantly different from other boys, yet the strangeness of his oddly colored hair causes people to *infer* that he must be different and strange in other ways too. If his associates base their reactions to him on this inference, then the boy's personality and behavior are likely to be affected. He may even learn to consider himself strange and unusual since his attitude toward himself will be affected by the way others react to him. The initially irrelevant difference will then have become a difference that makes a difference.

Differences in Others

Many people are prone to make illogical generalizations on the basis of irrelevant differences. At one time or another we have all heard someone say of members of an ethnic group, "They are all alike;" or "I can't tell them apart." The social distance that often separates two groups prevents the members of one from recognizing the wide range of individual variation among the members of the other.

This failure to recognize individual differences among members of a group characterizes the prejudiced person and accentuates intergroup conflict. Those who are prejudiced may see all Negroes as lazy, all Jews as materialistic, all Irish as irresponsible. A dark skin, a name that sounds Jewish, slanted eyes—characteristics that mark people as non-Caucasian or non-Gentile—start the sparks flying in the minds of the prejudiced and prevent them from seeing that the people who manifest these characteristics are not all alike. Those who are prejudiced are unable to judge individuals *as* individuals. Instead, they prejudge each individual according to some one distinguishing—and irrelevant—trait, and so react to everyone having the same trait as though he were identical with all the others. A prejudiced person's mind is full of stereotypes, that is, preconceived and rigid notions of what all members of another group are like.

Such a person will not permit himself to become involved with other people (or groups) until he is sure that they conform to his own standards. And when he has once developed hostility toward another person he will resent any implication that he himself resembles him in any way. True, most of us find it disconcerting to be told we resemble someone we dislike, especially if we regard that person as somehow inferior. But the prejudiced person may carry this reaction farther and regard differences as justification for actual hostility.

It is not only among members of ethnic groups that we fail to recognize individual differences. The woman who has found she can be domineering and overbearing in her family may fail to realize that such behavior will alienate her friends. A mother may be puzzled because two-year-old Johnny does not respond to the same treatment that succeeded with his sister Jane at age two. Jane loved to play by herself for hours; Johnny frets and cries unless someone is with him every minute. Both of these women have failed to realize that people differ and must be approached in different ways.

Recognition and acceptance of individual differences is a basic requirement for good human relationships, whether on the interpersonal, intergroup, or international level. Such recognition and acceptance will not necessarily resolve conflicts, but it can provide an opening in the direction of resolution. We must remember, however, that even when we are fully aware of these differences we still may not know how to approach other people or how to establish a friendly understanding with them.

Differences in Ourselves

So far we have talked primarily about how our relationships to others are influenced by our recognition or lack of recognition of individual differences. But we must also realize that differences between ourselves and others influence our own self-concepts as well. It is inevitable that we shall meet people who are better informed than we are on certain questions—people who can write, sing, or paint better, people who can make friends more easily. We should not become so blinded by such circumstances that we can only recognize differences that make us appear inferior. We must evaluate ourselves in order to develop our awareness of things we ourselves can do well, things for which our friends and acquaintances may have no talent. We must learn to accept ourselves in spite of our shortcomings, to utilize our assets to the fullest, and to avoid being defeated by our deficiencies.

Self-acceptance, however, should not lead to complacency. Even when we accept ourselves we can continue to try to improve ourselves. In this process of self-evaluation we can also profit by discovering those idiosyncrasies in ourselves that may irritate others. Some of these we can discard or alter. Others may be so important to our growth and development that we must retain them as they are or effect some sort of compromise. Here again we must distinguish between relevant and irrelevant differences. Let us look at an example.

A young man who feels that his parents are "cramping his style" may rebel against them. He may take issue with everything they do—their ways of dressing and serving meals, their forms of relaxation, their political opinions, their religious beliefs. In his rebellion everything becomes grist for his mill. He is determined to change it all.

But surely not all of these items merit equal scorn or censure, even for his rebellious purposes. Let us grant that some of the issues may be vital to him. They may derive from convictions he cannot give up without losing his self-respect. But he might learn to modify his attitudes toward other issues—toward habits of eating or dressing, for example—without damaging his integrity.

Conflicts arising from differences can produce different reactions. Some people openly rebel, as in the previous example. Some seek new social environments in which they can feel less at odds with their associates. Others withdraw from society, thereby relieving themselves of the necessity of adjusting to differences.

Individual differences are integral parts of our lives. And the personal welfare of each of us depends on his ability to recognize and use, play down or accentuate, his own differences in structure, aptitudes, abilities, interests, and opportunities.

The Sources of Individual Differences

Our relationships with others are influenced not only by their characteristics but also by our opinions about the origins of those characteristics. Most of us make assumptions about how individual differences arise. These assumptions reveal themselves in such remarks as: "He acts that way because he was born with a silver spoon in his mouth," and "She never had a chance. Look at the drunk she had for a father."

Such assumptions inevitably influence our behavior. The following imaginary case illustrates the importance of understanding the sources of individual differences.

> One way in which individuals differ sharply from each other is generally not known to them. To about 70% of all Americans, a weak solution of a chemical substance known as phenyl-thiocarbamide (P.T.C. for short) has an intensely bitter taste; to the other 30% it is tasteless. This difference is inherited, and it is not influenced by any known changes in the environment.
>
> Now imagine that P.T.C. is used as a disinfectant in drinking water in a town in which no one has heard of the difference between "tasters" and "taste blinds." When the first complaints of bad-tasting drinking water are received an inspector is sent to investigate. The investigator, who is taste blind, reports that he can't see what all the fuss is about and ascribes the complaints to prejudice or "trouble-making." This does not make the water taste any better to those who have complained and gradually two opposed parties emerge, a pro-P.T.C. and an anti-P.T.C. An election puts in the antis, who have a 70% majority, and disinfection with P.T.C. is discontinued.
>
> To the 30% who are pro-P.T.C. (because they can't taste it) the whole procedure has been unreasonable in the extreme. Because of an obstinate majority they have been deprived of protection against infection. If they feel badly enough about this they may rebel and attempt to evade the majority decision in some extralegal way.
>
> This is a train of events which is not only possible but probable where the cause of conflict between two groups rests on a difference between persons which is not known or understood. When it is gen-

erally recognized that an inherited influence is at the bottom of it, each side may be expected to understand the position of the other and they may then work together to find an acceptable solution.

In this case the fact that the majority was right was due to the biological accident that the hereditary factor for taste blindness is not very common. The reverse situation is readily imaginable. Although P.T.C. is not used as a disinfectant and the above events are not known to have happened, there is no doubt that many human conflicts have arisen because inborn differences have been ascribed to prejudice and vice versa.[1]

Whether heredity or environment is a more influential source of personality traits or characteristics is a question that has long plagued psychologists in their study of personal differences. The question has important implications. On one hand, if mechanical, musical, clerical, or executive abilities are *acquired*, anyone who receives the necessary training should be able to develop them. On the other, if such special abilities are *inherited*, selecting the right people to work in these fields becomes more complicated. Again, if individual differences are *acquired*, slum clearance, environmental improvement, and education are the only means of reducing crime. But if individual differences are *inherited*, then perhaps criminal tendencies can be eliminated, as some authorities suggest, by sterilizing all adults who manifest such tendencies.

Three methods have been developed to determine the relative importance of heredity and environment in individual differences. They are the *genealogical*, the *statistical* and the *biological*. None of the methods is perfect. Accurate genealogical information is difficult to obtain because hereditary and environmental influences cannot be clearly separated, especially when the study is carried back many years. The statistical method depends on the accuracy of the statistical data under consideration, and the accuracy of such data is not always easy to establish. The biological method is experimental, and since human beings are usually reluctant to serve as guinea pigs, whether to test a new recipe or a new vaccine, most of our biological information on the influence of heredity and environment concerns fruit flies, mice, and monkeys.

[1] L. C. Dunn and T. Dobzhansky, *Heredity, Race and Society* (New York: New American Library of World Literature, 1952). By permission of the authors and the New American Library of World Literature.

In some characteristics, such as eye color, taste-blindness, and albinism, the hereditary influence is clearly decisive. In others, environmental influences just as clearly predominate. The language a person speaks, for example, is almost entirely a product of the cultural environment in which he grows up. A child of French parents raised in the United States by an American couple will speak English, not French. In the evolution of many characteristics, however, heredity and environment interact so closely that isolating one set of influences in order to determine its impact is extremely difficult. Early psychologists were inclined to view heredity and environment as two separate and distinct factors. Recent approaches do not make this sharp distinction. They attempt to discover, rather, to what extent heredity is susceptible to modification by environmental factors.

But whatever the influences, a wide range of human variability is possible. Either heredity or environment alone is capable of producing vast differences. Together their influence is that much greater.

Hereditary Influences

When we speak of heredity, we mean biological inheritance, the handing down of characteristics from one generation to the next. This process is carried on by the genes, microscopically small bodies contained in the chromosomes—minute bodies in the nucleus of a cell which play a determinative part in hereditary transmission. Each individual receives half of his chromosomes from his father and half from his mother, 48 altogether. The total number of genes carried by both father and mother is much greater. Geneticists have estimated that one man alone can carry a minimum of 12,000 pairs of genes. Many different combinations of genes, therefore, are possible, and the chance that brothers and sisters will inherit the same or even similar combinations is negligible, unless they happen to be identical twins, who develop from a single egg and have the same genes. If each parent possessed only 10 different genes, the number of possible combinations would be over a thousand. This number grows to more than a million with 20, and to more than a billion with 30 different genes. This seems reason enough to assert that every human being is unique, without even taking into consideration the *learned* differences that each acquires. Acquired characteristics and behavior, however, are not biologically inherited, although many a folk tale about prenatal maternal experiences would have us believe that they are. A parent's crippled arm or leg cannot be passed on to the child.

Geneticists make a distinction between function and structure. Functions include breathing, emotional reactions, changes in metabolism, and glandular activities. Structure refers to the actual construction of the body. Geneticists have concentrated primarily on the study of structure because structure is relatively easy to observe and to manipulate. The study of structural inheritance has led some researchers to assume that certain functions are also inherited. But the lack of definite means for studying functions has thwarted efforts to verify this assumption. Musical and artistic talents, for example, are too elusive and indefinite to lend themselves to this type of interpretation.

Environmental Influences

Having examined briefly how heredity contributes to human variability, let us consider now the influence of environmental conditions. We have called attention to these conditions before, in dealing with work adjustment, psychosexual adjustment, family adjustment, and so on. Here we shall outline some major sociocultural characteristics that affect the development of individual differences.

A rich and complex culture nourishes personality by affording a variety of challenges and opportunities for putting skills and talents to work. A restricted and limited culture, on the other hand—a culture in which skills and talents are cramped and suppressed—will be less productive, no matter what its people's innate intelligence may be. A culture that has no use for scientific knowledge, for example, is barren ground for the development of scientific abilities. The more opportunities for diverse activities within a culture, the greater will be its range of individual variability.

We pointed out earlier that each group accepts and supports a certain range of individual differences. Those who fall outside this range are the deviants and misfits. This is true not only of relatively small groups, but also of cultures as a whole. In some societies, members have to conform within a relatively narrow range of approved behavior; in others they are permitted a wide leeway in expression, and correspondingly more individual differences are possible. Societies also differ in their treatment of those falling outside the sanctioned range. One society may regard the deviant as silly but harmless. Another may exclude him from certain activities. Still another may punish him severely. The severity of punishment will tend to limit the number of those willing to risk deviation.

One culture may allow a much wider scope of permissive behavior than another. Thus one society may be permissive politically but strict regarding religious conformity. Or there may be loose controls where sexual activity is concerned but rigid regulation of economic activity. The fact that each society has its own unique set of regulations provides the basis for our ability to distinguish members of one from members of another, even when their physical characteristics seem almost identical.

The quality of leadership is an important factor in the range of individual differences in a group. The behavior of group members will vary according to the permissiveness or strictness of their leadership. In one experimental study, separate groups of children were exposed to democratic, autocratic, or laissez-faire leadership. The greatest expression of individual differences occurred among children in the democratic group, slightly less was observed in the laissez-faire group, while the range of individuality was much reduced in the autocratic group.[2]

Measuring Individual Differences

The fact that each individual has his own unique personality does not mean that no laws concerning human personality and human behavior can be established. Although no two human beings are exactly alike, all share certain fundamental needs that must be satisfied for the sake of survival and psychological well-being. Deprivation or

[2] Ronald Lippitt and Ralph K. White, "An Experimental Study of Leadership and Group Life," in *Readings in Social Psychology,* eds. Maccoby, Newcomb, and Hartley (1958), pp. 496-511.

frustration of these needs will elicit certain predictable responses that differ from those elicited by their satisfaction.

In studying any psychological phenomenon, two approaches are possible. We may concern ourselves with the general nature of the phenomenon and attempt to determine the basic processes underlying it and the conditions causing it, or we may focus on the variability of the phenomenon as manifested in individual cases. Thus, we may concentrate on the general principles of personality organization or on the personality of a given individual. We may consider the laws of perception or the way in which a particular person perceives a situation. We may investigate the principles of learning or examine the way one student learns. The two approaches are complementary.

The approach dealing with individual cases is known as the *idiographic* approach. Its source material consists of personal documents—autobiographies, diaries and letters—and expressive and projective documents, such as literary works and various other art forms. Robert W. White's book *Lives in Progress*[3] is an example of this approach. In it he describes the lives of three people in great detail —a physician and scientist, a business assistant, and a housewife and social worker. He introduces information on biological roots, social forces, and psychodynamics of development. His presentation of these three different personalities demonstrates the valuable contribution that such source material can make toward the understanding of an individual personality.

The approach that aims at generalization is called the *nomothetic*. Its source material consists primarily of data collected through questionnaires, standardized interviews, and controlled experiments on large numbers of people. This approach may utilize personal documents, but with the intent of discovering statistical generalizations or uniformities of behavior, rather than the nature of a single personal life.[4]

Both the idiographic and nomothetic approaches are essential to our understanding of human behavior. Both utilize the human differences factor. There would be no need to accumulate comparable data

[3] Robert W. White, *Lives in Progress* (New York: Dryden, 1952).

[4] Gordon W. Allport, *The Use of Personal Documents in Psychological Science* (New York: Social Science Research Council, Bulletin No. 49, 1942).

on large numbers of people—as the nomothetic approach does—if all people were alike. One person would do as well as another, and one would be sufficient.

Major Developments in Measurement

Let us now consider in some detail the methods and devices that have been used in the study of individual differences.

Strangely enough, the first systematic investigation of individual differences came not from a psychologist but from an astronomer. One night in 1796, in the observatory at Greenwich, an assistant named Kinnebrook was bent over his telescope busily recording the instant when certain stars crossed his field of vision. At the same time, Maskelyne, the astronomer royal of the observatory, was making a similar record. But when the two men sat down to compare figures, Kinnebrook's times were found to be almost a second later than Maskelyne's. On the assumption that Kinnebrook was incompetent, he was dismissed. Twenty years later, Bessel, an astronomer at Koenigsberg, read about the incident in a history of the Greenwich observatory and began to ask himself if Kinnebrook had really been incompetent or whether some other factor was responsible for the unfortunate assistant's apparent error. His curiosity aroused, Bessel began to collect data on the records of several trained observers and discovered the same kind of variations that had cropped up at Greenwich 20 years earlier. Continuing his study, he soon arrived at two significant conclusions. The first was that observers' records differed because some reacted more quickly than others. One person might be able to make a reading and translate it onto paper in one half or one quarter the time it took another to do so. The second point was that differences appeared not only from one person to the next but also at different times in the same person's record. Bessel's study is the first published account we have on individual differences—on the psychological factor that has since become known as the *personal equation.*

Since Bessel's time, psychological tests have been devised to measure many different aspects of personality. But before we describe the tests, let us note some of the general developments in techniques and their objectives.

Early investigators of individual differences were concerned almost exclusively with measuring sensory and intellectual functions. Today, testing techniques have been extended to measure emotional characteristics, social behavior, and a wide range of aptitudes. There has been a definite trend away from the measurement of segmented, isolated aspects of personality and toward a study of the total personality.

The first tests were individually administered. They helped to establish good rapport between tester and subject and made it easier to observe the subject's reactions while he was being tested. But they hindered the rapid accumulation of data. When large groups were to be tested, individual administration became too time-consuming. Psychologists, therefore, became interested in constructing tests that could be given quickly to large numbers of people. The desire for mass testing of recruits in World War I added impetus to their work. Out of World War I emerged such group tests as the *Army Alpha*, an intelligence test for soldiers who understood English, and the *Army Beta*, a "non-verbal" intelligence scale for those whose English was poor, either because of lack of education or because English was not spoken at home. During World War II, the Army General Classification Tests were used to select candidates for training programs.

At every stage of development in testing, validity was an important concern. It was one thing to construct a test. It was another to construct a test that would measure what it was supposed to measure. As each new test or technique appeared, it was subjected to close scrutiny and critical examination. Did an intelligence test actually measure "native" intelligence? Did a questionnaire designed to measure emotional maturity really measure it? These were the kinds of questions that were being raised, and that are still being raised today as new tests continue to be developed. The checking became more rigorous as more complex personality traits began to be tested. Today we have scores of books, monographs, and articles dealing with test construction and the adequacy of test material. Improvements are constantly being made as more refined statistical methods and measuring techniques are developed.

Although the testing movement was in part a response to practical demands, it also stemmed from certain significant theoretical developments. In 1869, Sir Francis Galton, British scientist and statistician, wrote: "I have no patience with the hypotheses occasionally expressed, and often implied, especially in tales written to teach children to be good, that babies are born pretty much alike, and the sole agencies in creating differences between boy and boy, man and man, are steady application and moral effort. It is in the most unqualified manner that I object to pretensions of natural equality." [5] Galton thus rejected the concept that the mind was a *tabula rasa,* a wax tablet, that merely accumulated facts as it was exposed to them. He stressed the importance of heredity, believing that heredity sets limits on individual accomplishments. It was this same native or hereditary intellectual ability that Alfred Binet, a French psychologist, wanted to measure when he developed, with Theophile Simon, the intelligence scales known as the Binet-Simon tests. "Our purpose," he said, "is to evaluate a level of intelligence. It is understood that we here separate natural intelligence and instruction. It is the intelligence alone that we seek to measure, by disregarding, insofar as possible, the degree of instruction which the subject possesses. He should, indeed, be considered by the examiner as a complete ignoramus knowing neither how to read nor write." [6]

We note that Binet said to disregard *insofar as possible* the degree of instruction, indicating that he was aware of the difficulty of separating what was inherited from what was acquired.

Standardized Measuring Techniques

Today, psychological tests are used in many different fields: in schools and colleges, in vocational guidance, in employee selection in business and industry, in the psychological clinic, and in hospitals for the mentally ill. The different tests may be

[5] Wayne Dennis, ed., *Readings in the History of Psychology* (New York: Appleton-Century-Crofts, 1948), p. 231. From: Francis Galton, *Hereditary Genius: An Inquiry into Its Laws and Consequences.* American edition published by D. Appleton and Co., 1870. By permission of Appleton-Century-Crofts, Inc.

[6] Dennis, *Readings in the History of Psychology,* p. 416. From: Alfred Binet and Theophile Simon, *The Development of Intelligence in Children.* Translated by Elizabeth S. Fite. Published by the Training School at Vineland, N. J., 1916. By permission of Appleton-Century-Crofts, Inc.

Figure 1. Test item from the Stanford-Binet test. (From Lewis M. Terman and Maud A. Merrill, Stanford-Binet Intelligence Scale, *3rd revision, 1960. Boston: Houghton Mifflin Company, 1960. By permission of the Houghton Mifflin Company.)*

grouped into six major categories: (1) intelligence tests, (2) aptitude tests, (3) achievement tests, (4) interest tests, (5) tests measuring attitudes and opinions, and (6) personality tests.

INTELLIGENCE TESTS The first widely used intelligence test was developed by Binet and Simon when, in 1904, they were asked by the French school authorities to assist in the placement of school children. In contrast to earlier psychologists who had tested rather narrow aspects of mental activity, such as reaction time and rote memory, Binet and Simon undertook to measure the general level of intelligence, concentrating particularly on the higher mental processes. To judge well, to comprehend well, to reason well—these they believed to be the essential ingredients of intelligence.

The best known revision of the Binet-Simon test is the *Revised Stanford-Binet Tests of Intelligence,* constructed by Lewis M. Terman and Maud A. Merrill. (See Figure 1, page 395.) The test is scored according to *intelligence quotient,* abbreviated IQ. The IQ is the ratio of mental age to chronological age:

$$IQ = \frac{MA}{CA}(100)$$

Thus a child who performs at the 5-year level on the test is given a "mental age" of 5. If his chronological age is also 5, his IQ is 100. If his MA is 10 and his CA is 5, he has an IQ of 200; i.e. he has superior intelligence. If his MA is 5 and his CA is 10, he has an IQ of 50; i.e. he is feebleminded.

The Stanford-Binet test is an individually administered test, primarily of the verbal type—i.e. the person taking the test has to be able to use and understand words. Subsequent developments in intelligence testing have resulted in the construction of group and performance tests. We have already mentioned the *Army Alpha,* the *Army Beta,* and the *Army General Classification Tests* developed during the two world wars. Since then a civilian edition of the Army General Classification Test has been constructed. Other intelligence tests, of either the individual or group type, stressing either the verbal or performance aspects, have also been developed. (See Figure 2.) There

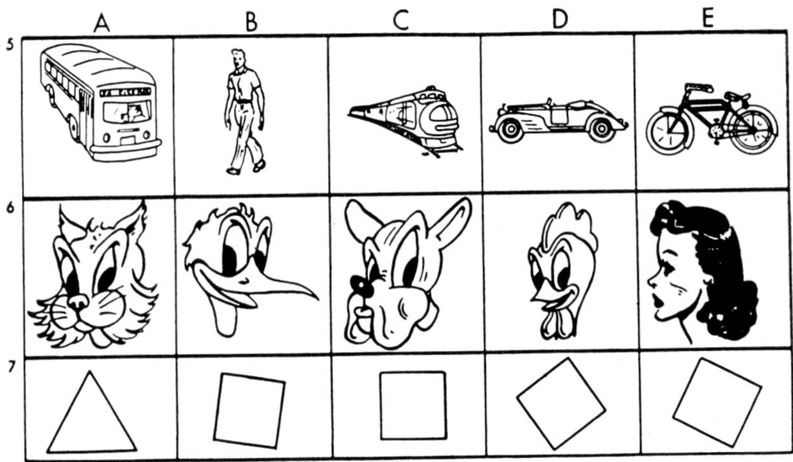

Figure 2. A non-verbal test. Practice item from the SRA Non-Verbal Classification Form, Form AM, prepared by Robert N. McMurry and Dale L. Johnson. (Courtesy Science Research Associates, Inc.)

are special performance tests for children whose language development is limited or handicapped, children with speech defects and deaf children, for example. The Goodenough *Draw-a-Man Scale* can be used with such children as well as with pre-school children.

An individual test that gives both a verbal and performance score, and is styled especially for adults, is the *Wechsler Adult Intelligence Scale.* (See Figure 3.) One form of the Wechsler scale is also adapted for children. This test is constructed in such a way that the scoring shows the pattern of an individual's mental functioning, indicating his strengths and weaknesses.

One major advance has been the development of diagnostic mental tests that seek to measure different aspects of intelligence. Some tests distinguish between abstract, concrete, and social intelligence. Others attempt to assess such intellectual abilities as verbal understanding, word fluency, number facility, space perception, reasoning, and shape recognition. When graphed, the results from such tests give a profile of strong and weak points in the subject's fundamental abilities and thus afford a more detailed picture than a single IQ score.

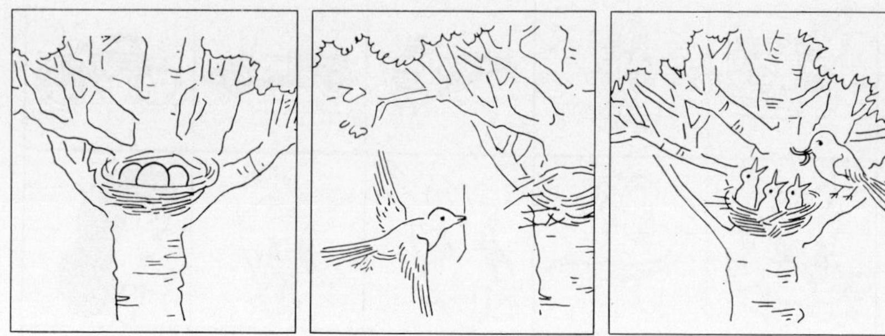

Figure 3. NEST *item of the picture arrangement subtest of the Wechsler-Bellevue Intelligence Scale. (Reproduced by permission from the Wechsler Adult Intelligence Scale, copyright © 1955, The Psychological Corporation, New York, N. Y. All rights reserved.)*

Figure 4 shows an example of items used to measure space perception.

APTITUDE TESTS Aptitude tests are designed to measure potential ability to perform a particular activity. Actually, intelligence tests are aptitude tests in a broad sense, but the term *aptitude test* usually

In the two rows below, mark an X in the box of EVERY figure which is LIKE the first figure in that row. If you wish to change an answer, draw a circle around this box like ⓧ. Then mark the new answer in the usual way.

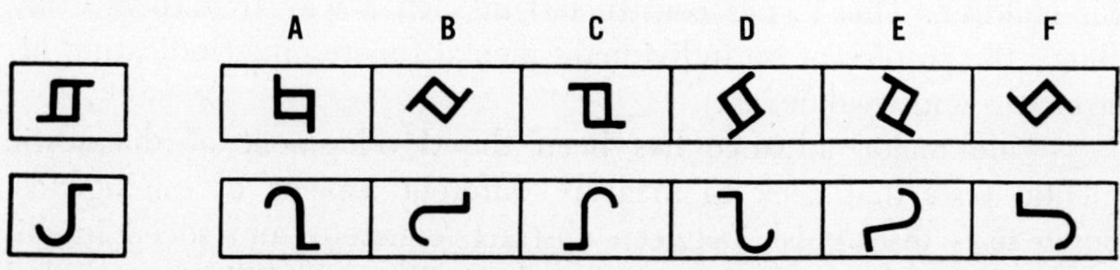

In the first row, you should have marked [A], [D], and [F]. In the second row, you should have marked [C] and [F].

Figure 4. Practice item from the space series of the SRA Primary Mental Abilities Test, prepared and copyrighted, 1947, by L. L. Thurstone and Thelma Gwinn Thurstone. (Courtesy Science Research Associates, Inc.)

refers to those tests that are used to measure a specific capacity. The two most common forms of aptitude tests are mechanical and clerical.

But general aptitudes, such as mechanical or clerical, are often difficult to measure because many kinds of activity may be called for in a given mechanical or clerical task. This difficulty can be overcome, however, either by using tests that measure different aspects of aptitude or by including various subtests. Thus the *MacQuarrie Test for Mechanical Ability,* primarily a paper-and-pencil test, has seven subtests, measuring manual dexterity, spatial visualization, and speed of perception. The *Minnesota Spatial Relations Test* and the *Minnesota Paper Form Board* measure aptitude in visualizing spatial relations. Both require matching of shapes and sizes, but in the first the shapes are actually manipulated while in the second all the matching is done mentally. Some aptitude tests are paper-and-pencil tests, while others, such as the *Minnesota Rate of Manipulation Test,* are manual per-

This student is taking one of the pegboard tests that measure manual dexterity. (From Monkmeyer, by Nancy Hays.)

formance tests, involving motor activities considered essential in various occupations. Still others are actual work samples.

Clerical aptitude, like mechanical aptitude, calls for several abilities. Extensive work in this field, however, indicates that the most important factors in clerical aptitude are perceptual speed and accuracy in checking numerical and verbal symbols. These are primarily the factors the *Minnesota Clerical Test* measures.

In the field of artistic and musical aptitude, the *Seashore Measures of Musical Talent,* the *Meier Art Judgment Test,* and the *Knauber Art Ability Test* are the best known. More recent tests in this field are the *Horn Art Aptitude Test* and the *Musical Aptitude Test* of the California Test Bureau.

Another development in the field of aptitude testing has been the construction of custom-built groups of tests (called *batteries*) for testing specific occupational aptitudes. Some of these tests are for general use; others are restricted for use in professional schools. The *Ferson-Stoddard Law Aptitude Test* and the *George Washington University Series of Nursing Tests* are examples of such group tests. So is the *Medical Aptitude Test* for which a new form is constructed each year for the Association of American Medical Colleges.

In recent years, standard batteries have been developed with norms for specific occupations. One of these is the *General Aptitude Test Battery* of the United States Employment Service that gives scores for ten different aptitudes, including intelligence, verbal aptitude, numerical aptitude, spatial aptitude, form perception, clerical perception, eye-hand coordination, motor speed, finger dexterity, and manual dexterity. Another example is the *Differential Aptitude Test* of the Psychological Corporation, New York City, which measures eight abilities, such as verbal reasoning, language usage, and spatial relations. The *Flanagan Aptitude Classification Tests,* published by Science Research Associates, includes twelve different tests relevant to successful performance in different occupational tasks. The tests measure the ability to read tables and charts, to read with understanding, and to reason logically. The main use of aptitude tests is in vocational guidance and in hiring personnel.

A number of tests have been developed to help teachers, counselors, and students in assessing students' capacity for future academic training. The *Cooperative School and College Ability Test* is one example of these.

ACHIEVEMENT TESTS An aptitude test measures potential ability; achievement tests measure what and how much a person has learned or how well he can perform a given task. However, the dividing line between these two kinds of tests is not always clearly drawn. Aptitude tests do measure abilities that have been practiced and developed by the individual; and achievement tests, although they measure a person's present knowledge and performance, also may indicate an individual's future potentialities and in that sense are indexes of aptitude.

Achievement tests may be grouped into two main categories: educational achievement tests and tests of vocational proficiency. Some educational achievement tests measure achievement in a single subject, such as history or arithmetic. Others cover many different areas of school achievement and thus make possible a comparison of a student's knowledge in one field with his achievement in other areas. The *Cooperative General Achievement Tests,* the *Metropolitan Achievement Tests,* the *Stanford Achievement Tests,* and the *Tests of General Educational Development* are all examples of this latter type.

Since reading is an essential tool in educational achievement, a great many reading tests have been developed. Many of these indicate not only how well a student can read, but also serve as diagnostic tools enabling a teacher to locate sources of the students' reading difficulties. One example of a diagnostic reading test is the *Iowa Silent Reading Test,* which reports nine scores from subtests on rate of reading, word meaning, and sentence meaning. In order to assess a child's readiness for reading, many schools use *Reading Readiness Tests* in the first grade.

Vocational proficiency tests are achievement tests used mainly to measure a trained candidate's possible success in a job. When a firm is seeking a capable typist or experienced bookkeeper, a proficiency test will often indicate which candidate comes closest to meeting its requirements. Achievement tests in typing, bookkeeping, and stenography are available. In addition, the United States Employment Service is at present working to develop trade questions, designed for measuring ability in various trades. The test for carpenters and plumbers, for example, includes such questions as "What are the two most commonly used methods of testing plumbing systems?" These tests are constructed and scored to distinguish between novices, apprentices, journeymen, and experts. One difficulty connected with drawing up trade questions, however, is that rapid technological changes make it necessary to revise the questions frequently.

MEASUREMENT OF INTERESTS The main impetus to the development of measures of interest has come from psychologists working in the field of vocational adjustment. *Strong's Vocational Interest Blank* and *Kuder's Preference Record* are the best known, most widely used measures of interest. (See Figure 5.) Investigation into preferences has established that people engaged in similar occupations share characteristic patterns of likes and dislikes. Preference tests, then, enable the test taker to compare his interests with those of people successful in occupations he is considering. A young man interested in engineering, for example, can compare his interests with those of successful engineers.

Measures of interest have revealed differences between men and women. Using the *Allport-Vernon Study of Values*, it was found that women are generally more interested in activities related to aesthetic, social, and religious values, whereas men usually prefer activities of theoretical, economic, or political interest. The following questions illustrate the nature of the questions asked in the test: "Would you prefer to hear a series of lectures on (a) the development of child-care centers in large cities or (b) contemporary poets?" Or "Assuming you have the ability, with salary identical, would you prefer to be a physicist, politician, or minister?"

As always when we deal with group differences, whether between occupational groups or the sexes, we have to keep in mind that we are dealing with general trends and averages. There are engineers, physicians, and teachers who do not share the interests of most of their colleagues. Some women are not interested primarily in religious and social activities, but instead favor things that most frequently appeal to men. There is, in all such measures, a great deal of overlapping among groups.

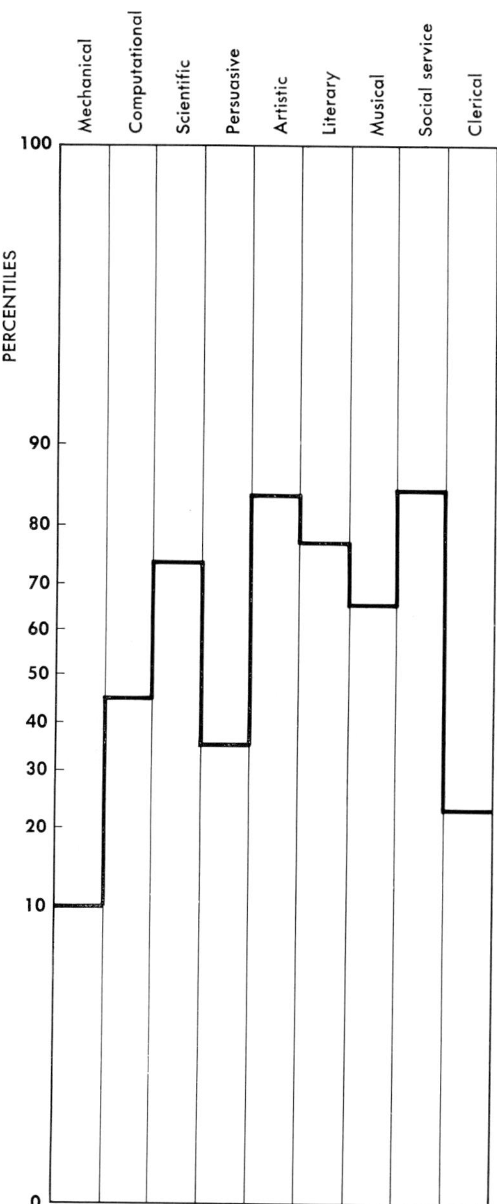

Figure 5. Profile of a college girl on the Kuder Preference Record. Test by G. Frederick Kuder. (Courtesy Science Research Associates, 1942.)

MEASUREMENT OF ATTITUDES AND OPINIONS The measurement of attitudes and opinions has become a major American industry. Almost every day, commercial polling agencies publish the results of their latest findings in the daily newspapers. They design special attitude surveys to measure attitudes toward almost any person, public issue, or product.

Most measurement of attitudes and opinions is done through questionnaires consisting of carefully standardized items or propositions. The respondent either rejects or endorses these propositions or indicates to what extent he agrees or disagrees with them. Scales have been developed to measure attitudes toward a wide range of subjects —war, capital punishment, birth control, labor, management, the church.

One area in particular that has received much attention has been attitudes toward national, ethnic, or religious groups. One of the earliest measuring instruments in this field is the *Social Distance Scale*, constructed by Bogardus. In this questionnaire the respondent is asked about his willingness to accept members of various ethnic groups into his social groups: his family, his club, his neighborhood. In recent years, the most extensive study of prejudice against minority groups has been made by several psychologists at the University of California at Berkeley. As part of their study they developed an *Ethnocentrism Scale*, which has been widely used since their research study was published, under the title, *The Authoritarian Personality*.[7] Like many other social scientists investigating attitudes and opinions, they were concerned not merely with determining the extent or the intensity of a person's prejudice but also with finding out how consistent it was with other beliefs or opinions, with assessing various social influences in the development of such attitudes, and with relating the prejudice to other aspects of the personality.

MEASUREMENT OF PERSONALITY Although intelligence, attitudes, and interests are elements of personality, we are usually looking for the emotional elements of behavior, interpersonal relations, and the different kinds of adjustment the individual has made when we administer personality tests. There have been two main approaches to

[7] T. W. Adorno, Else Frenkel-Brunswik, D. J. Levinson, and R. N. Sanford, *The Authoritarian Personality* (New York: Harper, 1950).

the study of personality, the *clinical* and the *psychometric*. The clinical approach includes interviews and case histories; the psychometric approach uses standardized tests and questionnaires, some of which are administered to individuals, others to groups.

Personality questionnaires are widely used. Some measure different areas of adjustment, others personality traits, still others clinical reaction patterns. The *Bell Adjustment Inventory* is an example of the first, measuring a person's home, health, social, and emotional adjustment. Responses to the *Bernreuter Personality Inventory* are categorized in terms of personality traits—neuroticism, self-sufficiency, introversion, social dominance, self-confidence, and sociability. The *Guilford-Martin Personnel Inventory* measures cooperativeness as opposed to fault-finding, objectivity as opposed to self-centeredness, and agreeableness as opposed to belligerence. *The California Test of Personality* gives separate scores for self-adjustment and social adjustment. Questions concerning self-adjustment deal, for example, with self-reliance and a sense of belonging; those concerning social adjustment refer to social standards and skills, family and school relations. All these tests are used in educational and vocational counseling and in personnel selection.

The *Minnesota Multiphasic Personality Inventory* was developed as a clinical instrument for use in psychiatric diagnosis and has scales which measure defensiveness, hypochrondriasis, depression, hysteria, character disorders, sexual problems; and paranoid, psychasthenic, schizoid, and hypomanic characteristics. The following questions are characteristic of the kind used in personality questionnaires: Do you feel that your parents have been unduly strict with you? Do you feel tired most of the time? Do you usually enjoy spending an evening alone? Do you try to avoid bossy people?

Another technique for studying personality is *behavior sampling*. This technique is used particularly in studying children and involves making a close observation of the child's actions—how he reacts to other children, how he treats his toys, how he responds to discipline.

One of the most significant developments in the field of personality measurement, however, is in *projective techniques*. A projective test provides the subject with a stimulus situation into which he can project his own feelings and needs, his own perceptions and interpretations. It is designed to call forth responses that will reveal the subject's feelings, values, motives, and characteristic modes of adjustment. Through his interpretations and creations he projects the inner aspects of his personality, involuntarily revealing traits he is unaware of and which would not be elicited in response to the direct questions of a personality questionnaire.

Many projective techniques have been developed, a few of which will be described here. Probably the two most widely used and best known are the *Rorschach Inkblot Test* and the *Thematic Apperception Test.* (See Figures 6 and 7.)

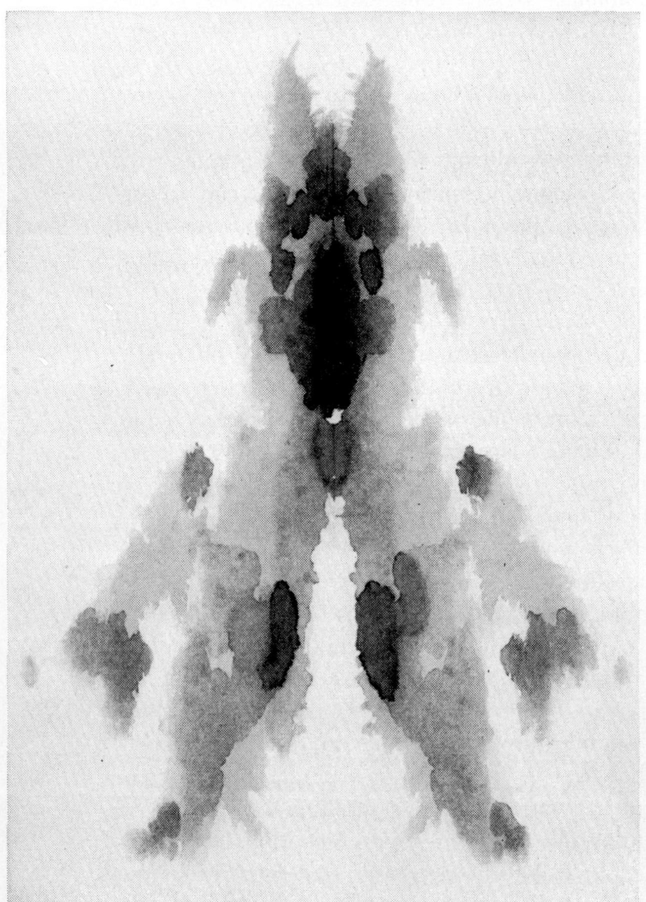

Figure 6. An inkblot. (From Harry W. Hepner, Psychology Applied to Life and Work, *3rd ed. New York: Prentice-Hall, Inc., 1957, p. 236.)*

Figure 7. Card from Thematic Apperception Test. (Reproduced from Henry Alexander Murray, Thematic Apperception Test, 1943, by permission of the President and Fellows of Harvard College.)

The *Rorschach Inkblot Test,* developed by the Swiss psychologist, Hermann Rorschach, consists of 10 cards, each containing one bilaterally symmetrical inkblot. Five cards are shaded in black and white; the other five contain varying amounts of color. The cards are presented to the subject one at a time in a prescribed sequence, and he is asked to tell what he sees in them. After the subject has seen all ten cards, the test administrator begins to ask questions to learn just what parts or aspects of the blots the subject perceived and responded to, and to give the subject an opportunity to add to or clarify his original responses. Interpretation of the subject's responses is a time-consuming task requiring considerable training, but the test provides important information about his personality—his intelligence as indicated in part by the originality and complexity of his responses, his emotional control or instability, the nature of his relations to other people, the richness of his imaginative life.

The *Thematic Apperception Test* was developed by the clinical psychologist, Henry A. Murray. It consists of 20 cards having pictures which resemble actual scenes or objects, but which are still ambiguous enough to allow the subject leeway in interpreting what he sees. As each card is given to the subject, he is asked to tell a story about it—what is happening, what led up to it, and what will be the outcome. Thus some see in the picture of the older and younger woman (page 407) a story of conflict between them, preceded by many quarrels because the older woman has always sought to dominate the younger one, and ending with the younger woman leaving. Others perceive in the picture a friendly relationship, with the older woman giving sympathetic support to the younger one. Each subject sees what he needs to see in the picture. The content of each is analyzed in terms of its underlying themes—whether the plot is happy or tragic, with whom the subject identifies, the influences in the environment that the subject takes into account as he tells what is happening to the people.

The Rosenzweig Picture-Frustration Test consists of 24 cartoon-like pictures, each showing two people involved in a common, mildly frustrating situation. The test is intended to reveal the subject's characteristic responses to common stress-producing or frustrating situations. In each picture the figure at the left is represented as making a statement that either describes the frustration of the second individual or is itself actually frustrating to the second person. (See p. 112, for sample test item.) The caption box above the figure on the right of each picture is blank. The subject is asked to study each picture and then to write in the blank box the first appropriate response that occurs to him. The assumption is that the subject identifies himself, consciously or unconsciously, with the frustrated individual in each situation and that his replies will indicate the way he would act if confronted with a similar situation. The scoring of the responses is based upon (1) the direction of aggression and (2) reaction type. Under direction of aggression, three forms of expression are distinguished: extrapunitiveness, in which the subject blames the environment for his predicament; intrapunitiveness, in which the subject blames himself; and impunitiveness, in which the subject evades aggression or avoids blame. Under reaction type, the following three classes of responses are distinguished: obstacle dominance, in which the subject emphasizes the barrier that stands between him and the solution to his problem; ego-defense, in which the subject's ego predominates and in which he tries to protect his self-esteem; and need-persistence, in which the subject emphasizes the solution of the frustrating problems.

Frustrations are common experiences. The way a person adjusts to them provides significant clues about his behavior and personality organization.

A number of projective techniques have been developed primarily for use with children. Many of these involve manipulation of materials rather than verbalization. Doll-play; building a world (out of a set of toy houses, vehicles, and people); and finger painting are examples of such techniques. (See Figure 8, pages 410-411.)

Personality inventories and questionnaires differ from projective techniques in the following ways:

1. A projective technique is much less structured than a personality questionnaire. A personality questionnaire asks the person how he feels or acts in a variety of typical situations that are definitely structured. For example, representative questionnaires pose such questions as, Would you rather be a chemist than an artist? Do you prefer working alone or in a group? Projective techniques involve no such specific questions. However, the degree of structuring may vary for different projective techniques. The Thematic Apperception Test, for example, is more structured than the Rorschach.

2. Personality questionnaires generally attempt to portray the individual segmentally, emphasizing what are considered to be the important segments of his personality. A projective test, on the other hand, attempts to view and understand the personality as a whole.

3. Projective techniques are more sensitive to the unconscious aspects of personality.

4. Projective techniques are usually less obvious in what they

attempt to measure and thus can be less easily faked by the subject.

Three basic assumptions underlie the use of projective techniques:

First, all behavior manifestations express the individual's personality. Any aspect of an individual's behavior offers some insight into his personality: his needs, goals, defenses, and the like.

Second, the subject will reveal through the answers he gives some aspects of his personality that he either will not or cannot reveal otherwise. Projective tests usually involve the presentation of purposely ambiguous or unstructured material. It is assumed that when the individual attempts to explain these apparently objective bits of material he will disclose his preoccupations, his wishes, his fears, and his aspirations without suspecting that he is doing so. His resistance to disclosing personal and sometimes painful information will, therefore, be substantially diminished.

Third, each response is assumed to have its cause in the psychological make-up of the subject. Many critics of projective techniques have objected to the Thematic Apperception Test, for example, on the grounds that the subject may merely recount the plot of a movie he has seen or the content of a book he has read recently, instead of producing personally meaningful information. This objection, however, disregards the fact that from all the experiences a person has had, he selects certain ones to remember and to recount, and that these selections in turn have personal meaning.

The Importance of Measuring Individual Differences

What is the value of measuring individual differences? What purposes will such measurement serve? To answer these questions it may help to look at the results of one test.

The scores from a mechanical aptitude test are plotted on page 412. The graph shows a "normal distribution curve," the kind usually found in testing large groups. The most frequent scores range around 50, and are represented by a peak in the center of the graph. To either side the lines curve down, describing lower and lower frequencies as the scores approach the low extreme of 10 and the high extreme of 90. Very few of the subjects got scores near the extremes—that is, very few had extremely low or extremely high aptitudes.

How can we make use of such scores? That depends on our purpose. Let us look at a few possibilities.

Figure 8. Projective techniques with children. Three photos showing children's construction with the World Test. (Left) Sue's "world" is aggressive, hostile, and at the same time strangely chaotic. (Middle) Noreen's "world" is rigid, schematic, and expressive of anti-social feelings. There are no people at all; the school is pushed far to the corner. (Right) Angela's "world" is completely chaotic, though populated and unaggressive. It is a widely spread town but lacks any over-all plan. (From Childhood Problems and the Teacher, *by C. Buhler, F. Smitter, S. Richardson, and F. Bradshaw, copyright 1952, Holt, Rinehart and Winston, Inc. By permission.)*

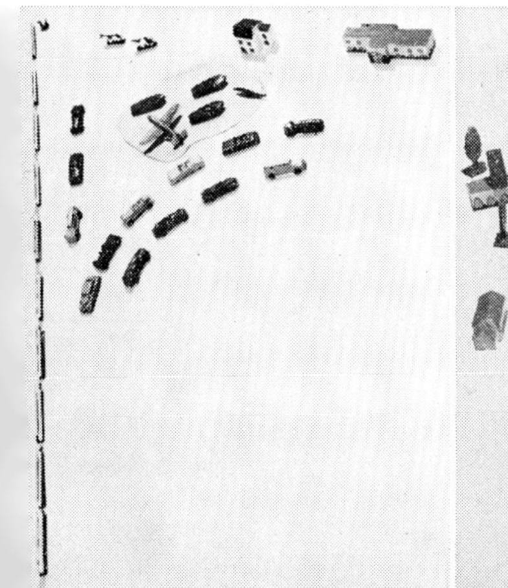

If we are hiring people for jobs that require a certain type of knowledge, we may find it advisable to hire those who fall in the range from 60 to 80 in our distribution. For we know from past experience that those with lower scores cannot perform the tasks well, and that those with the higher scores are too good for the job and will become dissatisfied because the work is not stimulating enough.

Or let us assume we are dealing with a group of adults who want to improve their reading proficiency. With the help of tests we can find out how quickly they read and how well they understand what they read. Again we find a normal distribution of scores. In this case we may decide that we can teach them more effectively if we divide them into three groups, putting together the low-scorers, the middle-scorers, and the high-scorers.

The information psychologists have accumulated on individual differences has led to far-reaching changes in all levels of our educational procedures, in personnel practices in business and industry, in civil service, in fact in almost every area of life.

We realize today that we may find high mental ability at any socio-economic level, that children may be brighter than their parents, or that not all bright parents have bright children. And we realize the

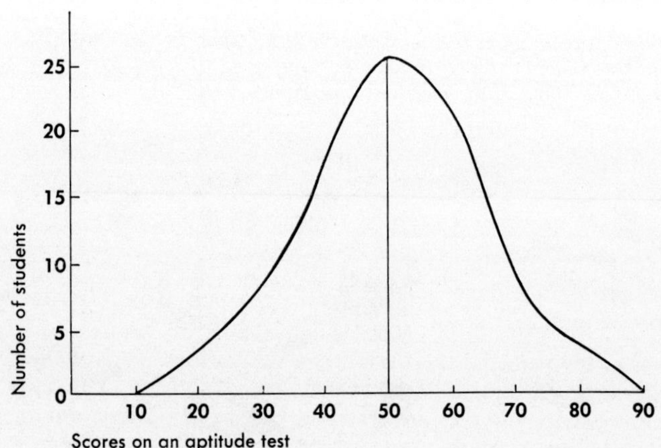

Figure 9. A normal distribution curve.

importance of using an individual's assets to the best possible advantage, both for his own good and for the good of society. Our greatest asset is our people—and their *various* abilities. It would be a dull, perhaps unbearable, world if we were all alike, if we all had the same interests, the same likes and dislikes.

Systematic and extensive measurement of individual differences has made a significant contribution to our knowledge of human ability and personality, particularly insofar as the diagnosing and predicting of human behavior are concerned. The question of individual differences is important in educational and vocational guidance and in marriage counseling. The clinical use of tests can help the psychologist to detect instances of unusual or abnormal behavior that may indicate maladjustment, or worse, may be the forerunner of a serious breakdown. Having detected such behavior, he can take steps to prevent further disturbances by helping the person to achieve a better adjustment.

For Additional Reading

Abt, Lawrence E. and Leopold Bellak, eds., *Projective Psychology. Clinical Approaches to the Total Personality*. New York: Knopf, 1950.

Adorno, T. W., *et al.*, *The Authoritarian Personality*. New York: Harper, 1950.

Allport, Gordon W., *The Use of Personal Documents in Psychological Science*. New York: Social Science Research Council, Bulletin No. 49, 1942.

Anastasi, Anne, *Psychological Testing*. New York: Macmillan, 1961.

Anderson, H. H. and G. L. Anderson, *Introduction to Projective Techniques*. Englewood Cliffs, N. J.: Prentice-Hall, 1951.

Benedict, Ruth, *Patterns of Culture*. New York: Penguin, 1947.

Boring, Edwin G., *A History of Experimental Psychology*. New York: Century, 1929.

———, *Psychology at Large*. New York: Basic Books, 1961. See especially the chapter on Lewis M. Terman, pp. 266-294.

Cattell, R. B., *Description and Measurement of Personality*. Yonkers, N. Y.: World Book, 1946.

Cronbach, Lee J., *Essentials of Psychological Testing* (2nd ed.). New York: Harper, 1960.

Dennis, Wayne, ed., *Readings in the History of Psychology*. New York: Appleton-Century-Crofts, 1948.

Dressel, Paul, *et al.*, *Evaluation in Higher Education*. New York: Houghton Mifflin, 1961.

Dunn, L. D. and Theodosius Dobzhansky, *Heredity, Race and Society* (rev. ed.). New York: New American Library of World Literature, Inc., 1952.

Eysenck, H. J., *The Scientific Study of Personality*. New York: Macmillan, 1952.

Frank, Lawrence K., *Projective Methods*. Springfield, Ill.: Thomas, 1948.

Freeman, Frank S., *Theory and Practice of Psychological Testing* (3rd ed.). New York: Holt, Rinehart and Winston, 1962.

Goodenough, Florence L., *Mental Testing—Its History, Principles and Applications*. New York: Rinehart, 1949.

Gulliksen, Harold, *Theory of Mental Tests*. New York: Wiley, 1950.

Hunt, J. McV., *Intelligence and Experience*. New York: Ronald, 1961.

Jenkins, James J. and Donald G. Paterson, eds., *Studies in Individual Differences: The Search for Intelligence*. New York: Appleton-Century-Crofts, 1961.

Johnson, Wendell, *People in Quandaries*. New York: Harper, 1946.

Kahn, Theodore C. and Martin B. Giffen, *Psychological Techniques in Diagnosis and Evaluation*. New York: Pergamon, 1960.

Klopfer, Bruno, *et al.*, *Developments in the Rorschach Technique: Technique and Theory*. New York: Harcourt, Brace, 1954.

Lindzey, Gardner, *Projective Techniques in Cross-Cultural Research*. New York: Appleton-Century-Crofts, 1961.

Lyman, Howard C., *Test Scores and What They Mean*. Englewood Cliffs, N. J.: Prentice-Hall, 1963.

Murphy, Gardner, *An Historical Introduction to Modern Psychology*. New York: Harcourt, Brace, 1938.

Murray, Henry A., *Explorations in Personality*. New York: Oxford University Press, 1938.

———, and Clyde Kluckhohn, "Outline of a Conception of Personality," in *Personality in Nature, Society, and Culture* (2nd ed.), eds. Clyde Kluckhohn, Henry A. Murray, and D. Schneider. New York: Knopf, 1953, pp. 3-52.

Murstein, B. I. and R. S. Pryer, "The Concept of Projection: A Review," *Psychological Bulletin*, LVI (1959), 353-374.

Mussen, Paul H., ed., *Handbook of Research Methods in Child Development*. New York: Wiley, 1960.

Piaget, Jean, *Psychology of Intelligence*. Peterson, N. J.: Littlefield, Adams, 1960.

Rabin, Albert J. and Mary R. Haworth, eds., *Projective Techniques with Children*. New York: Grune and Stratton, 1960.

Sarason, Irwin G., ed., *Contemporary Research in Personality*. Princeton, N. J.: Van Nostrand, 1962.

Stern, G. G., M. I. Stein and B. S. Bloom, *Methods in Personality Assessment*. Glencoe, Ill.: Free Press, 1956.

Super, Donald E. and John O. Crites, *Appraising Vocational Fitness by Means of Psychological Tests* (rev. ed.). New York: Harper, 1962.

Terman, Lewis M. and Maud A. Merrill, *Stanford-Binet Intelligence Scale. Manual for the Third Revision Form L-M*. Boston: Houghton Mifflin, 1960.

——— and Melitta H. Oden, *Genetic Studies of Genius: V. The Gifted Group at Mid-Life: Thirty-five Years' Follow-up of the Superior Child*. Stanford, Calif.: Stanford University Press, 1959.

Tomkins, Silvan S., *The Thematic Apperception Test: The Theory and Technique of Interpretation*. New York: Grune and Stratton, 1947.

Tyler, Leona E., *Tests and Measurements*. Englewood Cliffs, N. J.: Prentice-Hall, 1963.

Wechsler, D., *The Measurement and Appraisal of Adult Intelligence* (4th ed.). Baltimore: Williams and Wilkins, 1958.

———, *The Range of Human Capacities*. Baltimore: Williams and Wilkins, 1952.

Witkin, H. A., *et al.*, *Psychological Differentiation. Studies of Development*. New York: Wiley, 1962.

Wrightstone, J. Wayne, Joseph Justman, and Irving Robbins, *Evaluation in Modern Education*. New York: American Book, 1956.

For Directory of Test Publishers, see p. 468.

Psychotherapy

15

Psychotherapy

is a process for treating a problem

or an illness

by psychological methods.

It is a learning situation,

involving two or more persons,

in which an attempt is made

to correct

the effects of disruptive experiences

or of certain deficiencies

in learning.

During this process the patient strives to attain, insofar as is possible for him, the characteristics of satisfactory adjustment. These characteristics will be described in Chapter 16.

What constitutes adjustment for one person, however, may differ markedly from what constitutes adjustment for another. Personal comfort, creativity, happiness, mean different things to different people. Psychotherapy, therefore, focuses on the individual and his own needs. It emphasizes that each must learn to adjust in the manner that suits him best, regardless of what goals others may be seeking. But it also insists that this adjustment must involve satisfactory interaction with others, since it cannot be attained through isolation.

Problems treated by psychotherapy are usually emotional or psychological in origin. But psychotherapy may also be used as an adjunct to medical treatment—when, for example, a physical ailment, such as an ulcer, is related to emotional disturbances. The *psychotherapeutic* process is effective mainly in *psychogenic*, that is, functional, diseases.

In psychotherapy the psychologist, psychiatrist, or analyst attempts to create for the patient an environment conducive to mental health. The different approaches of these specialists will be described later in the chapter; but in general their methods are based on psychological dynamics, which involve a special understanding of the cause-and-effect relationships operating in our feelings, thoughts, and interactions with others. In discussing defense mechanisms, neuroses, and psychoses we touched on some of these dynamic factors that relate to psychological disturbances. In this chapter we shall discuss how a person's adjustment to himself and to his environment becomes more satisfactory as he is helped to alter his thoughts, feelings, and behavior.

Since psychotherapy is a process for changing behavior, it can be thought of as a special kind of learning situation. As a first step in understanding it, therefore, let us consider the relationship between psychotherapy and learning.

Psychotherapy as a Learning Process

We develop our behavior patterns through a series of experiences that teach us how to think, feel, and act. These behavior patterns may enable us to adjust satisfactorily, or they may cause us to be maladjusted. People who are frequently angry or aggressive, for example, have developed maladjustive techniques for handling their problems. Those who are well-adjusted have learned to approach their problems calmly and rationally, firmly believing they can solve them by applying lessons they have learned in the past.

But since new situations may confront us with problems we have never had to solve before, solutions that have worked in the past may be inapplicable. If we rely too heavily on familiar, tried-and-true techniques, our approaches to problems may become rigid and unimaginative. Psychotherapy can show us how to *alter* our behavior by modifying our approaches. It can teach the neurotic person to replace inappropriate habits with constructive techniques.

Let us illustrate briefly how a particular experience might produce neurotic behavior and how the psychotherapeutic learning process might modify this behavior. Suppose a small child has been severely frightened by a dog that jumped on him and knocked him down. The child's *observable behavior* may exhibit the following pattern: He may not only avoid the dog that frightened him but may begin to avoid all dogs, thus *generalizing* his fear. Consequently, at the sight of any dog he may run, or begin to cry, or seek comfort and shelter with adults. The comments by which he reveals his *feelings and emotions* may indicate that he is tense, anxious, fearful, perhaps even physically upset. His *thoughts and fantasies* may also be affected by his fear of dogs. He may imagine that vicious dogs are following him wherever he goes, or waiting around every corner to pounce on him. He may spend much of his time dreaming up ways of escaping them. His mind may, in fact, be so full of his fears that he sees dogs where there are none.

Psychotherapy could help this child to *learn* that his fears were unfounded—that many dogs, perhaps the majority, are gentle, affectionate, and playful. It could help him, through learning, to develop a more realistic attitude.

However, since a single experience would not seem sufficient to produce such a pervasive anxiety, it would be advisable to explore the matter further during the psychotherapeutic process in order to understand the additional causes of this intensive reaction.

Let us look at another example of the effects of psychotherapeutic learning. Mrs. A sought therapy because she suffered intense feelings of inferiority, loneliness, and anxiety, which produced violent temper outbursts. Mrs. A had been born with one leg shorter than the other, and because of this handicap she had, as a child, been teased and humiliated by other children. As an adolescent she had been excluded from such normal activities as sports and dancing, and had been rejected by boys.

The humiliating experiences Mrs. A remembered suffering as a crippled girl in a culture where physical beauty and perfection are highly valued had prevented her from participating in the activities of the other children. Thus her interactions with others had led to the development of behavior patterns and attitudes (including her bursts of temper and the feelings that produced them) that created difficulties and prompted her to seek therapy.

At the commencement of therapy Mrs. A's behavior was forceful, aggressive, and domineering; but she reported that she often felt anxious, fearful, and insecure. She further recounted certain recurring thoughts and fantasies, in which she saw herself winning foot races or beauty contests or being complimented on her dancing ability.

Through psychotherapy Mrs. A learned to modify her attitudes and her behavior so that she no longer felt it necessary to try to compensate for her handicap. She learned that her extreme sensitivity as a child had probably caused her to misinterpret a few, isolated experiences and to conclude on the basis of this false interpretation that all people rejected her. She had reacted by developing aggressive tendencies. As she grew older, it was not her physical handicap that caused people to reject her but rather the aggressive tendencies which she had developed in an effort to compensate for the handicap. If she had been pleasant and cooperative instead of aggressive and domineering she would probably have had a wide circle of friends.

Once she had learned through psychotherapy to understand the real reason for her unsatisfactory interpersonal relationships, Mrs. A was able to alter her behavior and to become cooperative and friendly. If she had been able to learn this lesson as a child, the difficulty might never have arisen. Psychotherapy, therefore, may be regarded as a technique that serves to remove the learning lag reflected in maladjustment.

This example illustrates how psychotherapy is a process of *un*-learning and *re*learning. Before we can learn correct attitudes and procedures we must unlearn the incorrect ones that are blocking our way. These incorrect approaches can stem from any number of sources. In psychotherapy we must discover some of these sources and unlearn the attitudes and behavior they have created.

In discovering these sources we may find that it is possible for a particular behavior pattern to spring from a single, isolated stimulus in our physical environment. This can be illustrated by the proverb, *the burned child fears the fire*. A child must be burned only once to learn to fear the fire. When we consider this phenomenon in relation to the thousands of stimuli we receive from our physical environment, and then introduce into the picture the millions of social stimuli we receive through our relationships with other people, we begin to realize how involved the process of learning and reacting to learning can become.

All of these minute learning situations act upon us, transforming us from mere biological organisms at birth into highly socialized, civilized adults. So complex is the world we live in, so varied and often bewildering the demands made on us, so involved and hectic the problems we face, that it is easily possible for us to fail to learn some of the things we need to know or to mislearn others. Either of these conditions can lead to maladjustment.

Among the kinds of mislearning which psychotherapy seeks to correct is the mislearning that leads us to make *generalizations*—sweeping inferences or conclusions based on impressions gained from a few isolated examples. A young man's father, for example, may have been an insensitive tyrant, and, as a result, the young man may have generalized that *all* men in authority are insensitive tyrants. He may regard them all with the same mixed feelings of fear and hatred he felt for his father. Such a generalization might cause serious interpersonal disturbances. It might lead him to try to defend himself against difficulties that exist only in his imagination. And this defensive behavior might in turn invite exactly the reaction he fears, thus reinforcing his generalized belief. He may refuse to cooperate. He may react to suggestions as though they were threats. He may constantly complain that he is being bullied or overworked or otherwise treated unfairly. Then, when his superiors lose patience with him and rebuke him for his attitude, he may convert their actions into motives for overgeneralizing about his inability to get along with people in authority. He may say to himself, "I can *never* work for this man again," or, "*Nobody* understands me." When we stop to analyze, during the therapeutic process, what a patient means by the remark, "Nobody understands me," we may discover that he has established this attitude on the basis of a few isolated incidents in which someone unintentionally caused him to feel rejected.

People beset by intense emotional reactions often think in terms of such absolutes. They may believe that *all* persons in authority are *always* tyrannical and that they *never* understand or appreciate the problems of *anyone* who works for them. In cases of neurotic overgeneralization, the therapist's job is to help the patient to make finer and more valid discriminations between persons, events, and experiences—to learn, for example, that not all people in responsible positions are arbitrary and tyrannical, even though his father was.

Sometimes people overgeneralize by confusing the past with the present. The neurotic, because of his inability to distinguish past and present, tries to interpret today's events in the light of yesterday's reactions. He brings into the present, where they are not appropriate, feelings and reactions he should already have discarded. In this connection, the patient must learn to distinguish between childhood and adult roles. He must re-evaluate his childhood inadequacies in the light of his adult capacities and accomplishments. The adult who says, "I was shy as a child," must discover the source of these childhood feelings in order to see that his timidity need not continue to plague him as an adult.

From this description of a neurotic's maladjustive generalizations, we can see that he is his own worst enemy. Many neurotics possess great potentialities for success and yet cannot succeed. The bright student who fails in school, the beautiful woman who can't get or stay married, the mother who can't love her children, the executive who can't deal with his subordinates—all these people offer examples of self-defeating behavior. This is especially true in the spheres of human relations and emotions. Although all of us experience emotions, we often find them difficult to describe and name, either for ourselves or for others. And because we cannot define them we are frequently at a loss as to how to deal with them.

By providing the patient with new names or labels for his disruptive experiences and feelings, the therapist helps him to increase his awareness of cause-and-effect relationships. By enabling the patient to re-evaluate his attitudes, feelings, and defenses, and so replace his *unrealistic generalizations* with *constructive discriminations*, the therapist helps him to modify his behavior.

To sum up, in psychotherapy the patient learns to alter his feelings and attitudes. He learns to make fewer generalizations and finer discriminations; he learns to stop thinking in absolutes; he learns to react to others according to their actual characteristics, rather than according to his own biases toward them. Just as the small child learns that not all men are his father, so the neurotic adult learns, that people cannot be classified according to his extreme "either-or" categories.

Out of the therapeutic process comes a new process of controlled, responsible evaluation—free from the emotional distortion and anxiety-produced defenses of the past—that helps to remedy the patient's deprivations and to provide him with reinforcements and rewards.

The Patient-Therapist Relationship

The kind of relationship established between the patient and his therapist is believed to have a decisive influence on the success of the therapy. The patient-therapist relationship is a special kind of association encountered nowhere else. It offers the patient, through the behavior and attitudes of the therapist, a unique learning situation. He and the therapist work together, the therapist helping the patient to recognize his deficiencies, to understand their sources, and to work out satisfactory ways of resolving them. The psychotherapeutic setting is consciously designed to promote this kind of learning. It provides (1) a sheltered atmosphere, (2) understanding, (3) an attitude of acceptance, (4) permissiveness, and (5) feelings of support. Let us consider each of these factors briefly.

Sheltered Atmosphere

The therapist provides for the patient a sheltered atmosphere in which he can *test reality*—an atmosphere in which he can analyze, explore, and test his ways of thinking and feeling. The therapeutic setting is a kind of laboratory in which the patient may experiment and perhaps make all sorts of errors without having to experience the feelings of failure, shame, or disappointment that might result if he made them in the outside world. For this reason he is able to experiment with progressively more difficult situations. The more he experiments and explores, regardless of errors, the more successfully he utilizes the therapeutic situation.

Understanding

The psychotherapeutic situation is an encounter between two (or more, as in group therapy) human beings, and is a new situation for the therapist as well as for the patient. Even when the therapist has seen the patient's case history, even when he already knows something of his background and his present problems, he interacts with a human being, not with a set of symptoms. Background information is valuable; thorough training in therapeutic skills is essential; but every patient presents a new situation.

The therapist must be willing and able to understand the patient and his world, a world which may be very different from his own. The therapist must be willing to expose himself not only to a new world, but also to an individual whose personal style of integration and organization are unfamiliar to him. He must be willing to experience attitudes and values which may open up to him a way of life different from but not necessarily inferior to his own, even though it has created problems for the patient. Thus the psychotherapeutic situation is a new learning situation for the therapist too, and may provoke anxieties in him as well as in the patient.

Satisfactory communication between therapist and patient is essential for understanding. At times this may be difficult not only for the patient but also for the therapist. Our methods of communication are affected by our social backgrounds and by our particular experiences. If wide differences exist it may be difficult to bridge the gap.[1]

Therapists agree that the patient must establish an adjustment pattern in keeping with his personal make-up and values and his particular environment. Yet the therapist's own value system may intrude itself in many ways into the therapeutic process. Even though he may not state his values explicitly, the therapist may communicate them in various subtle ways which influence the patient. If the value systems of patient and therapist are not compatible, the intrusion of the therapist's values may cause the psychotherapeutic effort to fail.

Attitude of Acceptance

The therapist must be able to accept the patient, to empathize with him, and through his behavior and attitudes make the patient aware of this empathy. A feeling of acceptance must be transmitted to the patient no matter what his problems or characteristics may be.

Acceptance of the patient by the therapist leads to what psychologists call *positive transference.* In positive transference the patient becomes strongly attached to his therapist. He may view him as an idealized parent, husband, wife, or lover. In what is called *negative* transference, however, the patient may detest the therapist. It frequently happens that the patient loves the therapist one moment and hates him the next. Through all of his changing moods and attitudes, the therapist must continue to accept the patient with warmth and understanding, remaining aware that when the patient hates him it is because he hates what the therapist is helping him to learn about himself, or because he wishes the therapist would help him to learn

[1] For a discussion of social class, mental illness and therapy, see especially August B. Hollingshead and Frederick C. Redlich, *Social Class and Mental Illness* (New York: Wiley, 1958).

faster. If the therapist ever gives the impression that he is not accepting the patient, serious new problems may arise. This is why it is so important for the therapist to be thoroughly trained, as well as emotionally stable and well adjusted in his own right.

The therapist is careful not to criticize the patient. He tries to prevent his own feelings from influencing his responses to the patient. He refrains from making judgments. His only aim, as far as the patient is concerned, is to help him to attain a better understanding of himself. This sort of non-judgmental, non-prejudicial, non-condemning attitude is almost never present when a person tries to discuss his problems with a parent, marriage partner, minister, or friend. Such people have their own particular frames of reference, their own values, their own attitudes; and through their personal reactions and advice they may try to influence the patient to accept a view or solution that fails to take into account his actual needs.

The therapist's acceptance leads the patient to feel intellectually understood, emotionally accepted, and sympathetically supported in all his reactions during therapy—in other words, leads him to feel safe. The constant encouragement provided by the therapist enables the patient to face, explore, and eventually overcome his problems.

Permissiveness

The therapist is permissive. He has no ready answers to give. Rather, he listens while the patient talks about things he cannot discuss with anyone else. By talking freely about them to the therapist, without fear of criticism or censure, the patient is able to extinguish disturbing reactions, such as fear or guilt feelings, which he has formerly associated with the things that have been bothering him. This chance to talk freely produces catharsis—a feeling of emotional release that the patient experiences as he unburdens himself of tensions that may have been bottled up inside him for years.

Most of us harbor thoughts and feelings we fear to disclose to others. In the protected, permissive atmosphere of therapy, the patient can talk such feelings over, confident that the therapist will understand his doubts and fears. The more the patient talks, the more his confidence returns, and the more freely he discloses previously repressed feelings and thoughts or previously concealed behavior. He may suddenly find himself talking about things he had forgotten—or had not permitted himself to think about—for years.

Feelings of Support

In order to bolster the patient's self-confidence, the therapist tries to reassure him by providing him with needed information, and even at times by offering judicious suggestions. If he believes the patient's environment needs to be altered, the therapist may help him to find a new job, to make new friends, or to develop more meaningful activities. If it seems necessary he may also take steps designed to improve the patient's home environment.

The therapist may also direct his patient toward certain groups which can help with specific problems. Alcoholics Anonymous, Divorcees Anonymous, or various forms of group therapy may have great therapeutic value. For some patients participation in religious activities and the support they derive from religious inspiration may provide a valuable adjunct to therapy.

The Goals of Psychotherapy

At first glance it might seem that the goal of psychotherapy would be simply to get rid of maladjustive or neurotic symptoms. But symptoms are only indicators, and just as a mechanic cannot repair a car by merely tampering with the gauges on the dashboard, so a therapist cannot modify behavior by merely treating reaction patterns. We do not cure the alcoholic by hiding his whiskey.

The principal goal of psychotherapy is to modify our reactions to problem situations. In order to do so it is necessary to explore cause-and-effect relationships and thereby discover the sources of the patient's problems. A new appreciation of how cause-and-effect relationships function in our behavior is one of the major benefits to be derived from psychotherapy.

Before we can modify behavior, certain other modifications must take place. In order to discuss them let us divide the goal of psychotherapy into seven interrelated subgoals: modification of (1) feelings,

(2) perceptions, (3) interpretations, (4) judgments, (5) motivation, (6) awareness, and (7) behavior.

Modification of Feelings

During the psychotherapeutic process, the patient describes his behavior, both past and present. In doing so he gives vent to certain feelings. Usually he is apprehensive at first and gives only superficial, rehearsed information, hoping to stave off a deep, intensive examination of his personality. But gradually he

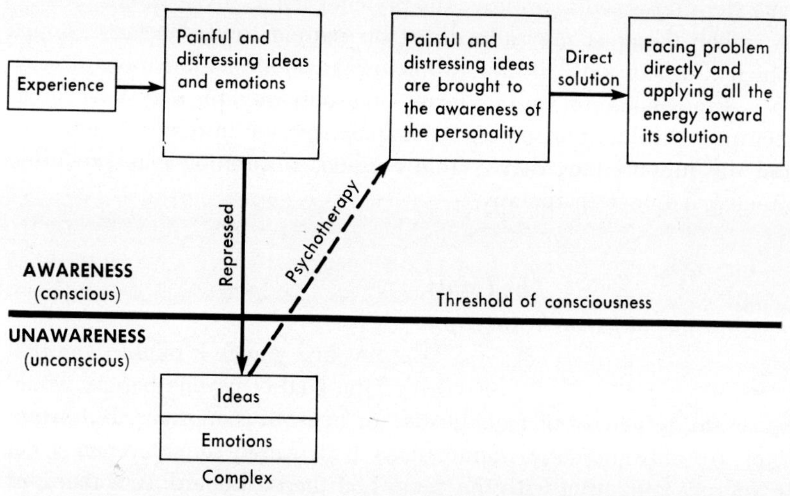

Figure 1. The application and functioning of psychotherapy. (From Barney Katz and George F. J. Lehner, Mental Hygiene in Modern Living. *New York: The Ronald Press Company, 1953, p. 492.)*

begins to express more and more of his true feelings. As he does so the therapist tries to clarify and explain the feelings. Where the patient, reluctant to display signs of anxiety or anger, may formerly have repressed such emotions, he now discovers that he is free to reveal them. As he brings them out into the open he is able to look at them more objectively, guided by the therapist, and he is able to discard some of them and to modify others.

Modification of Perceptions

Perception is a process by which we give meaning to our sensations. If we see a red light flashing from a traffic pole, for example, we know it is not a decoration. It is a stop signal. If we thoughtlessly drive through it and then see a policeman, we perceive him as a source of punishment. If, on the other hand, we see a policeman when we are lost in a strange town, we perceive him as a source of assistance. Perceptions may at times be unrealistic, and since we react to people and events as we perceive them, unrealistic perceptions can lead us into difficulties. Neurotic persons are especially prone to distort reality by perceiving it in the light of their warped attitudes.

Psychotherapeutic treatment, therefore, is aimed at helping the patient to realize that his disturbing impressions are merely a reflection of his own insecurity, and that when other people seem disagreeable they may merely be reflecting his own hostility. This new awareness can help him to see that his subjective perceptions are rooted in his own feelings and that they must be modified to conform to reality. Through therapy the patient may regain an objective, realistic relationship to his environment.

Modification of Interpretations

In addition to altering perceptions, psychotherapy can also modify one's interpretations of events. When a maladjusted person perceives really friendly people as hostile, unfriendly, or threatening, he cannot interpret their actions correctly. His viewpoint limits his reactions, his motives, and the scope of his behavior. The boundaries of his understanding are so narrow that to understand, predict, or interpret behavior—his own or that of others—is impossible for him. This weakness leaves him puzzled, disturbed, and anxious.

Psychotherapy attempts to alter the manner in which the maladjusted person makes interpretations and the kind of interpretations he habitually makes. He is led to examine his own motives and those of others in order to see how his interpretations reflect his own needs. He is stimulated to become aware of the infinite number of forces that influence behavior. He learns to avoid basing his interpretations on a few inadequate and unfounded generalizations. Once he acquires the understanding that enables him to make realistic and meaningful interpretations, his own behavior as well as the behavior of others becomes more intelligible and predictable to him.

Modification of Judgments

Judgment is the process by which, through comparisons and discriminations among items or events, we *make decisions and assign values.* It involves relating persons and events to our own frame of reference or philosophy of life. Judgment is a highly subjective process that gives expression to our personal interpretations, often in terms of approval or disapproval. A maladjusted person who has acquired a distorted set of values is likely to make judgments that lead him further into difficulties. He may be hypercritical, always ready to denounce even when he has no real basis for denunciation. He may often feel compelled to display his judgments, no matter how vague his understanding of a situation may be. Frequently he wants a decision, an answer (often he demands a simple "yes" or "no" answer), even when decisions and answers cannot be easily provided.

The ability to *suspend* judgment involves an emotional maturity the maladjusted person often lacks. Psychotherapy attempts to help the patient to acquire this type of maturity. It helps him to evaluate the process by which he makes judgments and reaches decisions. It also attempts to divert his attention from the process of judging to the process of understanding—to substitute objectivity for subjectivity.

Modification of Motivation

We have remarked many times that it is important to understand our own needs. These needs, as we know, motivate our behavior. They determine our goals, our self-concepts, and the way we make interpretations or judgments. Psychotherapy attempts to help the patient to recognize the needs motivating him, to see where they are leading him, and to understand the central role they play in his behavior. When he comes to understand his motives, he may relinquish old, unattainable goals, set his sights on new goals that are more within his reach, and come to realize the importance of constantly examining and re-examining his goals and his motives in the light of his needs.

Modification of Awareness

Psychotherapy attempts to make the patient more aware of all the factors, conscious and unconscious, that affect his behavior. Increased awareness is sometimes called *insight* and may be related to a better appreciation of how we perceive, interpret, judge, and are motivated. In psychotherapy much of our improvement in self-awareness comes about through uncovering long-forgotten and suppressed experiences and the thoughts and, especially, the feelings associated with them. Psychologists sometimes call this process "making the unconscious conscious."

Modification of Behavior

The therapist's ultimate objective is to modify the behavior of his patient along the lines we have been discussing. But the therapist is interested in eliminating not only behavioral symptoms, but also the problems that produced them. Of course the compulsive patient who eats or drinks too much, who suffers from phobias and irrational fears, who is depressed, or who exhibits physical symptoms without any organic basis, wants first of all to be relieved of his symptoms and the suffering they bring him. He might in fact measure the therapist's proficiency by his success in removing these symptoms. The therapist, however, looks at the situation differently. For him the symptom, although important in itself, is viewed as a sign of a deeper, more fundamental trouble. He is interested in the underlying behavior patterns that caused the symptoms, and he must distinguish between symptom treatment (such as giving an aspirin for a headache), and problem treatment (finding the cause of the headache). Modifying behavior through therapy, therefore, involves changes at both the symptom level and the problem level.

In general terms, the goal of therapy is to make the patient feel more secure, to increase his self-esteem, and to sharpen his insight. In this way therapy can help him to accept himself and to achieve greater spontaneity and creativity. In accomplishing these aims psychotherapy removes the barriers that have prevented him from becoming well adjusted.

Theories of Psychotherapy

The differences between the various "schools" of therapy are often less matters of fundamental divergences than they are differences in emphasis placed on certain theoretical ideas. All schools of therapy, for example, recognize the value of catharsis. But therapists differ in the methods by which they approach it and the theoretical importance they assign to it in their systems. Different schools and theories of psychotherapy frequently employ similar methods and concepts.

We might say that therapists are often more easily distinguished by their terminology than by their practices—by what they say rather than by what they do. The factors conducive to learning, which we described earlier, are probably used by all therapists, regardless of their theoretical orientation. All therapists are increasing their concern with the psychodynamics of learning. The effectiveness with which they use them depends, of course, on their ability, training, and experience.

Differences do exist, however, in both theory and technique. We shall describe the general characteristics of the following techniques: (1) psychoanalytic therapies, (2) directive therapy, (3) non-directive therapy, (4) relationship therapy, (5) group therapy, and (6) self-analysis.

Psychoanalytic Therapies

Psychoanalysis, whether we consider the views of Freud, Jung, or Adler, is a theory of personality as well as a therapeutic technique. Many of the therapeutic procedures and ideas about personality originally developed by Freud, Jung, or Adler have now been absorbed into the general body of psychotherapy. In psychoanalysis, as distinguished from other therapeutic methods, we generally find a heavy emphasis on such techniques as free association, dream analysis, and systematic use of interpretation, catharsis, and emotional re-education. Crucial to the psychoanalytic process is the relationship between the therapist and the patient, involving transference, which provides the emotional leverage for therapy. In general the goal of psychoanalysis is to uncover and resolve emotional conflicts in the patient, many of which stem from early childhood experiences.

It should also be mentioned that since its introduction by Freud psychoanalysis has gone through several stages of development. At different times different concepts have been stressed—catharsis, free association, and the transfer neuroses, for example. Today the tendency is to emphasize emotional re-learning. This emphasis is particularly apparent in the recent developments involving so-called "brief" psychoanalysis, which appears to be more like re-education than therapy in the conventional sense. This new approach emphasizes further the close relationship between psychotherapy and the learning process discussed earlier.

FREUD The most elaborate and systematic attempt to explain the origins, development, and cure of psychological disturbances was made by Sigmund Freud. From his early publications in the 1880's until his death in 1939, Freud continued to examine and theorize about the causes, psychodynamics, and manifestations of mental disorders, and to promulgate a method of psychotherapy. He was an acute, sensitive observer of human nature, and many of his ideas, although controversial when introduced, have become part of our everyday thinking.

Freud believed that all of us, while infants and small children, pass through certain stages of development marked by a concentration of interest in particular bodily areas or functions. At each of these stages we encounter different social learning problems. First comes the so-called *oral-erotic* stage, during which the child derives his chief emotional satisfactions from nursing, thumb-sucking, biting, and chewing. In this stage the child also encounters his first major psychological frustration—weaning. This weaning frustration provides the child with his first indication that he is a separate person from his mother.

Second comes the *anal-erotic* stage, during which the child is concerned with the process of controlling the expulsion and retention of feces. The main frustration appearing at this time concerns toilet training. Freud believed that this frustration led to the development of further self-awareness and the beginning of a sense of responsibility. Toilet training taught the child that he had certain obligations to fulfill and that he must adjust to certain social and physical demands in his pursuit of pleasure.

The third stage Freud called the *genital* or *phallic* stage, during which the child derives emotional pleasure and satisfaction from discovering, exploring, and using his sex organs. Frustrations at this stage arise from the suppression of the sexual urges that develop toward the parent of the opposite sex. Freud stressed the frustrating Oedipal situation of the son in love with his mother or the daughter in love with her father. He believed that these frustrations helped the youngster to develop a sense of self-reliance and responsibility that enabled him to become independent of his parents, to stand alone in society, and to form new attachments with other adults, leading to the establishment of a family of his own.

Freud felt that the basic groundwork of personality was laid during infancy and early childhood. He believed that later breakdowns or maladjustive behavior resulted from a fixation at the oral or anal stage arising from inadequate development. This emphasis upon childhood experiences explains why his therapy stresses examining the infancy of the patient in order to determine at which stage his development lagged or was diverted from the normal developmental channels. The process by which childhood experiences are retraced is known as *free association.* In free association, the patient is asked to say anything that occurs to him, regardless of how insignificant or irrelevant it may seem or how reluctant he may be to express it. He is asked to assume a detached attitude toward his own thoughts and to exert as little direction and control over his associations and ideas as possible. The patient's ability to free-associate is facilitated by the permissive atmosphere created by the therapist and by the objectivity with which the therapist approaches everything the patient says.

These free associations sooner or later lead the patient back to his adolescence and infancy and involve, of course, his parents and possibly other authority figures. Reliving these infantile experiences may cause the patient to react emotionally to the therapist in the same way that he previously reacted to his parents. This is the transference situation, mentioned previously, in which the patient comes to project onto the therapist the feelings of love or hatred he formerly felt toward his parents. This transference phenomenon and the strong emotional interactions between the patient and therapist constitute an important aspect of the therapeutic process. Through the transference situation, the patient gains new insights into his feelings, attitudes, and behavior.

Another technique that helps the patient to remember and to disclose material about his early life and development is the *analysis of dreams.* In dreams the patient's feelings, hopes, and wishes visit him in disguise and the therapist can help him to see through this disguise to recognize the latent content of the dream, and to understand its real significance. Dreams and the symbolism in which they express themselves are often unconscious efforts at wish fulfillment.

JUNG An early co-worker of Freud, and a man who made important contributions to psychoanalysis, was Carl J. Jung, a Swiss psychiatrist. Jung's system of psychoanalysis is known as *analytic psychology.* He came to disagree with Freud primarily about the concept of libido, which for Freud meant the total life urge based mainly on love and sex. Jung defined the concept more broadly as a general life urge, not merely sexual in nature, but connected with all pleasures, especially social pleasures.

Jung also differed from Freud in his views about the unconscious. Jung's theory postulated both an *individual unconscious,* consisting of repressed personal experiences, and a *collective unconscious,* consisting of inherited predispositions toward archaic ways of thinking. Thus, dreams for Jung involved interpretations related to racial unconscious motives as well as to personal unconscious motives. The concept of the racial unconscious led him to undertake intensive study of the folklore and symbolism of both primitive and modern cultures.

Jung placed great emphasis upon dream analysis and upon the artistic productions of the patient. He also used free association but developed specially controlled association techniques in which the therapist provides a word and the patient responds with the first association that occurs to him. Through the use of the controlled association technique, Jung uncovered what he called *complexes,* which are clusters or patterns of emotional ideas and wishes related to certain objects or experiences.

Jung's view of personality structure and development posited a psychological pattern of opposite qualities and tendencies, such as thoughts *vs.* feelings, sensations *vs.* intuition, and extraversion *vs.* introversion. In the normal person, these contradictory poles are integrated, enabling him to achieve maximum development and to realize his potentialities fully. The neurotic, however, has allowed one tendency to develop out of all proportion to the others.

Jung, then, believed that analysis could help a person to discover which tendency had become exaggerated and how he should go about redressing the balance. Jung stressed the wholeness of personality and believed that a person must combine the rational and irrational aspects of his make-up in order to live a happy, well-adjusted life.

ADLER Alfred Adler, originally a member of Freud's group of analysts, later broke with Freud and developed his own views, which have come to be called *individual psychology.* Adler rejected Freud's concepts of the unconscious and repression, and also his emphasis upon the psychosexual origin of personality characteristics. Adler accepted Freud's insistence on psychological determinism, but felt that the source of the determination was man's *will to power.* He believed this was man's primary motive—the will to excel in social, economic, and sexual competition. Failure to excel in these areas, Adler asserted, led to an *inferiority complex,* which in turn was responsible for efforts to compensate for defects. These compensatory efforts, Adler believed, restricted personality growth.

According to Adler, personality development progressed along a road paved with evidences of either personal superiority or inferiority. As infants—small, helpless, inexperienced—we are especially subject to the whims of others and vulnerable to inferiority feelings. As we grow older, both family and society emphasize the advantages of size, beauty, and strength; and there develops within us a continual conflict between our wishes and dreams for superiority, our attempts to achieve it, and the social realities that may make us feel inferior.

This striving for prestige, which Adler called the *masculine protest*, occupies a place in his theory similar to that of the Oedipus situation in Freudian theory. A person develops into a normal adult or a neurotic or psychotic personality as the result of this struggle between the masculine protest and social reality.

In Adlerian therapy, which differs considerably from either the Jungian or orthodox Freudian therapy, no distinction is made between conscious and unconscious material. The Adlerian analyst, for example, uses dreams to discover the "style of life" of the patient, i.e. the type of defenses he utilizes in trying to establish his superiority. The therapist tries to analyze the inferiority feelings that stem from real or fancied personal deficiencies, particularly so-called organ deficiencies (such as defective vision), or from organic inferiority (weak heart), some form of which everyone is assumed to possess. Next he proceeds to examine the patient's marital, vocational, and social adjustments. Here he dwells on how the patient has maintained or achieved superiority in each of these major areas of life and examines the inferiority feelings that plague the patient. A primary goal of Adlerian therapy is to show the patient the overcompensations and defensive patterns he has acquired and to help him to find better ways of succeeding in his marital, vocational, and social strivings.

Directive Therapy

Considerably more directive than the psychoanalytic theories is the psychological approach worked out by the American psychiatrist, Adolf Meyer.[2] Meyer's theory incorporates parts of the findings of the psychoanalytic school but stresses more heavily influences of social experience and learning. It emphasizes the importance of viewing the person as a whole in the total environment. To this point of view, Meyer gave the name *psychobiology*. For him (in contrast to Freud) the sexual area of behavior becomes merely another area in which maladjustment can occur. He is inclined to discount transference phenomena and the role of the unconscious.

Meyer postulated a developmental theory similar to Freud's and stressed similar points, but he interpreted these points differently.

[2] Alfred Lief, ed., *The Commonsense Psychiatry of Dr. Adolf Meyer* (New York: McGraw-Hill, 1948).

For example, a maladjusted psychosexual development, Meyer believed, involved the acquisition of maladjustive habit patterns and social and personal attitudes. Accordingly, in order to attain maturity, a person must develop (learn) new habit patterns as old ones are found wanting. If an inappropriate set of habits is retained, the adult will become insecure and dissatisfied, and he will need either to build up a system of ideas, attitudes, and responses that will in some way explain his inappropriate habits, or else free himself from the intolerable situation.

Followers of Meyer emphasize direct instruction in therapy. The patient is told about the nature of his difficulties, their sources, and their incidence in the general population. A program is planned for him, sometimes covering his activities down to the last hour of his day. Situations are manufactured and forced upon him so that reconditioning techniques can operate. Thus, when the patient presents himself for therapy, the therapist takes command and, because of his prestige, expects implicit obedience. The therapist also stresses summarizing or synthetizing each session's dicussions, thereby stimulating the patient's natural capacity to integrate his experiences—something the maladjusted person finds very difficult to do.

Directive therapy assumes that a patient can be helped best by active intervention in and direction of his life. He is encouraged and given support; he is compelled to go through a period of relatively complete dependency at first. Later, the therapist will *require* him to show more and more independence and, finally, to break off and guide his own life.

Nondirective Therapy

In contrast to Meyer's approach, the nondirective view, developed by Carl Rogers, holds that a patient can best develop insight into and remedy his difficulties if he is permitted to proceed under his own power and at his own pace. The task of the analyst is to provide the proper atmosphere and clarification; his job is to reflect or mirror the feelings expressed by the patient so that he can hear them expressed in a social situation and become familiar with their implications. Thus, the therapist offers no new, interpretive material. He does not lead; he follows.

In Rogers' view behavior disorders are presumed to arise because the patient has had no opportunity to clarify his feelings and emotions. As a result the patient is powerless to understand or to explain his feelings, impulses, and conduct or to see that they differ from social and conscious reality. He therefore misinterprets some facets of reality and develops maladjustive patterns of responding. It is because of this misinterpretation of reality that some people, regardless of their success, can never classify themselves as succesful. They have established a self-concept of themselves as failures. Regardless of how well they perform, they always feel compelled to apologize for their poor performance. In nondirective therapy the patient is given the opportunity to evaluate his self-concept.

Rogers assumed that everyone has a natural capacity for personality growth and adjustment and that in the maladjusted person this natural drive has been thwarted or deflected by environmental obstacles and emotional blocks. The task of the therapist is to get the process of growth going again by removing these troublesome blocks. Since he has the natural growth forces of a person's personality for allies, the therapist can restrict himself to a passive role. By his permissive, accepting attitude, he encourages the patient to unburden himself of suppressed feelings. Through the technique of reflection (mirroring the patient's own feelings), he helps the patient to recognize, clarify, and accept these feelings and, finally, to develop new insight. By striving to keep his own personality unobtrusively in the background, the therapist minimizes the danger of forcing the patient's growth in the wrong direction.

Rogers holds that nondirective therapy, when skillfully applied, leads to an orderly and predictable sequence of development, the major therapeutic steps being the expression of feelings, the recognition of feelings, and the initiation of new behavior patterns. As this last stage is reached, the patient begins to feel less and less dependent on the therapist. He begins to realize, at first timidly and then with fewer qualms, that the therapeutic relationship must eventually end. The initiative in making the final break is left to him. And since this step is frequently accompanied by a new upsurge of anxiety, in the final interview the therapist assures him that he may come back if he feels he needs to.

Relationship Therapy

The therapies we have just discussed recognize, of course, the importance of the interaction between patient and therapist and between the patient and his social surroundings. But relationship therapy emphasizes this interaction even more. In effect, relationship therapy maintains that errors occurring during interpersonal relationships—errors, that is, that are made while relating to parents, children, friends, and the like—are responsible for maladjustment. The therapist tries to rectify these errors by assuming the roles of these other people in the hope that the patient will identify with him and gain a better understanding of what is involved in such relationships.

An important tool in relationship therapy is psychodrama. In this technique the therapist suggests a social situation that appears important to the patient and has him act out the roles of the various individuals involved. This acting out produces a catharsis and helps to lessen the patient's social deficiencies. The patient acquires the habit of picturing how others will react to his behavior, and in this way he learns which habits or traits to discard and which to retain and develop. The psychiatrist Harry Stack Sullivan [3] has contributed much to the ideas and procedures of relationship therapy.

Group Therapy

An important recent development in psychotherapy is group treatment. The therapist selects a group of patients (usually six to eight but sometimes more) who have disorders and complaints neither too different nor too similar. The group meets for about one and a half hours, one to three times a week. Advocates of group therapy believe it has certain advantages over individual psychotherapy. Group participation reduces the artificiality of the therapeutic situation, providing a more natural, everyday setting. The group also provides a certain social support for each member, a "we" feeling that may reduce the patient's anxiety about his own problems.

The group gives patients a special social "testing situation" in

[3] Harry Stack Sullivan, *The Interpersonal Theory of Psychiatry* (New York: Norton, 1953).

Child-guidance clinics give help to parents by providing opportunities for them to talk over their problems with other parents under the direction of a psychologist. (Courtesy the Los Angeles County Association for Mental Health—successor to the Southern California Society for Mental Hygiene—and Hal Adams, photographer.)

which each can learn how to improve his social relations, test his methods of dealing with others, identify himself with other persons and their problems, and obtain comfort through mutually sharing problems. The patient, becoming aware that other people suffer from problems similar to his own, is apt to lose much of his own sense of social rejection and isolation. As he observes the other members of the group, he begins to realize that they too have problems just as he does—some even worse, in fact. This helps to bolster his courage.

Through group discussion the patient's resistance is overcome. Hearing others talk about their problems often encourages the more inhibited patient to do the same. Positive and negative transferences may occur.

Group therapy is frequently used in combination with individual therapy. The patient may have one or two hours of individual therapy and one group session per week. Many group therapists use the individual sessions to acquire information that can later be used to guide the group discussion. The individual sessions, for example, may be used primarily to get at the root of the neurotic conflict while the group study may serve mainly for exploratory purposes and as a medium for trying out new forms of behavior related to the neurotic conflict. The new therapy appears to have been successful in treating fairly severe neuroses of the obsessional or anxiety type. It appears to be less valuable in treating hysterical disturbances and in working with manic-depressive patients. The group-therapy technique is currently undergoing much research, and it seems fairly certain that it will be used more and more as time goes on.

Self-Analysis

At this point the student may well be wondering, "How can I help myself? Can I myself eliminate anxiety, a phobia, a compulsion, or other maladjustive symptoms?" The answer may be either yes or no, depending on what is implied in the questions. To the extent that we can modify our behavior through learning, it must follow that we can bring about many changes in ourselves without the help of a therapist. And there are others besides therapists who can help us with our problems—parents, teachers, clergymen, counselors, coaches, friends.

In the light of what we have already said about psychotherapy, it might be argued that therapy is primarily a method of helping the individual to help himself by creating an atmosphere conducive to learning. Since the individual is the only one who has the power to change himself, any improvement in his behavior is essentially self-improvement. Even with the help of the best therapist, successful therapy is still, in a sense, a "self-cure."

Perhaps the question we should ask ourselves is this: Can we help ourselves or provide self-therapy when our behavior shows excessive emotional or psychological maladjustments that are revealed through certain symptoms? Have we any evidence to help us answer this question?

One of the most comprehensive discussions of self-therapy is contained in the book *Self-Analysis*, by the late Karen Horney.[4] She believed that self-analysis is possible in many cases and discussed the theoretical and practical aspects of the process in her book. Another interesting discussion of self-analysis is given by the biologist E. T. Farrow in his book, *Analyze Yourself*.[5] He indicates that after two hundred hours of analysis under two different systems of analysis he decided to try to analyze himself. His book describes in detail the progress of his self-analysis, the techniques he evolved, and the results he obtained. Farrow adapted the method utilized by Freud in analyzing his dreams, writing down everything that came to his mind during specified periods. He maintains he was able to re-create the emotional experiences of incidents as early in his life as six months of age. Following this re-creation of his emotional crises an improvement in his health and sense of well-being occurred. (It might be mentioned in passing that Freud analyzed his own dreams, although his theoretical orientation in psychoanalysis and his emphasis on the transference phenomenon as a tool for successful psychotherapy deny the feasibility of self-analysis.)

But self-analysis has its drawbacks. Horney discussed several difficulties, including the difficulty of maintaining high motivation without a therapist and the danger of stopping too soon, of removing a few difficulties or blocks, for instance, and then arranging one's life to fit the part of the neurosis which was not worked through. Furthermore, the patient in self-analysis may find it impossible to deal with the problems he uncovers.

And even if we accept the theoretical possibility of self-therapy for some people, in practice many others would require the help of a therapist. Some, such as psychotics, would not even be aware that they needed help, no matter how obvious their mental and emotional predicament might be to others. Others might be aware of the existence of a problem but might completely misinterpret its nature. For example, a person suffering from conversion symptoms, such as colitis, an ulcer, or certain kinds of asthma or allergy, would recognize his symptoms but attribute them to an organic cause and not even realize that

[4] Karen Horney, *Self-Analysis* (New York: Norton, 1942).

[5] E. T. Farrow, *Analyze Yourself* (New York: International Universities Press, 1945).

they actually stemmed from psychological causes. To suggest psychological self-analysis to such a person would strike him as ridiculous.

Still another person might be aware that a problem of psychological origin existed and yet lack confidence in the ability of his organism to cure itself, just as it lacked the ability to avoid the symptoms of the problems in the first place. Such a person might reason that since his neurotic symptoms indicated that he had been unable to handle a problem, he should not expect now to be able to work through the problem that led to the symptoms.

Probably there are people who can help themselves by self-therapy. Such people can recognize the psychological nature of their problem, analyze the difficulties, and work through their own psychological dynamics to provide solutions. Into this group would fall the generally well-adjusted individual who suddenly developed a special problem and discovered his own methods for working it out.

We have already spoken about the importance of obtaining insight in psychotherapy. If such insight appears to result from the interactions of the patient and therapist, we might conclude that if the patient had, without help, developed this insight earlier, he would not have developed his present neurotic symptoms. His symptoms, in other words, indicate that he was not able to achieve this insight alone. We might even carry this reasoning a step further and say that if insight is the key to curing one's psychological difficulties, it must also be the key to solving any problem that arises, thereby preventing symptoms from developing. This raises the related question, "Why do psychological difficulties arise?" Or, in other words, "Why does one person develop psychological symptoms while another does not, when both are confronted with the same situation?" The answer lies in the fact that not everyone has sufficient insight to handle his problems.

Specialists Who Practice Psychotherapy

The person who is emotionally disturbed needs the help of someone who understands the psychodynamics underlying maladjustment. Sometimes, of course, emotional disturbances are temporary surface phenomena, just as are many physical ailments; and the help and care of family and friends may be all that is needed to recover from them. But if a disturbance occurs repeatedly or if it is severe, then expert help is needed, and one of the following specialists in personality disorders should be consulted: (1) a psychiatrist, (2) a clinical psychologist, or (3) a psychoanalyst.

The Psychiatrist

The psychiatrist is a physician who also has had special training in the diagnosis and treatment of mental illness. Therefore, he is equipped to determine both the organic and the psychological bases of personality disorders. Frequently an illness manifesting itself primarily in physical symptoms—a headache or excessive fatigue, for example—may be caused, or at least aggravated, by emotional disturbances. Or a patient who shows symptoms of emotional disturbance may be suffering from some organic injury, such as brain damage. The psychiatrist has been trained to detect both kinds of symptoms and to recognize what they mean.

The psychiatrist who has specialized in the function of the nervous system is called a *neuropsychiatrist.* If he has been trained especially in operations on the brain and the spinal cord, he is a *neurosurgeon.* Ordinarily psychiatrists are members of the American Psychiatric Association, and the American Orthopsychiatric Association. Neuropsychiatrists usually also belong to the American Neurological Association.

The Clinical Psychologist

The clinical psychologist is a specialist whose training has been at an accredited university, who has a Ph.D. in clinical psychology, and who has had at least a year's internship at a mental hospital or clinic. The clinical psychologist, like the psychoanalyst, has in many cases also been psychoanalyzed. Because so much of psychotherapy involves the dynamics of the learning process, the clinical psychologist receives extensive training in this area, as well as in diagnosis and research techniques. Efforts are now being made in many states to obtain licensing for qualified clinical psychologists in order to guard against quacks infiltrating the profession.

The clinical psychologist is generally a member of the American Psychological Association and an increasing number are Diplomates in Clinical Psychology, American Board of Examiners in Professional Psychology. The clinical psychologist usually works in close cooperation with physicians to be sure that all medical aspects of a case are carefully covered.

The Psychoanalyst

The psychoanalyst is a psychiatrist or psychologist with special training in psychoanalysis. He may practice psychoanalysis exclusively or he may use other methods of treatment. The training of the psychoanalyst requires that he himself undergo psychoanalysis by a recognized psychoanalyst. The two main methods that the psychoanalyst uses are free association and dream analysis. Usually the psychoanalyst belongs to the American Psychoanalytic Association.

The Team Approach

In recent years an increasing number of clinics maintaining teams of professionally trained people have been set up. The minimum staff of such a team consists of a psychiatrist, a clinical psychologist, and a psychiatric social worker. Such teams are widely used today in child-guidance clinics, in neuropsychiatric out-patient clinics, in prisons, and in student counseling agencies.

Locating a Therapist

In addition to the specialists in the field of mental illness—the psychiatrist, the psychoanalyst, the clinical psychologist—there are others who may have received therapeutic training to help a person with his adjustment problems. This might include your pastor, school psychologist, or vocational counselor. But some people, aware of their problem and knowing the type of treatment they require, do not know where to find competent psychologists and psychiatrists. Here are some suggestions:

Call or write to the psychology department at the university nearest to you. The faculty will be able to refer you to qualified clinicians. Or contact the local office of the American Medical Association, or ask your doctor. In many cities you will find a branch of the National Association for Mental Health. These local organizations ordinarily maintain an information and referral service, and although they will not recommend any one therapist, they will give you a list of qualified people in your area. The American Medical Association follows the same procedure. Some communities have compiled a directory of psychiatric and psychological clinics, especially for people in the low-income brackets. Finally, the state governments maintain mental hygiene clinics that will send you an application blank on request and schedule an appointment for you.

For Additional Reading

Adler, A., *The Practice and Theory of Individual Psychology*, translated by P. Radin. London: Kegan Paul, Trench, Trubner, 1929.

Alexander, Franz, *The Scope of Psychoanalysis: 1921-1961*. New York: Basic Books, 1962.

Alexander, Franz and Thomas M. French. *Psychoanalytic Therapy*. New York: Ronald, 1946.

Alexander, Theron, *Psychotherapy in Our Society*. Englewood Cliffs, N. J.: Prentice-Hall, 1963.

Ansbacher, H. L. and Rowena R. Ansbacher, eds. *The Individual Psychology of Alfred Adler*. New York: Basic Books, 1956.

Axline, Virginia M., *Play Therapy*. Boston: Houghton Mifflin, 1947.

Bach, George R., *Intensive Group Psychotherapy*. New York: Ronald, 1954.

Bion, W. R., *Experiences in Groups*. New York: Basic Books, 1961.

Buhler, Charlotte, *Values in Psychotherapy*. New York: The Free Press of Glencoe, 1962.

Colbry, Kenneth M., *A Primer for Psychotherapists*. New York: Ronald, 1951.

Dollard, J. and Neal E. Miller, *Personality and Psychotherapy*. New York: McGraw-Hill, 1950.

Farrow, E. T., *Analyze Yourself*. New York: International Universities Press, 1945.

Fenichel, Otto, *The Psychoanalytic Theory of the Neuroses.* New York: Norton, 1945.

Frank, Jerome D., *Persuasion and Healing: A Comparative Study of Psychotherapy.* Baltimore: Johns Hopkins University Press, 1961.

Freud, Sigmund, *A General Introduction to Psychoanalysis.* New York: Garden City, 1938.

——, *Collected Papers,* Vols. I-IV, London: Hogarth, 1949.

Hoch, Paul H. and Joseph Zubin, eds., *Psychopathology of Communication.* New York: Grune and Stratton, 1958.

Hollingshead, August B. and Frederick C. Redlich, *Social Class and Mental Illness.* New York: Wiley, 1958.

Horney, Karen, *Self-Analysis.* New York: Norton, 1942.

Jaco, E. Gartley, ed., *Patients, Physicians and Illness.* Glencoe, Ill.: The Free Press, 1958.

Jung, C. G., *The Integration of the Personality.* New York: Farrar and Rinehart, 1939.

Kubie, Lawrence S., *Practical and Theoretical Aspects of Psychoanalysis.* New York: International Universities Press, 1950.

Lief, Alfred, ed., *The Commonsense Psychiatry of Dr. Alfred Meyer.* New York: McGraw-Hill, 1948.

Mowrer, O. Hobart, *Psychotherapy—Theory and Research.* New York: Ronald, 1953.

Reik, T., *Listening with the Third Ear.* New York: Farrar, Strauss, 1949.

Rogers, Carl R., *Client-Centered Therapy.* Boston: Houghton Mifflin, 1951.

——, *Counseling and Psychotherapy.* Boston: Houghton Mifflin, 1942.

——, *On Becoming a Person: A Therapist's View of Psychotherapy.* Boston: Houghton Mifflin, 1961.

Rotter, Julian B., *Social Learning and Clinical Psychology.* Englewood Cliffs, N. J.: Prentice-Hall, 1954.

Ruesch, Jurgen, *Therapeutic Communication.* New York: Norton, 1961.

Seward, Georgene, *Psychotherapy and Culture Conflict.* New York: Ronald, 1956.

Slavson, S. R., *Analytic Group Psychotherapy.* New York: Columbia University Press, 1950.

Snyder, William U., *The Psychotherapeutic Relationship.* New York: Macmillan, 1961.

Stein, Morris I., ed., *Contemporary Psychotherapies*. New York: Free Press of Glencoe, 1961.

Sullivan, Harry Stack, *The Interpersonal Theory of Psychiatry*. New York: Norton, 1953.

Vance, Forrest L. and Theodore C. Volsky, Jr., "Counseling and Psychotherapy," *American Psychologist*, XVII (August 1962), 565-570.

A SENSE OF INDIVIDUALITY

A SENSE OF INDEPENDENCE

CONFIDENCE

ACCEPTANCE OF SELF AND OTHERS

A SENSE OF SECURITY

A SENSE OF RESPONSIBILITY

GOAL-ORIENTATION AND A SENSE OF DIRECTION

A SENSE OF TIME PERSPECTIVE

PERSONAL VALUES AND PHILOSOPHY OF LIFE

A PROBLEM-SOLVING ATTITUDE

Characteristics of Satisfactory Adjustment

16

As we discuss the *characteristics*
of *satisfactory adjustment*
we shall be describing
the healthy personality.
We shall be emphasizing
qualities to strive for
rather than faults to avoid.
We reflect our mental health
through our attitudes.
Our personality characteristics
provide clues to these attitudes.

Psychological maturity is measured not by a single characteristic but by the manner in which we have coordinated and integrated many different characteristics.

It is not necessary for a mentally healthy person to possess every one of the characteristics we shall describe here. Nor are these characteristics found in everyone to the same degree. We need not be disappointed or alarmed, therefore, if we find we lack some of these characteristics, or if we find that friends and acquaintances seem, on the basis of them, to be better adjusted than we are. But knowing what they are—and how they affect personal adjustment—can facilitate our efforts to improve our mental health.

We might also remember that many great achievements have been made, and will continue to be made, by persons who were not well adjusted according to these standards. Van Gogh and Nietzsche, to mention but two examples, were severely disturbed, but this does not detract from their achievements. Mental health is *one* value but not the only one. Individual make-up and the pressure of particular circumstances determine a choice in which other values may take precedence.

It is also important to remember that adjustment is a continuing process, since different demands are made on us at different periods of our lives, and since our abilities, our needs, and our goals change. Neither the problems a child faces nor the resources he possesses to meet them are the same as the problems and resources of the adolescent or adult. With these qualifications in mind, then, we can proceed with our discussion of the characteristics of satisfactory adjustment.

A Sense of Individuality

The child learns very early that he is separate and different from others around him. If his development through adolescence into maturity is a healthy one, his sense of self, or individuality or *ego-identity*, will be continually confirmed. Most of the time he will have a basic understanding of what he is capable of doing, what he is willing to do, and what he will not do. This does not mean that he self-consciously considers every action at every moment but rather that he is capable of this awareness when necessary. Only when he is aware of his past achievements and failures and of his potentialities and future goals can he choose among them; and, having chosen, be responsible for his actions.

At times the well-adjusted individual can yield to others and conform readily to social demands. At other times he feels that he must refuse to compromise or to conform. Yielding too often, submitting without question to an authority figure, overconforming for the sake of gaining approval—all these cause the ego-identity to become obscured. The well-adjusted individual, even though possibly unaware of this danger, tends to assert himself in self-defense. This happens frequently among adolescents, for example, and must be understood as their defense against fears arising from new demands that threaten their ego-identities. A certain amount of self-assertion is a healthy sign at any age, but if it develops into intolerance for others it is no longer healthy.

Since neither blind conformity nor intolerance nor rebellious isolation from others (exaggerated individuality) are signs of a healthy personality, we see that a person in good mental health must be capable of conforming to the norms of his society and, at the same time, be capable of deciding when it would be undesirable for him to conform. He is an *autonomous* person, aware of others, responsive to them, but capable of making choices in accordance with his own individuality.

A Sense of Independence

The ability to make such choices requires a sense of independence, a certain self-sufficiency that permits us to carry out our wishes and to work toward our goals without being constantly concerned about what others may think or say. A sense of independence permits us to show more initiative, to be more creative, to depend more on our own judgment, and to utilize whatever qualities of leadership we may possess. We can set our own goals, work toward them, and attain them—all under our own power.

The struggle for independence, for *autonomy*, begins early in life. Parents can encourage their children in this struggle by helping them to learn to express themselves and to stand on their own feet. If, on the other hand, parents discourage their children and cause them to feel ashamed of their early failures and setbacks, or if other people tease them or laugh at them, they will learn to doubt their own abilities, and their sense of independence will be damaged.

At the same time, however, children must be protected against dangers in their environments and against any potentially destructive inner impulses they have not yet learned to recognize or to control. It is up to the parents, therefore, to achieve a delicate balance between protection and autonomy.

Confidence

If we lack confidence in ourselves, our development may be crippled. If we lack confidence in others, our social relationships may be disturbed. Confidence in both ourselves and others is essential to the formation of warm, close relationships and is basic to a healthy personality. Children develop self-confidence in the same way they develop independence—through parental encouragement.

To be self-confident we must be able to appraise our assets and shortcomings realistically. Exaggerated expectations of what we can do can lead to *over*confidence. All of us have encountered, for example, brash, swaggering classmates who thought they already knew more than their professors could teach them, who were sure they could pass their examinations without bothering to study. How did they look when their grades appeared? Abject and crestfallen. They needn't have suffered this defeat if they had viewed their own abilities more realistically.

Memories of past successes help to reinforce confidence in present efforts. If we have a sense of basic trust or confidence, if we can view our opportunities optimistically, we are much more likely to take temporary setbacks in stride and to persist along the path we have marked out for ourselves.

Confidence in others involves, basically, the ability to trust others and depends, to a great extent, upon the sort of treatment we are accustomed to receiving from others. It is important to learn that some people can be trusted even if others may have deceived us at times. We need to have confidence in our ability to determine which ones we can trust. If we feel tempted to generalize that, because a few people have proved to be untrustworthy, all people must therefore be untrustworthy, our chance to achieve satisfactory adjustment will be threatened.

Acceptance of Self and Others

Closely related to confidence is acceptance. We must be able to accept ourselves, to like ourselves, to have confidence in ourselves in spite of the defects we are sure to find in ourselves. In other words, we must find our self-concept acceptable, even though we are aware of our shortcomings and know that we have made mistakes. Similarly, we must be able to accept others in spite of the defects we see in them and the mistakes we know they have made.

This ability to accept is fundamental to the ability to love. If we cannot accept ourselves we cannot consider ourselves worthy of love, and if we cannot accept others we cannot love. Just as the ability to give and to accept love is a sign of good mental health, so the inability to form close attachments, the inability to give or to receive love, is a sign of emotional disturbance and poor mental health. If we view others with suspicion, if we fortify ourselves against the pain we expect them to inflict, or if we fear to respond to kindness and affection because we doubt that they are genuine, we will never achieve satisfactory adjustment.

To love means to extend one's sense of self to include others. It is a characteristic of our human development that, as we grow older, other people become important to us, are included in our concerns and considerations. Moreover, we learn to express these concerns and considerations in a manner appropriate to the kind of relationship involved. Some relationships are intimate. Others are casual. Each calls for a different method of interacting. Competence in interpersonal relationships means, among other things, the ability to take into account differences in the nature of relationships and to be sensitive to the requirements of a particular interpersonal situation.

The world is full of people who want to love others and make friends but who are unable to do so. As a result of damaging personal experiences, which may have occurred in early childhood, they are afraid to break out of the shells they have built around themselves, both consciously and unconsciously. They are afraid to participate in the process of giving and accepting that love requires. The psychotic person manifests the inability to love in its most extreme degree.

Interpersonal relationships are most satisfying when the needs of each of the individuals involved are satisfied. In a love relationship, this means satisfaction of both the need to give and the need to receive love. We cannot expect to receive love if we refuse to give it. Nor can we, as a rule, expect some one to persist in giving it if we refuse to accept it. The well-adjusted person needs to give love as much as to receive it.

A Sense of Security

If we are confident of ourselves and others, and if we accept ourselves and others, we can develop a sense of security that reflects the inner harmony and self-confidence we need to possess if we are to be at peace with ourselves. The amount of acceptance and love we received as children contributes significantly to the development of a sense of security.

If we lack a sense of security we are afraid not only of others but also of ourselves. Plagued by feelings of doubt and distrust, we betray our inner turmoil by such statements as, "I know that what I'm doing is wrong, and I know what I *should* be doing, but somehow I cannot bring myself to do it."

The secure person, by contrast, feels confident of his ability to choose and to follow an acceptable, effective course of action. He feels certain that, with reasonable effort, he can achieve his aims and satisfy his emotional needs.

A Sense of Responsibility

A sense of responsibility means both taking into account the consequences of our own actions and being sensitive and responsive to the needs of others. Our actions often affect the feelings of others. A responsible person, therefore, is a considerate person. He is alert to the needs and feelings of others and careful not to hurt them by a thoughtless word or deed. He will not, for example, commit the sort of error an insensitive mother commits when she permits her daughter to hear her say to a friend, "My child will never be a beauty." Such a remark, which disregards the feelings of the child and overlooks possible consequences, reveals that the mother is insensitive and therefore irresponsible.

A responsible person will also consider the long-range effects of his behavior. He may give food to a hungry beggar as a means of temporary assistance, while at the same time recognizing his responsibility to help to alter conditions that require people to depend upon handouts for survival.

Different persons have different ranges of responsibility. Some feel a sense of responsibility only toward those who are very close to them. Some feel a sense of responsibility only toward groups in dire distress—refugees from disasters, starving children in underprivileged countries or in tenement neighborhoods. Others feel a sense of responsibility toward all mankind.

We can develop a sense of responsibility only if we feel that we can be effective in our interpersonal relationships. If we feel inadequate, if we feel that no one cares what we do, if we feel that our efforts could never produce any useful or desirable results, we are not likely to feel particularly responsible for anything that happens. But if we feel that others respect us and appreciate our efforts, and if we can at the same time recognize the rights and needs of others, our sense of responsibility will develop accordingly. If we believe, for example, that we can exert an influence on events—perhaps help to create a new community facility or to shape a group policy—and if we are concerned about or vitally interested in such a project, we may feel it worthwhile to cooperate with others who are interested. The stronger we feel about the project the more active and intense our participation is likely to be.

Some people are appalled at the complexity of modern life and at the bewildering variety of forces that seem to spring up to challenge them every day. They feel that their efforts can have little or no effect on what goes on around them, either at the local, state, national, or international level. They should remember, however, that any group achievement is merely the sum total of multiple individual efforts.

The responsible individual is concerned not only about himself but also about his fellow man. The responsible individual recognizes the value of effective interpersonal relationships. The responsible individual does what he can to remove prejudice, reduce hatred, and promote understanding, insight, and mutual appreciation among the members of his society.

Goal-Orientation and a Sense of Direction

Whether or not we derive satisfaction and pleasure from our activities largely depends on the goals we have set for ourselves and on the manner in which we have channeled our energies and efforts to attain these goals. This holds not only for occupational goals but also for such goals as finding a wife or husband, establishing a home, raising children, achieving financial security, and having time for recreational activities. Purposeful striving and a kind of directed productivity and creativity make the attainment of goals possible. Such a sense of direction also prevents us from remaining static. It compels us to continue to grow and to develop. The well-adjusted person is motivated to strive, to seek new experiences, to realize more and more of his potentialities.

Many of our more important goals can be reached only in the distant future. If these are to have meaning for us in the present, we must be fairly certain that our present activities will help us to reach them. It is possible to set goals and levels of aspiration so high that they become a source of frustration simply because we cannot believe we shall ever really attain them. As a result, we may lose hope and incentive and allow actual accomplishment to give way to dreaming and fantasy. Goals set realistically indicate satisfactory adjustment. A realistic goal is one we can feel reasonably certain of attaining if we persevere. This *hope* of attainment will stimulate constructive activity and help to reduce the tension that comes from delayed satisfaction. Hope of success increases the amount of frustration we can endure and helps to prevent slackening of effort. Thus a person who knows he has the ability to fill a certain job well will search for it longer than will a person who is seeking a job for which he knows he is not qualified. The first few rejections will have a more damaging effect on the latter. Hope, then, is an important factor in goal-orientation.

The person who seems to have no goals, or who revises his goals every day, is wasting his potentialities. Such a person may change jobs every month. He may become enthusiastic about an activity one day only to drop it the next. The jack-of-all-trades and the dilettante are examples of persons who have failed to acquire a consistent, highly motivated goal-orientation.

The ability to handle frustrations and irritations without becoming upset requires a high degree of goal-orientation, as contrasted to self orientation. The self-oriented person, when caught up in a frustrating situation, is primarily concerned with protecting his ego. The goal-oriented person, by contrast, is primarily interested in working out his problem and proceeding toward his goal. Although he may be temporarily baffled by a situation and may even, for a time, succumb to despair, the goal-oriented person will eventually rally his resources and renew his efforts to resolve the conflict.

If we are sure of our goals and of our plan for attaining them, we are better able to tolerate frustration and tension without becoming emotionally upset—without immediately going to pieces or losing our temper, for example. But if we are not sure what we want or how to get it, we are not likely to achieve a sense of accomplishing anything.

A Sense of Time Perspective

Each of us lives in the present, but this present is related to the past and to the future in a manner that affects our current feelings, attitudes, and actions. When we are children, the present is narrowly defined because we have few past experiences to draw upon and cannot envision far beyond today. But as we grow older our time perspective broadens. We can see beyond the immediate necessities of the day. We can plan ahead—set our sights on distant goals. We can utilize our many past experiences.

As we have already seen, an excessive dwelling on the past is a symptom of maladjustment. Some persons who are unhappy in the present and for whom the future holds little promise derive their greatest comfort and pleasure from looking back on the "good old days." Memories become their substitute for future plans and present actions. Others, tormented by shame and guilt about past experiences, are unable to live happily and constructively in the present. For them the present is wasted, and this wasted present becomes, in turn, an additional source of regret tomorrow. The well-adjusted individual, however, does not blot out the present by reliving the past or dreaming about the future. He utilizes his past experiences as guides for present and future action.

Personal Values and Philosophy of Life

The acquisition and understanding of personal values has occupied the attention of men for a long time. Traditionally, it has been the concern of philosophers and theologians. More recently, both physical and social scientists have taken it into consideration. It has increasingly become a matter of concern for the clinical psychologist as well, since judgments of value enter, implicity or explicitly, into therapeutic relationships with patients.

Our choice of friends, our religious beliefs, our political convictions—all these represent values. The mature, well-adjusted person explores these values in order to understand himself and to control his reactions. He comes to see his values more objectively; that is, he maintains a problem-solving attitude toward them and learns that these subjective, and often very important, values can be understood and modified. He is able to reconsider values acquired as a child, and to change and modify them as he develops intellectually and emotionally.

How can we assess our values? Because they are personal and highly subjective (even though they are socially derived) many people believe we cannot assign a rating to them except in terms of the meaning they hold for us personally. Nevertheless, the following useful criteria have been suggested: [1]

1. *Inclusiveness.* A value that affects *all* men rather than *some* is, other things being equal, superior. For example, freedom for all is of greater value than freedom for only a few.

2. *Permanence.* A value that lasts is superior to a temporary one.

3. *Irrevocability.* A value that is not replaceable or readily created by human effort is superior to one that can be produced easily. For example, the books of brilliant thinkers and the paintings of gifted artists are worth more than mediocre products.

4. *Congruency.* A value that harmonizes with a person's total pattern of beliefs is superior to one that is inconsistent with it.

5. *Cognitive completeness.* A value based on full information and broad experience is superior to one resting on partial and fragmentary knowledge.

6. *Survival.* A value that contributes to the life of the individual or the survival of the race is superior to one that leads to the extinction of either.

Value judgments are an integral part of a personal *philosophy of life,* by which we mean the system of values by which we live. This philosophy of life includes our aims, ideals, and manner of thinking —the principles by which we guide our behavior and conduct our affairs. Many people have built their life philosophies around re-

[1] George W. Hartmann, "Pacifism and Its Opponents in the Light of Value Theory," *Journal of Abnormal and Social Psychology,* XXXVI (1941), p. 164.

ligious concepts. Others have developed humanitarian or materialistic or pragmatic or opportunistic approaches to life. Whatever its form, a philosophy of life will have meaning to a person only according to the value he assigns to it.

Every culture has its basic assumptions and beliefs, and every generation has to re-examine these beliefs in its search for meaning. As we saw in Chapter 1, man has always sought to erect systems of thought that would aid him in understanding more about himself, about the nature of some final reality, about the universe. Such explanations help man to feel at home and secure in his world. Whether they are "right" or "wrong" is often immaterial. The belief that an erupting volcano was caused by a god's sneezing served the same reassuring psychological function for primitive man that our more scientific explanation does for us today.

This does not mean that one belief can reassure us as effectively as another. The explanations, beliefs, and theories that make up an individual's philosophy of life must be able to stand the test of reality. They must, that is, fit the real world and provide some means by which the person can predict and control events and direct his own behavior. If the system falls short of this requirement, disillusionment, anxiety, even panic may result. When our philosophy of life reveals itself to be inadequate or invalid, we feel lost, at sea, desperate to find something to replace it with. An example of this might be seen in the behavior of certain ex-communists who have sought solace in religion or some other "system" after the shattering effects of losing their faith in communism. One study of prejudice had this to say about the significance of personal philosophy:

> We are saying that prejudice will be prevented only if the philosophical mould of one's life is sound. A sound mould requires a basic trust of mankind, freedom from the jungle-outlook, from rigid categories, from the paranoid inability to take blame upon oneself or to adopt the point of view of the other fellow. A sound mould requires one to know the extent of one's hostile attitudes, and to feel some shame in having them, and to understand their probable roots in his home environment, in his school, or in his own temperament.[2]

[2] Gordon W. Allport and Bernard M. Kramer, "Some Roots of Prejudice," *Journal of Psychology,* XXII (1946), 36. By permission of The Journal Press.

A Problem-Solving Attitude

A problem-solving attitude is indicated by a willingness to apply the scientific approach in solving our own problems. To apply this approach we (1) carefully define and analyze the problem, (2) evaluate various possible approaches, and (3) apply the method that seems to offer the best chance of solving it.

Willingness to face a problem, to try to understand it, to work on it distinguishes the well-adjusted person. He is objective, he understands cause-and-effect relationships, and he is flexible. At times, of course, he may misjudge some aspect of the problem and his solution may fail. But then, like the scientist in the laboratory, he will try another approach.

Why *must* we face and solve our problems? The answer lies in the fact that an unsolved problem obstructs our progress just as a boulder obstructs a highway. It prevents us, emotionally, from solving other problems or accomplishing other aims. Failure to solve one problem jeopardizes our chances of solving the next. Each problem that arises, therefore, must be solved so that it can serve as a stepping-stone rather than as an obstruction.

The neurotic person, as we saw earlier, is one who has failed to identify, analyze, and solve his problems. He has become fixated at that point in his development where he encountered a problem he was unable to solve. An unsolved problem may thus have a kind of derailing effect and prevent us from reaching our goals.

The problem-solving attitude requires *self-objectivity.* To be objective about ourselves we must be willing to see ourselves as others might see us, not as we *wish* to see ourselves. We must be ready to examine ourselves realistically, to evaluate our assets and liabilities, strengths and limitations, shortcomings and talents, and our potentialities for growth. And we must acquire a certain degree of insight into our motivations, goals, and defenses and into the way our behavior affects others. Allied with self-objectivity is a sense of humor. The man who can laugh at himself reveals a certain detached awareness of his own foibles and idiosyncrasies. His sense of humor prevents him from taking himself and his problems too seriously.

Fundamental to the problem-solving attitude is the assumption of cause-and-effect relationships. Without this assumption, any attempt to solve a problem or to attain a goal is meaningless. For if we cannot anticipate the effect of our actions, we cannot distinguish the sensible course of action from the potentially harmful. Thus we are unable to predict the consequences of our behavior or to control a situation.

Some element of uncertainty always exists, of course, and the more complex the problem, the larger this element is likely to be. An unforeseen event may make havoc of our most carefully laid plans. When we say, "If all goes well, then . . . ," or, "Unless something unexpected happens . . . ," we indicate our awareness of uncertainties. But even so we do not abandon all planning. Nor do we consider our basic assumption of cause-and-effect relationships invalid.

Sometimes when we have acted unwisely we try to excuse ourselves by insisting that we had no way of foreseeing the effects of our behavior. A parent whose harsh discipline has made his child neurotic may wring his hands and declare that he would have been less tyrannical if he could have foreseen the consequences of his actions. True, we cannot always anticipate every possibility. But the chances are that if we weigh our actions carefully and make an effort to anticipate the possible consequences of our behavior, we will not often be tempted to make a decision that we will regret later on.

A child, as we know, has a limited understanding of cause-and-effect relationships, and therefore cannot analyze his behavior or predict its consequences. Unfortunately many adults are just as incapable as children of analyzing their behavior rationally. Such adults feel themselves in the grip of forces beyond their control and eventually adopt attitudes of helplessness and irresponsibility. We call this kind of irresponsibility in an adult *infantile* behavior.

To be sure, there are situations which are beyond our control, and it would be foolhardy to assume that we can shape everything to our own desires. A feeling of omnipotence is as much a sign of maladjustment as is a sense of helplessness and defeat. In either case the person is out of touch with reality. Appraisal of a problem requires consideration of what we *cannot* do as well as what we *can* do.

Another characteristic of the problem-solving attitude is flexibility. Flexibility implies that we can either adapt our behavior to the special requirements of a situation or learn how to modify the situation. In a changing world the inflexible person is an anachronism. The whole process of living requires constant adjustment, constant change. And the person who is unable or unwilling to take this change into account, who stubbornly clings to a course of action that is inappropriate to the situation, is maladjusted.

Finally, related to flexibility is creativity, the opposite of rigidity. To see new approaches to a problem, new versions of old facts, new significance in common phenomena implies a productive flexibility called *creativity*. Creativity is the mark of the great artist, writer, scientist, or statesman; but it is something that all of us possess in varying degrees. It is found not only in intellectual achievements but also in human relations. We can be creative in bringing up our children, in our relationships with our co-workers, in the kinds of activities we select for our leisure-time enjoyment. Whenever we help to bring about, either in ourselves or in others, a change in the direction of further growth, we are being creative.

For Additional Reading

Allport, Gordon W., *The Nature of Prejudice*. Cambridge: Addison-Wesley, 1954.

———, *Pattern and Growth in Personality*. New York: Holt, Rinehart and Winston, 1961.

Anderson, Harold, ed., *Creativity and Its Cultivation*. New York: Harper, 1959.

Andrews, Michael F., ed., *Creativity and Psychological Health*. Syracuse, N. Y.: Syracuse University Press, 1961.

Barron, Frank, *Creativity and Psychological Health*. Princeton, N. J.: Van Nostrand, 1963.

Coleman, James C., *Personality Dynamics and Effective Behavior*. Chicago: Scott, Foresman, 1960.

Erikson, Erik H., "Growth and Crises of the Healthy Personality," in *Personality in Nature, Society, and Culture* (rev. ed.), eds. Clyde Kluckhohn, Henry A. Murray, and David M. Schneider. New York: Knopf, 1953, pp. 185-225.

Foote, N. N. and L. S. Cottrell, Jr., *Identity and Interpersonal Competence*. Chicago: University of Chicago Press, 1955.

Frank, Lawrence K., *Nature and Human Nature. Man's New Image of Himself*. New Brunswick, N. J.: Rutgers University Press, 1951.

French, Thomas M., *The Integration of Behavior*. Vol. 1, "Basic Postulates." Chicago: University of Chicago Press, 1952.

Fromm, Erich, *The Art of Loving*. New York: Harper, 1956.

——, *Man for Himself*. New York: Rinehart, 1947.

Gurin, Gerald, Joseph Veroff and Sheila Feld, *Americans View Their Mental Health: A Nationwide Interview Survey*, Joint Commission on Mental Illness and Health, Monograph Series No. 4. New York: Basic Books, 1960.

Jahoda, Marie, *Current Concepts of Positive Mental Health*, Joint Commission on Mental Illness and Health, Mongraph Series No. 1. New York: Basic Books, 1958.

Katz, Barney and George F. J. Lehner, *Mental Hygiene in Modern Living*. New York: Ronald, 1953.

Lecky, Prescott, *Self-Consistency—A Theory of Personality*. New York: Island Press, 1945.

Leighton, Alexander H., John A. Clausen and Robert N. Wilson, eds., *Explorations in Social Psychiatry*. New York: Basic Books, 1957.

Lichtenberg, Philip, Rhondda K. Cassetta, and John C. Scanlon, "Mutual Achievement Strivings: A Continuum for Mental Health," *Journal of Abnormal and Social Psychology*, LXIII (November 1961), 619-628.

MacKinnon, Donald W., "The Nature and Nurture of Creative Talent," *American Psychologist*, XVII (July 1962), 484-495.

Maslow, Abraham H., ed., *New Knowledge in Human Values*. New York: Harper, 1959.

——, "Self-Actualizing People: A Study of Psychological Health," in *The Self. Explorations in Personal Growth*, ed. Clark E. Moustakas. New York: Harper, 1956, pp. 160-194.

——, *Toward a Psychology of Being*. Princeton, N. J.: Van Nostrand, 1962.

Nunnally, J. C., Jr., *Popular Conceptions of Mental Health: Their*

Development and Change. New York: Holt, Rinehart and Winston, 1961.

Opler, Marvin K., ed., *Culture and Mental Health: Cross-Cultural Studies*. New York: Macmillan, 1959.

Riesman, David, *The Lonely Crowd. A Study of the Changing American Character*. New Haven: Yale University Press, 1950.

Roe, Anne, "Man's Forgotten Weapon," *American Psychologist*, XIV (June 1959), 261-266.

Rose, Arnold, ed., *Mental Health and Mental Disorder*. New York: Norton, 1955. See especially Section VII: "Contribution to the Understanding of Mental Health."

Sawrey, James M. and Charles W. Telford, *Dynamics of Mental Health: The Psychology of Personal and Social Adjustment*. Boston: Allyn and Bacon, 1963.

Scott, William A., "Research Definitions of Mental Health and Mental Illness," in *Mental Hygiene*, ed. Peter T. Hountras. Columbus, Ohio: Merrill, 1961, pp. 16-39.

Smith, M. Brewster, "Research Strategies Toward a Conception of Positive Mental Health," *The American Psychologist*, XIV (November 1959), 673-681.

Symonds, Percival M., *The Ego and the Self*. New York: Appleton-Century-Crofts, 1953.

Taylor, Calvin W. and Frank Barron, *Scientific Creativity: Its Recognition and Development*. New York: Wiley, 1963.

Tillich, Paul, *The Courage To Be*. New Haven: Yale University Press, 1952.

White, Robert W., *Lives in Progress: A Study of the Natural Growth of Personality*. New York: Dryden, 1952.

Directory of Test Publishers

Acorn Publishing Co., Inc.
Rockville Centre, New York

Bureau of Educational Measurements
Kansas State Teachers College
Emporia, Kansas

Bureau of Educational Research
and Service
State University of Iowa
Iowa City, Iowa

Bureau of Publications
Teachers College
Columbia University
New York 27, New York

California Test Bureau
5916 Hollywood Boulevard
Los Angeles 28, California

Consulting Psychologists' Press
577 College Avenue
Palo Alto, California

Division of Applied Psychology
Purdue University
Lafayette, Indiana

Educational Records Bureau
21 Audubon Avenue
New York 32, New York

Educational Test Bureau
Educational Publishers, Inc.
720 Washington Avenue, S.E.
Minneapolis, Minnesota

Educational Testing Service
Princeton, New Jersey

Evaluation Division
Bureau of Educational Research
Ohio State University
Columbus, Ohio

Harvard University Press
Cambridge 38, Massachusetts

Houghton Mifflin Co.
2 Park Street
Boston 7, Massachusetts

Knauber, Alma J.
6988 Warder Drive
Cincinnati 24, Ohio

Personnel Press, Inc.
180 Nassau Street
Princeton, New Jersey

Psychological Corporation
522 Fifth Avenue
New York 36, New York

Public School Publishing Co.
204 West Mulberry Street
Bloomington, Illinois

Science Research Associates
259 East Erie Street
Chicago 11, Illinois

Stanford University Press
Stanford, California

C. H. Stoelting Co.
242 North Homan Avenue
Chicago 24, Illinois

U.S. Department of Labor
Bureau of Employment Security
U.S. Employment Service
Washington, D.C.

World Book Co.
313 Park Hill Avenue
Yonkers 5, New York

Index

Index

A

I

J

K

N

O

P

R